THE DICKENS COMPANIONS

General editor Susan Shatto, Associate editor Michael Cotsell

The Companion to *Bleak House*

THE DICKENS COMPANIONS

[1]

The Companion to *Our Mutual Friend*
MICHAEL COTSELL

[2]

The Companion to *The Mystery of Edwin Drood*
WENDY S. JACOBSON

[3]

The Companion to *Bleak House*
SUSAN SHATTO

The Companion to
Bleak House

———————

SUSAN SHATTO

London
UNWIN HYMAN
Boston   Sydney   Wellington

Published by the Academic Division of
Unwin Hyman Ltd
15/17 Broadwick Street, London W1V 1FP

Allen & Unwin Inc.,
8 Winchester Place, Winchester, Mass. 01890, USA

Allen & Unwin (Australia) Ltd,
8 Napier Street, North Sydney, NSW 2060, Australia

Allen & Unwin (New Zealand) Ltd in association with
the Port Nicholson Press Ltd,
60 Cambridge Terrace, Wellington, New Zealand

First published in 1988

British Library Cataloguing in Publication Data

Shatto, Susan
    The companion to Bleak House. — (The Dickens companions).
1. Dickens, Charles, *1812–1870*. Bleak House
I. Title   II. Dickens, Charles, *1812–1870*.
Bleak House   III. Series
823′.8   PR4556
ISBN 0-04-800047-7

Library of Congress Cataloging in Publication Data

Shatto, Susan
    The companion to Bleak House/Susan Shatto
p.   cm. – (The Dickens companions)
Bibliography: p.
Includes index
ISBN 0-04-800047-7 (Alk. paper)
1. Dickens, Charles, 1812–1870. Bleak House.
I. Dickens, Charles, 1812–1870. Bleak House. II. Title. III. Series.
PR 4556.S43 1988
823′.8 – DC19

Typeset in 10 on 11 point Erhardt by Fotographics (Bedford) Ltd
and printed in Great Britain by Biddles Ltd, Guildford, Surrey

CONTENTS

page

List of Illustrations   vi

General Preface by the Editors   vii

Acknowledgements   x

Abbreviations for Dickens's Works and Related Material   xi

Bibliographical Symbols and Abbreviations   xii

Introduction   1

A Note on the Text   9

How to Use the Notes   10

The Notes   11

Appendix: Alternative Titles   298

Select Bibliography   302

Index   313

LIST OF ILLUSTRATIONS

page

1 The cover of the monthly parts of *Bleak House*, by 'Phiz' (Hablot Knight Browne)   12

2 The Court of Chancery in Lincoln's Inn Hall, by T. H. Shepherd, in *London Interiors*, 2 vols (1841–4)   21

3 Megalosaurus. From Richard Owen, *Geology and Inhabitants of the Ancient World*, 1854   24

4 Lincoln's Inn Hall, Chapel, and Chancery Court, by T. H. Shepherd, in *London Interiors*, 2 vols (1841–4)   50

5 Caroline Chisholm in 1853, engraved by J. B. Hunt   53

6 'Sir Leicester Dedlock', by H. K. Browne, in the fourteenth monthly number of *Bleak House*   66

7 Leigh Hunt in 1850. From *The Autobiography of Leigh Hunt*, 3 vols, 1850   69

8 'The Bands of Hope'. From *Punch*, 22 (6 March 1852), 103   89

9 Walter Savage Landor in 1839, by W. Fisher   95

10 Maria Manning, as she appeared at Union Hall Police Court in 1849. From a verbatim report of the trial, in the British Library   121

11 George IV in 1822, by Sir Thomas Lawrence   135

12 'A Model of Parental Deportment', by H. K. Browne, in the eighth monthly number of *Bleak House*   137

13 Samuel Rogers, by Daniel Maclise. From *Fraser's Magazine*, 1830   170

14 Inspector Charles Field in 1856   178

15 'Friendly Behaviour of Mr. Bucket', by H. K. Browne, in the sixteenth monthly number of *Bleak House*   180

16 A map of the London of *Bleak House*   300

17 A map of the Inns of Court and Inns of Chancery   301

GENERAL PREFACE
BY THE EDITORS

The Dickens Companions series provides the most comprehensive annotation of the works of Dickens ever undertaken. Separate volumes are devoted to each of Dickens's fifteen novels, to *Sketches by Boz* and to *The Uncommercial Traveller*, the five Christmas books are treated together in one volume. The series will be completed by a General Index, making nineteen volumes in all.

The nature of the annotation is factual rather than critical. The series undertakes what the general editors of the Clarendon Dickens have called 'the immense task of explanatory annotation' of Dickens's works. Each Companion will elucidate obscurities and allusions which were doubtless intelligible to the nineteenth-century reader but which have changed or lost their meaning in a later age. The 'world' of Dickens passed away more than a century ago, and our perceptions and interpretations of his works can be sharpened by our having recalled for us a precise context or piece of information.

The annotation identifies allusions to current events and intellectual and religious issues, and supplies information on topography, social customs, costume, furniture, transportation, and so on. Identifications are provided for allusions to plays, poems, songs, the Bible, the Book of Common Prayer and other literary sources. Elements of Dickens's plots, characterization and style which are influenced by the works of other writers are also identified. When an aspect of the text can be shown to have been influenced by Dickens's own experience, this is indicated. The work of Dickens's illustrators is also discussed. Finally, although the Companions do not attempt the work of a modern scholarly edition, material from Dickens's manuscripts and proofs is included when it is of major significance.

The main part of the information in each Companion is arranged in the form of notes presented for convenient use with any edition of Dickens's works. The information is thus placed where it is most relevant, enabling the notes to be used to elucidate a local difficulty, or to pursue the use of a certain kind of material or the development of a particular idea. To facilitate their use, the notes are cross-referenced, and each Companion contains a comprehensive index. The introduction to each Companion traces the major influences and concerns revealed by the annotation and, where appropriate, demonstrates their place in the genesis and composition of the text.

Dickens's vital and imaginative response to his culture is a familiar fact, but The Dickens Companions demonstrate and explore this response more fully and in far greater detail than has ever been attempted. Hitherto, Dickens's works have been annotated only on a modest scale. Many modern editions of the novels contain some notes, but there is not space in one volume for both the text of a novel and a comprehensive annotation of the text. Because most volumes of The Dickens Companions are devoted to a single work, the series can provide the full-scale, thoroughgoing annotation which the works of Dickens require. The completed series will compose a uniquely comprehensive archive of information about Dickens's world, affording the modern reader an unparalleled record of Dickens's concerns and the sources of his artistry. For many kinds of scholar, not merely Dickensians, The Dickens Companions will provide a fundamental tool for future critical and historical scholarship on various aspects of nineteenth-century British culture. They open up Dickens's texts to both related literary texts and the 'text' of their society, thereby enlarging the traditional boundaries of literary studies.

To undertake the 'immense task' of annotation, the Editors have assembled a team of Dickens scholars who work closely together and with the Editors in order to enhance the depth and scope of each Companion. The series is not a variorum commentary on Dickens: it does not consist of a survey or a selection of comments by other annotators and scholars. Previous scholarship is, in general, cited only when it is considered to identify an important piece of information about the historical, literary and biographical influences on Dickens's works.

The annotation in The Dickens Companions is based on original research which derives for the most part from the writings of Dickens's own time, the reading available to him and the books he is known to have read. The annotation is not perfunctorily minimal: a large number of notes are substantial essays and all are written in a readable style. Nor does the annotation consist of narrow definitions of what the reader (in the opinion of another reader) 'needs to know' in order to 'understand' the text. Rather, the annotation attempts to open up the actual and imaginative worlds which provided the sources and the backgrounds of Dickens's works in the belief that what interested, engaged and amused Dickens can hardly fail to interest, engage and amuse his readers. Our largest hope for The Dickens Companions is that the volumes will be read with a pleasure akin to that with which Dickens's own writings are read, and that they will be genuine Companions to both his works and his readers.

The idea of providing each of Dickens's major works with a companion volume of annotation originated with the late Professor T. J. B. Spencer. It is to his memory that the series is gratefully and affectionately dedicated.

SUSAN SHATTO
MICHAEL COTSELL

For K. J. Fielding

ACKNOWLEDGEMENTS

I wish to express my gratitude to the Leverhulme Trust for again supporting my work in Victorian studies. Their generosity, on this occasion through the University of Edinburgh, helped me to initiate the Dickens Companions series during my tenure as Leverhulme Research Fellow in English Literature. I am also very indebted to the University of Edinburgh and to the Department of English Literature.

Four people have made substantial contributions to the present volume, and I am especially grateful to them for their interest: the late T. J. B. Spencer, who conceived the idea of the Dickens Companions and who supervised an early version of this volume; Michael Cotsell, whose valued friendship has made our mutual task of editing so agreeable; Philip Collins, who has in various ways and for many years contributed more than anyone else to my work on Dickens and Tennyson; and K. J. Fielding, whose unstinting encouragement and advice enabled the Dickens Companions to be initiated in Edinburgh.

For allowing me to examine manuscripts, printed texts and illustrations in their collections, and for giving permission to quote from or reproduce them, I wish to thank the following individuals and institutions: the Curator of the Dickens House, London; the Henry E. Huntington Library and Art Gallery, San Marino, California; the Chief Librarian, the National Art Library, Victoria and Albert Museum, London. For permission to reproduce certain illustrations, I wish to thank the Trustees of the National Portrait Gallery (Plates 5, 9) and the Trustees of the Wallace Collection (Plate 11).

The staff of the National Library of Scotland and of the University of Edinburgh Library have patiently and courteously given me much assistance, and I am particularly indebted to them.

On behalf of the contributors to the Dickens Companions, it is a pleasure to be able to express our deep appreciation to our past and present editors at Unwin Hyman, Keith Ashfield and Jane Harris-Matthews, without whose support the series could not have been published and so handsomely produced. We are all of us also very grateful to Edward Leeson for his punctilious and scholarly copy-editing, and to Kevin Harris, whose analytical expertise provides the volumes with richly informative indexes.

Finally, several friends and colleagues have given me much help, and I wish to thank them most sincerely: Elsie Duncan-Jones; Angus Easson; Wendy Jacobson; John McVeagh; David Paroissien; and David Stock.

University of Edinburgh   SUSAN SHATTO

ABBREVIATIONS FOR DICKENS'S WORKS AND RELATED MATERIAL

1. Works: Principal

AN	*American Notes*
BH	*Bleak House*
BL	*The Battle of Life*
BR	*Barnaby Rudge*
C	*The Chimes*
CC	*A Christmas Carol*
CH	*The Cricket on the Hearth*
CHE	*A Child's History of England*
DC	*David Copperfield*
DS	*Dombey and Son*
GE	*Great Expectations*
HM	*The Haunted Man*
HT	*Hard Times*
LD	*Little Dorrit*
MC	*Martin Chuzzlewit*
MED	*The Mystery of Edwin Drood*
MHC	*Master Humphrey's Clock*
NN	*Nicholas Nickleby*
OCS	*The Old Curiosity Shop*
OMF	*Our Mutual Friend*
OT	*Oliver Twist*
PI	*Pictures from Italy*
PP	*The Pickwick Papers*
SB	*Sketches by Boz*
TTC	*A Tale of Two Cities*
UT	*The Uncommercial Traveller*

2. Works: Miscellaneous Writings

CP	*Collected Papers*
MP	*Miscellaneous Papers*
RP	*Reprinted Pieces*

AYR	*All the Year Round*
HW	*Household Words*

CD	Charles Dickens Edition, 21 vols (1867–[74])

3. Related Material: Basic Sources

Forster   John Forster, *The Life of Charles Dickens*, 3 vols (1872–4)
Letters   *The Letters of Charles Dickens*, ed. Madeline House and others, Pilgrim
               Edition (1965–   )
Letters: Coutts   *Letters from Charles Dickens to Angela Burdett-Coutts, 1841–1865*, ed. Edgar
               Johnson (1953)
Nonesuch   *The Letters of Charles Dickens*, ed. Walter Dexter, Nonesuch Edition, 3 vols
               (1938)
Speeches   *The Speeches of Charles Dickens*, ed. K. J. Fielding (1960)

BIBLIOGRAPHICAL SYMBOLS
AND ABBREVIATIONS

MS   Manuscript
< >   Deletion in MS or proof
∧ or △   Addition or substitution in MS
∧ OR △   Addition or substitution in proof
illegible word   Signifies an unreadable word in MS

INTRODUCTION

'The Moving Age'

A commonplace in the criticism of *Bleak House* is that it reflects the condition of England in two different periods – about 1830, the period of Dickens's youth, and the early 1850s, the period in which he composed it. The commonplace, which derives from valuable studies by Humphry House in 1941 and John Butt and Kathleen Tillotson in 1957, is in fact a myth based on impressionistic and partial analyses of the actual events, issues and personalities which invigorate the imaginative world of the novel.

Esther does indeed say that she writes her part of the narrative 'full seven years' after the occurrence of the events she recounts, and it is true that a sense of the past is created by such statements as 'it is a long time ago' (chapter 30), 'there were at that time a number of poor Spanish refugees' (chapter 43), 'It was a night's journey in those coach times' (chapter 45) and 'Railroads shall soon traverse all this country' (chapter 55). But, far from being indications of the date of the setting of the novel, such statements are merely authorial feints. Dickens may have intended *Bleak House* to be a 'romance', but the 'past' in the world of the novel is for the most part not the relatively distant past of the 1820s, but the very recent past of the 1840s. This is indicated even in the authorial feints: for example, the mail-coach system operated up to 1846, and railway lines were being laid in the north-east up to 1850. Other red herrings are the Spanish refugees: Dickens may well have seen them in the late 1820s, but his mention of them in the novel derives from the description in Carlyle's *Life of John Sterling*, published in 1851.

The life which Dickens responds to in *Bleak House* is the life that was going on around him as he wrote. This can be demonstrated by a table listing the most prominent elements in the novel to which dates can be assigned. Sixty-six per cent date from 1851–3, the period of composition, and 72 per cent date from 1850–3:

The Contemporaneity of *Bleak House*

(An asterisk denotes *terminus a quo* and/or *terminus ad quem* for references or scenes in the novel.)

Date of event/ issue/person	Event/issue/person alluded to or mentioned	Chapter
May 1853	Chancery judge at Mansion House	Preface
1830s–present [1851–3]	Wrongful imprisonment for lunacy	Preface
1849	Chancery case described in 1849 pamphlet (model for Gridley's case, chapter 15)	Preface

1

Date of event/ issue/person	Event/issue/person alluded to or mentioned	Chapter
1834–present	Day Chancery suit	Preface
1700–present	Jennings Chancery suit	Preface
1828–32	Lord Lyndhurst (the Lord Chancellor)	1, 3
1851	Megalosaurus (discovered 1823) described in *HW*	1
1820s–present	Chancery reform movement	1 onwards
1830s	Miss R— (Miss Flite)	1–
1843*	Six Clerks' Office (abolished 1843)	1
1852*	Copying of legal documents by hand (discontinued by Act of Parliament, 1852)	1–
present	Lord Lansdowne's gout (partly the model for Sir Leicester's?)	2–
1820s–1830s	Richard Sharp (Mr Kenge)	3–
present	Caroline Chisholm (Mrs Jellyby); foreign missionary societies	4–
1841–8	Niger expedition (1841); Dickens reviews published account (1848)	4
1851–present	St Albans election reveals widespread electoral corruption (Dickens sites Bleak House near St Albans)	6–
present	Leigh Hunt (Harold Skimpole)	6–
1830s–1840s	Sloman's sponging house (Coavinses)	6–
1840s	Chartism	7
1846*	Guppy and Jobling and Esther and Charley travel by mail-coach (mail-coach system ended 1846)	7, 45
present	Evangelical philanthropy, women with a 'mission', district visiting, sanitary reform movement Oxford Movement and 'papal aggression': papal bull, 1850; Ecclesiastical Titles Assumption Act, 1851	8–
February 1852	Band of Hope meeting at Exeter Hall (Infant Bonds of Joy)	8
1845–present	Potato famine in Ireland (1845–9) causes mass immigration of Irish poor to Britain (brickmakers whom Esther meets are Irish)	8–
present	Walter Savage Landor (Lawrence Boythorn)	9–
1841–51	Chinese Exhibition (1841), the Chinese Junk (1848), Great Exhibition (1851)	9, 14
1848, 1851	Tooting baby-farm disaster (1848); Apprentices and Servants Act, 1851 (Guster)	10
present	Widespread use of opium by the poor is associated with countless accidental deaths and suicides	10, 11
present	Redundancy of beadles	11
January 1850	Inadmissible evidence of George Ruby (Jo)	11
1840s–1850	Abuses of intramural burials; Metropolitan Interments Act, 1850	11, 16
1840–7*	Dedlocks journey to France and back by road (rail journey possible after 1847)	12
1849	Maria Manning and her husband are tried and executed for murder (Hortense)	12

Date of event/ issue/person	Event/issue/person alluded to or mentioned	Chapter
present	Oxford Movement and Young Englanders; appointment of Lord John Manners as Commissioner of Woods and Forests	12
1851	Ministerial crisis	12, 40
1830s–present	Discrimination against naval surgeons	13
present	Campaign to abolish Smithfield market	14, 16, 32
1770s, 1820s–1830s	Lord Chesterfield, George IV, John Henry Skelton (Mr Turveydrop)	14–
1840–7*	St Giles's rookery mostly demolished by 1847 (Tom-all-Alone's)	16, 22, 46
present	Society for the Propagation of the Gospel in Foreign Parts	16
present	Prevalence of street-musicians	16, 42, 60
1845–present	Franklin polar expedition; Livingstone and Gordon-Cumming in Africa	18
1830s–present	Vogue for travelling to the Middle East	19
1841–4	Public debate on the punishment of attempted suicides	19
present	Whiskers become fashionable	20, 40
1852	The legal fictions of 'John Doe and Richard Doe' abolished	20
present	Samuel Rogers and his sister Sarah (Grandfather and Grandmother Smallweed)	21
1850–1	The Birds and the Sloanes convicted for cruelty to servants; Apprentices and Servants Act, 1851 (Charley Neckett)	21
present	Inspector Charles Field (Mr Bucket)	22
1820s–present	Typhus fever epidemics	22
1848–present	British troops dispatched to quell civil unrest in Ireland	24
1830s–1840*	Esther and friends travel by hackney-coach (hackney-coaches were superseded by cabs in the 1830s, were scarce by 1840 and nonexistent by 1850)	24
1846*	The Fleet Prison (abolished in 1846)	24
present	Accidents in gasworks and firework factories	26
1840s–present	Railways in London replace coach travel	27
1840s–present	The captain of industry a Carlylean hero	28
1840s	Craze for exhibitions of American Indians	30
present	Women with a 'mission'	30
1837–present	Smallpox epidemics	31
present	Death by spontaneous combustion	33
present	Campaign for conferral of honours on deserving professional men	35
1840s–1850*	Campaign to abolish duelling made it virtually defunct by 1850	40
1852	Lord John Russell sponsors Bill to extend the franchise	40
1852	Opening of Holloway House of Correction, with treadmills for female prisoners	42

Date of event/ issue/person	Event/issue/person alluded to or mentioned	Chapter
1820s/1851	Spanish supporters of Torrijos settle in London (1820s); Dickens reads of them in Carlyle's *Life of John Sterling* (1851)	43
1820s–1840s	Political economy theories flourish	43
1840–7*	St Giles's rookery: before its demolition in 1847, the breeding-place of disease	46
1846–present	Public Baths and Wash-houses Act (1846) provides these amenities at low cost for the poor	47
1840s–present	Private madhouses a topical issue	47
November 1852	State funeral of the Duke of Wellington (an influence on the funeral of Tulkinghorn)	53
1839*	Chelsea Bun House (demolished 1839)	53
1840s–1850s*	Railway lines laid in north-east; Great Northern line opens (1850)	55
1850–present	Royal Commission on Divorce established to consider reform of procedure (1850)	58
1840–present	Steam hammer patented (1840); wide applications in industry	63

In the light of these largely contemporaneous elements, *Bleak House* might be considered a speculum reflecting Dickens's examination of the best and the worst of his times – reflecting and refracting the transformations, the 'movements' and 'reforms', which he witnessed, sometimes with approval and sometimes with contempt. The 'impress from the moving age' and the 'rushing of the larger worlds', of which the Dedlocks, in their narrow social world, attempt to remain oblivious, are images of the activity and progress which the novel shows as (a) dispersing the curtain of fog which does not lift on the opening chapter, and (b) displacing the 'jeweller's cotton and fine wool' which enshroud the Dedlocks from the present.

The constituents which animate 'the moving age' in the world of the novel are not merely real events – electoral corruption, ministerial crises and the campaign to abolish Smithfield market, for example – but also real people, or historical memories of them: Lord Chesterfield, Caroline Chisholm, Charles Field, George IV, Leigh Hunt, Walter Savage Landor, Lord Lyndhurst, Maria Manning, Samuel Rogers and Richard Sharp – to name only the better known. Vitality is further enhanced by the several glimpses into Dickens's own life: his enthusiasm for conjuring tricks and shower-baths; his favourite hotel in Paris; and, in Mr Boythorn's tame canary (' "the most astonishing bird in Europe!" '), a portrait of Dickens's own beloved pet, 'Dick'. Moreover, his chronically insolvent father, John Dickens, and his father's embezzling father-in-law, Charles Barrow, seem to have partly suggested the occupation and bankruptcy of the unfortunate Mr Jellyby.

In different ways, other real people inspire characters in the novel. The trend towards professionalization which was gradually tightening the hitherto slack or nonexistent standards of education and qualification in every major profession and field of employment created a new social type, the professional man, the figure

4

most representative of the middle years of the nineteenth century. Himself a self-made man, Dickens's admiration for the rigorously trained and qualified professional knew no bounds, as is evidenced by the extraordinary number of doctors, soldiers and policemen who are depicted respectfully and even heroically in *Bleak House*.

The irresolution of Richard in choosing a career enables Dickens to demonstrate his knowledge of the efforts within the medical reform movement to regularize the state of medical education and practice and to rectify the disparity in benefits afforded to surgeons in the Navy as compared to those in the Army. Richard's medical mentors, Mr Badger and Allan Woodcourt, display between them the characteristics of the new generation of doctor: a concern for proper qualifications, social responsibility towards the poor (Badger works for a 'large public institution') and, above all, compassion. Likewise, Richard's instructor in military life, Mr George, with his friend the ex-artilleryman Mr Bagnet, together represent the products of current army policy to engender a professional competence among both enlisted men and officers. As for the policemen, the efficient but humane Mr Bucket of the Detective Police, along with his constable and the three phlegmatic policemen in chapters 11 and 57, all exemplify in their business-like attitudes the principle of 'omnicompetence' which Edwin Chadwick embodied in the Police Acts of 1829 and 1839 in order to strengthen the effectiveness of the new professional force.

Parallel measures to instigate professionalism were also being effected within the law in regard to the training and qualification of both junior and senior lawyers, and some improvements and progress towards this end had been made before Dickens began to write *Bleak House* and continued to be made during the course of its composition. Considering the thematic and narrative centrality of the dilatoriness of the Court of Chancery, however, it is not surprising that the law is the one profession shown to be embedded in the past, thereby functioning as a milestone against which to measure the distance covered and the advances made by its faster-moving sister professions.

The Literary Inheritance

Enhancing the contemporaneity of the events, issues and personalities which inform *Bleak House* is the nature of its literary inheritance, including the literary allusions which enrich its texture. What can be educed from them is that, rather like the poet in Tennyson's 'The Epic' (1842), Dickens seems to have felt that 'a truth/ Looks freshest in the fashion of the day'. Certainly, in terms of the extent of the material alluded to and the manner in which it is deployed, the novel's greatest indebtedness is to the writings of Dickens's contemporaries.

Many of the contemporaries were also contributors to his weekly journal, *Household Words*, the articles of which were for the novels of Dickens what Holinshed's *Chronicles* and North's Plutarch were for the plays of Shakespeare. The celebrated description of the fog, mist and mud at the opening of *Bleak House*, for example, derives from the opening paragraphs of two articles published in *Household Words* in 1850 and 1851: 'A Crisis in the Affairs of Mr. John Bull. As Related by Mrs. Bull to the Children', an attack by Dickens himself on the papal bull establishing a Catholic hierarchy of bishops in Britain, and 'Twenty-four Hours in a London Hospital', by Frederick Knight Hunt, a journalist who was a qualified surgeon (2.193–6, 457–65). Another example is 'A Guild Clerk's Tale', which was published just when Dickens had begun to turn his mind to writing *Bleak House*. The story, by William Moy Thomas, seems to have suggested the relationship between John Jarndyce and Esther (see note to chapter 8, p. 82). Countless other examples of the influence of *Household Words* on *Bleak House* are cited in the annotation.

Many aspects of the Dedlock plot and of the portrayal of aristocratic resistance to social change show an indebtedness to two adjacent articles published in 1834 in *Blackwood's Edinburgh Magazine*: 'Hints to the Aristocracy. A Retrospect of Forty Years', by the prominent historian and journalist, Archibald Alison, and 'The Baronet's Bride', chapter 15 of a serialized novel by Samuel Warren, *Passages from the Diary of a Late Physician* (35.68–80, 81–121) (see headnote to chapter 2).

Aspects of the depiction of Harold Skimpole suggest that Dickens was as familiar with Leigh Hunt's recently published *Autobiography* (1850), and with some of his miscellaneous writings, as he was with Leigh Hunt himself. Two serious poems by Thomas Hood, 'Moral Reflections on the Cross of St Paul's' (1826) and 'The Bridge of Sighs' (1844), underlie and enhance the dramatic episodes of Jo at Blackfriars Bridge (chapter 19) and of Bucket's and Esther's search along the riverside for the body of Lady Dedlock (chapter 57), and their eventual discovery of her (chapter 59). The stylistic and imaginative texture of the novel is further enriched by subtle echoes of the poems of many other of Dickens's contemporaries and near-contemporaries, including, of course, Thomas Moore, Byron, Wordsworth and Tennyson.

No one familiar with *Bleak House* needs to be told of the pervasive influence on it of Carlyle, whose unmistakable rhetoric gave voice to the thoughts of many. While the annotation evidences the novel's indebtedness to *Sartor Resartus* (1833–4), *The French Revolution* (1837), *Past and Present* (1843), *Latter-Day Pamphlets* (1850), and numerous critical essays, arguably it might have given more evidence. But in support of the rationale observed in the annotation, which gives preference to the citation of probable sources over correlative passages, what could be argued is that countless thoughtful Englishmen of Carlyle's day would have made the same observations – albeit not in the same tones – even in the absence of the indisputable organ-voice of nineteenth-century England.

For different reasons, Dickens's contemporary in America, Nathaniel Hawthorne, has been shown recently to have had as great an impact on *Bleak House* as Carlyle. Although Dickens admitted to Forster in 1851 that he thought the 'psychological part' of *The Scarlet Letter* (1850) 'very much overdone' (Forster 2.410), and although there is no record of his having read *The House of the Seven Gables* (1851), a wealth of internal evidence demonstrates the powerful effect on Dickens of his reading Hawthorne's two pensive romances on the eve and in the midst of composing a pensive romance of his own. Elements of the relationship between Roger Chillingworth and Hester Prynne in *The Scarlet Letter* find their

6

counterparts in the hold which Tulkinghorn gains upon Lady Dedlock, and the characterization of Tulkinghorn is further affected by Jaffrey Pyncheon, the black-mailing villain in *The House of the Seven Gables*. The especially dominant influence of this novel on *Bleak House* is displayed in such elements as the family curse on the Dedlocks and the legend of the Ghost's Walk, the depiction of Bleak House itself, and the portraits of Harold Skimpole and Volumnia Dedlock.

Above all, the character in *The House of the Seven Gables* who is most reflected in *Bleak House* is the young, efficient and housewifely Phoebe Pyncheon, whose name is intended to suggest Phoebus, the god of prophecy and the god who brings back sunshine and light in spring. It is Phoebe, repeatedly identified with sunshine, and with 'a kind of natural magic', who is responsible for introducing light, cheerful-ness and order to the dour, dilapidated and east-wind-buffeted House of the Seven Gables (see notes to chapter 3, which derive from Stokes, 1969, 1985, and Stamon, 1983).

The general influence of *Jane Eyre* (1847) on the character of Esther Summerson has been recognized by previous critics, notably Ellen Moers in 1973. The annotation, by identifying a number of significant verbal parallels between passages in Esther's narrative and those in Charlotte Brontë's novel, provides evidence that Dickens had read his contemporary's book with care, and that Esther's streak of self-reliance and independence is inherited from the spirited and wilful Jane just as much as her goodness and housewifely virtues derive in part from Phoebe.

Counterbalancing the familiar criticisms of Esther and her narrative as insipid, static and flat is Dickens's virtually equal distribution between Esther's 'portion of these pages' and that of the omniscient narrator of the vast number of allusions – biographical, topical and literary – which inform the novel, complicating and deepening its resonances. Dickens allows Esther, for instance, to voice some of his own most fervent convictions on the mental anguish suffered by prisoners in solitary confinement (chapter 52), and on the affection and education which can alleviate the afflictions of deaf and dumb children (chapter 67). Moreover, his own attitude towards an important issue of the day is reflected in Esther's assuring Miss Flite that 'it was not the custom in England to confer titles on men distinguished by peaceful services, however good and great; unless occasionally, when they consisted of the accumulation of some very large amount of money' (chapter 35).

The extent to which Esther's narrative is informed by the Bible and by proverbial phrases has so often been remarked upon and cited as a re-enforcement of her blandness that the other works which in the world of the novel she might be said to have read have been overlooked. For example, her celebrated, much analysed dreams of the colossal staircases and flaming necklace, described in the account in chapter 35 of the fever which accompanies her smallpox, are closely modelled on passages in De Quincey's *Confessions of an English Opium-Eater* (1821; 1822) in which he describes his sufferings under the influence of opium, his being shown by Coleridge Piranesi's set of engravings representing the artist's dreams whilst in a fever, and his quoting lines by Wordsworth about an imaginary mighty city ablaze with jewels, gold, silver and stars.

No less in Esther's narrative than in that of the omniscient narrator, the

7

annotation amply demonstrates Dickens's well-known intimacy with Shakespeare. Some of Esther's allusions particularly enhance the complexity of her characterization and the richness of her imaginative life, such as her likening herself to Desdemona falling in love with Othello in the course of his account of 'the battles, sieges, fortunes' of his life (chapter 35) and, again in relation to Allan Woodcourt, her identifying with the Ghost when it bids farewell to Hamlet ('Pity me not . . . adieu, adieu! Remember me') (chapter 45).

Perhaps most interesting of all is the Shakespearian scene which underlies the final scene of the novel, in which Esther describes herself as sitting one evening on the porch of the new Bleak House (' "The moon is shining so brightly . . . and the night is so delicious" ') awaiting Allan's return home from his work of treating the sick people in a poor Yorkshire village. That Dickens chose to conclude *Bleak House* with a reminiscence of the closing scene of *The Merchant of Venice* does more than merely lend support to his conception of the novel as a romance. It suggests a reading of *Bleak House* as a novel concerned to show a moribund and disease-ridden Venice-like world, depicted in the opening chapter as one 'gone into mourning . . . for the death of the sun' and gloomily illuminated by haggard gas-light, as a world being supplanted – indeed, spontaneously combusted – by the quiet triumph of a nineteenth-century Belmont, a new world which not only represents the social reforms of 'the moving age' but also embodies the values of love, redemption, and individual acts of goodness. The injunction of Christ in the Sermon on the Mount which informs Shakespeare's Belmont scene, 'Let your light so shine before men, that they may see your good works, and glorify your Father which is in heaven', itself informs the Belmont scene at the close of *Bleak House*, with its implicit reminiscence of the lyrical exclamation of Portia:

> How far that little candle throws his beams!
> So shines a good deed in a naughty world.

A NOTE ON THE TEXT

The text of *Bleak House* quoted throughout this volume is that of the Norton Critical Edition of the novel, edited by George Ford and Sylvère Monod (1977) ('*Norton*'). The notes on the variant readings from the manuscript, work plans and proofs, and the transcription of the work plans and list of alternative titles, are based on the author's examination of the holographs and printed texts in the Forster Collection of the Victoria and Albert Museum, London.

Like the manuscripts of Dickens's other late novels, the manuscript of *Bleak House* is heavily corrected, and Dickens also made many substantive emendations at proof stage. For these reasons, only a selection of the variant readings are quoted or commented on in the annotation.

HOW TO USE THE NOTES

To help the reader locate in the novel the word or phrase quoted in an entry, the notes are presented in this way: the opening phrase of the paragraph which includes the entry is quoted as a guide and printed in italics; the entry itself appears in bold-face type. This system should also help the reader who turns from the novel in search of a note on a particular word or phrase.

Documentation within the notes is kept to a minimum by the use of an abbreviated form of referencing. Works of literature are referred to by their parts: *Vanity Fair* 12; *Past and Present* 3.2; *The Faerie Queene* 2.12.17.14–16; 'The Idiot Boy' 8–10. Frequently cited works of criticism and other secondary sources are referred to by author, part (where relevant) and page: '(Collins 171–2)', '(Mayhew 3.106–7)'. References to infrequently cited sources add the date of publication: '(Sala, 1859, 23)'. Complete details are given in the Select Bibliography.

The articles quoted from *Household Words* and *All the Year Round* always antedate or are contemporary with the composition of the novel unless the reference indicates otherwise.

The notes indicate the divisions of the novel in its first published form as a series of nineteen monthly parts (the final part a double number), published from March 1852 to September 1853.

The Work Plans

The notes include transcripts of the sheets of memoranda on which Dickens sketched out his ideas for each monthly number. He folded each sheet once to make two pages, and he referred to the sheets as 'Mems'. In the present volume they are referred to as 'work plans'. To distinguish the pages from each other, the left page is described as the 'number plan' and the right page as the 'chapter plan'. In the notes which follow, the work plans are located among the notes to the first chapter of each monthly number.

Sources

The majority of the annotation is original to this volume. Notes on topography and buildings which are not attributed to a particular source derive from Timbs (1855), or Thornbury and Walford (1873–8), or both. When notes derive from those in *Norton*, this is stated. Notes which seem to derive from *Norton* but which do not acknowledge it as a source derive from an unpublished dissertation by the author (1974).

*The
Notes*

1   The cover of the monthly parts of *Bleak House*, by 'Phiz' (Hablot Knight Browne)

BLEAK HOUSE

Dickens filled ten half-sheets in the MS with ten alternative titles, seven of which contain the name 'Tom-All-Alone's' linked with different subtitles: 'The Ruined House/That got into Chancery/and never got out', or 'The Solitary House/where the grass grew', or 'The Ruined Mill', and variants of these (see Appendix). The name 'Tom-all-Alone's' derives from a house near Chatham which Dickens knew as a boy. The owner was a recluse called Tom Clarke (Langton, 1891, 60; see also headnote to chapter 16, p. 141).

'Bleak House Academy/The East Wind', 'Bleak House/and The East Wind/ How they both got into Chancery/and never got out', and finally 'Bleak House' also appear among the alternative titles. That 'Bleak House and the East Wind' is written as a headline on the folio on which chapter 1 begins and on the folios containing the chapter plans for the first two monthly numbers suggests that this was the title Dickens originally chose from among the alternatives, and that 'Bleak House' (the last-composed of the alternatives and the only one written with a different pen) was chosen as an afterthought.

It has been conjectured that when Dickens decided to name the country house 'Bleak House' he applied the left-over name of 'Tom-all-Alone's' to the urban slum. And instead of putting the country house in Chancery, as some of the subtitles indicate he had intended to do, he put the slum in Chancery and linked it to the house by making it the property in the Jarndyce suit (Ford, 1969).

Several actual houses have been proposed as the original of Bleak House (including Fort House, Broadstairs, which Dickens rented during the summer and autumn for many years), but all the claims are without foundation.

[DEDICATION]

DEDICATED, AS A REMEMBRANCE OF OUR FRIENDLY UNION, TO MY COMPANIONS IN THE GUILD OF LITERATURE AND ART]   The dedication was first published along with other preliminary matter in the final double number of the monthly parts, following the last chapter. The Guild of Literature and Art was conceived in 1847 by Dickens and Bulwer-Lytton as a scheme to assist impoverished authors and artists of established reputation and mature years. Essentially a provident fund and benefit society, the Guild was also intended to provide a college and home for its members at specially built houses in Stevenage, Hertfordshire. The institution was endowed from proceeds of performances by Dickens's amateur theatrical company, with which he had just completed touring when he settled down to write *BH*. In a *HW* article published in May 1851, 'The Guild of Literature and Art' (3.145–7), he announced the scheme and explained how it would work, but his proposed prospectus (printed in *Letters* 5.700–2) was never issued, and in spite of careful planning the ambitious scheme completely failed (see *Speeches* 351–2).

PREFACE

The Preface was first published along with other preliminary matter in the final double number of the monthly parts, following the last chapter.

A Chancery Judge

A Chancery Judge once had the kindness to inform me, as one of a company of some hundred and fifty men and women . . . that the Court of Chancery . . . was almost immaculate.]   The occasion was a banquet given by the Lord Mayor at the Mansion House on 2 May 1853 in honour of judges and other official dignitaries. The judge referred to was Vice-Chancellor Sir William Page Wood. In a speech, the Vice-Chancellor said

> that the court had been blamed much more than it deserved. The parsimony of the public had long limited the Chancery judges to two – the number that had existed in the reign of George III – but its business had continued to increase. However, there were now seven judges, and each case would be examined on its merits. Everything brought before the court, he thought, would be decided within a few months. (*Speeches* 164)

not labouring under any suspicions of lunacy]   The Commissioners in Lunacy, who certified the insane, were under the jurisdiction of the Court of Chancery, which was also responsible for protecting the estates of lunatic heirs. Because the perimeters of certifiable insanity were so broad as to encompass all types of abnormal, excessive or irrational behaviour, wrongful imprisonment for lunacy occurred with increasing frequency during the 1830s and 1840s.

the shining subject of much popular prejudice (at which point I thought the Judge's eye had a cast in my direction)]   The judge would have been reading the monthly parts of *BH*. He could also have had in mind the *HW* articles on Chancery abuses and the Chancery prisoner and poor cobbler whom Mr Pickwick meets in the Fleet (see note to chapter 1, p. 29).

This seemed to me

one of SHAKESPEARE'S Sonnets.]   Sonnet 111:

> O, for my sake do you with Fortune chide,
> The guilty goddess of my harmful deeds,
> That did not better for my life provide

14

Than public means which public manners breeds.
Thence comes it that my name receives a brand,
And almost thence my nature is subdu'd
To what it works in, like the dyer's hand.
Pity me then, and wish I were renew'd. (1–8)

But as it is wholesome

The case of Gridley is in no essential altered from one of actual occurrence]
A few days after the publication of the first number of *BH*, a Mr W. Challinor of
Leek, Staffordshire, sent Dickens a pamphlet describing the case of a particular
Chancery suitor: *The Court of Chancery; Its Inherent Defects as Exhibited in Its System
and Written Proceedings* (1849). According to Forster:

> Dickens was encouraged and strengthened in his design of assailing Chancery
> abuses and delays by receiving . . . a striking pamphlet on the subject containing
> details so apposite that he took from them, without change in any material point,
> the memorable case related in his fifteenth chapter . . . The suit, of which all
> particulars are given, affected a single farm, in value not more than £1200, but all
> that its owner possessed in the world, against which a bill had been filed for a
> £300 legacy left in the will bequeathing the farm. In reality there was only one
> defendant, but in the bill, by the rule of the Court, there were seventeen; and,
> after two years had been occupied over the seventeen answers, everything had to
> begin over again because an eighteenth had been accidentally omitted . . . The
> costs already incurred in reference to this £300 legacy are not less than from
> £800 to £900, and the parties are no forwarder . . . the defendants who own the
> little farm left by the testator have scarce any other prospect before them than
> ruin.
>
> (3.29–30)

The case Challinor described is one which he had already brought to the
attention of the Chancery Reform Association at a meeting on 30 January. A
detailed report appeared in *The Times* the next day (Butt and Tillotson 184).

**At the present moment there is a suit before the Court which was
commenced nearly twenty years ago]**　　In August 1853, three weeks before
he completed *BH*, Dickens wrote to his subeditor at *HW*, W. H. Wills, to ask for
details of the Day Chancery case because he wanted to 'glance at it in the Preface'
and to 'be *within the facts*'. Wills replied that, since the case began in 1834, £70,000
had been spent in costs, sometimes thirty or forty counsel appeared ('it used to be
said the whole Bar'), and the end of the case was 'as far off as ever' (7 August 1853,
Nonesuch 2.481–2).

**There is another well-known suit in Chancery, not yet decided . . .
swallowed up in costs.]**　　It has long been known that Dickens modelled
Jarndyce and Jarndyce on the notorious Jennings case, a Chancery suit with costs

15

over £140,000, which originated at the turn of the century and dragged on until 1878. All the property was consumed in costs. A miser named Jennings (or Jennens) who lived in a deserted mansion in Acton, Suffolk, died in 1798 at the age of 97. The will he had made could not be found, nor could any executors. Finally the heir-at-law was discovered to be the great-great-grandson of C. Jennens of Gopsal, the eldest uncle of the testator. The heir entered into possession of the property, but the case lingered in the courts until eighty years after the miser's death (Fitzgerald, 1895, 239–40).

There is only one other point

The possibility of what is called Spontaneous Combustion] See note to chapter 33, pp. 216–18.

In Bleak House

In Bleak House, I have purposely dwelt upon the romantic side of familiar things.] The interpretation of the nineteenth century as an 'age of romance' was a contemporary notion. Carlyle expressed the idea in *The Diamond Necklace* (1837), the first chapter of which is entitled 'Age of Romance':

> The Age of Romance has not ceased; it never ceases; it does not, if we will think of it, so much as very sensibly decline . . . you ask, Where is the Romance? In the Scotch way one answers, Where is it not? . . .
> Such being the intrinsic quality of this Time, and of all Time whatsoever, might not the Poet who chanced to walk through it find objects enough to paint? What object soever he fixed on, were it the meanest of the mean, let him but paint it in its actual truth, as it swims there, in such environment; world-old, yet new and never-ending; an indestructible portion of the miraculous All, – his picture of it were a Poem.

Dickens's interpretation of the idea is elaborated in 'A Preliminary Word', the leading article in the first issue of *HW* (1.1): 'To show to all, that in all familiar things, even in those which are repellant on the surface, there is Romance enough, if we will find it out . . . is one main object of our Household Words' (1.1). (See also Hawthorne's explanation in his preface to *The House of the Seven Gables* (1851) – the novel to which *BH* is most indebted – of why he has called his work 'a Romance'.)

In the MS and the printed texts up to and including 1853, the present final sentence was followed by an envoi: 'I believe I have never had so many readers as in this book. May we meet again! London, August, 1853.' Letters written during the serialization of the novel express his delight with its wide circulation; in May 1852 he exclaimed to Mrs Watson: 'Five and thirty thousand every published day, is the present mark of Bleak House, thank God!' (Rolfe, 1942, 163). Two days later he wrote to W. F. de Cerjat:

> I hope you will like Bleak House better and better as you go on. It is a most

enormous success; all the prestige of Copperfield (which was very great) falling upon it, and raising its circulation above all my other books. (8 May 1852, *Nonesuch* 2.394)

When he had completed the novel he wrote to Mrs Watson:

The story has taken extraordinarily, especially during the last five or six months, when its purpose has been gradually working itself out. It has retained its immense circulation from the first, beating dear old Copperfield by a round ten thousand or more. I have never had so many readers. (27 August 1853, *Nonesuch* 2.483)

[Dickens left this side blank]

(Bleak House <and the East Wind> – No. I.)

Chapter I.

In Chancery

The great cause of Jarndyce and Jarndyce

Chapter II.

In < the fashionable world> fashion

Lady Dedlock. / Open country house picture.

Sir Leicester Dedlock

Law Writer. (Chapter III.

Mr Tulkinghorn

moment

Work up from this

A Progress.
Esther Summerson.

Lady Dedlock's child.

Chapter <III> IV.

Telescopic Philanthropy

The two Wards, the subjects of the unhappy story of
Jarndyce and Jarndyce

Richard Carstone
Ada

Mrs Jellyby. Her daughter Caddy Jellyby. The children
& household

Chapter 1   First monthly number
                                                 March 1852

IN CHANCERY.

London. Michaelmas Term

Michaelmas Term]   The names of the terms or sessions of the High Court
and also of Oxford and Cambridge and some other universities derive from the
names of feast-days in the English church calendar. As the feast of St Michael is
celebrated on 29 September, Michaelmas denotes the autumn term, the dates of
which vary from year to year but which fall between October and December. The
next term, Hilary (or Lent), begins in January, followed by the Easter and Trinity
terms. Between the Trinity and Michaelmas terms falls the Long Vacation,
described in chapter 19.

the Lord Chancellor]   The Lord High Chancellor, the first judge of the
realm, is the head of the Court of Chancery and a member of the Cabinet. He
receives a peerage with his appointment and sits on the woolsack as Speaker of the
House of Lords. The sympathetic depiction of the Lord Chancellor in Esther's
narrative in chapter 3 suggests that he is modelled on John Singleton Copley the
younger, Lord Lyndhurst (1772–1863), who was three times Lord Chancellor
(1827–30, 1834–5, 1841–5). Dickens saw Lyndhurst sitting and reported cases in
his court on several occasions when, after leaving his post as office boy in the law
firm of Ellis & Blackmore, he worked as a shorthand writer in Doctors' Commons
from 1828 to 1832 (Forster 1.67). Lyndhurst was renowned for his eloquence and
courtesy and was listened to eagerly, both in court and in Parliament.

Lincoln's Inn Hall]   (Plate 2.) The Court of Chancery sat in Lincoln's Inn Hall
out of session; in session, it sat at Westminster Hall (see note to chapter 19, p. 154).
Lincoln's Inn, which lies between Lincoln's Inn Fields and Chancery Lane, is one
of the four Inns of Court, the others being Gray's Inn, the Inner Temple and the
Middle Temple. In the Middle Ages, the Inns were the hostels and abodes of
lawyers and law students from the nobility and rich gentry. The sons of merchants
and others who could not afford the great expenses of the Inns of Court were
accommodated in one of the ten Inns of Chancery, five of which are mentioned in
BH: Thavies Inn (chapter 4), Staple Inn (chapter 10), Serjeants' Inn (chapter 19),
Clifford's Inn (chapter 34) and Symond's Inn (chapter 39).
　　By the nineteenth century, the Inns of Court and Inns of Chancery had evolved
to become legal societies, but barristers were required to be members of one of the
Inns of Court, which had a monopoly on calling to the Bar. In charge of all the pre-
trial details of cases were the attorneys, who practised in the common law courts,
and the solicitors, who practised in the equity courts; attorneys and solicitors were
not members of the Inns of Court and so could not plead in court.

2   The Court of Chancery in Lincoln's Inn Hall, by T. H. Shepherd, in *London Interiors*, 2 vols (1841–4)

The Old Hall of Lincoln's Inn was erected in the fifteenth century and was used by the Court of Chancery from about 1737. By the 1840s dining facilities had become inadequate, and the New Hall was erected in 1842–5. The reference here is to the Old Hall.

Implacable November weather.] The descriptions in the opening paragraphs of the novel of the mud, mist, darkness and fog so thick that it penetrates indoors are indebted to the opening paragraphs of two *HW* articles – one of them by Dickens – which had been published within the last sixteen months. In the issue of 23 November 1850, Dickens's own leading article, 'A Crisis in the Affairs of Mr. John Bull. As Related by Mrs. Bull to the Children', opens with a passage of scene-setting:

> Mrs. Bull and her rising family were seated round the fire, one November evening at dusk, when all was mud, mist, and darkness, out of doors, and a good deal of fog had even got into the family parlor. To say the truth, the parlor was on no occasion fog-proof, and had, at divers notable times, been so misty as to cause the whole Bull family to grope about, in a most confused manner, and make the strangest mistakes. (2.193)

This introduction inspired the opening paragraphs of a leading article published three months later, 'Twenty-four Hours in a London Hospital', by Frederick Knight Hunt (8 February 1851). In turn, Hunt's mention of the slippery walk up Ludgate Hill, the Thames fog and sea-coal smoke, crowds of pedestrians, and the drovers and their animals (compare Dickens's 'husbandman and ploughboy') occasioned the same or similar details in *BH*:

> It is slippery walking up Ludgate Hill, early on a mid-winter morning, with an atmosphere well mixed with Thames fog and sea-coal smoke, after a week of rainy days. Look up for the dome of St. Paul's, and so much of it as you can see looks unusually magnificent, half-hidden in its bath of London yellow clouds . . . Turn to the left up the Old Bailey, and the scene changes . . . Pass on from the Old Bailey towards Smithfield, and the crowd thickens and thickens, and, at each step you take, up splashes the thick yellowish-black slush that, literally, floats on all sides. Thousands of oxen . . . acres of sheep . . . drovers are yelling to dogs, and dogs plunging amongst herds yet unpenned . . . The human throng is as thick almost as the quadruped one. (2.457)

mud in the streets]
The *detritus* of the streets of London assumes many forms, and is known by many names, according as it is combined with more or less water . . . When in combination with a small quantity of water . . . the detritus is known by the name of "mac mud," or simply "mud," according as it proceeds from a macadamized or stone paved road.

Thus Mayhew begins his meticulously comprehensive analysis of London street-dirt – its types, origins, effects, quantities, costs, uses and collection (2.181–202). According to his calculations, four-fifths of the street-dirt consisted of horse manure and cattle dung, of which one hundred tons ('a low estimate') was dropped in the streets each day. Although scavengers defined mud as the dirt yielded by a street paved with granite, wet weather made it virtually impossible to separate mud from manure, dung, dust and 'mac'. Great quantities of mud (mixed with 'mac' and animal droppings) were collected daily and carted off to manure-barges, the owners of which sold each load for from £5 to £6. Some manure-barges were moored in the Thames, but the majority were found in the waterways which intersected the city – the Paddington, Regent's and Surrey canals.

as if the waters had but newly retired from the face of the earth]　An allusion to the end of the flood described in Genesis 8; compare especially 8.3: 'And the waters returned from off the earth continually: and after the end of the hundred and fifty days the waters were abated.'

Megalosaurus]　Of the many dinosaurs which had been discovered between the end of the eighteenth century and the early nineteenth century, the Megalosaurus gained the most notoriety because of its gigantic size. Parts of its skeleton were discovered in 1823 by the geologist William Buckland (1784–1856), who described it and named it in 1824 ('Notice on the Megalosaurus or Great Fossil Lizard of Stonesfield', *Transactions of the Geological Society*, 2nd ser., 1.391–6). Buckland estimated that the length of the creature would have exceeded forty feet, its height seven feet, and that its bulk would have equalled an elephant's, and in 1854 a drawing by the anatomist Richard Owen reconstructed the Megalosaurus to look like a large squat quadruped (Plate 3). This is the shape which Owen gave the Megalosaurus when he built life-size replicas of several dinosaurs for the Crystal Palace at Sydenham in 1854; the replicas are still on display in the gardens. (Because Buckland and Owen possessed only detached parts of imperfect skeletons, they greatly underestimated the actual size of the Megalosaurus and misrepresented its shape: it was actually an agile biped, fifteen feet high.) Three months before Dickens began to compose *BH*, a precise description of the Megalosaurus – as it was imagined by Buckland and Owen – appeared in the *HW* article by Henry Morley, 'Our Phantom Ship on an Antediluvian Cruise':

> His teeth look too decidedly carnivorous. A sort of crocodile, thirty feet long, with a big body, mounted on high thick legs, is not likely to be friendly with our legs and bodies. Megalosaurus is his name, and, doubtless, greedy is his nature. (3.494)

The echo of Genesis juxtaposed with the mention of the Megalosaurus and the image of pedestrians 'adding new deposits to the crust upon crust of mud' seems an allusion to one of the great controversies of the period: the extent to which new scientific discoveries, particularly in the areas of geology, biology and astronomy, could be used to support or to discredit the revelations of the Bible (see Shatto, 1976).

23

3   Megalosaurus. From Richard Owen, *Geology and Inhabitants of the Ancient World*, 1854

Holborn Hill]   The steep descent from Holborn to the Fleet River formed an impediment to carriage traffic until 1869, when Holborn Viaduct was constructed.

Smoke lowering down from chimney-pots, making a soft black drizzle] Coal, the fuel most widely burnt in the metropolis since 1600, produced a greater quantity of soot and black smoke than any other fuel. Mayhew, reporting that the 'peculiarities' of a smoky and sooty atmosphere were more strongly developed in London than elsewhere, cited an authority on air pollution who gave evidence to a committee of the House of Commons:

> on one occasion at the Horse Guards the amount of soot deposited was so great, that it formed a complete and continuous film, so that when I walked upon it I saw the impression of my foot left as distinctly on that occasion as when the snow lies upon the ground. (2.341)

the death of the sun]   The notion that the sun was growing colder and that the solar system would eventually become merely dead matter revolving in space was the 'nebular hypothesis' of Laplace (1749–1827). Tennyson had given his impression of the resulting chaos in *In Memoriam* (1850):

> 'The stars,' she whispers, 'blindly run;
>   A web is wov'n across the sky;
> From out waste places comes a cry,
>   And murmurs from the dying sun . . .
> (3.5–8; final version of lines composed in 1833–4)

Fog everywhere

Fog everywhere.]   As reported by Mayhew, the nuisance of the notorious November fogs was increased by the smoke from furnaces and private coal-fires, the mixture of vapour saturated with carbon particles producing the peculiar yellow-brown colour of the fogs. Their frequency in the metropolis was believed to be due to the presence of the river and to the fact that the higher temperature of the town created conditions similar to those which occur upon rivers and lakes (2.339–40; see also Timbs, 1850, 353–4).

It has been suggested that in these opening paragraphs of the novel Dickens had in mind one passage or another from Carlyle, but references to fog and the use of it as a metaphor are so commonplace in the writings of the period, and the influence of Carlyle on the novel is so pervasive, that it would be misleading to suggest here a particular indebtedness to Carlyle.

Fog up the river, where it flows among green aits]   The area described is Brentford, Isleworth and Twickenham.

the tiers of shipping]
The docks of London are entirely the growth of the present century, and the result of the vast increase in the commerce of the preceding 25 years . . .

From near the Tower to Blackwall, or nearly four miles, is now occupied by five Docks, comprising 450 acres, and accommodation for 1,200 ships and 530,000 tons of goods: the mass of shipping, the vastness of the many-storied warehouses, and the heaps of merchandise from every region of the globe, justify the glory of London as "the great emporium of nations". (Timbs 254)

the waterside pollutions of a great (and dirty) city.]   Prior to 1847, when the Towns Improvement Clauses Act enforced the conveyance of sewage into public sewers, nearly all London households had cesspools, and a large proportion were without any drains whatever. Unfortunately, the 'improved' system of drainage effected by the Act resulted in the waste from private households, as well as the refuse of gut, glue, soap and other factories, and of animal and vegetable offal, all being discharged from the new sewers into the largest open sewer of all, the Thames. Because the river was tide-locked for the five or six miles into which the sewers emptied, the sewage was confined for twelve hours a day, during which time it gave off its stench not only in the immediate area of the river but also – via the elaborate system of drains and sewers – into streets and houses miles away. Worse still, six of the nine water companies supplying London drew their water from the river, and none of the companies filtered the water (*HW* 1.49–54; 'The Main Drainage of London', *The Times*, 19 July 1859, 5).

Dickens became actively involved in the programme to reduce water pollution in 1849, when he took an interest in the scheme for sewage disposal promoted by his brother-in-law, Henry Austin, an architect and civil engineer who was secretary to the General Board of Health. Together with Forster, they were the probable authors of two articles on the subject published in the *Examiner* in 1849: on 14 July 'Drainage and Health of the Metropolis', and on 4 August 'The Sewers' Commission' (*Letters* 5.564 n., 710–11). Moreover, the launch of *HW* in 1850 provided Dickens with his own forum in which to expose the horrors of water pollution and promote action for reform: see, for example, 'The Troubled Water Question' (1.49–54), 'The Water-Drops. A Fairy Tale' (1.482–9), and 'Father Thames' (2.445–50). For Dickens's interest in other aspects of the sanitary reform movement, see notes to chapters 11 and 46, pp. 114, 253–4.

cabooses of collier-brigs]   A caboose, the on-deck cook-room or kitchen, is described in 'The True Story of a Coal Fire' as 'a square enclosure, not unlike a great black rabbit-hutch, open at both sides' (*HW* 1.91).

Greenwich pensioners]   The retired and disabled seamen of the Royal Navy resident at Greenwich Hospital. The antiquated costumes worn by the pensioners made them an attraction for visitors to London.

people on the bridges peeping over the parapets . . . with fog all round them, as if they were up in a balloon, and hanging in the misty clouds.]

This description, together with that above of the river traffic and the 'yards, and . . . rigging of great ships', seems a reminiscence of a passage in 'Ballooning', the *HW* article by R. H. Horne which was published three months before the first number of *BH*:

> We look over the side of the car. We do this very cautiously . . . holding on by the edge, we carefully protrude the peak of our travelling-cap, and then the tip of the nose, over the edge of the car, upon which we rest our mouth . . . soon we thrust the chin fairly over the edge, and take a good stare downwards . . . As for the Father of Rivers, he becomes a dusky-grey, winding streamlet, and his largest ships are no more than flat pale decks, all the masts and rigging being fore-shortened to nothing . . . all is lost in air. Floating clouds fill up all the space beneath. (4.99)

Horne's article is an example of the popularity of balloon ascents, which had become a craze in the 1780s following the flight of the Montgolfier brothers over Paris in 1783 and of Vincenzo Lunardi over London in 1784. By the 1850s, balloon ascents had become so commonplace a pastime that *Punch* announced that the police planned to regulate 'the now inconveniently crowded balloon traffic of the Metropolis' and that newspapers would need to introduce a new column, 'Ballooning Intelligence' (21 (5 July 1851), 16; 22 (15 September 1852), 173). Dickens described balloon ascents in 1836 in 'Vauxhall Gardens by Day' (*SB*); and in his *HW* article of October 1852, 'Lying Awake', he repeatedly calls to mind (in an unsuccessful attempt to occupy himself with pleasant thoughts) 'The balloon ascents of this last season' (6.145–8).

Gas looming through the fog

Most of the shops lighted two hours before their time – as the gas seems to know, for it has a haggard and unwilling look.] 'As is well known, [the London fogs] are often so dense as to require the gas to be lighted in midday, and they cover the town with a most dingy depressing pall' (Mayhew 2.340). Gas distilled from coal began to be developed for use as a convenient and economic substitute for oil-lamps and candles in the 1790s. Soon after the introduction of gas-lighting around 1803, it was adopted by all the principal towns in Britain for lighting streets, shops and public buildings, and by 1823 215 miles of London streets were illuminated by gas-lamps. Private households adopted it less quickly, partly on account of fears about the danger of using it, but by 1842 there were few private houses in large towns not either partially or entirely lit by gas.

The raw afternoon is rawest

that leaden-headed old obstruction, appropriate ornament for the threshold of a leaden-headed old corporation: Temple Bar.] Temple Bar was a triple gateway of Portland stone, designed by Wren, erected in 1670 and completed in 1672, which stood where the Strand and Fleet Street join, before the

Inner Temple and the Middle Temple, marking the entrance to the City. Moreover, it was at the centre of the legal district of London, an area of two square miles which encompassed all the important buildings associated with the law. The severed heads and limbs of executed traitors were displayed on iron spikes above the pediment of Temple Bar up until 1746, when the practice came to be considered barbaric. In the nineteenth century, Temple Bar became a notorious traffic hazard and was taken down in 1878 and re-erected at the entrance to Theobalds Park, Hertfordshire; there are plans, however, for it to be returned to the City and placed in the churchyard of another Wren monument, St Paul's.

'Leaden-headed' refers not to any leaden ornaments (the statues of monarchs in the four niches, and all the minor sculptures, are of stone), but to the stupidity of City dignitaries. Perhaps there is also a hint of wordplay on Leadenhall Street and Leadenhall Market, situated in the heart of the City.

High Court of Chancery]   The Court of Chancery, which considered cases involving disputes over legacies, wills and trusts, had been criticized and satirized for more than a century on account of the gross delays and inequities caused by its bureaucracy.

During the Regency, 'in chancery' became a slang pugilistic term for the position of the head when held under the left arm of the opponent, who could pummel it with his right hand whilst the victim was unable to retaliate effectively. The term derived from the tenacity and absolute control with which the Court of Chancery held on to anything, and the certainty of cost and loss to property (*OED*; noted in Shatto, 1974 diss.).

The Chancery reform movement, which began in the 1820s with the establishment of the Chancery Commission, was associated with the larger series of legal reforms initiated in part by the general trend towards professionalization which was taking place simultaneously in medicine, the military, the church and government. When the Chancery Commission reported in 1826, its proposals fell far short of the overhaul of the system which was required, and by the 1840s and 1850s the Court of Chancery had become a national scandal. Its abuses were numerous. The officials of the court were wholly inadequate to cope with its business, the work was done by underpaid deputies, and the machinery was medieval, but the many survivals of old rules and practices which increased delay and expense could not be abolished because court officials had a vested interest in maintaining them. In the course of the many years that a suit might last, the proceedings were further lengthened by the system requiring that each time someone was 'born into the cause', 'married into it', or 'died out of it' (chapter 1), a new bill had to be filed to bring the new party before the court or out of the suit. Evidence was given in writing, not orally, and the mode of taking it was a complicated system of interrogation conducted in technical language which the witness could not understand and which lasted for months. The Masters and the Six Clerks' Office (see notes below, pp. 31, 33) caused some of the worse delays and incurred the greatest expense.

Moreover, a case could come before the court many times because at all stages motions might be made for many purposes. Any number of counsel could be briefed at the hearing of these motions, for the court desired every piece of evidence to be presented and discussed, every point of law to be made, and every argument to be freely debated ('Eighteen of Mr. Tangle's learned friends, each armed with a little summary of eighteen hundred sheets, bob up like eighteen hammers in a piano-forte').

The abuses of Chancery feature as an incident in Dickens's first novel, when Mr Pickwick, imprisoned in the Fleet, encounters a Chancery prisoner who dies of consumption after twenty years, and a cobbler, imprisoned for twelve years, who was ruined by having money left him. The extended treatment of the Court of Chancery in *BH* results largely from the combination of Dickens's personal experience of the court in 1844 and the prominence given to Chancery reform by the press in 1850 and 1851. Dickens's sympathy with Bentham's campaign for legal reform has been discussed by Stone (1985).

In 1844, acting on the advice of Serjeant Talfourd and Forster, both lawyers, Dickens sued a number of small publishers, booksellers and printers, and became the plaintiff in no less than five Chancery actions to restrain breaches of copyright. He won his case, but 'after infinite vexation and trouble, he had himself to pay the costs incurred on his own behalf' (Forster 2.75). When he was advised to take further proceedings for more piracies two years later, he wrote to Forster:

> My feeling . . . is, that it is better to suffer a great wrong than to have recourse to the much greater wrong of the law. I shall not easily forget the expense, and anxiety, and horrible injustice of the *Carol* case, wherein, in asserting the plainest right on earth, I was really treated as if I were the robber instead of the robbed.
>
> (Forster 2.75–6; *Letters* 4.650–1)

The attention which *The Times* focused on Chancery reform has been documented by Butt (1955). Demands for reform culminated in 1850 in two Acts, passed in July and August respectively: the Court of Chancery Act diminished the delay and expense of proceedings of the court in England, and the Court of Chancery Act (Ireland) regulated the proceedings of the court in Ireland. In spite of the new legislation, *The Times* did not desist from its criticisms, and throughout the summer and autumn of 1851 – the period when Dickens began to turn his mind to the composition of *BH* – it carried on with articles on the inadequacies of legal education and on eminent lawyers who were opposed to reform. Meanwhile, Dickens had been publishing articles about Chancery in *HW*. In December 1850 and February 1851, for example, a two-part article by a barrister, Alfred Cole, 'The Martyrs of Chancery', recorded cases of persons imprisoned for contempt of court (2.250–2, 493–6); see also 'The Last Words of the Old Year' by Dickens (2.339) and 'The Law' by Charles Knight (2.408).

While the novel was being serialized, an important instalment of reforms came into effect with the Chancery Procedure Act (1852) and the Suitors in Chancery Relief Act (1852). These were followed in 1854 by the Common Law Procedure Act. Together, the legislation amended both the pleading of the court and its system of procedure. Further abuses were effectively curtailed by the culminating piece of legislation, passed three years after Dickens's death, the Judicature Act of 1873. (See: Holdsworth, 1928, 79–114; Hamer, 1970; Duman, 1982, *passim*.)

Caricatures of the legal system feature prominently on the cover for the monthly parts (Plate 1): the top panel depicts lawyers tripping over the woolsack whilst playing Blind Man's Buff; the side-panels show a lawyer burying (or digging up) documents, lawyers playing battledore and shuttlecock and a game of chess, and a law-writer copying documents. The scenes are partly modelled on the three illustrations which Cruikshank designed for Gilbert Abbot à Beckett's *The Comic Blackstone* when it was published in volume form in 1846. (It was serialized in *Punch* from October 1834 to December 1844 but with illustrations by another artist.) Browne most closely followed Cruikshank in the depiction of counsel playing battledore and shuttlecock, for this is the vignette which serves as the tail-piece to *The Comic Blackstone* (Tye, 1973).

On such an afternoon

with a foggy glory round his head]   This is reminiscent of Dickens's description of the frescoes ruined by damp on the houses at Albaro, in 1844: 'Sometimes (but not often) I can make out a Virgin with a mildewed Glory round her head; holding nothing, in an indiscernible lap, with invisible arms' (22 July 1844, *Letters* 4.160).

goat-hair and horse-hair]   The wigs of judges and Queen's Counsel were made of goat-hair, those of barristers and other court officials of horse-hair. Carlyle used 'horsehair' as an image of empty legal verbiage in 1850: 'to go blindly floundering along, wrapt-up in clouds of horsehair, bombazeen, and sheepskin officiality . . . is indeed fatal' ('Model Prisons', *Latter-Day Pamphlets* 2).

a long matted well (but you might look in vain for Truth at the bottom of it)]   The space on the floor of the court between the judge's bench and the last row of seats occupied by counsel was covered by coconut matting. The allusion is to the proverb, 'Of truth we know nothing, for truth is in a well'.

silk gowns]   Used allusively to indicate the rank of a Queen's Counsel.

bills, cross-bills]   Bills of complaint in Chancery were the written statements of a case, usually by the plaintiff, which set forth the fraud or injury done, or wrong sustained. A cross-bill was the defendant's answer to a bill of complaint.

answers, rejoinders]   Answers are the written defences made by a defendant to the allegations contained in a bill or to information filed by the plaintiff against him. Rejoinders are the second pleading on the part of the defendant, being his answers to the plaintiff.

affidavits]   Rather than use oral witnesses, the Court of Chancery worked only by affidavits, read aloud by counsel. Gridley, Miss Flite and Richard attend court only to listen to the proceedings: their presence is unnecessary to the progress of their cases. The acceptance of oral evidence from witnesses was one of the reforms instituted by the Chancery Procedure Act of 1852.

references to masters]   A Master in Chancery is one of a number of subordinate judges, the chief of whom is Master of the Rolls, who serve as assistants to the Lord Chancellor. Masters have referred to them disputes or controversies related to a case for their consideration, decision or settlement. The rank still exists.

its decaying houses and its blighted lands]   One of the concerns of the court was the maintenance of trusts in land made either by testators or by the court itself to safeguard the inheritance of young heirs.

Who happen to be in the Lord Chancellor's court

petty-bags, or privy purses]   The three clerks of the 'Petit bag' were officers of Chancery who kept their records in a little leather bag. The Keeper of the Privy Purse is not an officer of Chancery (as Dickens well knew) but the officer of the Royal Household who is charged with the payment of the private expenses of the sovereign.

no crumb of amusement ever falls]   A variation of 'crumb of comfort', deriving from two parables in the New Testament (Matthew 15.27, Luke 16.21).

a little mad old woman ... She carries some small litter in her reticule which she calls her documents]   The probable original of Miss Flite was a well-known deranged woman who frequented the Court of Chancery in the late 1830s; she was described by 'Paul Pry' in *Oddities of London Life* (2 May 1838) 2.113–19:

> To those whose business or pleasure calls them within the vicinity of the courts of law or police, the eccentric figure of Miss R—must be sufficiently familiar . . . She invariably carries with her a reticule strapped round her, adorned with fine bows, and in size and weight equal to a small coal-sack. This bag contains a collection of papers – mouldy crusts – bottles of discoloured water – and scraps of rubbish – all evidences, according to her perverted notions, of daily attempts to poison and assassinate her . . . The court of chancery in particular has, more than once, been visited by this lady, and its gravity has often been upset by the ludicrous misunderstandings which have occurred. On the appointment of a new Lord Chancellor, Miss R—is indefatigable in seeking an interview. (Noted by Butt, 1959, 303)

squeezed bonnet]   The modest poke bonnet, fashionable during the 1840s and 1850s, was tied close around the face.

A sallow prisoner]   'Sallow' was added in MS. Sallowness is one of the symptoms of jaundice, the syndrome marked by excessive bile in the blood which also seems to affect two other characters associated with the Court of Chancery, Mr Vholes and Richard – of whom Mr Jarndyce (whose name sounds similar to 'jaundice') remarks in chapter 35: ' "His blood is infected, and objects lose their natural aspects in his sight." ' In the nineteenth century, jaundice was considered to be a somatic disease which could be initiated by depression, bad news, fits of anger, fear or alarm. Contemporary descriptions of the symptoms include languid-ness and a diminished appetite, with eruptions or boils occurring occasionally (Vholes is described as 'a sallow man' with red eruptions on his face, a 'lifeless manner' and impaired digestion). Emaciation and debility would become more marked towards death (as with Gridley and Richard), in which case death was seldom long postponed.

"to purge himself of his contempt"]   Gridley's plight is that suffered by the two dozen innocent prisoners described by Alfred Cole in the first of his two *HW* articles (mentioned above, p. 29), 'The Martyrs of Chancery':

> Disobedience of an order of the Court of Chancery – though that order may command you to pay more money that you ever had, or to hand over property which is not yours and was never in your possession – is contempt of court . . . For this there is no pardon. You are in the catalogue of the doomed, and are doomed accordingly. (2.250–1)

A month after the appearance of this article, Sir Edward Sugden wrote to *The Times* (7 January 1851, 5) to state that imprisonment for contempt of the Court of Chancery had been prohibited by an Act of Parliament which he himself had framed in 1830. His letter initiated Cole's second article (written with W. H. Wills), which replied that the fact that two dozen persons were still in prison for contempt, in spite of the Act, was a mockery of the administration of the law and a condemnation of the Court of Chancery (2.494).

Jarndyce and Jarndyce drones on

bills of mortality]   A periodically published official return of the deaths (later, also of the births) in a certain district.

Jarndyce and Jarndyce still drags its dreary length before the Court]   A reminiscence of Pope, *An Essay on Criticism* 356–7: 'A needless Alexandrine ends the Song, That like a wounded Snake, drags its slow length along.' Dickens alluded to the lines during a visit to Scotland in 1841, when he wrote to Forster describing Loch Earn: 'the loch, twelve miles long, stretches out its dreary length before the windows' (5 July 1841, *Letters* 2.323).

Jarndyce and Jarndyce has passed

"in it"]   A legal expression for being involved in a case.

benchers]   The senior members of the Inns of Court who manage the affairs of each Inn and possess the privilege of calling to the Bar.

Mr. Blowers, the eminent silk gown]   Dickens may have derived the name from Mr Joseph Blower, a Chancery solicitor who was examined in 1824 by the Chancery Commission appointed to inquire into the practice of Chancery (*Parliamentary Papers* 15, 1826, app. A, 273). The case about which Blower was giving evidence, Stevens v. Guppy, may have also suggested the name of Mr Guppy, the solicitor's clerk (Newsom, 1977, 96).

How many people out of the suit

Jarndyce and Jarndyce has stretched forth its unwholesome hand to spoil and corrupt]   Compare the dialogue between Satan and God in Job 1.11–12:

> But put forth thine hand now, and touch all that he hath, and he will curse thee to thy face. And the Lord said unto Satan, Behold, all that he hath is in thy power; only upon himself put not forth thine hand.

the Six Clerks' Office]
The continued existence of the Six Clerks' Office is one of the great abominations of the court. The officers there are the porters of the Court of Chancery. Every suitor is not only obliged to pay them heavy admittance fees before he may enter the dreaded gates of the court, but is also obliged to fee them further every term in which his cause is moved on the smallest jot.
(Westminster Review 40, 1843, 227–8)

The office was abolished in 1843.

Chancery-folio-pages]   Copying clerks and hired writers were paid per folio, reckoned as either seventy-two or ninety words. Part of the expense of long legal suits resulted from the need for every legal document in a case to be copied so that all the parties concerned received a copy; the cost of the work was charged to the estate. The Chancery Procedure Act of 1852 discontinued the practice of bills being copied by hand and instituted the use of printing. The companion piece of legislation, the Suitors in Chancery Relief Act, replaced the allowances paid to copying clerks with a system of professional pay determined by the Lord Chancellor.

Mr. Chizzle, Mizzle, or otherwise]   In a *HW* article of 1850 (1.134) this style of naming indistinguishable persons is called 'going through the whole alphabet of . . . "make-believe" names', an anticipation of 'the device of ringing alphabetical changes' on the names of fictitious clients which is practised by the bored law clerk in *OMF* (1.8).

Leaving this address

(delivered like a sepulchral message) ... the fog knows him no more. Everybody looks for him. Nobody can see him.] Compare Job 7.8–10:

> mine eye shall no more see good. The eye of him that hath seen me shall see me no more: thine eyes are upon me, and I am not. As the cloud is consumed and vanisheth away: so he that goeth down to the grave shall come up no more. He shall return no more to his house, neither shall his place know him any more. (Noted by *Norton*)

The Chancellor is about to bow

blue bags] Junior barristers carried documents in blue bags; Queen's Counsel used red bags.

If all the injustice it has committed, and all the misery it has caused, could only be locked up with it, and the whole burnt away in a great funeral pyre] The passage is partly informed by the sentiments expressed about Krook's death by spontaneous combustion at the end of chapter 32, but in light of similar ideas Dickens spoke about in 1855, the passage may also be an allusion to the destruction of both Houses of Parliament by fire in October 1834. Until 1826 the Exchequer accounts were kept on splints of wood called 'tallies', but in 1834 it was decided to burn the great accumulation of these antiquated and useless sticks in a stove in the House of Lords. Unfortunately, the fire resulted in a spectacular conflagration engulfing the Lords and Commons which was witnessed by thousands. Dickens drew a moral from the incident in a speech to the Administrative Reform Association in 1855:

> I think we may reasonably observe, in conclusion, that all obstinate adherence to rubbish which time has long outlived, is certain to have in the soul of it more or less that is pernicious and destructive; more or less that will some day set fire to something or other; more or less, which, freely given to the winds would have been harmless, which persistently retained, is ruinous. (*Speeches* 206)

Chapter 2

IN FASHION.

The chapter was composed and interpolated after the first number had been completed: the chapter plan and the pagination of the MS show that the first number was originally intended to comprise only three chapters, 'In Chancery', 'A Progress' and 'Telescopic Philanthropy', but Dickens found he had not composed enough folios to fill the required number of thirty-two printed pages and so completed five further folios to make a new chapter. As a result of the interpolation, the main plot of the novel is introduced sooner than was originally intended.

The depiction of the Dedlocks and their social circle in this chapter and throughout the novel mocks the characteristic elements of the fashionable or 'silver fork' novel, at its height in the 1820s and 1830s but in decline during the next decade. The countless *romans de société* by such writers as Lady Blessington, Lady Charlotte Bury and Mrs Gore, and the early works of Disraeli and Bulwer-Lytton, feature the essential ingredients of the genre: characters drawn almost exclusively from the upper class and the aristocracy, some having equivocal pasts; scenes of high life, descriptions of elegant surroundings and house-parties at country seats; dandies and society toadies; the use of French phrases; the pose of ennui; illegitimacy, blackmail, and the appetite for gossip and scandal which was nourished by the gutter press. Throughout the 1840s the fashionable novel was parodied by other novelists, notably by Thackeray in 'Lords and Liveries . . .' in *Punch's Prize Novelists* (1847), *The Book of Snobs* (1846–7; 1848) and *Vanity Fair* (1847–8), and by Dickens, in his burlesque, *The Lady Flabella*, which Kate Nickleby reads to the languid Mrs Wititterly in *NN* (28). In 'The Dandiacal Body' in *Sartor Resartus* (1843), Carlyle criticized the genre and attacked one of its most prominent exponents and a dandy himself, Bulwer-Lytton.

It seems likely that Dickens derived aspects of the Dedlock plot and of his portrayal of aristocratic resistance to social change from two adjacent articles in *Blackwood's Edinburgh Magazine* 35 (1834), 'Hints to the Aristocracy. A Retrospect of Forty Years' (68–80) and 'The Baronet's Bride' (81–121). The first article, 'Hints to the Aristocracy', was composed by the historian and Tory, Archibald Alison (1792–1867), a prolific and influential journalist. Alison likens the growth of democracy since the 1832 Reform Bill (referred to as the 'Revolution of 1832') to the period in France immediately before and after the Revolution; and, although he recognizes the importance of the British aristocracy in the social order, he nevertheless identifies their conduct as the major cause of current social discontent. He makes frequent use, incidentally, of images similar to Sir Leicester's favourite clichés – 'the framework of society', 'the obliteration of landmarks', 'the opening of floodgates' and 'the uprooting of distinctions' – and he also likens the present age to that of Sir Leicester's greatest bugbear, Wat Tyler:

> The great wave of democracy has not only broken down the barrier of the constitution, but it has rushed into every corner and crevice of the state . . .
> . . .The present convulsion is less directed against the Crown than the Aristocracy: what is complained of, is not the weight of the prerogative, but the usurpation of an Oligarchy. . . . This is by far the worst symptom of the times; it is a feature unknown in the former history of England, save during the frenzy of Wat Tyler and Jack Cade; it is a proof that the genuine democratic poison is at work amongst us, and that our people have tasted of the fruits, not merely of British freedom, but French equality.
> . . .we know from study and observation the vital importance of the nobility, to uphold the fabric of liberty not less than order, and that the moment they are

swept away, there is no barrier remaining to protect ourselves or our children from the worst of tyrannies – the tyranny of a multitude of tyrants. (70, 71, 79)

Alison admits that this public discontent is partly the result of contributory factors – notably industrialism, the rise of the middle class and the education of the masses – but he maintains that, powerful as has been the influence of these causes, they alone could not have been adequate to 'overturn the English Constitution' were it not for what he terms the '*exclusive system*' which characterizes the conduct and manners of the aristocracy, a system 'which distinguishes the present from any other popular convulsion in English history' (72). His depiction of 'secluded and exclusive Aristocratic families' who 'lead a luxurious, indolent life, associated solely with each other, studiously keeping their neighbours at a distance, and knowing as little of the people . . . as they do of the Kalmucs or Hindoos' consists of country house-parties, fashionable company and journeys to the Continent in private carriages, scenes identical to those in *BH*.

Along with many of his contemporaries, notably Carlyle, Alison believes that the aristocracy, both Whig and Tory, must change in order to preserve their influence: casting off the 'fastidious pride' and 'cold reserve' which he considers to be 'the mania of fashion and a foolish etiquette', they must begin to associate with the middle ranks of society. The type of able, accomplished and educated middle-class man whom he urges them to accept on an equal footing is a man such as Dickens's self-made captain of industry, Rouncewell:

> It is . . . by selecting the able, the worthy, and the accomplished, out of the *whole classes* in their vicinity, whose manners and acquirements fit them for their society; by drawing the vast, intelligent, and powerful body of the middling ranks towards them, by the bonds of mutual interest, affection, and gratitude, that that cordial co-operation of all the respectable classes can alone be secured, which is now the only barrier that exists between our present state and revolutionary anarchy . . . (77)

The article which follows 'Hints to the Aristocracy' in *Blackwood's* seems to have suggested some aspects of plot and characterization for *BH*. 'The Baronet's Bride' is chapter 15 in *Passages from the Diary of a Late Physician*, a novel by Samuel Warren (1807–77) serialized in *Blackwood's* in eighteen instalments. The story tells of Sir Henry Harleigh, 'descendant of an ancient house', who, although he marries a woman of contrasting character, the beautiful Lady Anne, is generally considered to have made a fortunate and harmonious marriage. His demeanour is identical to Sir Leicester's:

> His manners were marked by a dignity that often froze into hauter, and some-times degenerated into almost surly abruptness . . . Towards his beautiful wife, however, he preserved a demeanour of uniform tenderness. She could not form a wish that he did not even personally endeavour to secure her the means of gratifying. (82)

During her first London season as the baronet's wife, Lady Anne establishes herself as 'the star of fashion', who is 'followed by crowds of flatterers', including a simpering 'sickly scion of nobility' whose languid speech recalls that of Sir Leicester's debilitated cousin. The *soirées* and *conversaziones* which she gives in her elegant townhouse are reported by journalists in the 'obsequious morning prints'. After she and Sir Henry summer in Switzerland, they retire to their country seat, the grounds of which are sometimes 'drenched' and made 'gloomy' by torrential rain. Here she becomes prey to languor and anxiety. Her husband tells the doctor these are signs of ennui but then announces that his wife is insane. In fact Lady Anne is concealing the secret that it is her husband who has gone mad, and she fears that if this were generally known they would become 'the topic of conversation and discussion . . . of general enquiry and speculation'.

Meanwhile, the family solicitor threatens to bring ruin on Sir Henry and 'exposure of the most public nature' by revealing that a stranger is laying claim to Sir Henry's title and fortune. Both the resulting lengthy lawsuit and Sir Henry's insanity soon become public knowledge, exciting numerous rumours and reports in the press. During this time, the mad Sir Henry – like the 'mad' Chancery suitor, Gridley – composes 'a rambling, exaggerated account of his own lawsuit'. On the morning the cause goes to trial, the plaintiff is found dead in bed as a result of intoxication the previous night. Sir Henry wins the case but does not recover his sanity. His wife, broken-hearted, declines into a long illness, eventually dying on 'a wretched November night' not dissimilar to that on which Lady Dedlock is found dead: 'The country all around was wrapped in a dreary winding-sheet of snow; the sleet came down without ceasing; and the wind moaned as [if] it were a dirge for the dead' (117). She is buried in the family mausoleum, as is Lady Dedlock.

As well as to the fashionable novel, the Dedlock plot shows a general indebtedness to the 'urban Gothic' genre represented by Victor Hugo's *Notre-Dame de Paris* (1831), Eugène Sue's *The Mysteries of Paris* (1842–3) and G. M. Reynolds's *The Mysteries of London* (1845–8). Another novel of Reynolds has also been suggested as a possible analogue, *The Seamstress; or, The White Slave of England*, serialized in his *Miscellany* from 23 March to 10 August 1850 and published in volume form in 1853. The seamstress falls in love with a marquis, but marriage is unthinkable until it is revealed that she is the long-lost daughter of the marquis's haughty stepmother, the Duchess of Bellamont, who had fallen in love with a penniless lieutenant in her youth and had been forced to disown her child at birth (Wilkins, 1976, 68; Maxwell, 1977, 188–99).

It is but a glimpse

oversleeping Rip Van Winkles, who have played at strange games through a deal of thundery weather]   In the story of Rip Van Winkle in Washington Irving's *The Sketch Book* (1819), Rip helps a strange figure carry a heavy keg to a destination where a number of curious figures are playing at ninepins, which make a sound like rolling peals of distant thunder. He drinks from the keg, falls into a stupor and sleeps for twenty years. On waking, he finds the world much changed.

sleeping beauties, whom the Knight will wake one day, when all the stopped spits in the kitchen shall begin to turn] In 'The Sleeping Beauty in the Wood', one of Charles Perrault's *Contes du Temps Passé* (1696) translated into English in 1729, the enchanted princess and everyone in her castle are put to sleep for one hundred years, during which time all activity ceases: 'The very spits at the fire, as full as they could hold of partridges and pheasants, also slept' (1729 edn). The princess is finally released from enchantment when a young prince appears in her golden chamber.

It is not a large world

It is not a large world . . . it is a very little speck.] As a synonym for 'fashionable society', 'world' was frequently used by 'silver fork' novelists. Disraeli mocked the term in *Tancred; or, The New Crusade* (1847):

> To the great body, however, of what is called 'the World,' the world that lives in St. James' Street and Pall Mall, that looks out of a club window, and surveys mankind as Lucretius from his philosophic tower . . . the Duke and Duchess were absolutely unknown . . . It was clear, therefore, that the Bellamonts might be very great people, but they were not in 'society'. (1.2)

(as your Highness shall find when you have made the tour of it] An imitation of the style of Swift's 'Epistle Dedicatory' to 'His Royal Highness Prince Posterity' in *A Tale of a Tub* (1697). Throughout the dedication, Swift adopts a worldly-wise tone, as in this sentence:

> I know very well, that when *Your Highness* shall come to riper Years, and have gone through the Learning of Antiquity, you will be too curious to neglect inquiring into the Authors of the very age before You.

My Lady Dedlock has returned

The fashionable intelligence says so] 'Fashionable intelligence' was the conventional newspaper heading for reports of society figures. The description throughout the novel of Lady Dedlock being 'hotly pursued' and 'hunted down' by gossip-mongering journalists is reminiscent of Disraeli, *Tancred; or, The New Crusade* (1847):

> In the meantime Tancred was launched, almost unconsciously, into the great world. The name of the Marquess of Montacute was foremost in those delicate lists by which an eager and admiring public is apprised who, among their aristocracy, eat, drink, dance, and sometimes pray. From the saloons of Belgrave and Grosvenor Square to the sacred recesses of the Chapel Royal, the movements of Lord Montacute were tracked and registered, and were devoured every morning, oftener with a keener relish that the matin meal of which they formed a regular portion. (2.6)

her "place" in Lincolnshire.] Dickens admitted to modelling aspects of Chesney Wold on Rockingham Castle in Northamptonshire, the home of the Honourable Mr and Mrs Richard Watson, whom he met in Lausanne in 1846 and to whom he affectionately dedicated *DC* in 1850. He first visited Rockingham in 1849 and went again in 1851. That he liked it as much as he liked its owners is indicated in a letter to Forster written during his first visit: 'Of all the country-houses and estates I have yet seen in England, I think this is by far the best' (30 November, *Letters* 5.662). Soon after completing *BH* he wrote to Mrs Watson: 'In some of the descriptions of Chesney Wold, I have taken many bits, chiefly about trees and shadows, from observations made at Rockingham. I wonder if you have ever thought so!' (*Nonesuch* 2.484). Charles Dickens the younger, citing this letter as an example that his father 'very rarely thought it necessary to actually reproduce the first sketch in the finished picture', notes that the long drawing-room and the terrace walk of Chesney Wold were also 'transferred from Rockingham'. He adds:

> But Rockingham Castle stands on a breezy hill in Northamptonshire, and Chesney Wold is placed in a flat, watery Lincolnshire landscape, and in scarcely any respect except that which I have mentioned is there any likeness between the two houses. (1896, 347)

Rockingham Castle is only a few miles south of Lincolnshire, and the name of the Dedlocks' house may have been inspired by the name of the fourth bishop of Lincoln, Robert de Chesney (d. 1166). The castle was royal property from the time of William the Conqueror until it was sold by James I in 1619. Little remains of the original fortress except for the grand arched gateway, which is flanked by two massy bastion towers. The great hall was built by Edward I and the house was largely rebuilt after 1544. It has been suggested that Dickens chose Lincolnshire as the location of the Dedlocks' country house because it was one of the counties which was the least industrialized and most wholly agricultural (and thus 'feudal'). Moreover, one of the favourite butts of *Punch* from the 1830s into the 1850s was a Lincolnshire MP, Colonel Sibthorp, a crackpot ultra-Tory who held the seat for Lincoln for nearly thirty years (Collins, 1974, and 1984, 12).

"bored to death."] The pose of boredom, usually described as 'ennui', was one of the affectations of the dandies and of fashionable society in general.

Therefore my Lady Dedlock has come away

The pictures of the Dedlocks past and gone] The metaphoric role given to these ancestral portraits throughout the novel (chapters 7, 12, 16, 29, 40, 48, 66) is one of many examples of the influence of Hawthorne's *The House of the Seven Gables* (see Introduction, pp. 6–7). Invested with the life of their dead subjects, the pictures are reminiscent of the portrait of Colonel Pyncheon and of the mysterious 'large, dim looking-glass', both of which become major images in Hawthorne's novel.

Sir Leicester Dedlock is only a baronet

Sir Leicester]   The ancient line of the earls of Leicester gives the name aristo-cratic associations; perhaps it was suggested by the fact that Rockingham Castle is twenty miles south-east of Leicester.

Sir Leicester is twenty years

a twist of the gout]   His affliction is later referred to as 'a demon of the patrician order' (chapter 16). Because of its high rate of occurrence among the aristocracy, gout has been traditionally referred to as the monarch of diseases and the disease of monarchs. Its social distinction derives from its being an inherited complaint more common among men than among women and from its association with indulgence in certain rich foods, port and other strong wines. Nineteenth-century medicine had no cure for gout, although there were many quack remedies and learned theories. Sir Leicester's attitude towards the family gout – 'the Dedlock family have communicated something exclusive, even to the levelling process of dying, by dying of their own family gout' (chapter 16) – is representative of the late eighteenth century, the heyday of the disease and the period when it made its greatest impact on culture and society (see Rogers, 1981, the definitive essay on gout and literature; Franks, 1984).

The depiction of Sir Leicester as afflicted with the gout may be in part an allusion to the elderly and gouty Whig, Lord Lansdowne (1780–1863), leader of the House of Lords since 1846. In a letter of 1849, Dickens expressed his irritation with the statesman: 'There has been a kind of grim imbecility and gouty Chester-fieldianity about Ld. Lansdowne this year, remarkable to behold' (21 July, *Letters* 5.580). By December 1852, Lansdowne was so crippled with gout that he was forced to decline the offer to form a government on the resignation of Lord Derby.

his fine shirt-frill, his pure white waistcoat, and his blue coat with bright buttons always buttoned.]   The costume was popularized by Beau Brummell; the buttons would be brass or gilt. In *The Chimes* (First Quarter), Dickens adopted the outfit as representative of a 'real good old city tory' (Alderman Cute) – as he told Forster when describing his plans for the story:

> As you dislike the Young England gentleman I shall knock him out, and replace him by a man . . . who recognizes no virtue in anything but the good old times, and talks of them, parrot-like, whatever the matter is. A real good old city tory, in a blue coat and bright buttons and a white cravat, and with a tendency of blood to the head. (?1–2 November 1844, *Letters* 4.209)

Indeed, he married her for love

at the top of the fashionable tree.]   This seems to have been an expression in vogue: it is italicized in Pierce Egan's *Life in London* (1821), which describes 'A morning at Tattersal's, among the *top-of-the-tree* heroes in society' (2).

How Alexander wept when he had

How Alexander wept when he had no more worlds to conquer, everybody knows] Perhaps the best-known example of the commonplace is Juvenal's tenth satire, on 'the vanity of human wishes': 'One globe is all too little for the youth of Pella [Alexander the Great]; he chafes uneasily within the narrow limits of the world.'

not into the melting, but rather into the freezing mood.] Othello describes himself after the death of Desdemona as

> one whose subdu'd eyes,
> Albeit unused to the melting mood,
> Drops tears as fast as the Arabian trees
> Their med'cinable gum.   (5.2.351–4)

She has beauty still

the Honourable Bob Stables . . . observes . . . that she is the best-groomed woman in the whole stud.] His name is reminiscent of Bob Acres in Sheridan's *The Rivals* (1775). The description of women in terms of horses is noted as a characteristic of aristocratic speech in the *HW* article by G. A. Sala, 'Slang', which mentions a young lord who refers to a pretty young lady as a 'neat little filly' (8.76).

With all her perfections

With all her perfections on her head] *Hamlet* 1.5.78–9: 'No reck'ning made, but sent to my account/With all my imperfections on my head.'

an old-fashioned old gentleman] The depiction of Mr Tulkinghorn is indebted to two of Hawthorne's characters, Judge Pyncheon in *The House of the Seven Gables* (1851) and Roger Chillingworth in *The Scarlet Letter* (1850). Both Judge Pyncheon and Tulkinghorn are blackmailers on the verge of destroying their victims when they are struck by sudden death – which, incidentally, prevents them both from enjoying rare old bottles of wine. Moreover, Dickens's description of Tulkinghorn lying dead in his chambers (chapter 48) is highly reminiscent of Hawthorne's celebrated chapter, 'Governor Pyncheon' (18), on the dead Judge sitting through the day and night whilst the narrator rehearses the important events he is missing (Stokes, 1985, 57–8; Stamon, 1983, 56–8).

Even closer parallels have been noticed between Tulkinghorn and Hawthorne's villain in *The Scarlet Letter*. Roger Chillingworth, an aged and learned Englishman, arrives in seventeenth-century Boston to find his young wife publicly pilloried for having committed adultery and borne an illegitimate child. He obtains from Hester an oath that she will conceal his identity, assumes the character of a physician and sets about discovering her lover. Hawthorne's depiction of the stages of discovery and of the husband's cruel and torturing attitude towards the lovers reveals the gradual moral degradation of Chillingworth himself.

Dickens gives to Tulkinghorn Chillingworth's role of investigator of secret guilt and self-ordained agent of retribution. Tulkinghorn is also given many of his prototype's characteristics: they are both professional men of mature years who dress in black; they have defective vision but are acutely perceptive; their demeanour of calm inscrutability serves to mask malign motives; and they are associated with images of mortality and burial which are related to images of secrecy and concealment. Tulkinghorn is also attributed with an ability to make sudden appearances, an element reminiscent of Hawthorne's interest in the supernatural (Stokes, 1969). See also note to chapter 41, p. 240. Tulkinghorn's depiction as a type of Devil (traditionally referred to as 'the old gentleman', 'the old scholar' and 'the old man'), and the influence on Dickens of a book he read in 1837, Defoe's *Political History of the Devil*, have been established by Georgas (1982).

attorney-at-law, and eke solicitor of the High Court of Chancery]   An attorney practised in the courts of common law and a solicitor in the courts of equity.

cast-iron boxes]   Such boxes, not actually of cast iron, crowd the chambers in Lincoln's Inn Old Square of the solicitor described in *Heads of the People* (1841 supplement):

> The uninitiated reader sees no great grandeur in dwelling amid tin boxes; but read the names that adorn them: – "The Duke of ——," "Marquis of ——:" mercy on me, all the magnates of the land have their title-deeds boxed up in that dingy retreat!   ('The Solicitor', 178)

the coin of the conjurer's trick . . . constantly being juggled through the whole set.]   A keen amateur conjuror, Dickens practised this trick himself and described it in a bill he drew up to advertise one of his conjuring performances in 1849:

THE PYRAMID WONDER

> A shilling being lent to the Necromancer by any gentleman of not less than twelve months, or more than one hundred years, of age, and carefully marked by the said gentleman, will disappear from within a brazen box at the word of command, and pass through the hearts of an infinity of boxes, which will afterwards build themselves into pyramids and sink into a small mahogany box, at the Necromancer's bidding.   (*Letters* 5.706)

conducted, by a Mercury in powder]   The graceful and athletic god Mercury, who wore winged sandals for swift travel, served as a guide and as the messenger of the gods. Throughout the novel, the Dedlock footmen are referred to as 'Mercuries in powder' (the tax on hair powder is mentioned in chapter 58), and their elegant livery the colour of peach blossom is occasionally alluded to (chapters 48, 53). The style which dictated that footmen in fashionable families should be clad in the costume of the eighteenth century was derided in 1851 by an authority on etiquette and dining:

> The fashion (what a perversion of the word!) of plastering the heads of servants with powder is one that ought to be exploded. To see a huge footman with his pate like a college pudding, covered with pomatum and powder, as if he had borrowed the lard from the cook, and the flour from the dredger, is a most untidy and sorry sight. Nothing, too, can be more unmeaning than to see this miserable relic of bygone times of swords, buckles, garters, gold lace coats, embroidered vests, and cocked hats, kept up in these days of plain liveries and cleanly habits. (*London at Table*, 1851; 1858 edn, 35–6)

Dickens mocked the costume in his pastiche of the fashionable novel in *NN* (28). For the fine physiques typical of fashionable footmen, see note to chapter 53, p. 270.

The old gentleman is rusty

Mr. Tulkinghorn]   Throughout the proofs of this chapter, his name reads 'Talkinghorn' – presumably a compositorial error, for Dickens emended it to the MS reading, 'Tulkinghorn'.
-

knee breeches tied with ribbons, and gaiters or stockings.]   The costume was generally superseded by longer styles of trousers during the first decade of the nineteenth century, but elderly gentlemen occasionally wore knee breeches into the middle of the century.

Has Mr. Tulkinghorn any idea

the Italian Opera]   The theatre at Covent Garden was given the name The Royal Italian Opera in 1847 when it was reopened, having been converted from a theatre into an opera-house. The building was destroyed by fire in 1856.

a new dwarf or giant]   Of the numerous dwarfs and giants exhibited in London in the nineteenth century, the greatest amount of aristocratic patronage was given to the celebrated American midget 'General Tom Thumb' (Charles Sherwood Stratton), who toured England in 1844–6 under the management of P. T. Barnum. His successful reception by the royal family and the aristocracy initiated a craze for midgets and dwarfs, who descended on London from Scotland, Holland and Spain. More numerous than dwarfs were giants (in girth more often than in height), notably the 'French giant', the 'Celebrated Canadian Giant' and a 'Swiss giantess' who could lift three hundredweight with one hand (Altick, 1978, 253–6).

who, in hooking one, hook all and bear them off, as Lemuel Gulliver bore away the stately fleet of the majestic Lilliput.] In Swift's *Gulliver's Travels* (1726), Gulliver recounts how he captured the Lilliputian fleet of Blefuscu with a cable of packthread and bars like knitting-needles by fastening a hook to the prow of each ship, tying all the cords together and pulling them away (5).

Blaze and Sparkle the jewellers . . . Sheen and Gloss the mercers . . . Mr. Sladdery the librarian] The frequent mention of well-known firms, a feature of Byron's poems, became a characteristic of the fashionable novel and was mocked by Thackeray in *Punch's Prize Novelists* (1847) (Tillotson, 1954; 1971, 86). 'Mr Sparkle, the jeweller' is mentioned in a *HW* article of 1851 (4.178).

Sir Leicester has no objection

Wat Tyler] Leader of the Peasants' Revolt in southern England in 1381, Tyler was slain, the revolt was crushed and many of the rebels were executed. The sympathetic account of the Peasants' Revolt which Dickens gives in *CHE*, and which he published in *HW* three months after the publication of the present number, reflects contemporary popular radical opinions:

> Wat was a hard-working man, who had suffered much, and had been foully outraged; and it is probable that he was a man of a much higher nature and a much braver spirit than any of the parasites who exulted then, or have exulted since, over his defeat . . . The King's falsehood in this business makes such a pitiful figure that I think Wat Tyler appears in history as beyond comparison the truer and more respectable man of the two. (5.306)

'Wat Tyler' was also the nickname of a northern Chartist leader who gained national notoriety in rebellious disturbances during 1848 (Sucksmith, 1975, 119–23). For the cancelled passage in proof showing Dickens's intention to link Wat Tyler with the inventor James Watt, see note to chapter 7, p. 76.

Mr. Tulkinghorn takes out

a golden talisman of a table] In the second half of the eighteenth century, much drawing-room furniture was flamboyantly gilded with filmy thin gold leaf.

"Is it what you people

law-hand] A round style of handwriting employing contractions and abbreviations and deriving from early Latin legal documents written on vellum. The style is reproduced in the letter which Esther receives from Kenge & Carboy in chapter 3.

Chapter 3

A PROGRESS.

In the MS, 'A Progress' was the second chapter of the novel until Dickens interpolated 'In Fashion' (see headnote to chapter 2).

I have a great deal

I have a great deal of difficulty in beginning to write my portion of these pages]   There are numerous traces in *BH* of the influence of Charlotte Brontë's *Jane Eyre* (1847), the most obvious similarities being that both Jane and Esther are orphan girls who narrate their own stories. (For close verbal echoes of *Jane Eyre* in chapter 37 of *BH*, see p. 225; also see notes below, pp. 45–6, 47.) It has been suggested that Dickens may have conceived the character of Esther, a strong-minded girl who is nevertheless mild, selfless and benevolent, as a rival to the abrasive and egotistical heroine of Charlotte Brontë (Moers, 1973, 22). That the character of Esther is closely modelled on Phoebe Pyncheon in Hawthorne's *The House of the Seven Gables* has been noticed independently by Stamon (1983) and Stokes (1985, 50-2), both of whom suggest that Esther's surname was inspired by the reiterated association of Phoebe with sunshine. Moreover, with a 'genial activity pervading her character', Phoebe is bright, orderly, efficient and 'a nice little housewife', and with her 'gift for practical arrangement' which gives 'a look of comfort and habitableness to any place' she works the same effect on the dark and cursed old House of the Seven Gables as Esther works on Bleak House. What might also be suggested is that Phoebe's relationship with her elderly spinster cousin, Hepzibah, provided a model for Esther's relationship with John Jarndyce. For example, when Phoebe arrives at the House of the Seven Gables, Hepzibah tells her:

> But, Phoebe, this house of mine is but a melancholy place for a young person to be in. It lets in the wind and rain – and the snow, too . . . but it never lets in the sunshine! And as for myself, you see what I am; – a dismal and lonesome old woman . . . whose temper, I am afraid, is none of the best, and whose spirits are as bad as can be! . . .
> "You will find me a cheerful little body," answered Phoebe smiling, and yet with a kind of gentle dignity. (5)

(For the influence of Hepzibah on the depiction of Volumnia, see note to chapter 28, p. 200.)

My dear old doll!

My dear old doll!]   This paragraph suggests the influence of *Jane Eyre*:

To this crib I always took my doll; human beings must love something, and, in the dearth of worthier objects of affection . . . I doted on this little toy, half fancying it alive and capable of sensation. I could not sleep unless it was folded in my night-gown; and when it lay there safe and warm, I was comparatively happy, believing it to be happy likewise. (4)

I was brought up

I was brought up . . . like some of the princesses in the fairy stories . . . by my godmother.]   Esther seems to conflate 'godmother' with the stock figure in fairy-tales. 'Cinderella' is the best-known fairy-story which features a wicked stepmother, but Dickens may also have known analogous stories such as 'The Rose-Tree' (also called 'The Wicked Stepmother'), 'The Princess with the White Petticoat', 'Rosy' and 'The Cruel Stepmother and Her Little Daughter' (listed in Briggs, 1970, 1.45, 452–4, 472–3).

I had never heard my mama

Mrs. Rachael]   In Genesis, Rachael is the initially barren wife of Jacob whom God enables to bear Joseph and who dies giving birth to Benjamin. Mrs Rachael becomes the wife of the Old Testament-quoting Rev. Mr Chadband.

Although there were seven girls

Esther Summerson]   In the Bible, the orphaned and low-born but beautiful Esther is chosen queen from among many virgins and becomes the saviour of her people. Hester, a variant of Esther, is the name of the heroine in *The Scarlet Letter* who served Dickens as a model for aspects of Esther's adulterous mother (see notes to chapters 2 and 41, pp. 41, 240). In the nineteenth century, 'Esther' was generally (but incorrectly) assumed to mean 'star'.

"Your mother, Esther

pray daily that the sins of others be not visited upon your head, according to what is written.]   Exodus 20.5: 'for I the Lord thy God am a jealous God, visiting the iniquity of the fathers upon the children unto the third and fourth generation of them that hate me'.

It must have been

reading, from St. John . . . let him first cast a stone at her!' "]   The story of the woman taken in adultery is told in John 8.3–7. Christ dismisses the woman, telling her to sin no more, and disperses her accusers by reminding them of their own sins.

" 'Watch ye therefore!

" 'Watch ye therefore! . . . Watch!' "]   Esther's aunt defies the passage from
St John by citing the admonition about the second coming of Christ in Mark
13.35–7:

> Watch ye therefore: for ye know not when the master of the house cometh, at
> even, or at midnight, or at the cockcrowing, or in the morning: Lest coming
> suddenly he find you sleeping. And what I say unto you I say unto all, Watch.

She was laid upon her bed.

She was laid upon her bed . . . her frown remained unsoftened.]   This
passage shows the influence of the scene in *Jane Eyre* in which Jane visits the death-
bed of her own cruel aunt:

> The well-known face was there: stern, relentless as ever – there was that peculiar
> eye which nothing could melt, and the somewhat raised, imperious, despotic
> eyebrow . . . I stooped down and kissed her: she looked at me . . . I knew by her
> stony eye – opaque to tenderness, indissoluble to tears – that she was resolved to
> consider me bad to the last; because to believe me good would give her no
> generous pleasure: only a sense of mortification. (21)

"Pray be seated – here

Miss Barbary's]   The name chosen for Esther's aunt – who, as a young
woman, had broken off her engagement to Mr Boythorn (chapter 43) – is the
name of the jilted servant mentioned by Desdemona:

> My mother had a maid call'd Barbary:
> She was in love; and he she lov'd prov'd mad,
> And did forsake her.   (*Othello* 4.3.25–7; noted by Friedman, 1986, 91–2)

Of course, 'Barbary' is also the maiden name of Esther's mother, who never
married Captain Hawdon.

"Miss Barbary, sir, " returned Mrs. Rachael

the Seraphim]   The highest of the nine orders of angels; they are distinguished
by the attribute which Miss Barbary lacked, fervour of love.

He appeared to enjoy beyond everything

**he formed himself on the model of a great lord . . . he was generally called
Conversation Kenge.]**   'Conversation Sharp' was the nickname of Richard
Sharp (1759–1835), the wealthy radical MP and member of the Holland House

circle who was renowned for his conversational talents. A friend of the most eminent literary men of the day, he was described by Byron in 1816 as 'the "Conversationist", as he was called in London, and a very clever man' (recorded by Thomas Moore).

"Mr. Jarndyce," he pursued

to discharge her duty in that station of life unto which it has pleased – shall I say Providence? – to call her."]   In the Catechism the catechumen promises 'to do my duty in that state of life, unto which it shall please God to call me'.

"Now, what does our young friend

I pause for her reply.]   The words of Brutus in *Julius Caesar* 3.2.32: 'If any, speak; for him have I offended. I pause for a reply.'

This interview took place

Windsor . . . I left it, inside the stage-coach, for Reading.]   The distance of the journey is fifteen miles. The short stage would be performed by a two-horse coach which made several journeys a day. The inside fare on a stagecoach was about five pence a mile, the outside fare about three pence, and the seats had to be booked several days in advance, when at least half the fare was paid. Esther's later mention of the straw on the floor (used for warmth) makes the description of her journey reminiscent of Dickens's own account of leaving Rochester as a young boy:

> As I left Dullborough in the days when there were no railroads in the land, I left it in a stage-coach. Through all the years that have since passed, have I ever lost the smell of the damp straw in which I was packed – like game – and forwarded, carriage paid, to the Cross Keys, Wood-street, Cheapside, London? (*UT*)

We were twelve boarders

my qualifications as a governess . . . helping to instruct others.]   In becoming apprenticed at the school where she was a pupil, Esther follows the regular procedure for providing such schools with junior staff; Jane Eyre spends her years at Lowood in a similar way. That apprentices were sometimes disdained by the regular pupils is indicated by the treatment of Miss Edwards at Miss Monflathers's establishment in *OCS*. Teaching or becoming a governess were two of the few occupations open to a middle-class girl who needed to make her own living – thus Ralph Nickleby recommends them to Kate in *NN* (3) (Collins, 1961).

Six quiet years

a Ward of the Ct in this cause]   A legatee under the age of 21 who derived his subsistence from an estate which was in Chancery was directly subject to the authority of the court. Mr Jarndyce, as guardian of Ada and Richard, acts as an agent of the court.

White Horse Cellar, Piccadilly]   A house widely renowned in coaching days which stood on the corner of Down Street. It was the starting-point for mail-coaches to the West Country, including the coach on which Mr Pickwick and his friends depart for Bath (*PP* 35).

And when the two Miss Donnys

grieved as much to part with me, as the least among them]   Matthew 25.40: 'And the King shall answer and say unto them, Verily I say unto you, Inasmuch as ye have done it unto one of the least of these my brethren, ye have done it unto me.'

I had been the light of his eyes]   Psalms 38.10: 'My heart panteth, my strength faileth me: as for the light of mine eyes, it also is gone from me.'

He was very obliging

a fly]   A two-wheeled one-horse covered carriage, such as a cab or hansom, with room for two passengers inside and a seat for the driver above and behind the cab. A fly was let out on hire for three pence per mile.

"Oh dear no, miss," he said.

a London particular."]   The *OED* cites this 'humorous name for a London fog' as the earliest printed example of the usage, but Dickens used the expression in a *HW* article (composed with W. H. Wills) published a few months before he began work on *BH*. In 'Spitalfields', a weaver describes how his white satins have been ruined by ' "the two-days' fog . . . The blacks (London genuine particular)" ' (3.27).

We drove slowly through the dirtiest

the dirtiest and darkest streets that ever were seen]   This would be the rookery of St Giles's, the model for Tom-all-Alone's (see note to chapter 16, pp. 141–2). The most direct route from White Horse Cellar to Lincoln's Inn was along Piccadilly, through the rookery to High Holborn, and then down Chancery Lane.

and old gateway . . . a silent square . . . a churchyard . . . some cloisters]
Plate 4. A brick gatehouse built in the early sixteenth century stands at the Chancery Lane entrance to Lincoln's Inn and gives access to Old Square, also called Old Buildings. Beside Lincoln's Inn chapel is a graveyard, and beneath the chapel is a crypt on open arches which was built as a place for students and lawyers to perambulate.

4 Lincoln's Inn Hall, Chapel, and Chancery Court, by T. H. Shepherd, in *London Interiors*, 2 vols (1841–4)

"Miss Ada," said Mr. Kenge

Ada] A name of German origin which means 'happy', Ada was a popular name, an early example being Byron's daughter, Augusta Ada.

We conversed in a low tone

bag wig]   So called because the black hair was enclosed in an ornamental bag of silk usually tied with a silk bow.

"Mr. Jarndyce of Bleak House

"Mr. Jarndyce of Bleak House is not married?"]   It was possible for an estate-owner who sought the guardianship under the court of a female minor to marry her and so join their estates. The provision of a female companion for Ada helps the Lord Chancellor to approve of the arrangement (Hamer, 1970, 344).

We looked at one another

the children in the wood]   'The Children in the Wood' is a popular old English ballad, described by Addison as 'one of the darling songs of the common people' and 'the delight of most Englishmen in some part of their age' (*Spectator* 85). It tells of a brother and sister who, having inherited money from their dead parents, fall prey to their wicked uncle who hires ruffians to murder them. One ruffian kills the other and abandons the children in the wood, where they wander until 'death did end their grief'. The final stanza shows the relevance of Esther's allusion:

> You that executors be made,
>   And overseers eke
> Of children that be fatherless,
>   And infants mild and meek;
> Take you example by this thing,
>   And yield to each his right,
> Lest God with such like misery
>   Your wicked minds requite.

"Right! Mad, young gentleman," she returned

I expect a judgment. Shortly. On the Day of Judgment.]   The arrival of the Day of Judgement before a law case ends is a joke which dates from the Middle Ages and which is found in all countries as part of the satire against lawyers (Hamer, 1970, 346).

the sixth seal mentioned in the Revelations is the Great Seal.]   Revelation 6.12–17:

And I beheld when he had opened the sixth seal, and, lo, there was a great earth-quake; and the sun became black as sackcloth of hair, and the moon became as blood; And the stars of heaven fell unto the earth . . . For the great day of his wrath is come; and who shall be able to stand?

The sixth seal is equated with the Great Seal of England, which is kept by the Lord Chancellor. The Great Seal bears a likeness of the sovereign and is used to authenticate important documents issued in the name of the sovereign.

Chapter 4

TELESCOPIC PHILANTHROPY.

"In-deed! Mrs. Jellyby," said Mr. Kenge

Mrs. Jellyby . . . devotes herself entirely to the public.]　　The reputed original of Mrs Jellyby is 'the emigrant's friend', Caroline Chisholm, *née* Jones (1808–77) (Plate 5). The daughter of a philanthropist, she married a captain in the service of the East India Company and settled in Madras, where she established the Female School of Industry for young girls and orphans of poor soldiers. Leaving India in 1838 to settle in Sydney, Australia, she opened a home for the reception of newly arrived colonists. Her unlimited energy enabled her to extend the scheme, and in 1846 she left Australia for a nine-year sojourn in England, where she publicized her activities and successfully influenced the Government's policies on emigration by writing two pamphlets, *Emigration and Transportation Relatively Considered* (1847) and *The ABC of Colonisation* (1850).

She met Dickens in February 1850 as a result of his interest in her Family Colonisation Loan Society, established to assist families of slender means who were desirous of emigrating. Dickens had subscribed to the scheme in October 1848 (*Letters* 5.416), and he co-authored with Mrs Chisholm an article promoting it in the first number of *HW*, 'A Bundle of Emigrants' Letters' (1.19–24). A later article, 'Family Colonisation Loan Society' (by Samuel Sidney), describes in detail how the scheme operated (1.514–15). Although he admired Mrs Chisholm's public activities (his *HW* article describes her 'great exertions in reference to the emigration of the poor, especially of her own sex'), he had anxieties about her neglect of her family, as he confessed to Miss Coutts in 1850: 'I dream of Mrs. Chisholm, and her housekeeping. The dirty faces of her children are my continual companions' (4 March 1850, *Letters: Coutts* 166). Two further characteristics of Mrs Chisholm are given to Mrs Jellyby: her assertive manner and her use of one of her children as an amanuensis (see Collins, 1960, 348–9). For Dickens's attitudes towards philanthropic schemes and women with a 'mission', see notes to chapter 8, pp. 83–4, 86, 87.

5   Caroline Chisholm in 1853, engraved by J. B. Hunt

devoted to the subject of Africa . . . and the happy settlement, on the banks of the African rivers, of our superabundant home population.]   What Dickens described as his 'invention' of the cause of emigration to Africa was partly inspired, of course, by Mrs Chisholm's Family Colonisation Loan Society. The depiction of Mrs Jellyby's African scheme was attacked in 1852 by Lord Denman, a former Lord Chief Justice, in a series of newspaper articles reprinted as a pamphlet in 1853, *Uncle Tom's Cabin, Bleak House, Slavery and Slave Trade* (Butt and Tillotson 183, n. 1). (The first of many English editions of Harriet Beecher Stowe's novel was published shortly after the present number of *BH*.) Dickens commented on the pamphlet in a letter to Lord Denman's daughter on 20 December 1852:

> Mrs. Jellyby gives offence merely because the word "Africa" is unfortunately associated with her wild Hobby. No kind of reference to Slavery is made or intended, in that connexion . . . it is one of the main vices of this time to ride objects to Death through mud and mire, and to have a great deal of talking about them and *not* a great deal of doing – to neglect private duties . . . for . . . public hullabaloo . . . and thus seriously to damage the objects taken up . . . I *know* this to be doing great harm. But, lest I should unintentionally damage any existing cause, I invent the cause of emigration to Africa. Which no one in reality is advocating. Which no one ever did, that ever I heard of.   (cited in Butt and Tillotson 195, n. 1)

The bottom vignette on the cover of the monthly parts (Plate 1) shows Mrs Jellyby (in the midst of other philanthropists gathered around Mr Jarndyce) embracing two black children and standing alongside a figure in a fool's cap who wears a board reading 'Exeter Hall' (Butt and Tillotson 195; Steig, 1978, 132–6).

The 'subject of Africa' had been topical and contentious since the 1770s, when comparisons began to be made by both abolitionists and anti-abolitionists between the slaves in Africa and the West Indies and the factory workers at home. The metaphor was soon appropriated by industrial reformers and social critics, including Cobbett, who coined the image of 'white slaves'. The charges of hypocrisy against a middle class which exerted itself on behalf of blacks in the colonies but remained apathetic to the plight of industrial workers in Yorkshire continued to be made during the first half of the nineteenth century (Gallagher, 1985, 3–8). Another reason why Africa was in the news was because Britain made attempts in 1850 to interfere with the slave trade of other nations by patrolling the coasts of Africa with naval vessels, a controversial venture which was debated in Parliament and in the press. Opponents objected not just on moral grounds but also because of the unnecessary expense.

Although the slavery issue had been settled in Britain, an increasing number of foreign missionary and philanthropic societies were established to assist the natives of Africa and the West Indies – as well as India, China and the South Seas. Sampson Low's *The Charities of London* (1850) lists more than twenty-five such societies, including the Aborigines Protection Society, the African Civilization Society, the African Native Agency Committee, the Society for Advancing the

Christian Faith in the British West Indian Islands and the Mico Fund for the Education of the Negro and Coloured Population of the West Indies. In August 1850, *Punch* mocked the evangelical movement's sympathy with Africans in an article which mentions 'the Savages' Friend Society – if there is one' and 'the Philanthropophagi and Negro-Fanciers of Exeter Hall' (19.89).

The foreign missionary society movement, which began to flourish in the last decades of the eighteenth century, gained notoriety in 1841 as a result of the failure of Sir Thomas Fowell Buxton's ambitious Niger expedition, the particular object of Dickens's satire on 'Borrioboola-Gha, on the left bank of the Niger'. Buxton (1786–1845), a prominent philanthropist and evangelical, sponsored the scheme with the object of ending the slave trade, encouraging legitimate commerce and establishing a model farm and the settlement of missionaries among the natives. Six months after the expedition's frigate and two steamers had sailed from England, fever broke out in all the vessels, killing forty-one of the 301 Europeans and bringing the venture to an end (Charles Buxton, *Memoirs of Sir Thomas Fowell Buxton*, 1848, 441–52, 514–28, 533–51). Buxton's son believed that the venture would have been entirely successful but for the Niger climate (' "The finest climate in the world!" said Mrs. Jellyby').

When a two-volume narrative of the journey was published in 1848, Dickens reviewed it in the *Examiner* on 19 August and used the occasion to condemn Exeter Hall evangelicalism in general and foreign philanthropy in particular:

It is not, we conceive, within the likely providence of God, that Christianity shall start to the banks of the Niger, until it shall have overflowed all intervening space. The stone that is dropped into the ocean of ignorance at Exeter Hall, must make its widening circles, one beyond another, until they reach the negro's country in their natural expansion . . . Believe it, African Civilisation, Church of England Missionary, and all other Missionary Societies! The work at home must be completed thoroughly, or there is no hope abroad. To your tents, O Israel! but see they are your own tents! (*MP* 1.133–4)

Dickens had expressed the same sentiments in 1836–7, in Mr Weller's complaint about his wife's church society providing the 'infant negroes in the West Indies with flannel waistcoats and moral pocket handkerchiefs':

'Wot aggrawates me, Samivel, is to see 'em wastin' all their time and labour in making clothes for copper-coloured people as don't want 'em, and taking no notice of the flesh-coloured Christians as do.' (*PP* 27)

Carlyle discussed the issue in 1849 in his attack on Negroes and foreign philanthropists which was inspired by his recent visit to Ireland and first-hand experience of the potato famine, 'Occasional Discourse on the Nigger Question' (*Fraser's Magazine*, December 1849; reprinted as a pamphlet, 1853).

"I don't say that," returned Mr. Kenge

Mr. Jellyby . . . is . . . Merged – in the more shining qualities of his wife."]

Archibald, the husband of Mrs Chisholm, is described as a man 'who for many years ably supported his wife in all her charitable undertakings' (*DNB*). He survived her by only four months.

He then rang a little bell

Guppy]   For the possible source of his name in a Chancery case of the 1820s, see note to chapter 1, p. 33.

"No distance," said Mr. Guppy

Thavies Inn]   The distance was roughly a quarter of a mile, for the Inn was situated directly south of Holborn Circus. It was formerly an Inn of Chancery appertaining to Lincoln's Inn, which sold it in 1771, when it was subsequently destroyed by fire. A range of private buildings was then erected on the site. Although the area was bombed in the Second World War and completely rebuilt, Thavies Inn still exists in name.

"Only round the corner," said Mr. Guppy.

as near as a toucher]   A colloquial or slang expression for 'very nearly', 'all but', derived from the game of bowls.

Nobody had appeared belonging to the house

pattens]   Sandals of wooden soles on iron rings which served to raise the ordinary shoes off the ground. Pattens were especially worn by girls when doing chores (Charley Neckett and the Bagnet daughters wear them) and, less often, by women out of doors in bad weather.

Mrs. Jellyby, whose face reflected

with handsome eyes, though they had a curious habit of seeming to look a long way off. As if . . . they could see nothing nearer than Africa!]   In *The Mudfog and Other Sketches*, Mr Tickle 'displayed his newly invented spectacles, which enabled the wearer to discern, in very bright colours, objects at a great distance, and rendered him wholly blind to those immediately before him'. When the President of the Association objects that he did not know that the eye worked in this manner, Tickle replies that 'a large number of most excellent persons and great statesmen could see, with the naked eye, most marvellous horrors on West Indian plantations, while they could discern nothing whatever in the interior of Manchester cotton mills' (Report of the Second Meeting).

But what principally struck us

the feather of her pen]   Steel pens did not come into general use until the middle of the century.

"– I shall then have finished

Caddy]　Her nickname may be inspired by that of Carolina ('Caddy') Boyle, the elder sister of Mary Louisa Boyle, whom Dickens first met in 1849 and with whom he developed a close friendship. The sisters were friends of Walter Savage Landor, at whose house Dickens met Carolina (letter to Forster, 30 November 1849, *Letters* 5.662).

The evening was so very cold

the boiler]　A boiler built into the kitchen cooking range was developed about 1806. One version had a tube on the boiler with a brass cock which projected into the kitchen to give hot water when needed. A later model supplied up to fourteen gallons of boiling water from one small fire (Wright, 1960, 188).

We begged her not to

Little Red Riding Hood]　Esther later reads aloud 'Puss in Boots'; both stories are from the well-known collection by Charles Perrault.

When we went down-stairs

a mug, with "A Present from Tunbridge Wells" on it]　This town in Kent first gained popularity as an inland watering-place in the eighteenth century, when its springs and romantic situation recommended it as a favourite resort of Queen Anne. In the next century, the South-Eastern Railway made Tunbridge Wells easily accessible to Londoners.

"It's disgraceful," she said.

Priscilla drinks – she's always drinking.]　The joke is that 'Priscilla' was a favourite name with Puritans in the seventeenth century.

The purblind day was feebly struggling

purblind]　Revised in proof from the MS reading, 'benumbed'. 'Purblind' was a poeticism in the nineteenth century, in use by Carlyle and Scott.

Chapter 5

A MORNING ADVENTURE.

What with the bustle

Some pewter-pots and a milk-can hung on the area railings]   Customers of public houses who took their beer home at night hung the pots, of pewter or tin, on the railings for collection by the potboy in the morning. The milk-cans would be filled by the milkman on his next round.

she had been to see what o'clock it was.]   A euphemism for going to a public house. Clocks in private households were taxed by Parliament in 1797, and the same law required public houses to install clocks, called 'Parliamentaries', for the convenience of their customers.

"I don't care!" she said.

as old as Methuselah]   The oldest man in the Bible: he died aged 969 (Genesis 5.27).

"But for all that, I say again

I wonder the very paving-stones opposite our house can have the patience to stay there, and be a witness]   A conflation of passages from *Macbeth* and the Bible:

> The very stones prate of my whereabout
> And take the present horror from the time,
> Which now suits with it. (2.1.58–60)

And he answered and said unto them, I tell you that, if these should hold their peace, the stones would immediately cry out.   (Luke 19.40)

I could not but understand

the extraordinary creatures in rags, secretly groping among the swept-out rubbish for pins and other refuse.]   Mayhew describes a great variety of what were called 'scavagers', street-finders who sifted and collected anything which had a resale value, including bones, rags, bits of metal, old wood and cigar ends. They were rarely self-employed and generally worked for dust-contractors (2.136–80).

"When the leaves are falling

nosegays for the Lord Chancellor's court] Judges were traditionally presented with fragrant bouquets of wild flowers in order to ward off unpleasant odours associated with the accused person in consequence of his confinement in a prison cell. Aromatic leaves were also sprinkled over the tables and in front of the accused.

It was quite true

a narrow back street . . . "This is my lodging.] Charles Dickens the younger unequivocally identified the house that served as model for Krook's shop as being located in Chichester Rents, which then gave access from Chancery Lane to the side-entrance of New Square. Visiting the site, he further recognized Miss Flite's large room at the top of the house and noted the parapet outside on which Krook's cat waits to pounce on Miss Flite's birds (1896, 347).

She had stopped at a shop

KROOK, RAG AND BOTTLE WAREHOUSE ... DEALER IN MARINE STORES.] This kind of shop is described by Mayhew:

> The principal purchasers of any refuse or worn-out articles are the proprietors of the rag-and-bottle-shops. Some of these men make a good deal of money . . . The stench in these shops is positively sickening. Here in a small apartment may be a pile of rags, a sack-full of bones, and many varieties of grease and 'kitchen-stuff,' corrupting an atmosphere which, even without such accompaniments, would be too close. The windows are often crowded with bottles, which exclude the light; while the floor and shelves are thick with grease and dirt . . .
>
> The 'rag-and-bottle' and the 'marine-store shops' are in many instances but different names for the same description of business. The chief distinction appears to be this: the marine-store shopkeepers (proper) do not meddle with what is a very principal object of traffic with the rag-and-bottle man, the purchase of dripping, as well as of every kind of refuse in the way of fat or grease. The marine-store man, too, is more miscellaneous in his wares than his contemporary of the rag-and-bottle store ... [but in] perhaps the majority of instances there is little or no distinction between the establishments. (2.108)

It has been suggested that the depictions of Krook's shop and of Krook himself were influenced by Dickens's reading Mayhew's articles on the London poor which began to appear in the *Morning Chronicle* in 1849 and which were published as a collection in 1851 (Dunn, 1970).

a picture of a red paper mill, at which a cart was unloading a quantity of sacks of old rags.] Woollen rags were sent off for hop-manure, but white linen rags were sold by the pound for paper-making. Working-class women would sell

Introduce the old marine store dealer <u>who has the papers</u>

<u>2</u>

Bleak House and John Jarndyce.

       Leonard Skimpole

<u>3</u>

Foreshadowing legend of the country house

  Mrs Rouncewell – two sons

    Grandson, Watt
    Rosa

Chapter V.

A Morning Adventure.

Chapter VI.

Quite at Home.

Chapter VII.

The Ghost's Walk.

their rags either to marine-store dealers or to the street-buyers of rags, metal, glass and bones who called periodically (Mayhew 2.104–5; *HW* 1.380).

BONES BOUGHT ... KITCHEN/STUFF BOUGHT ... OLD IRON BOUGHT ... WASTE PAPER BOUGHT ... LADIES' AND GENTLEMEN'S WARDROBES BOUGHT.] Bones were bought for a halfpenny per pound or three pounds for a penny and then sold to the soap-boiler, who boiled out the fat and marrow for use and then crushed the bones and sold them for manure. 'Kitchen-stuff' included dripping, grease, soup-stock and broken bread, which were the perquisites of the cook, kitchen-maid or servant-of-all-work. Grease was sold to the tallow-maker or soap-boiler. Dripping was used by the poor as a substitute for butter and sold at three and a half to five pence per pound. Old iron was sold to the manufacturers to be remelted or rewrought. Old keys were purchased in great quantity. 'Old metal' meant copper, brass and pewter, the cheaper substances being iron or lead. Every kind of paper was purchased by street-buyers and rag-and-bottle shops, and attorneys' offices were important sources for the dealers, who then sold the waste paper to cheesemongers, buttermen, butchers, fishmongers, poulterers, pork and sausage sellers, sweet-stuff sellers, tobacconists, chandlers and generally all who sold provisions. Old clothes were sold by rag-and-bottle dealers to nearly all working people (Mayhew 2.40, 106-14; *HW* 1.380).

dirty bottles]   All glass vessels were sold to old-glass shops. A street-buyer of bottles and old glass complained to Mayhew: 'It's a trade would starve a cat, the buying of old glass . . . it's coming to be all up with street glass-people; everybody seems to run with their things to the rag-and-bottle shops' (2.107).

blacking bottles]   Dickens's work as a young boy in Warren's Blacking warehouse was a part of his past which he hid from all but his wife and his closest friend, John Forster. The reference here may be the same kind of private joke as that in *GE*, where Joe tells how he and Mr Wopsle went to look at the blacking warehouse when they arrived in London (27).

counsellors' bands]   Lawyers attached to their collars a broad strip of starched white muslin which was fastened to a tape tied round the neck.

to make the picture complete.]   All the items noticed by Esther are depicted by Browne in the plate, 'The Lord Chancellor Copies from Memory', but also included is a black doll suspended in the window, a detail which features in two other plates, 'The Appointed Time' and 'Tom-all-Alone's'. Black wooden dolls in white dresses were hung over the doors of marine-store shops and rag-and-bottle shops to indicate that they functioned as 'dolly shops', essentially pawnshops for the very poor (Mayhew 2.110).

As it was still foggy and dark

a hairy cap]   Fur caps made of cat skin were worn by persons of the lower class:

Jo wears one, as does the waterman Rogue Riderhood (*OMF* 3.3), the chimney-sweeper Mr Gamfield, and the thief Tom Chitling (*OT* 3, 18).

"You see," said the old man

sacks of ladies' hair]   There was a sizeable trade throughout Europe in the purchase and sale of human hair, used to make wigs and perukes for men, false hairpieces for women and items of hair jewellery, a fashion at its height in the 1840s and 1850s. 'Several Heads of Hair' (*HW* 9.61–5) is a detailed account of the Continental hair-market and of the high prices fetched by the best-quality hair. In Britain the demand for hair was so great that five tons of it were imported annually from foreign countries. The hair in Krook's shop would have come from local poor women, compelled to sell their hair to provide for their families.

"You see I have so many things here," he resumed

Lady Jane]   Krook's cat is named after Lady Jane Grey (1537–54).

"She'd do as much for any one

"I deal in cat-skins]   Cat skins provided a cheap kind of fur, like Krook's cap. Live cats were often stunned and their skins 'stripped off', as Krook says. Dead cats, to be found at the dust-heaps, were generally the perquisites of the women searchers, who would come to the dust-field or wharf every night and pay 'sixpence for a white cat, fourpence for a coloured cat, and for a black one according to her quality' (*HW* 1.380).

"Extremely honoured, I am sure," said our poor hostess

I am sorry I cannot offer chocolate.]   Chocolate (which is also drunk by Mr Turveydrop) was a more old-fashioned breakfast drink than its rival, coffee; moreover, at sixpence a pound, chocolate was cheaper than coffee (a shilling a pound) or tea (three shillings).

She partly drew aside the curtain

larks, linnets, and goldfinches]   Mayhew reports that Londoners could purchase a wide variety of birds from shopkeepers and itinerant street-sellers. Because they offered 'one of the peculiar pleasures of the country', singing birds were bought generally by the city-bound working class and by tradesmen, who would pay from threepence to fourpence for a young bird and up to two shillings and sixpence for a mature singing bird. Larks and linnets did not adapt easily to caged life and suffered a high mortality, but goldfinches, the longest-lived of the small caged birds, often survived for fifteen to sixteen years. They were also always in demand because of their liveliness and beauty (2.58–64).

"I cannot admit the air freely," said the little old lady

the wolf of the old saying]   'To keep the wolf from the door' is to fend off starvation.

"The only other lodger," she now whispered

The children in the lanes here, say he has sold himself to the devil.]   This seems to be a boyish taunt, as Krook and Mrs Piper also imply (chapters 10, 11). David Copperfield explains that the drunken madman to whom he sold his clothes 'was well known in the neighbourhood, and enjoyed the reputation of having sold himself to the devil, I soon understood from the visits he received from the boys, who continually came . . . shouting that legend' (13).

In half an hour after our arrival

Newgate market]   A quarter of a mile from Thavies Inn, Newgate Market was a bustling meat-market which stood on the site of Paternoster Square. It was demolished in 1869 when the Central Meat Market was formed.

She was by that time

barouche]   A four-wheeled carriage with a half-head behind which could be raised or lowered, a seat in front for the driver and seats inside for two couples to sit facing each other.

Chapter 6

QUITE AT HOME.

The extensive number of alterations and cancellations in this chapter result from Dickens's attempts to shorten the amount he had overwritten and to tone down Skimpole's resemblance to Leigh Hunt (*Norton*).

The day had brightened

we went westward.]   Their route would be rather north-north-west, through Islington, Holloway, Highgate, Whetstone, Barnet and South Mimms. The distance from London to St Albans is twenty-one miles.

"The whole road has been

my namesake Whittington]   Richard Whittington (d.1523), the son of a mercer, rose to be thrice Lord Mayor of London. According to a popular seventeenth-century legend and ballad, while running away in his youth from his master's house, he rested at Holloway and heard Bow Bells ringing what he imagined to be the words 'Turn again, Whittington,/Lord Mayor of London'.

He had all our names in his hat.

his hat . . . (which was like a soft bowl)]   This was a Bollinger, a predecessor of the bowler, which was worn by cab drivers.

The roads were very heavy

At Barnet there were other horses waiting for us]   Barnet was an important coaching stage on the Great North Road. The 'old battle-field' is the site of the battle of Barnet (1471) during the Wars of the Roses.

St. Albans; near to which town Bleak House was]   Dickens's original idea for the novel seems to have been to focus attention on a decaying country house in the Stroudwater Valley, Gloucestershire. Forster recorded Dickens's early plan in August 1851: 'for the time he was eager to open it in that prettiest quaintest bit of English landscape, Strood Valley, which reminded him always of a Swiss scene' (3.20). (Forster's confusing Strood, Kent, with Stroud, Gloucestershire, which Dickens visited in September 1851, is noted by *Norton*.) For the choice of 'Bleak House' as the name of Jarndyce's home and as the title for the novel, and for comment on the alleged originals of the house, see p. 13.

Dickens was familiar with St Albans because his brother Frederick lived there for a while and because as a young man he went there on riding excursions with Forster (De Vries, 1971, 62). The town had featured prominently in the press and in *Punch* since the spring of 1851, when a parliamentary election disclosed the existence of widespread and long-standing bribery and corruption in the borough. The St Albans Bribery Commission was established in October to inquire into the alleged corrupt transactions, and its investigations revealed a system of bribery so extensive that no measure short of disfranchisement seemed adequate to remedy the evil. An Act 'to disfranchise the Borough of Saint Alban' was passed in March 1852, and the Corrupt Practices at Elections Act, passed in June, established a procedure to deal with further suspected cases. The topicality of the subject seems to be reflected in the bribery hinted at in the election discussed in chapter 40, 'National and Domestic'.

While Ada was speaking

a handsome, lively, quick face]   As depicted by Browne in two plates, 'The Family Portraits at Mr. Bayham Badger's' and 'Sir Leicester Dedlock', Jarndyce's features are those of Walter Savage Landor, the original of Lawrence Boythorn (Plates 6, 9; see note to chapter 9, pp. 93–4).

6 'Sir Leicester Dedlock', by H. K. Browne, in the fourteenth monthly number of *Bleak House*, showing the resemblance of Jarndyce to Landor and of Skimpole to Leigh Hunt

"She means well," said Mr. Jarndyce

"The wind's in the east."]   In chapter 8, Jarndyce tells Esther that when he is deceived or disappointed he blames it on the east wind and takes refuge in his room called the Growlery. The association of trouble with the east wind derives from the Old Testament (for example, Genesis 41.5–6, Exodus 10.13, Psalms 48.7, Ezekiel 17.10, 27.26) and had become a commonplace. Dickens referred to the 'East Wind' in a letter of 1849 mentioning the auction of the contents of Gore House to pay off Lady Blessington's debts, and in a speech to the Metropolitan Sanitary Association in 1851 he commented: 'the air from Gin Lane will be carried, when the wind is Easterly, into May Fair' (30 April 1849, *Letters* 5.530; *Speeches* 128).

Jarndyce's retreat may derive from essays in the *Spectator* (424, 429, 440) describing a group of friends who spend the summer in the country, where they are 'provided of a great House, where there is not only a convenient Apartment for every particular Person, but a large Infirmary for the Reception of such of them as are any way indisposed, or out of Humour'. One particular day found many of the friends in an ill humour and voluntarily shut up in the Infirmary, the cause of their indisposition being attributed to a prevailing easterly wind (440) (Lovett, 1963, 124; Goldfarb, 1981, 14–15).

Three of the ten alternative titles for the novel refer to the east wind (see Appendix). Moreover, the east wind is illustrated implicitly – in the form of a weathervane and chimney smoke – in the central panel of the cover of the monthly parts (Plate 1). It has been noticed that Browne inaccurately depicted the direction the weathervane points towards in relation to the drift of the smoke (Steig, 1978, 134; Miller, 1986).

It was one of those delightfully

It was one of those delightfully irregular houses]   The extensive revisions to this passage in MS intensify the cosy charm of Bleak House and the jovial hospitality of its owner, attention being drawn to the mazy quaintness of the house, the pretty gardens and expansive views, the curious miscellany of furniture and the spartan nature of Jarndyce's habits.

Hawthorne's descriptions of the 160-year-old House of the Seven Gables have been shown to be an influence on the descriptions of Bleak House, Tom-all-Alone's and (more generally) Chesney Wold – all properties which come to symbolize for their inhabitants 'received tradition and inherited sins' (Stamon, 1983). Bleak House itself – which has three gables in the roof in front – most closely resembles the House of the Seven Gables, which is repeatedly depicted as 'picturesque and romantic', 'desolate, decaying, gusty, rusty' and a prey to the prevailing east wind.

a Native-Hindoo chair, which was also a sofa, a box, and a bedstead] India and the Orient manufactured lightweight varieties of convertible multi-purpose furniture, a style popular during the earlier decades of the nineteenth century but tending to be relegated to servants' rooms and attics later on.

cold-bath]   A hip-bath. Cold-bathing, which had been recommended as healthy since the eighteenth century, was particularly in vogue in the mid-nineteenth century because it was one of the therapies provided at water-cures. The practice was also promoted by Muscular Christians, such as Charles Kingsley, who advised that 'with a clean skin in healthy action and nerves and muscles braced by sudden shock [a cold bath], men do not crave for artificial stimulants. I have found that a man's sobriety is in direct proportion to his cleanliness' ('Great Cities and their Influence for Good and Evil', *Miscellanies* 2.289).

The furniture, old-fashioned

old-fashioned rather than old]   That is, dating from the eighteenth century. 'Old' would be in the style of William and Mary, or Jacobean.

the death of Captain Cook]   The gruesome and prolonged death inflicted by the Sandwich Islanders on the circumnavigator, James Cook (1728–79), was recorded by many eye-witnesses and became a popular pictorial subject. Paintings by John Webber (1784) and George Carter (1785) were both widely reproduced as engravings. A coloured engraving of the scene decorates the parlour of Mrs Whimple, with whom Magwitch lodges in *GE* (46).

the whole process of preparing tea in China, as depicted by Chinese artists]
Sets of pictures (in watercolour, gouache or oil) representing stages in the manufacture of products such as tea, cotton, rice, silk and porcelain were produced by Chinese artists around 1800 and occasionally imitated by European painters. A series of twelve paintings representing the cultivation and manufacture of tea (from hoeing the ground and planting the seed through to packing the chests at Canton for shipment to the Western market) hung in the Prince Regent's bedroom in the Royal Pavilion at Brighton (Patrick Conner, *The China Trade, 1600–1860* (Brighton, 1986), 62–4).

"I don't mean literally a child," pursued Mr. Jarndyce

He is grown up ... but ... he is a perfect child."]   Dickens modelled the character of Harold Skimpole on a real-life original, Leigh Hunt, and to a lesser extent a fictional prototype, Clifford Pyncheon in *The House of the Seven Gables.* While not acknowledging his indebtedness to Hawthorne's character, Dickens freely admitted that his original for Harold Skimpole was his friend, the amiably vivacious and perpetually insolvent critic, poet and essayist, James Henry Leigh Hunt (1784–1859) (Plate 7). One month before *BH* had completed serialization, Dickens wrote to his subeditor on *HW* about an article contributed by Leigh Hunt ('Gore House', 7.589–93), implying that Hunt was the model for Skimpole: 'It is Skimpole, you know – the whole passage. I couldn't write it more like him' (*Nonesuch* 2.480–1). He was more explicit the following month in a letter to Mrs Watson:

7   Leigh Hunt in 1850. From *The Autobiography of Leigh Hunt*, 3 vols, 1850

– Skimpole. I must not forget Skimpole – of whom I will now proceed to speak as if I had only read him, and had not written him. I suppose he is the most exact portrait that ever was painted in words! I have very seldom, if ever, done such a thing. But the likeness is astonishing. I don't think he could possibly be more like himself. It is so awfully true, that I made a bargain with myself 'never to do so, any more.' There is not an atom of exaggeration or suppression. It is an absolute reproduction of a real man. Of course I have been careful to keep the outward figure away from the fact; but in all else it is the Life itself. This in confidential reply to your enquiry.   (21 September 1853, autograph letter in the Henry E. Huntington Library, HM 17982)

Although Dickens says he has 'been careful to keep the outward figure away from the fact', Skimpole, like Hunt, is an animated slender man with delicate features and a dark complexion (Hunt's father was descended from one of the oldest settlers in Barbados). Moreover, Hunt's appearance is reflected in Browne's two depictions of Skimpole, 'Coavinses' and 'Sir Leicester Dedlock', even though this seems not to have been apparent to Dickens, who wrote to Forster on 7 March 1852: 'I enclose proofs of No. 2. Browne has done Skimpole, and helped to make him singularly unlike the great original' (*Nonesuch* 2.123) (Plates 6, 7). Forster's own opinion of the second number, however, was that 'the likeness was too like', and Dickens accordingly toned down the character and also altered 'Leonard', the Christian name originally given Skimpole, to 'Harold' (*Nonesuch* 2.383). But, for Dickens's oversights in emending the name (a Freudian slip?), see note to chapter 31, p. 208. 'Leonard' is as reminiscent of 'Clifford', incidentally, as of 'Leigh'. In general, the revisions in the proofs attempt to obscure the qualities which had been intensified in the additions to the MS: Skimpole's spontaneous, light-hearted manner of speech; his ignorance and dislike of worldly affairs; and his love of the beautiful.

Upon Hunt's death, a revised edition of his *Autobiography* was published by his eldest son, Thornton, in 1860. Thornton also demanded a public apology from Dickens, which took the form of an article in *AYR*, 'Leigh Hunt. A Remonstrance' (2.206–8) – a poor attempt at self-justification.

From 1833 to 1840, Leigh Hunt and his numerous family lived in a state of perpetual financial embarrassment in Cheyne Row, next door to Carlyle, who described Hunt in a letter on 27 June 1834:

An airy, crotchetty, most copious, clever Talker, with an honest undercurrent of *reason* too, but unfortunately not the deepest, not the most practical . . . His hair is grizzled, eyes black-hazel, complexion of the clearest dusky-brown; a thin glimmer of smile plays over the face of cast-iron gravity; giving him a singular, discrepant air.   (*Collected Letters of Thomas and Jane Welsh Carlyle* 7.225)

See also Carlyle's description of the disorderly Hunt household, quoted in note to chapter 43, p. 243.

The likeness between Harold Skimpole and Hawthorne's selfish sybaritic aesthete, Clifford Pyncheon, has been noticed by Stokes, who suggests that

Dickens was particularly influenced by Hawthorne's emphasis on Clifford's childishness and love of refined luxury (1985, 53–7). A further likely literary influence on the depiction of Skimpole is the attack on artistic bohemianism which was made in the two *HW* articles published less than a year before the present number of *BH*: 'Student Life in Paris' and 'The True Bohemians of Paris', by Sidney Laman Blanchard (3.286–8, 4.190–2) (Ericksen, 1973; his general argument expands on K. J. Fielding, 'Leigh Hunt and Skimpole: another remonstrance', 1968). Blanchard's disapproval of the picturesque but un-principled Parisian artists, writers and musicians is associated by Ericksen with Dickens's own well-known attacks on Pre-Raphaelitism and the germinal 'art for art's sake' trend in art and literature. Skimpole thus becomes a composite criticism both of Leigh Hunt and of philosophies which espoused the withdrawal of the artist from society and the absence of moral integrity in art.

"Why, just as you may suppose," said Mr. Jarndyce

Harold Skimpole's children have tumbled up somehow or other.]   Leigh Hunt and his wife Marianne had seven children. Little is known of the daughters, but the eldest son, Thornton, became a successful literary man, and in the preface to the revised edition (1860) of his father's *Autobiography* he recorded that Leigh Hunt's family 'increased faster than his means' (vii). One son died in youth and Hunt's favourite son, Vincent, in 1852, at the age of 30. The second-eldest, John, was brilliant but unstable, prone to attacking others with knives, and a persistent begging-letter writer. He died in 1846, aged 34 (*DNB*; Blunden, 1930, 209–10, 287; *Letters* 4.580-1).

Our luggage having arrived

my worldly goods]   From the Solemnization of Matrimony: 'with all my worldly goods I thee endow'.

a maid (not the one in attendance upon Ada]   Only families of some wealth could afford to keep a lady's maid: Mrs Beeton suggested that a man's annual income should exceed £1,000 before his wife maintained one. In very rich families it was not uncommon for the wife as well as each adult daughter to have her own maid, while in families with smaller incomes one maid might attend on two or three.

When we went downstairs

his neck-kerchief loose and flowing, as I have seen artists paint their own portraits)]   This seems to be a reminiscence of the collection of artists' self-portraits which Dickens would have seen at the Uffizi in Florence during his visit in 1845. Among the pictures are several in which the painters have depicted them-selves in wide-collared shirts open at the neck, and some are wearing neckerchiefs. In 1847, William Allingham described Leigh Hunt at home as 'a *young* man (though of sixty), with luxuriant if gray locks, open shirt collar and flowing dressing gown, bright face, and the easiest way of talking in the world' (11 July 1847, *William Allingham, a Diary*, 1907, 38). The engraving of Hunt by J. C. Armytage (from an unfinished miniature by Joseph Severn) shows him wearing a broad, open, flowing collar, and the portrait by Samuel Lawrence (1837) also shows him with an open collar.

I gathered from the conversation

educated for the medical profession, and had once lived . . . in the house-hold of a German prince.]   In fact, except for a short period as clerk in the law office of his brother, Leigh Hunt's entire life was devoted to literature. These details are obviously intended to disguise the resemblance to Hunt and to prepare for Skimpole's assessment of Jo's illness in chapter 31.

His good friend Jarndyce and some other of his good friends then helped him]   Leigh Hunt, who was in debt for most of his life and was repeatedly arrested for debt, lived for many years supported by the efforts of his literary friends, including Shelley, Byron, Macaulay, Carlyle, Forster, Bulwer-Lytton, Serjeant Talfourd, R. H. Horne and Dickens himself, who staged benefit performances on Hunt's behalf in 1847 and realized over £400.

fruit in the season . . . a little claret]   With the later reference to Skimpole's living on hothouse fruit, sponge cake and wine (chapter 43), this would seem to be an allusion to the four years in Leigh Hunt's youth when he ate special diets in an attempt to cure himself of melancholy (see the chapter, 'Suffering and Reflection', in his *Autobiography*, 1850, 1.294–5). As a mature man, however, Hunt actually lived on simple food, customarily drinking only water and eating only bread for supper.

Bristol-board]   Smooth-surfaced pasteboard used for drawing and painting.

Wear red coats, blue coats, lawn sleeves . . . aprons]   Red coats were worn by the Army, blue coats by the Navy, lawn sleeves by bishops and aprons by tradesmen.

"Well!" cried Mr. Skimpole

Age or change should never wither it.]   *Antony and Cleopatra* 2.2.239–40: 'Age cannot wither her, nor custom stale/Her infinite variety.'

Mr. Skimpole could play

the piano and the violoncello; and he was a composer]   Leigh Hunt described his love of music, particularly song, in his *Autobiography* (1850, 1.72–80). After *BH* was published, Dickens told Hunt that he had not known Hunt composed music (Forster 3.8). This seems hard to believe. K. J. Fielding, who assumes that

Dickens was telling the truth, has suggested that Dickens might have had in mind the Irish composer Thomas Moore, 'a man of the same stamp', who had died in February 1852 and who had been notorious among his fellow-authors for what they regarded as his toadying (1968, 6).

When I was shut out with her

Mr. Skimpole's room] Browne's illustration of the scene, 'Coavinses', includes several emblems of Skimpole's tastes, including a Chelsea shepherd and shepherdess (Cheyne Row is in Chelsea) and a statue of the Three Graces. The catalogue of Dickens's library at Gad's Hill shows that Dickens himself owned a plaster-cast copy of Canova's 'The Graces'.

"Coavinses?" said the strange man.

"Coavinses?" . . . "A 'ouse."] Persons arrested for debt were detained in a 'sponging house' for twenty-four hours, where they would be 'sponged' of all their money by the bailiffs who kept the house, and if their creditors were not paid during this time they would be sent to debtors' prison. Coavinses is modelled on Sloman's house at number 4 Cursitor Street, Chancery Lane, where Dickens's father was detained in 1834 and where Dickens visited him the next day to give him some money. A few months later, Sloman's featured in 'A Passage in the Life of Mr. Watkins Tottle' (*Monthly Magazine*, February 1835) under the guise of a house belonging to Mr Solomon Jacobs (Suzannet, 1939–40). Dickens also used Sloman's as the model for the house where Mr Pickwick is detained (*PP* 40). Disraeli's details of Sloman's sponging house in *Henrietta Temple* (1837) are very similar to those described in *SB* and *PP*. Colonel Crawley in *Vanity Fair* (1847–8) resides at Sloman's for a time (53).

"Then you didn't think

the birds, those choristers in Nature's great cathedral] Compare Shakespeare, Sonnet 73 (noted by *Norton*): 'Upon those boughs which shake against the cold,/Bare ruin'd choirs where late the sweet birds sang.'

It was late before we separated

the best of all ways, to lengthen our days, was to steal a few hours from Night, my dear!] From Thomas Moore, 'The Young May Moon', in *Irish Melodies* (1807–35):

> The young May moon is beaming, love,
> The glow-worm's lamp is gleaming, love,
>   How sweet to rove
>   Through Morna's grove,
> When the drowsy world is dreaming, love!
> Then awake! – the heavens look bright, my dear,

'Tis never too late for delight, my dear,
And the best of all ways
To lengthen our days,
Is to steal a few hours from the night, my dear!

"Well!" cried Mr. Jarndyce

Saint Michael's oranges]   A variety of the China orange grown at São Miguel in the Azores. Mrs Beeton refers to it as the 'Portugal orange'.

"Why, what a cod's head

what a cod's head and shoulders I am,"]   Cod's head and shoulders was a popular dinner-dish, the name of which became a colloquialism for 'What a fool I am!' Mrs Beeton's recipe for cod's head and shoulders recommends that it be served on a hot napkin and garnished with lemon and horseradish. Her coloured plate of the presentation shows that the fish does indeed look rather foolish.

Chapter 7

THE GHOST'S WALK.

While Esther sleeps

solitude, with dusky wings, sits brooding upon Chesney Wold.]   A reminiscence of Milton's apostrophe to the Spirit of God's creative power and wisdom at the beginning of *Paradise Lost*: 'thou from the first/Wast present, and with mighty wings outspread/Dove-like sat'st brooding on the vast abyss' (1.19–21).

So with the dogs

up-stairs, down-stairs, and in my lady's chamber.]   From the nursery rhyme, 'Goosey, goosey gander':

> Goosey, goosey gander,
> Whither shall I wander?
> Upstairs and downstairs
> And in my lady's chamber.

It has rained so hard

Mrs. Rouncewell, the old housekeeper ... a fine old lady, handsome,

stately, wonderfully neat]   The depiction of Mrs Rouncewell throughout this chapter is indebted to 'The Old Housekeeper' in *Heads of the People* (1840):

> We love, oh! how we love, to look upon her, that Old Housekeeper, as, in dark stuff gown, and snow white apron clad, with simple cap closely plaited over hair of almost equal whiteness, a silver headed walking stick, and, pendant from her side, a huge bunch of keys indicative of her vocation, she walks with hurried yet cautious step from room to room . . . for great is the responsibility of the House-keeper. (169–70)

There is no evidence to support the suggestion that Mrs Rouncewell is modelled on Dickens's paternal grandmother, Elizabeth Ball Dickens (1745–1824).

her stays . . . a broad old-fashioned family fire-grate]   When coal was introduced in the seventeenth century as a fuel for houses, a new style of fire-grate was invented. It was made wide, to fill the breadth of the hearth formerly used to burn long logs, and it was made of cast iron in the shape of a basket, the iron bars usually being bent in a slightly convex shape (Wright, 1964, 65–9).

The present representative

He supposes all his dependents to be utterly bereft of individual characters, intentions, or opinions, and is persuaded that he was born to supersede the necessity of their having any.]   Compare 'The Old House-keeper':

> The Old Housekeeper knows no other world than that which is comprised within the precincts of her Lord's domain – there all her hopes and fears, all her cares and anxieties centre; his will, and that of his lady, are the laws which govern her, and their opinion the tribunal at which alone she must be judged. (171–2)

Mrs. Rouncewell has known trouble.

went for a soldier]   For a man 'to go for a soldier' brought shame on his family because the Army had long had a reputation as a refuge for those who were social misfits, or who were unwilling to take on responsibilities (Trustram, 1984, 21).

steam-engines]   The steam-engine, patented in 1769 by James Watt (1736–1819), who improved an engine already in existence, was adapted during the nineteenth century for a multiplicity of uses in shipping, the railways and industry.

setting birds to draw their own water]   Mrs Rouncewell's son developed a sophisticated version of the commonplace trick of bird-fanciers, who trained caged birds to haul up a small bucket by a string from a glass out of reach and drink from it. In Poll Sweedlepipe's bird shop in *MC*, 'one unhappy goldfinch . . . drew the water for his own drinking, and mutely appealed to some good man to drop a farthing's worth of poison in it' (19).

to put his shoulder to the wheel]   A phrase derived from Aesop's fable of the man who lay on his back and cried for help when his cart was stalled. A friend advised him to whip his horses and put his shoulder to the wheel. The cliché is a favourite of Mr Vholes (chapters 39, 45).

power-loom]   Like the steam-engine, another product of the Industrial Revolution: the machine-operated power-loom was invented by Edmund Cartwright in 1785.

some Works. The iron country farther north]   Yorkshire, Lancashire and Durham are the industrial counties north of Lincolnshire; see note to chapter 63, p. 293.

some odd thousand conspirators . . . in the habit of turning out by torch-light . . . for unlawful purposes.]   The allusion is to Chartism, the political movement of the 1840s which began with workers who found that the Reform Bill had done little to improve their lives in general and, in particular, had not sufficiently extended the franchise. Meetings were held throughout England to arouse workers to a sense of their grievances, and, partly inspired by the revolutions on the Continent in 1848, violent outbreaks occurred in a few cities. Anticipating a siege of London in April, the government appointed 200,000 special constables and barricaded major buildings and bridges. The precautions succeeded in thwarting the thousands of workers who turned out on 10 April in an attempt to present their Charter of political demands to Parliament, and the Chartist movement gradually declined during the next decade. For aristocratic arrogance towards manufacturers and inventors, see note to chapter 28, p. 201.

Nevertheless Mrs. Rouncewell's son

a journey in far countries]   An echo of the parable of the prodigal son, who 'took his journey into a far country, and there wasted his substance with riotous living' (Luke 15.13; noted by Gill, 1967, 150). British manufacturers customarily travelled to the Continent to study foreign factory methods.

"And, again and again

Watt!]   After this exclamation, the following passage was cancelled in the first complete set of corrected proofs for the second number:

– Sir Leicester once remarked, in a moment of inspiration, that he considered the coincidence between the Christian name of his rock ahead the arch-rebel Tyler and the surname of the instructor [*corrected to MS reading* inventor] of the steam-engine to have meaning in it –

"Grandmother," says the young man

Rosa] A deletion in MS before 'Rosa' looks like 'Catherine' (the name of Dickens's wife).

"Yes, child. Daughter of a widow

She's an apt scholar . . . She shows the house already] The 'Old House-keeper' functions as a 'guide and walking catalogue' who 'can give the history of every article of furniture in the apartments, and of every picture that decorates the walls' (172).

"It's two young men

gig] A light two-wheeled one-horse carriage.

"If you please, he told me that!"

came from London only last night by the mail] The last express mail-coach operating from London ran in 1846, after which mail was delivered by train. Under the mail-coach system, which began in the late eighteenth century, well-appointed vehicles drawn by first-class horses in the charge of reliable coachmen and armed guards ran to regular times on routes radiating from London and leaving there in a group at eight o'clock each night. Horses were changed every six or eight miles and the average speed maintained on most roads was twelve miles per hour. The vehicles carried inside passengers only at fares far in excess of the regular coach fare.

"The terrace below is much admired.

It is called, from an old story in the family, The Ghost's Walk."] The story of the ghost of the wife of Sir Morbury Dedlock, who will not rest until disgrace comes to the Dedlock family, suggests the influence of several elements in *The House of the Seven Gables* (Stamon, 1983, 112–13; Stokes, 1985, 29–30). Just as the portrait of Colonel Pyncheon blights his descendants, so the curse of Matthew Maule on the colonel also blights them: 'old Matthew Maule, it is to be feared, trode downward from his own age to a far later one, planting a heavy footstep, all the way, on the conscience of a Pyncheon' (1). An even more obvious analogue is the story Hepzibah tells Phoebe about 'a certain Alice Pyncheon, who had been exceedingly beautiful and accomplished, in her lifetime, a hundred years ago':

This lovely Alice had met with some great and mysterious calamity . . . and gradually faded out of the world. But, even now, she was supposed to haunt the House of the Seven Gables, and, a great many times, especially when one of the Pyncheons was to die, she had been heard playing sadly and beautifully on the harpsichord. (5)

77

The story has nothing to do

She seats herself in a large chair . . . and tells them:]   Compare 'The Old Housekeeper':

> the hours we have spent ensconced in her old leather chair, listening to tales of other days, when the great, the gay, the young, of a generation almost forgotten, congregated there . . . never sure was leather chair so easy – never were tales so worthy of repetition. (169)

"In the wicked days

"In the wicked days . . . of King Charles the First – I mean, of course, in the wicked days of the rebels who leagued themselves against that excellent King]   Mrs Rouncewell naturally sides with the royalists, but – as her first remark hints at – Dickens's sympathies were with the other side, as he recorded in *CHE*:

> If twelve thousand volumes were written in his praise (as a good many have been), it would still remain a fact, impossible to be denied, that for twelve years King Charles the First reigned in England unlawfully and despotically, seized upon his subjects' goods and money at his pleasure, and punished according to his unbridled will all who ventured to oppose him. It is a fashion with some people to think that this King's career was cut short; but I must say myself that I think he ran a pretty long one. (33)

"Sir Morbury Dedlock," says Mrs. Rouncewell

the blessed martyr.]   Printed in the Book of Common Prayer until the middle of the nineteenth century was the 'form of prayer with fasting' for 'the day of the martyrdom of the Blessed King Charles I'.

Chapter 8

Third monthly number
May 1852

COVERING A MULTITUDE OF SINS.

The title derives from 1 Peter 4.8: 'And above all things have fervent charity among yourselves: for charity shall cover the multitude of sins.'

It was interesting

the Old Abbey Church, with its massive tower]   The outstanding feature of St Albans Abbey is the enormous Norman tower, 144 feet high, erected in 1115.

Mr. Skimpole was as agreeable

There was honey on the table, and it led him into a discourse about Bees.] The discourse derives from Leigh Hunt's *A Jar of Honey from Mount Hybla* (1848), the substance of which had been published in *Ainsworth's Magazine* in 1844. Essentially a retrospect of the mythology and history of Sicily with selections of classical legends and pastoral poetry, the volume includes a chapter on bees which considers, in part, the distinction between drones and workers (see Crompton, 1958, 297).

why the busy Bee should be proposed as a model]   The model is song 20, 'Against Idleness and Mischief', in Isaac Watts, *Divine Songs for Children* (1715):

> How doth the little busy bee
>   Improve each shining hour,
> And gather honey all the day
>   From every opening flower!. . .
>
> In works of labour, or of skill,
>   I would be busy too;
> For Satan finds some mischief still
>   For idle hands to do.   (sts 1, 3)

a Manchester man, if he spun cotton]   The Industrial Revolution made the city a major centre of commerce and the hub of the cotton-manufacturing trade. From the late 1840s into the middle of the next decade, the prominence in politics of John Bright and Richard Cobden, the leaders of the unpopular Manchester School radicals, helped to make 'Manchester', 'cotton' and 'cotton-spinning' derisive terms used to characterize so-called 'mammon-worshippers' who favoured a competitive free-trade economy.

Mems.

Richard and Ada – love.   <u>Yes</u>, slightly

Miss Jellyby?   <u>No</u>

Nemo?   <u>Yes</u>

New people – Mrs Pardiggle – New traits in Richard

                             <u>Yes</u>   <u>Yes</u> – slightly

Coavinses?   <u>No</u>.

(Bleak House – No. III.)

Chapter VIII.

Covering a Multitude of Sins.

Chapter IX.

Signs and Tokens.

Chapter X.

The Law-Writer

"Sit down, my dear," said Mr. Jarndyce.

the Growlery . . . When I am deceived or disappointed in – the wind, and it's Easterly, I take refuge here.] For the *Spectator* essays which may have suggested the connection between the Growlery and the east wind, see note to chapter 6, p. 67.

"Nonsense!" he said

I hear of a good little orphan girl . . . I remain her guardian and her friend.] A possible source for the relationship between Jarndyce and Esther is a *HW* story by William Moy Thomas, a journalist and scholar whom Dickens had met the previous year and whose ability and judgement he admired. 'A Guild Clerk's Tale' was published on 1 February 1851 (2.437–44), and later that month Dickens wrote to Mary Boyle about the new novel which was beginning to occupy his thoughts; he described himself sitting 'With the fire going out, and the first shadows of a new story hovering in a ghostly way about me (as they usually begin to do, when I have finished an old one)' (*Nonesuch* 2.274). It may be that 'A Guild Clerk's Tale' inspired one of these 'first shadows' which materialized into a major strand of the plot. The story is told by the guild clerk himself, 'the very type of an old bachelor', aged 45, who becomes the guardian of a pretty 19-year-old heiress. Gradually realizing that he loves her deeply, he is distressed when she tells him that she loves him as a father. When he discovers that she loves his own young clerk, who returns her love, he resolves to keep his passion secret, resigning himself to misfortune and reasoning that 'it was natural that the young should love the young before the old'. He encourages their union but goes away until after the wedding, when he returns to the silent guildhall to live alone once more. (Information on William Moy Thomas from Lohrli 445.)

"I don't know who does," he returned.

waltzing ourselves off to dusty death] 'Dusty death' is from *Macbeth* 5.5.22: 'And all our yesterdays have lighted fools/ The way to dusty death.' In the Dance of Death, the well-known medieval allegorical representation illustrated by Holbein (among others), Death leads all sorts and conditions of men in a dance to the grave.

"Why, yes, it was about a Will

Equity sends questions to Law] Before their fusion under the Judicature Act of 1873, there were two distinct tribunals of the Court of Chancery, the court of common law and the court of equity. The distinction was based upon the theory of the essential opposition between law and equity and the supposed natural superiority of conscience and equity over the strict law, but by the nineteenth century equity had long ceased to found itself on natural justice and had become as rigid as the common law.

like the history of the Apple Pie.]   An alphabet rhyme dating from the seventeenth century, 'A was an apple-pie' was first published in *The Child's New Play-thing* (1743) and subsequently appeared in many editions of Mother Goose. It begins, 'A was an apple-pie, B bit it, C cut it, D dealt it, E eat it . . .,' and ends, 'W wanted it, X, Y, Z, and ampersand All wished for a piece in hand'.

"Bleak House: true.

the children]   Exodus 20.5: 'for I the Lord thy God am a jealous God, visiting the iniquity of the fathers upon the children unto the third and fourth generation'.

"You are clever enough

" 'Little old woman, and whither so high?' –/'To sweep the cobwebs out of the sky.']   This rhyme was first published by John Newbery in *Mother Goose's Melody; or, Sonnets for the Cradle* (*c*.1760), a volume edited by Oliver Goldsmith:

> There was an old woman toss'd in a blanket,
>   Seventeen times as high as the moon;
> But where she was going no mortal could tell,
>   For under her arm she carried a broom.
> Old woman, old woman, old woman, said I!
>   Whither, ah whither, ah whither so high?
> To sweep the cobwebs from the sky,
>   And I'll be with you by and by.

This was the beginning

Old Woman, and Little Old Woman, and Cobweb, and Mrs. Shipton, and Mother Hubbard, and Dame Durden]   Esther's nicknames derive either from figures who attend to others or foster them, or from figures with prophetic ability. Cobweb is one of the fairy attendants of Titania in *A Midsummer Night's Dream*. Mother Shipton, according to tradition, was a witch and prophetess who lived in Yorkshire at the end of the fifteenth century. She is reported to have made predictions about members of the court of Henry VIII and to have foretold notable events. Old Mother Hubbard was a stock nursery-tale character made famous by Sarah Catherine Martin in her rhyme, *The Comic Adventures of Old Mother Hubbard and Her Dog* (1805). Dame Durden, the subject of a popular song, kept five men servants 'to use the spade and flail' and five women servants 'to carry the milken-pail'. The servants wed each other whilst the Dame remained unwed. It has been suggested that, although Esther's nicknames are endearments, they refer to ugly, wicked or comic women and widows and so indicate her fear that her illegitimate birth has made her unattractive and undesirable (Axton, 1966).

We lived, at first, rather a busy life

committees for getting in and laying out money.]   Dickens himself received innumerable requests for contributions to charitable organizations, and the extent of his benevolence has been documented by Pope (1978, 10). During the year 1846–7, for example, he planned and launched Urania Cottage, Miss Coutt's reformatory for women; supported thirteen hospitals and sanatoriums through speeches, charitable readings and subscriptions; and made at least forty-three donations to benevolent and provident funds. Nevertheless, he had reservations about large institutionalized philanthropy, particularly when it was identified with the evangelical movement and motivated more by self-righteousness than by disinterested charity. The *HW* article of 1850, 'The Subscription List' (by W. B. Jerrold and W. H. Wills), expresses Dickens's own sentiments:

> The regular charities . . . are, many of them, gigantic jobs; operating less for the excellent objects pretended in them than for the payment of large salaries to their officers and managers. Most of the subscribed capital goes to build magnificent palaces for a few children, who are supposed to be born in hovels; to pay the bills of treasurers, who manage to get elected as such because they are printers, or contractors for articles used in the institution, and enormously overcharged. The purest we believe to be medical charities; but some of these are full of abuses – abuses often occasioned by their very affluence, and which they have attained by means of a clever and constant working of THE SUBSCRIPTION LIST. (2.12)

The bottom vignette of the cover of the monthly parts (Plate 1) features Mr Jarndyce being petitioned by a variety of philanthropists, two of whom wear fool's caps and hold signs reading 'Exeter Hall' and 'Humbug', while another wears the broad-brimmed hat worn by Quakers which was used by *Punch* to characterize John Bright. Dickens's final treatment of a subject which he satirized throughout his career is the depiction of the loud-voiced Mr Honeythunder, who administers the Haven of Philanthropy in *MED* (6, 17).

subscription-cards]   Also called 'mendicity tickets', these were refundable for small sums of money and were given by charity subscribers to persons they wished to assist. The system prevented imposters from benefiting from a direct handout because the applicant's address was required to be written on the ticket so that the society could investigate his circumstances before giving him money. The *Quarterly Review* approved of the arrangement: 'The tender heart may be consoled by dispensing these touchstone tickets instead of pennies and sixpences, assured that if the distress is real it will receive suitable relief' (97, 1855, 424).

Their objects were as various as their demands.]   Nearly five hundred charities, with names as varied as the Bath Servant's Friend Society and the Forlorn Females' Fund of Mercy, are listed in Sampson Low's *The Charities of London. Comprehending the Benevolent, Educational, and Religious Institutions. Their Origin and Design, Progress, and Present Position* (1850). Low compiled the volume to help potential benefactors choose from among the vast number of charities, which he classified into eighteen categories, including: general medical hospitals; medical charities for special purposes; preservation of life and public morals;

reclaiming the fallen, and staying the progress of crime; relief of general destitution and distress; colleges, hospitals and other asylums for the aged; aiding the resources of the industrous; for the blind, deaf and dumb; charitable and provident, chiefly for specified classes; asylums for orphans and other necessitous children; educational foundations; Bible and missionary. Following his summary, Low exclaims:

> What an amazing comprehensiveness is here developed in the operations of Christian charity for the relief of suffering and dependent humanity, – how all classes of wretchedness and want are included, – and every description of need, infirmity, and ignorance, designed to be provided for! (453)

the Sisterhood of Mediaeval Marys]   The Oxford Movement and the associated Gothic revival in art and literature fostered the establishment of religious communities for women modelled on Continental Catholic communities. The first sisterhood in the Church of England, the Sisterhood of the Holy Cross, was founded in London in 1845 by Dr Pusey, and subsequent ones with similar names were founded in various cities during the next few years (Anson, 1955, 220–30; Butt and Tillotson 180). Dickens considered such communities to be 'in the practice of a perverted form of religion', an opinion expressed in 1849 in a letter to Miss Coutts about a pamphlet from the Church Penitentiary movement appealing for funds to establish 'Houses of Mercy' for penitent prostitutes (*Letters* 5.541–2). Two years later, again writing to Miss Coutts, he described Roman Catholicism as 'that curse upon the world' when he expressed his anxiety about the establishment of the Roman Catholic hierarchy in England by means of a papal bull in 1850. He also mentioned his concern that Roman Catholicism was being given a foothold in the Church of England by the Oxford Movement, which he blamed for 'the intolerable enormity it has dug out of the mire' (22 August 1851, *Letters: Coutts* 186; Butt and Tillotson 180). His dislike of Catholicism, a sentiment then shared by most English people, is apparent in *BR, PI* and *CHE*, and in *HW* articles published around the time of the establishment of the hierarchy of Catholic bishops and the subsequent passage in August 1851 of the Ecclesiastical Titles Assumption Act (see especially Dickens's leading article, 'A Crisis in the Affairs of Mr. John Bull', 2.193–6). *CHE* was written partly to guard against the 'horrible result' that his own son might be influenced by 'conservative or High Church notions' (3 May 1843, *Letters* 3.482). The notions he had in mind are described in his *Examiner* article on the Oxford Movement, 'Report of the Commissioners appointed to inquire into the condition of the persons variously engaged in the University of Oxford' (3 June 1843):

> A vast number of witnesses being interrogated as to what they understood by the words Religion and Salvation, answered Lighted Candles. Some said water; some, bread; others, little boys; others mixed the water, lighted candles, bread, and little boys all up together, and called the compound, Faith.   (*MP* 1.105)

they were going to have their Secretary's portrait painted, and presented to

his mother-in-law] The contemporary vogue for commemorating local worthies and national heroes was disparaged by Carlyle in 1850:

> Poor English Public . . . They would fain do honour to somebody, if they did but know whom or how.
> . . . Think of a proper Somebody. Almost anybody much heard of in the newspapers, and never yet convicted of felony . . . anybody of a large class, we are not particular, he will be your proper Somebody . . .
> Such I take to be the origin of that extraordinary population of Brazen and other Images which at present . . . solicit worship from the English people . . . These are not heroes, gods, or demigods; and it is a horrible idolatry, if you knew it, to set them up as such! ('Hudson's Statue', *Latter-Day Pamphlets*)

the women of England, the Daughters of Britain . . . the Ladies of a hundred denominations.] 'The women of England, the Daughters of Britain' alludes to the quartet of volumes on 'the subject of female duty' by Mrs Sarah Ellis: *The Women of England* (1839), *The Wives of England* (1843), *The Mothers of England* (1843) and *The Daughters of England* (1845).

Women were the backbone of Victorian charitable organizations. Prior to the early decades of the century, the majority of charity workers were women, but the management committees were exclusively made up of men. Henceforward, however, an increasing number of charities were jointly managed by men and women, and there was also a tremendous growth in the number of charities managed exclusively by women. These covered a wide range of interests but were notably dedicated to causes related to women and children. (See the definitive work on the subject by Prochaska, *Women and Philanthropy in Nineteenth-Century England*, 1980.)

canvassing and electing] Many charities were financed in part by subscriptions which entitled the donors to nominate needy candidates who were elected on a poll of the subscribers. A subscriber would canvas votes for his own candidate. In charitable educational foundations, however, a rich subscriber could ensure that his candidate was admitted to a place by making an additional donation. Like the dispensing of subscription cards, the right to nominate candidates was one of the privileges a subscriber received in return for making a donation.

Among the ladies who were most distinguished

Mrs. Pardiggle] Largely a representation of Dickens's hostility to evangelical philanthropy and feminism, Mrs Pardiggle has also been identified as a Puseyite on account of the names of her children and her daily attendance at matins. The inconsistency of her sympathizing with both the High Church and the evangelicals has been remarked on as an example of Dickens's greater concern to ridicule abuses than to be consistent (Pope, 1978, 134–5). Her peremptory tone of voice and great show of determination have suggested to Philip Collins that she is partly modelled on the original of Mrs Jellyby, Caroline Chisholm (1960, 348).

there were two classes of charitable people: one, the people who did a little and made a great deal of noise] Mrs Pardiggle is modelled on her predecessor, Mrs Bellows, in Dickens's *HW* article satirizing Bloomerism and women with a 'mission', 'Sucking Pigs':

> Mrs. Bellows has no business to be self-dependent, and to preserve a quiet little avenue of her own in the world, begirt with her own influences and duties. She must discharge herself of a vast amount of words, she must enlist into an Army composed entirely of Trumpeters, she must come (with the Misses Bellows) into a resounding Spartan Hall for the purpose. To be sure, however, it is to be remarked, that this is the noisy manner in which all great social deeds have been done. (4.146)

(For further examples of Dickens's attitude to women who entered public life, see the note on the feminist Miss Wisk in chapter 30, p. 208). That feminism is one of the contemporary issues given prominent treatment in *BH* is a subject interestingly discussed by Moers (1973).

"These, young ladies," said Mrs. Pardiggle

with great volubility] Added in MS. MS and proof revisions to six further passages in this chapter intensify her loud, harsh and clumsy manner.

Egbert . . . Oswald . . . Francis . . . Felix . . . Alfred] The names of saints or heroes of the early church (Butt and Tillotson 180). Charlotte M. Yonge's *History of Christian Names* (1878) notes that Francis was a name generally common only among Roman Catholics. The ninth-century King Alfred promoted ecclesiastical reform, founded monastic communities and was considered the pattern of a Christian king.

Tockahoopo Indians] The name sounds like 'Tuckahoe', the nickname for the lowlands of Virginia and the Indian inhabitants there. 'Tuckahoe' was well known from 1817 onwards and appeared in *Bartlett's United States Dictionary* of 1848. Dickens might have heard it when he visited Richmond in 1842, or he might have come across it in the *American Geography* he carried with him during his journey.

An early version of the criticism of the boy who contributes his pocket-money to the Indians is Mr Weller's comment on his wife's church society aiding West Indians (quoted in note to chapter 4, p. 55). A more recent complaint on the subject was 'The Nigger Question' (1849), Carlyle's protest at the plan of Lord John Russell to aid West Indian Negroes.

the Infant Bonds of Joy] In February 1852, three months before the publication of the present number, 6,000 children who had pledged to abstain for life from alcohol and tobacco attended Exeter Hall for a mass gathering of the Band of Hope. The event was widely reported and illustrated in the press. Organized in

1847 for Sunday-school children in Leeds, the Band of Hope expanded rapidly throughout the country, the majority of the children being recruited from the working class. The 'Band of Hope' name was copied by temperance and church organizations of various affiliations (including Anglicans, Wesleyans and Quakers) and became a generic term for all such children's groups. The children marched in parades, performed at temperance concerts, memorized a teetotal catechism which imitated the Christian catechism, and attempted to persuade their elders to become teetotallers (Plate 8) (Harrison, 1971, 192; Shiman, 1973).

That Dickens execrated the temperance movement and believed that drunkenness was not the cause but the symptom of social ills is well known. Two of his major attacks on temperance fanatics were published not long before *BH*: 'Demoralisation and Total Abstinence' (*Examiner*, 27 October 1849) and 'Whole Hogs' (*HW* 3.505–7).

We had never seen such dissatisfied children

The face of each child, as the amount of his contribution was mentioned, darkened in a peculiarly vindictive manner]   As a young boy, Dickens was himself apparently exhorted to contribute his pocket-money to a particular subscription. When he refused he was made to understand that he 'must dismiss all expectations of going to Heaven' ('Dullborough Town', *UT*).

All large charities had children's associations, and their financial contributions were enormous. Girls were more often involved than boys, the average age being from 12 to 13 years old, although it was not unusual for boys and girls aged 4 and 5 to work alongside older children. There was a range of activities designed for children, particularly in the evangelical missionary movement. In addition to accompanying their mothers on district visits ('I take them everywhere,' says Mrs Pardiggle), children were recruited to collect money and distribute tracts, and to join working parties to make items to sell at bazaars (Prochaska, 1980, 73–94).

"They attend Matins with me

(very prettily done)]   This was a religious cliché (House 118). It is used by Sam Weller at the end of the edifying discourse given by the Reverend Mr Stiggins: ' "Brayvo; wery pretty!" said Sam . . . "Wery pretty" ' (*PP* 45).

I am a School lady . . . a Visiting lady . . . a Reading lady . . . a Distributing lady; I am on the local Linen Box Committee]   Sunday schools, district visiting societies, Scripture reading societies and the Religious Tract Society (which distributed tracts to the poor) were all charitable activities promoted chiefly by the evangelicals (Pope, 1978, 134). Members of reading societies, such as the Scripture Readers' Associations, visited homes to read to the sick, needy, elderly and others who could not or did not attend church. Several charities supplied boxes of baby linen to pauper women with new babies. In *SB* the activities of 'the childbed-linen monthly loan society' are described sympathetically in 'The Ladies' Societies'.

THE BANDS OF HOPE;

OR, THE CHILDISH TEETOTAL MOVEMENT.

Grandpapa. " BUT FOR SEVENTY YEARS, MY CHILD, I HAVE FOUND THAT THE MODERATE USE OF THE GOOD THINGS OF THIS LIFE HAS DONE ME GOOD."

Young Hopeful Teetotaller. " ALL A MISTAKE, GRANDPA'. TOTAL ABSTINENCE IS THE THING. LOOK AT ME! I 'VE NOT TASTED WINE OR BEER FOR YEARS ! "

8   'The Bands of Hope'. From *Punch*, 22 (6 March 1852), 103

"You may have observed

some of the lists to which I have referred . . . I put down my mite first; then my young family enrol their contributions]   Mrs Pardiggle likens herself to the 'poor widow' praised by Christ because she threw into the treasury 'two mites':

> this poor widow hath cast more in, than all they which have cast into the treasury: For all they did cast in of their abundance; but she of her want did cast in all that she had, even all her living. (Mark 12.42–4)

In her pride at the publication of her family's names in the subscription lists, Mrs Pardiggle is modelled on Lady Bittern in 'The Subscription List' (*HW* 2.10–12):

> This expedient for spreading a small amount of charity over a large surface of publicity is more strikingly exemplified by the next entries: –

> The Right Honourable Lady Bittern .... 10s. 0d.
> The Honourable Blanche Bittern... 7 6d.
> The Honourable Fanny Bittern.. 5 0
> The Honourable Alicia Bittern... 2 6
> The Honourable Jemima Bittern... 2 6
> The Honourable Chas. de Brandenburgh Bittern............................ 2 6

> Lady Bittern is an economist. No one knows better than her ladyship how to lay out thirty shillings in charity with profit to the reputation of her numerous family.

O. A. Pardiggle, F.R.S.]   Mrs Pardiggle hopes people will think her husband is a Fellow of the Royal Society, but the initials also stand for the rather less eminent Friends' Relief Society.

"The loss is yours

Stationed in a waggon on this lawn]   Itinerant Methodist orators customarily preached from waggons – for example, Dinah Morris, the female preacher in *Adam Bede* (1859).

Ada told me afterwards

the bringing in of their rival candidates for a pension]   Benevolent societies established to help particular groups, such as gardeners or governesses, supplied small pensions from £20 to £30 a year to persons aged 60 or over. The candidates were elected as described in the note above (p. 86) on canvassing and electing. The *Quarterly Review* considered this type of charity especially worthy, remarking that canvassing for admittance was 'earnest', and that there was always a large number of disappointed candidates (97.416–17).

I am very fond of being confided in

"boned"]   Slang for 'stolen'.

I was glad when we came

the brickmaker's house . . . in a brickfield]   Machine-manufacture of bricks and drainpipes evolved during the 1850s and 1860s but, before the mechanization became widespread, brickmaking was a craft-centred trade which was most highly developed in or near towns, mostly in the eastern counties. Because their work was generally limited to the summer months only (see *Letters* 5.231 n. 3), brickmakers were often unemployed, and they had a particularly low reputation as drunkards, liars and profligates.

one of a cluster of wretched hovels . . . with pigsties . . . stagnant pools . . . a large dirt-pie.]   This description derives from 'A Suburban Connemara', a *HW* article published in March 1851 (2.562–5) which describes the squalid London district of Agar Town, inhabited by the destitute Irish who became refugees as a result of the successive failures of the potato crop in Ireland from 1845 to 1849. Other details in the novel suggest that the brickmakers whom Esther meets are intended to be Irish: Jenny's husband drinks, beats her and gets into fights – tendencies described as characteristic of the Irish in 'An Irish Peculiarity' (*HW* 1.594–6); in chapter 46, the scene featuring Jenny derives from Carlyle's description of the poor Irish widow in *Past and Present* (see note, p. 253); the low lodging-house where the brickmakers stay in chapter 46 would be of the worst sort – such as those described in 'On Duty with Inspector Field': 'none so filthy and so crowded as where Irish are' (*HW* 3.267). Moreover, in the sketch of 'The Brick-layer's Labourer' in *Heads of the People* (1841 supplement, 101–8), the bricklayer is an Irishman named Paddy. For the housing of the poor and the sanitary reform movement, see notes to chapter 46 (pp. 251–2).

"Then make it easy for her!"

drawed like a badger]   In badger-drawing or -baiting, dogs were set to draw out a badger from an artificial hole, such as a barrel. A *HW* article denounced the sport as 'an amusement which familiarised the spectator with violence and blood-shed . . . in an unworthy and contemptible degree' ('The Modern "Officer's" Progress', 1.306).

Now you're a-going to poll-pry and question according to custom]   The term 'poll-pry' originated with John Poole's comedy, *Paul Pry* (1825): Paul is an inquisitive and meddlesome fellow whose catchphrase is 'I hope I don't intrude'.

The objects of district visitors were to inquire into the condition of the poor, to give them advice on religion, health and sanitation, to provide occasional temporal relief (such as blankets, food and coal tickets) and to help them to obtain the aid of other charitable institutions. Designed to put the middle class in closer touch with the poor, visiting societies systematized the old casual custom of visiting the poor: the districts of each parish were divided into streets, the streets into households, and roughly one visitor was assigned to every twenty to forty families. The largest societies canvassed entire cities and looked into a wide range of problems. In London, which had a great number of visiting societies representing rival denominations – high and low church, Roman Catholics, Methodists, non-conformists – few poor families were not visited, and a family might be visited several times a month.

The thousands of voluntary visitors gave rise to a concern about the clumsy and tactless inexperienced visitor, and manuals of advice were widely circulated. Visitors were not only instructed on how to encourage industry, frugality, temperance, cleanliness and religion, but they were also reminded that it was a 'privilege', not a 'right', to enter the cottages of the poor, and that they should be sympathetic, not patronizing, a friend and not a 'relieving lady' (Prochaska, 1980, 111–13; see also Pope, 1978, 132–3).

In a speech to the Metropolitan Sanitary Association in 1851, Dickens expressed his conviction that sanitary reform was of far greater benefit to the poor than the message preached by district visitors representing religious societies:

> What avails it to send a Missionary to me, a miserable man or woman living in a foetid Court where every sense bestowed upon me for my delight becomes a torment, and every minute of my life is new mire added to the heap under which I lie degraded? . . . Would he address himself to my hopes of immortality? I am so surrounded by material filth that my Soul can not rise to the contemplation of an immaterial existence! (*Speeches* 129)

we've had five dirty and onwholesome children, as is all dead infants] *The Labourer's Friend* (1856) cites the calculation of a Medical Officer of Health that in the City of London 400 out of 1,000 persons, or two-fifths of the population, died before the age of 5 (84–6).

the little book wot you left . . . It's a book fit for a babby] The charitable societies published and circulated tens of thousands of religious as well as sanitary tracts which generally contained moral stories and appeals to the conscience of the reader phrased in childish language or in doggerel verse to assist the memory. The tone was frequently didactic, as in the penny pamphlet published by the Ladies' Sanitary Association, *The Power of Soap and Water* (n.d.): ' "I am sure, wife . . . if you keep a comfortable home over my head, I am not the man to go to the public house. I would rather come home and sit with you and the children any day" ' (cited in Wohl, 1983, 67–8).

Ada and I were very uncomfortable.

Robinson Crusoe] One of Dickens's favourite childhood books was Defoe's novel (1719) about a man shipwrecked on an island who manages to make himself comfortable during his solitude. Dickens mentions *Robinson Crusoe* fondly in 'Nurse's Stories' (*UT*).

Presently I took the light

what Our Saviour said of children]   'Suffer little children, and forbid them not, to come unto me: for of such is the kingdom of heaven' (Matthew 19.14, Mark 10.14).

Ada was so full of grief

Ada was so full of grief]   Between the end of this paragraph and the start of the next, Dickens cancelled a passage in proof which emphasized Jarndyce's limited perceptions about his friends:

> "Excellent people, you know," he said, beginning to walk about, "Mrs. Pardiggle and all the rest of 'em. Excellent people! Do a deal of good, and mean to do a good deal more. But they want one pattern out of all varieties of Looms, they *must* be in extremes, they *will* knock in tintacks with a sledge hammer, they make such a bustle and noise, and they are so confoundedly indefatigable! – O Lord, yes, I feel the wind all over me!"

Chapter 9

SIGNS AND TOKENS.

"Let me see!" he would say.

post-chaise]   A faster and more private mode of travel than a coach, the post-chaise was consequently more expensive to hire. It carried one or two passengers with their luggage and was drawn by two, three, or four horses, one of them (or one of each pair) ridden by a postilion. The disadvantge of travelling by post-chaise was that passengers had to change into a fresh vehicle at the end of each stage. In chapter 55, Mrs Rouncewell and Mrs Bagnet, in a hurry to get to London, travel by post-chaise from Lincolnshire.

"I went to school with this fellow

Lawrence Boythorn]   In a letter to Mrs Watson on 6 May 1852 (autograph, Henry E. Huntington Library, HM 17978), Dickens confided that Boythorn was 'a most exact portrait of Walter Savage Landor' (Plate 9). Through Forster, Landor's close friend and, later, his biographer, Dickens first met the celebrated author of *Imaginary Conversations* (1824–9) in 1840, when Landor was aged 64.

The men greatly admired each other, Dickens naming his second son Walter Landor Dickens, and they remained friends until the older man's death in 1864.

As a schoolboy, Landor established a reputation not merely for his skill at Latin poetry but also for his perversities of temper and violent opinions, and at Oxford he was regarded as a 'mad Jacobin'. His intention to become a model country gentleman at his sizeable estate in Wales was impaired by a series of litigious disputes with his neighbours and tenants which culminated in his leaving England for France in 1814, accompanied by his wife and four children. He finally settled in Italy, but in 1835 he separated from his wife following a quarrel and returned to live in England. His character was marked by his tremendous explosions of laughter and transient wrath, generous impulses, chivalrous sentiment, refined epicureanism and a love of the classics. In 1858 he retired to Italy, where he died (Super, 1957; *DNB*). Revisions in the MS and proofs enhance Boythorn's stature, boisterous exuberance, vehemence and paradoxical gentleness and gallantry. Perhaps because Boythorn does not appear in any of the illustrations to the novel, Dickens decided to compliment Landor further by asking Browne to give Landor's benign features to Mr Jarndyce instead (Plates 6, 9).

"By my soul, Jarndyce," returned his guest

the remotest summits of the Himalaya Mountains]   Various expeditions in the first half of the nineteenth century ascertained that the Himalayas were the highest mountain range in the world.

The subject of this laudation

a very little canary, who was so tame]   The bird is doubtless modelled on Dickens's own canary, named 'Dick' (1850–66), described by Forster as 'a canary very dear both to Dickens and his eldest daughter, who had so tamed to her loving hand its wild little heart that it was become the most docile of companions' (3.95).

"There never was such an infernal

"Nothing but a mine below it . . . and the whole blown to atoms with . . . gunpowder]   An allusion to the Gunpowder Plot of 1605, when Guy Fawkes and other Catholics placed large quantities of iron, gunpowder and faggots in the cellars of the Houses of Parliament in an aborted attempt to destroy its Members on the opening day of the session.

Accountant-General]   An officer of the Court of Chancery appointed by Act of Parliament to receive all money lodged in court and to place it for security in the Bank of England. The office was abolished in the late nineteenth century and the duties transferred to the Paymaster-General.

"By my soul!" exclaimed Mr. Boythorn

one within another, like the ivory balls in a Chinese carving.]   Though

9   Walter Savage Landor in 1839, by W. Fisher

Dickens had no doubt seen such carvings, this is a reminiscence of Tennyson, *The Princess* (1847), prologue 20, 'Laborious orient ivory sphere in sphere', a line which Dickens had echoed more closely in his *HW* article of 1851 (written with R. H. Horne), 'The Great Exhibition and the Little One': 'the laboriously-carved ivory balls of the flowery Empire, ball within ball and circle within circle, which have made no advance and been of no earthly use for thousands of years' (*HW* 3.358).

fire split peas at their legs]   Dickens would have known of one of Landor's antics which got him rusticated from Oxford for a year: he fired a gun at the windows of an 'obnoxious tory', but no harm was done because the shutters were closed.

I scarcely knew him again

lilac-kid gloves]   Coloured kid gloves were fashionable only in the evening, or at weddings.

bear's-grease]   A popular hairdressing which was sold in boxes or pots for a shilling up to as much as a guinea. The genuine article was made of fat cut from the bear and rendered down, but according to George Dodd's *Dictionary of Manufactures, Mining, Machinery, and the Industrial Arts* (1869) 'Bear's Grease seldom deserves the name given to it; it is more usually a mixture of beef marrow and hog's lard, with some kind of oil and perfume' (22). Bear's-grease was believed to promote the growth of hair and was worn by 'the young gentlemen about town' (*The Mudfog and Other Sketches*, 'Report of the Second Meeting'). David Copperfield uses bear's-grease when he courts Miss Larkin (18).

"Not half a glass?" said Mr. Guppy

My present salary . . . is two pound a week.]   Guppy represents one of the grades of lawyer's clerk described in chapter 31 of *PP*:

> There is the salaried clerk – out of door, or in door, as the case may be – who devotes the major part of his thirty shillings a week to his personal pleasure and adornment, repairs half-price to the Adelphi Theatre at least three times a week, dissipates majestically at the cider cellars afterwards, and is a dirty caricature of the fashion which expired six months ago.

the Old Street Road]   The road was that part of Old Street which extends from St Luke's Church to Shoreditch Church. By the early 1850s it had ceased to be the 'open, healthful ground' it had been in the past (Timbs 559).

Penton Place, Pentonville . . . considered one of the 'ealthiest outlets.]

> Never mind Pentonville, it is not now what it was, a place of some rural beauty. The fields . . . are now melancholy and cut up with . . . rows of houses, run up

during the paroxysm of the brick and mortar mania of times past, and now tumbling in ruins . . . The march of town innovation upon the suburbs has driven before it all that was green, silent, and fitted for meditation.   (A writer of 1833, cited in Thornbury and Walford 2.281)

Pentonville, in the parish of St James's, Clerkenwell, had cockney associations. Penton Street was the site of the celebrated cockney place of amusement, White Conduit House. Originally built in the reign of Charles I, the tavern grew depraved and debauched and was pulled down in 1849. George Cruikshank admitted that some of his early knowledge of cockney character and of City human nature derived from evenings at White Conduit House. In 'Chambers' (*UT*), the younger of the two lawyer's clerks 'leads the fashion at Pentonville in the articles of pipes and shirts'. Guppy's lodgings in Pentonville, and afterwards in Lambeth (see note to chapter 64, p. 294), combined with his use of slang and his flashy clothes, are details which characterize him as a cockney swell who likes to have a good time.

"I will, miss," said Mr. Guppy.

"As I love and honour, so likewise I obey.]   In the Solemnization of Matrimony it is the woman, not the man, who promises to obey.

Chapter 10

THE LAW-WRITER.

Law-writers, who copied or engrossed legal documents, are described by G. A. Sala in 'Legal Houses of Call':

> wretched men with red noses, hoarse voices, tattered apparel and trembling hands – so trembling, that you are amazed at their ability to execute the magnificent examples of penmanship by which they live . . . Of all the gifts, abilities, or varied craftsmanship they once possessed – of classical educations, splendid opportunities, honourable employments, they have left but this sole cunning of the hand. Here they wait in sodden silence, or shiftless gossip, until their services are called into request, until some piece of writing has to be executed for a neighbouring office. When their labour is over they drink the hire – then wait again, and write, and drink, and die.   (*HW* 7.257)

On the eastern borders

Cook's Court, Cursitor Street]   The original, Took's Court, Cursitor Street, was occupied largely by law-stationers and law-writers. 'Legal Houses of Call' describes 'Boot Lane', an area very like this part of Chancery Lane:

Know you the lane where the smell of parchment and red tape, the air redolent of wig-powder and pounce tell of the deeds that are done in their clime? Know you the lane that is narrow and crooked, and dirty, and ill-savouring as the laws which are twisted, and tortured, and garbled, and misconstrued, in the courts round about? . . .

Slinking out of this ill-omened thoroughfare, in a shabby, shambling, downcast manner, and not turning boldly out of it at a respectable angle, is a little frowsy street with no thoroughfare at the end thereof, save a maze of horrible little courts and alleys. (7.254–5)

Law-Stationer]   In addition to providing stationery and other articles required by the legal profession, law-stationers took in manuscripts and legal documents to be copied or engrossed. In the paragraphs introducing Mr Snagsby, the inverted pastoral imagery seems occasioned by the law-stationer's association with parchment (made from the skins of sheep).

pounce]   A fine powder of sandarac or cuttlefish bone used to prevent the ink from spreading in writing and to prepare the surface of parchment to receive writing.

wafers]   Small discs of flour and gum or of gelatine which were moistened and used to seal letters, attach papers or receive the impression of a seal.

red tape and green ferret]   The figurative meaning of red tape became current in the 1830s; for example, see Dickens's *HW* article on bureaucracy and ministerial irresponsibility, 'Red Tape' (2.481–4). Green ferret is a stout tape made of either cotton or silk.

bodkins]   Small piercing instruments for making holes to bind parchments together and for drawing tape or cord through them.

Peffer is never seen

St. Andrew's, Holborn]   A parish church designed by Wren on what was then Holborn Hill, between Shoe Lane and St Andrew Street.

admonished to return by the crowing of the sanguine cock . . . if Peffer ever do revisit the pale glimpses of Cook's Court]   A reminiscence of the opening scenes of *Hamlet*:

> *Bernardo.*   It was about to speak, when the cock crew.
> *Horatio.*   And then it started like a guilty thing
> Upon a fearful summons . . .   (1.1.147–9)

> *Hamlet.*   What may this mean
> That thou, dead corse, again in complete steel
> Revisits thus the glimpses of the moon . . .   (1.4.51–3)

the cellar at the little dairy]   A great number of London cows were kept in crowded sheds or damp cellars and fed on the refuse from vegetable markets and greengrocers. The sanitary reform movement urged the abolition of such places, and two *HW* articles supported the cause: 'Health by Act of Parliament' and 'The Cow with the Iron Tail' (1.462, 2.145–51).

In his lifetime, and likewise

too violently compressed about the waist . . . pints of vinegar and lemon-juice]   The fashion of tight-lacing to achieve a tiny waist was derided by Dickens in two *HW* articles, 'Sucking Pigs' and 'Frauds on the Fairies' (4.146, 8.98), and by Harriet Martineau in 'Malvern Water' (4.70). Women drank vinegar and lemon juice in an attempt to keep thin.

a rumour flying among them]   The image derives from the description of the 'monstrous Fantom', Fame, in the *Aeneid* (here translated by Dryden):

> Fame, the great Ill, from small beginnings grows.
> Swift from the first; and ev'ry Moment brings
> New Vigour to her flights, new Pinions to her wings . . .
> Swift is her walk, more swift her wingèd hast . . . (4.252–4, 259)

the many tongues of Rumour]   'Millions of opening Mouths to Fame belong;/And ev'ry Mouth is furnish'd with a Tongue . . .' (Dryden's *Aeneid* 4.263–4). There is also, of course, a reminiscence of 'Rumour', who enters 'painted full of tongues' in the induction to *2 Henry IV*.

Mr. and Mrs. Snagsby are not only

one bone and one flesh]   The phrase in the Solemnization of Matrimony, 'they two shall be one flesh', derives from Genesis 2.23: 'And Adam said, This is now bone of my bones, and flesh of my flesh.'

From beneath his feet . . . as from a shrill ghost unquiet in its grave]   A recollection of Hamlet's words when the Ghost cries 'Swear' from under the stage:

> *Hamlet.* Ha, ha, boy! say'st thou so? Art thou there, truepenny?
> Come on. You hear this fellow in the cellarage:
> Consent to swear . . .
> *Ghost.* Swear . . . Swear by his sword . . . Swear. (1.5.151)

This proper name, so used

a lean young woman from a workhouse . . . farmed or contracted for . . . by an amiable benefactor of his species resident at Tooting]   As an alternative

99

to living in the workhouse, many London pauper children were boarded out by the parish at contractors' farm schools in the suburbs. The abuses of the system are described in *OT* (2). The best-known baby farm was that of Peter Drouet at Tooting, which maintained the pauper children of many of the largest metropolitan parishes. In 1848 cholera broke out among the 1,400 overcrowded children, killing more than 150. Although the coroner's jury returned a verdict of manslaughter, Drouet was later found not guilty by the Central Criminal Court. Dickens wrote four articles for the *Examiner* which described the conditions at the farm, reported on the verdict of the coroner's jury, reproached the court reporter's complacent understatement of the tragedy and criticized the acquittal of Drouet ('The Paradise at Tooting', 20 January 1849; 'The Tooting Farm', 27 January; 'A Recorder's Charge', 3 March; 'The Verdict for Drouet', 21 April; see Brice and Fielding, 1968). Several of Dickens's *HW* articles of 1850 allude to the Tooting disaster (1.99, 171, 205), and in a *HW* article of 1853, 'Home for Homeless Women', he described a girl very like Guster who had also been brought up at Tooting (7.173).

The 12-year-old orphan servant girl from the Chatham workhouse who was employed by Dickens's parents when the family lived at Bayham Street and later Gower Street is reputed to have inspired 'the Orfling', the young girl from St Luke's Workhouse employed by the Micawbers in *DC*. It has been suggested that Dickens was moved to create Guster, and also Charley Neckett, the maid-of-all-work who is ill-treated by the Smallweeds, in order to remind the public of two recent scandalous cases which attracted widespread sympathy. During the winter of 1850 to 1851, Mr and Mrs Bird of Exeter were tried for murdering their servant, Mary Ann Parsons, a parish apprentice. They were acquitted but later sentenced to two years' hard labour for cruelty and assault. In December 1850, George Sloane, a special pleader in the Middle Temple, and his wife were tried for starving and maltreating their servant, Jane Wilbred, a 17-year-old girl from the West London Union workhouse. They were convicted and sentenced to prison for two years. Both cases were reported in Dickens's own *Household Narrative of Current Events* (Collins, 1960, 345–8).

Apropos of these cases and his depiction of Guster and Charley, Dickens might have had in mind the Apprentices and Servants Act of 1851, 'An Act for the better protection of persons under the care and control of others as apprentices and servants'. It required that a register be kept of young persons from workhouses who were hired as servants, and that they be regularly visited. It also made it a misdemeanour to neglect to supply food and, most important, it enabled the prosecution of persons found mistreating apprentices and servants.

Mr. Snagsby refers everything

loving to walk in Staple Inn in the summer time]　Originating in the fifteenth century, Staple Inn was one of the ten Inns of Chancery. Much rebuilt, the Inn which Dickens knew dated from the eighteenth century. Nathaniel Hawthorne described Staple Inn's peculiar charm on a summer afternoon in *English Notebooks* (1853–7):

there was a surrounding seclusion of quiet dwelling-houses, with beautiful green shrubbery and grass plots in the court and a great many sunflowers in full bloom . . . There was not a quieter spot in England than this, and it was very strange to have drifted into it so suddenly out of the bustle and rumble of Holborn; and to lose all this repose as suddenly on passing through the arch of the outer court. In all the hundreds of years since London was built, it has not been able to sweep its roaring tide over that little island of quiet.

There is a memorable description of the Inn, where Mr Grewgious has chambers, in *MED* 11. After being devastated in the Second World War, Staple Inn has been largely restored to its former style.

the Rolls Yard]   The yard of the Rolls House and Chapel in Chancery Lane, where the rolls and records of the Court of Chancery were kept until 1870.

a brook "as clear as crystial" once ran right down the middle of Holborn] Revelation 22.1: 'And he shewed me a pure river of water of life, clear as crystal.' The brook, or 'bourne', was the upper part of the Fleet river, which rises at Hampstead and enters the Thames at Blackfriars Bridge. *En route*, flowing through a deep valley, it gave its name to the broad thoroughfare of Holborn ('old bourne'). Once navigable by small cargo-boats, the Fleet had not been 'as clear as crystial' for many years, for it was covered over and turned into a drain in the late eighteenth century.

when Turnstile really was a turnstile]   Great Turnstile, on the south side of Holborn just west of Cursitor Street. In the seventeenth century the three passages from Holborn into Lincoln's Inn Fields derived their names from the revolving barriers erected to admit pedestrians into Holborn but exclude the animals which pastured in the fields.

The day is closing in

Lincoln's Inn Fields]   Hawthorne described them as 'truly . . . almost a field, right in the heart of London, and as retired and secluded, almost, as if the surrounding city were a forest, and its heavy roar were the wind among the branches' (entry for 6 December 1857, *English Notebooks*).

Here, in a large house

a large house, formerly a house of state . . . its painted ceilings, where Allegory . . . sprawls]   Tulkinghorn's house is modelled on 58 Lincoln's Inn Fields, the home of John Forster from 1834 to 1856. Originally one house with 57, number 58 was built in 1640 and divided in 1795. The houses around the Fields were traditionally inhabited by the nobility, and a previous tenant of number 58 was a Lord Chancellor. Eighteenth-century painted ceilings decorated great houses such as Windsor, Hampton Court, Blenheim Palace and Burghley House. The

101

baroque style for such *trompe l'œil* work had degenerated in lesser hands (as in the case of the Roman Allegory). Dickens's description, with the word 'sprawls', is a reminiscence of Pope, *Moral Essays*, Epistle to Burlington:

> On painted Ceilings you devoutly stare,
> Where sprawl the Saints of Verrio or Laguerre,
> On gilded clouds in fair expansion lie,
> And bring all Paradise before your eye. (145–8)

While admitting that his father had modelled Tulkinghorn's house on number 58, Charles Dickens the younger recorded that 'literal exactitude was by no means observed in the description of its rooms', and could 'not clearly remember whether the Roman existed in fact or only in fancy' (1896, 346–7).

Here, beneath the painted ceiling

Mr. Tulkinghorn is not in a common way.]   His services are not offered to the general public.

special-pleaders]   Advocates who were members of an Inn of Court and who devoted themselves mainly to the drawing up of formal allegations.

The middle-aged man in the Pew, knows scarcely more of the affairs of the Peerage, than any crossing-sweeper in Holborn.]   We immediately think of Jo, but this seems to have been a common expression, as in *MC* 26: 'yet know no more about us than you do of the crossing-sweeper at the corner'.

"Nemo, sir. Here it is.

Forty-two folio.]   That is 3,024 or 3,780 words; for how this is reckoned, and for the Acts of Parliament in 1852 which discontinued payment per folio and the copying of documents by hand, see note to chapter 1, p. 33.

"Nemo!" repeats Mr. Tulkinghorn.

"Nemo is Latin for no one."]   Also, it was the *nom de crayon* H. K. Browne first adopted as the illustrator of *PP*, and Dickens's use of the name here may have been a private joke between them (Steig, 1978, 132).

"Half after nine, sir," repeats Mr. Snagsby.

King's Bench Office]   In the Temple, where the Masters had their offices.

But Mr. Tulkinghorn does not go on

blot-headed candle]   Probably a candle blackened by the soot and smoke from the wick.

The air of the room is almost bad

a red coke fire]   The refuse cinders of coal obtained from gasworks, coke was much cheaper than coal and was bought by the poor from carts or from vendors carrying sacks of it on their backs (Mayhew 2.85).

Banshee]   A supernatual being supposed by Irish and Scottish peasants to wail under the windows of a house where one of the inmates is about to die. The juxtaposition of 'famine' and 'Banshee' suggests an allusion to the recent great potato famine in Ireland (1845–9).

For, on a low bed opposite the fire

winding-sheet]   The solidified drippings of grease which cling to the side of a candle and resemble the folded sheet in which a corpse is wrapped. Popular superstition regarded a winding-sheet on a candle as an omen of death or calamity (*OED*).

the bitter, vapid taste of opium.]   See note to chapter 11, p. 107.

Chapter 11   Fourth monthly number
                                                                                June 1852

OUR DEAR BROTHER.

The title derives from the Burial Service: 'Forasmuch as it hath pleased Almighty God of his great mercy to take unto himself the soul of our dear brother here departed, we therefore commit his body to the ground.'

"Run, Flite, run!

a . . . medical man . . . with . . . a broad Scotch tongue.]   Before the Medical Reform Act of 1858, the majority of qualified physicians and surgeons practising in England were graduates or licentiates of the medical schools in Edinburgh and Glasgow, for, unlike England, Scotland had established proper courses of medical education early in the eighteenth century. Moreover, because physicians were required to have a university degree for membership of the Royal College of Physicians of England, Englishmen who could not afford to go to Oxford or Cambridge, but who were determined to become physicians, went to Edinburgh or Glasgow. (The Royal College of Surgeons of England did not require its members to be university graduates.) A large proportion of the Scotsmen who had qualified

Coroner's Inquest.

Harmonic meeting-room

Little Cheeks

Swills } the comic vocalist

Beadle

Coroner   Boy. Jo.

churchyard & Broom

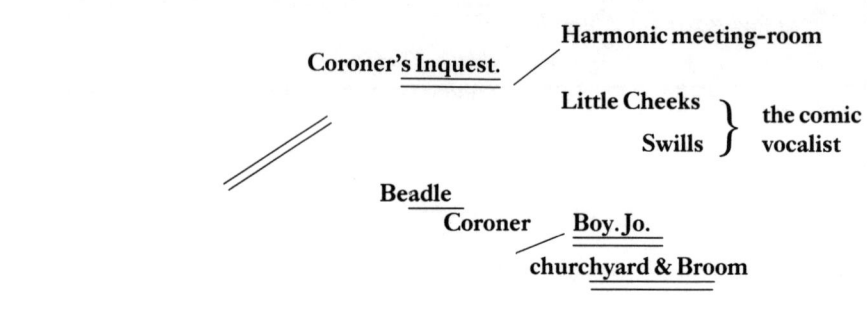

~~Picture~~

Chesney Wold

Rosa & Watt? Yes. Slightly.   <Carry on> Carry on

Esther.

Miss Jellyby? No.

(Bleak House – No. IV.)

Chapter XI.

Our dear brother.

Chapter XII.

On the Watch.

Country house – clear, cold day

Riding from Paris home

Brilliant and distinguished circle

French Lady's maid

Boodle
and
Buffy

Mr Tulkinghorn and Lady Dedlock. Each watching the other.

**Open that interest and
leave them so:—**

Chapter XIII.

Esther's Narrative.

as physicians or surgeons went to England to practise because more money could be made there, particularly in London, and because Scottish medical education was highly regarded (Newman, 1957, *passim*).

The dark young surgeon passes the candle

The dark young surgeon]   Dickens's decision to make Allan Woodcourt a surgeon rather than a physician may have been influenced by a desire to treat the topical issue of the discrimination affecting surgeons in the Navy: the subject is introduced in chapter 13, when Richard decides to train as a surgeon (see note p.127), and Woodcourt becomes a ship's surgeon himself in chapter 17.

Unlike the Scottish doctor (who is probably a physician), Woodcourt would have trained in London or (less likely) at one of the provincial medical schools recognized for the membership diploma of the Royal College of Surgeons. After a five-year apprenticeship to an individual physician or surgeon at a hospital or in general practice, medical students attended a course of lectures and a course of dissections, and then completed their education with a year of clinical experience which was referred to as 'walking the hospitals'. On completion of this year, students who had decided to become surgeons would have gained the Diploma in Surgery of the Royal College of Surgeons, the usual surgical qualification in England and Wales between 1843 and 1858. The majority would have also gained the medical qualification of the Society of Apothecaries (LSA) and have earned by examination Membership of the Royal College of Surgeons (MRCS), separate qualifications which became conjoined by custom and convenience.

In addition to his being an MRCS (as mentioned in chapter 13), other factors distinguish Woodcourt from doctors of the previous generation – such as the inadequately trained 'Fashionable Physician' satirized in *Heads of the People* (1840), Sir Courtney Palmoile, and Palmoile's counterpart in *DS*, the Court Physician Parker Peps. Woodcourt's 'professional' attitude and his interest in sanitary reform and social care reflect traits which earned wide public esteem for the new generation of doctors. The gradual professionalization of medical practice which occurred during the mid-century was the result of a long-running public debate initiated in 1837, the year in which a parliamentary Medical Reform Committee was established to investigate the disorganized state of medical education and practice. The haphazard, unsupervised way in which medical students were allowed to pursue their course enabled the undisciplined to lead lives of pleasure rather than study. There was also widespread concern about the enormous number of so-called doctors: charlatans and quacks who were allowed to practise because of the absence of regulations. The subjects were complex and contentious, and throughout the 1840s and 1850s they were kept before the public on account of a series of Bills brought before the House. Meanwhile medical examining bodies were beginning to regulate the profession and to institute new and stricter qualifications for eligibility. The debate and activity of twenty-one years culminated in the Medical Reform Act of 1858 which made education uniform throughout the country and registration of practitioners compulsory (Newman, 1957, *passim*; Cope, 1959, 59–85; Crosse, 1968, 39–41).

The new generation of doctor was frequently given a heroic stature in prose and fiction – for instance, Carlyle's 'humane Physician' in the passage in *Past and Present* which influenced the scenes involving Woodcourt in chapter 46 and 47 (see p. 253–4). Another example is the type of doctor praised at the end of 'The Medical Student', the *Heads of the People* essay which depicts a lackadaisical, vulgar man typical of those whom the contemporary reforms sought to weed out. In contrast to him,

> There are those who have adopted their profession as a branch of science, and a means of benefiting mankind . . . these are Philosophers, and so many as there are of them, so many gentlemen are there in the Medical Profession. (1840, 48)

And there is also the 'great Physician' in *LD*, whose

> equality of compassion was no more disturbed than the divine Master's of all healing was. He went, like the rain, among the just and unjust, doing all the good he could, and neither proclaiming it in the synagogues nor at the corner of the streets. (3.25)

"I knew this person by sight

"He has purchased opium of me]   Opium was widely used in pill and liquid form by doctors to treat the symptoms of major diseases for which cures were unknown, and even though it was referred to as a poison it was sold not only by doctors and chemists but also over the counter in any type of shop, including grocers' and general stores. The sale of opium was high in urban areas and among the poor, who used it as a cheap alternative to alcohol and also because they lacked adequate medical care. Largely because the drug was often used by persons committing suicide, and because there were numerous cases of accidental fatal overdosing, a campaign was mounted in the 1850s to restrict its availability, and the activity resulted in the Pharmacy Act of 1868. The 'poison' Krook finds by the bed would be laudanum (opium dissolved in alcohol), which had a distinctly bitter smell – as Woodcourt comments. That Nemo had purchased opium for a year and a half suggests that he had become addicted to drinking laudanum, the habit called opium-eating. Opium-smoking, as practised by John Jasper in *MED*, was in Britain an exotic method of taking the drug and was limited to the dockland communities frequented by Chinese sailors (Berridge, 1978; Wellcome Institute, 1984, 16–20; see also Jacobson, 1986, 21–30).

"About a year and a half ago," says Mr. Snagsby

she considered Nemo equally the same as Nimrod.]   Nimrod is 'the mighty hunter before the Lord' in Genesis 10.9.

By this time the news

A policeman . . . stands like a tower, only condescending to see the boys at

his base occasionally; but whenever he does see them, they quail and fall back.] But shortly the same boys, not awe-struck by the beadle, taunt that officer of the law. The contrast drawn between the attitudes of the public towards the policeman and the beadle seems to derive (along with later descriptions of the policeman) from the essay by Paul Prendergast, 'The Policeman', in *Heads of the People* (1841 supplement):

> The Policeman is also an object of much terror to all small boys . . . It is quite amusing to observe the rapidity with which his "Now then, young feller," makes one of these young gentlemen scamper. You may often be advertised of the approach of a Policeman, by seeing half-a-dozen of them dash by you at the turning of a corner . . . the same boys would hoot and bawl after a great fat beadle; but the Policeman is not to be played or trifled with . . . his presence inspires them with veneration and awe. (255–6)

The beadle, though generally understood

The beadle . . . a ridiculous institution . . . a remnant of the barbarous watchmen-times . . . something that must be borne with until Government shall abolish him.] Since the establishment of the Metropolitan Police in 1829, the redundancy of beadles and their insistence on the extent of their diminishing authority had become topical issues. *Punch* expressed the popular attitude in 'The Insolence of Beadledom', 19 (29 June 1850) 2:

> Beadledom has for some years been growing upon us, until at last it has come to be looked upon as one of the Institutions of the country, and as such it is liable to abuse . . . Beadledom, once confined to the parish, has crept into our squares, insinuated itself into our arcades, and, indeed, become so general, that to say we are literally swarming with beadles would be no extravagant figure . . . The cocked hat has been cocked up somewhat too high, and the staff has been brandished a little too boldly in these latter days.

(See also 22, 28 February 1852, 98.) That beadles had long represented petty tyranny and stupid officiousness is illustrated in Sir David Wilkie's painting, 'Parish Beadle' (1823), as well as in the depiction of Mr Bumble in *OT*. But Bung, the beadle in 'Our Parish' (*SB*), is likeable, efficient, respected and humane.

The insistence of beadles on retaining their old authority was part of the widespread reluctance of the public to accept certain aspects of the new legislation promoted by the sanitary reformer Edwin Chadwick (1800–90). The Police Acts of 1829 and 1839, embodying Chadwick's principle of 'omnicompetence', gave the new professional force wide-ranging powers, including those of preserving order, repressing mendicity and abating nuisances (Finer, 1952, 166–77; Rumbelow, 1971, 18–20).

By-and-by the beadle comes out

accessible by telegraph] The inhabitants of Took's Court have wild ideas about how the telegraph worked: although telegraphy came into use in England in the 1840s, a message could not have been sent to a ship on its way to China. *HW* praised the telegraph, 'this wonderful invention', in 'Wings of Wire' (2.241–5).

Lords of the Admiralty]   The governing body of the Royal Navy, impressively housed in Whitehall.

Taunts the beadle . . . with having boiled a boy; choruses fragments of a popular song to that effect]   'The Workhouse Boy' tells of boys in a workhouse who miss one of their friends after eating soup on Christmas Day:

> At length the soup copper repairs did need,
> The Coppersmith came, and there he seed,
> A dollop of bones lay a grizzling there,
> In the leg of the breeches the poor boy did vear!
> To gain his fill the boy did stoop,
> And, dreadful to tell, he was boil'd in the soup!
> And ve all of us say, and ve say it sincere,
> That he was push'd in there by an overseer.
> Oh the Poor Vorkhouse Boy.
> (st. 4, cited in Ashton, 1888, 351–2; noted by Sone, 1963, 309)

the unmoved policeman (to whom a little opium, more or less, is nothing)]   The policeman in Paul Prendergast's essay is similarly phlegmatic in the performance of his duties – such as dispersing a crowd around a Punch and Judy show: ' "Come, I say, none of this!" cried the imperturbable officer, whose gravity, or rather dulness, would have been proof against Momus or Grimaldi himself, "it's o' no use. Move on" ' (255). The imperturbability of the British policeman had become a commonplace, as Philip Collins has remarked (1962, 203), quoting *Punch* on this national characteristic:

> The Englishman is as laconic as an electric telegraph's message. The Frenchman is as lengthy and as pompous as an American President's message . . . The English Policeman says briefly and sharply, "Move on there."   ('French and English Policemen', 18, 1850, 77)

his shining hat, stiff stock, inflexible great-coat, stout belt and bracelet, and all things fitting]

> That the Policeman wears an oil-skin hat, and . . . a stout great coat . . . that his ordinary official costume is a sort of half-military uniform of blue ditto; that a leather belt encircles his waist; and while he is on duty, a piece of striped list the cuff of his coat; that his collar is so made as to defy retaliation . . . and that his somewhat soldier-like appearance . . . has made him the subject of an invidious comparison with a certain marine shell-fish in its uncooked state, are facts, which . . . nobody will dispute in the main. ('The Policeman', 249)

Next day the court is all alive

the Sol's Arms]   Perhaps this is a facetious conflation of 'sol' ('sun') and 'sol[icitor]'. Charles Dickens the younger identified the Old Ship tavern in Chichester Rents (which connected Chancery Lane with New Square, Lincoln's Inn) as 'unquestionably' the original of the Sol's Arms: 'it had a large room on the first floor in which the inquest *must* have been held', and it was opposite the house identifiable as Krook's (1896, 347).

Harmonic Meetings]   These popular musical evenings, held in public houses or 'song and supper rooms', were an early version of the English music-hall. Refreshments were served during the programme, which was announced by the landlord of the house, who served as chairman and sat surrounded by his friends at a table below the platform. A harmonic meeting is depicted in *SB* ('Scenes'), and in *PP* 20; another one – of a rougher sort – features in chapter 26 of *OT*, which describes the chairman, the singers and the low company of men and women who comprise the audience.

his friends will rally round him]   'Rally round' was a political expression much in vogue. In *OMF*, for instance, Veneering contemplates running for Parliament, 'but requires breathing time to ascertain "whether his friends will rally round him"' (2.3).

a pieman . . . his brandy-balls]   Brandy-balls were usually sold not by piemen (who sold meat, fish and fruit pies) but by street-sellers of confectionery. The sweet was made of sugar, water, peppermint and cinnamon (Mayhew 1.195, 203).

At the appointed hour arrives the Coroner

The Coroner frequents more public-houses than any man alive.]   The description of the inquest on Nemo is indebted to the eye-witness account which W. H. Wills wrote for *HW* in 1850, 'A Coroner's Inquest' (1.109–13). Wills described the proceedings at length, generally criticizing the informality with which they were conducted and the impropriety of holding them in public houses. In *OMF* the coroner's inquest on the body of the man believed to be John Harmon takes place at the Six Jolly Fellowship Porters (1.3).

So they go out in a loose procession

the public chroniclers of such inquiries, by the line]   Their style is parodied in chapter 33, where they describe Krook's death and recall Nemo's. While Dickens was still a schoolboy, he would sometimes take into the office of the *British Press* 'penny-a-line stuff', miscellaneous notices and police reports which were paid for at a penny a printed line (Hall, 1883, 111).

as familiarly and patronisingly mentioned as the name of the Hangman is, according to the latest examples.]   William Calcraft (1800–79) served as executioner in the City of London from 1829 to 1874, also flogging criminals and performing executions at Horsemonger Lane Gaol. Known for his jokes, oaths and drunkenness on the scaffold, he enjoyed considerable notoriety, and several cheap publications about him appeared in his own lifetime. The 'latest example' seems an allusion to the execution of Mr and Mrs Manning at Horsemonger Lane Gaol in 1849 (see note to chapter 12, p. 119).

Anastasia Piper, gentlemen.

Anastasia]   She can be identified as an Irish immigrant from her name, which occurred chiefly in Ireland in the nineteenth century.

Why, Mrs. Piper has a good deal to say

half-baptising . . . on accounts of not being expected to live]   Anyone present at what was believed to be the impending death of a child was allowed to baptize it, but if the child survived the proper rite was required to be performed.

Name Jo. Nothing else that he knows on.

Jo]   The reputed original of Jo was a boy crossing-sweeper named George Ruby who testified at the Guildhall on 8 January 1850 in a case at which Dickens was present, an assault on a policeman. Dickens may have taken particular interest in George Ruby because during 1848–9, when he was a regular contributor to the *Examiner*, the newspaper had published a series of articles reporting cases of children whose testimony was considered inadmissible because they did not know the answers to the Catechism. The *Examiner* reported the case of George Ruby (12 January, 15), and it is possible that Dickens was the author of the article (Fielding and Brice, 1968). The proceedings were also reported in the January issue of the monthly supplement to *Household Words*, the *Household Narrative of Current Events*. The articles which they provoked may well have been by Dickens himself; certainly, they are in his style (House, 1941, 32–3; Collins, 1960, 345; Fielding and Brice, 1968). The *Household Narrative* editorial on the proceedings observed:

> all he knew was how to sweep the crossing; while manifestly prominent among the things he did not know, was how to speak other than the truth. The latter was not the inference, however, of the worthy magistrate: he did not recognise the excellent soil, only barren because no seed had been sown there; but straightway after lamenting over the deplorable ignorance of the unfortunate child, he rejected his evidence peremptorily as that of a creature who knew nothing whatever of the obligation to tell the truth.

The testimony of George Ruby was quoted in part in a *HW* article by James Hannay published in the August following the trial, 'Lambs to be Fed' (3.548). Three months before the publication of the present number, an almost identical case was described twice in the *Household Narrative* (March 1852; noted by Suddaby, 1912).

In addition to the cases reported in the *Household Narrative* and the *Examiner*, there is the possibility of a further influence on the scene of Jo's testimony excluded from evidence, that of a similar scene in Carlyle's *Latter-Day Pamphlets* (see Fielding and Brice, 1968). On the style of Jo's answers at the inquest as an imitation of the reported speech in the legal proceedings and as used in parliamentary reports, see Harris, 1968, 49.

Never been to school.]   Poor children could attend the state-supported, under-financed ragged schools, but the teachers were often entirely untrained. The primary purpose of the schools was to prevent delinquency, and at first only religious instruction was offered, but later there were reading lessons and the children were given training to enable them to earn a living. In his *Ragged Schools; Their Rise, Progress and Results* (1852), John MacGregor mentions a boy whom Dickens sent to a ragged school and in whose conduct and career he took a very practical interest. It has been suggested that this boy may have partly influenced the characterization of Jo and also 'Deputy', the urchin in *MED* (personal communication from Philip Collins, to whom I am much indebted). Shortly after the present number was published, Dickens was criticized by members of the Ragged School Union for not having done justice to the efforts of the ragged schools to improve the lot of children like Jo (Collins, 1963, 86–93).

Knows a broom's a broom]   Crossing-sweepers constituted a large class of the metropolitan poor, according to Augustus Mayhew, the probable author of the chapter on crossing-sweepers in his brother's *London Labour and the London Poor*. The job was one of those resorted to as an excuse for begging without being considered a beggar. The sweepers were more or less under the protection of the police: if they kept their pathways well swept, the policeman of the district would protect the original sweeper of the crossing from the intrusion of a rival, but if a sweeper had not been given permission to sweep a particular crossing he could be moved on, as Jo is in chapter 19.

People were driven to take up sweeping either because they were physically unable to do rougher work or because it was the last resource open to them to earn a living. Many of the young sweepers Mayhew interviewed had begun at 10 or 11 years old, and they earned extra money by tumbling in front of gentlemen after the opera and behind omnibuses on Sundays, fetching cabs, opening cab doors and procuring prostitutes (2.496–7). A shilling was considered to be a good day's earnings. On the other hand, one of the advantages of being a crossing-sweeper was the small amount of capital which was required to set up in business, for a broom was all that was needed – however, as one boy remarked: 'A broom doesn't last us more than a week in wet weather, and they costs us twopence halfpenny each; but in dry weather they are good for a fortnight' (2.498).

Augustus Mayhew generally found the class of crossing-sweepers 'among the most honest of the London poor. They all tell you that, without a good character

112

and "the respect of the neighbourhood," there is not a living to be got out of the broom . . . and nearly all of them have had their minds so subdued by affliction, that they have been tamed so as to be incapable of mischief.' (2.466)

From the mid-1840s, the livelihood of London crossing-sweepers began to be encroached upon by 'street-orderlies', able-bodied paupers employed by the National Philanthropic Association (Mayhew 2.253–78).

For some little time the Jurymen

to go half-price to the play at night]   Patrons could be admitted to the pit for half-price if they were willing to come in halfway through a performance, or during the interval between two plays.

It is anything but a night of rest

Guster murders sleep]   *Macbeth* 2.2.35: 'Methought I heard a voice cry "Sleep no more;/Macbeth does murder sleep".'

Then the active and intelligent

a hemmed-in churchyard, pestiferous and obscene, whence malignant diseases are communicated to the bodies of our dear brothers and sisters who have not departed]   In 1868, in a letter to a Miss Palfrey, Dickens identified the graveyard in which he 'buried the "Nemo" of Bleak House', admitting to having had in mind the external details of the burying-ground of St Martin-in-the-Fields at the corner of Drury Lane and Russell Street (*Nonesuch* 3.642). For why Dickens was legally wrong in burying Nemo here, see note to chapter 59, p. 288.

The danger to health and insult to decency caused by intramural burials became an issue in the late 1830s, and during the next two decades the shocking evidence produced by medical and scientific investigators fomented a public outcry which ultimately led to reform. The abuses which concerned the sanitary reformers were numerous and chiefly affected the poor, who could not afford burial fees sufficient to ensure a decent and Christian burial. The pauper funerals provided by the parish were usually hasty affairs neglectful of religious observance. To avoid the indignity of a pauper's funeral, the working class made regular payments into 'burial clubs' to cover the expenses of a decent funeral, but the sum accumulated frequently tempted the desperate to premature collection, the chief victims being children. Undertakers and clergymen alike were involved in unscrupulous practices concerning burial fees, funeral expenses, speculation in burial-grounds and the sale of corpses for dissection. The overcrowding in many metropolitan graveyards was an abomination: by the early 1840s some intramural burial-grounds already contained more than 3,000 bodies per acre. Moreover, the churchyards and burial-grounds of the nonconformist sects, in addition to the eight commercial cemeteries established outside London, had all become inadequate. As the number of burials exceeded the rate of decomposition, the height of some burial-grounds rose. Bodies recently buried were disinterred to make room for later ones, mass graves were left open to save the gravediggers work, and coffins were crammed against each other, the topmost within a foot or two of the surface. Such conditions caused a pestilent stench which pervaded the grounds and gave rise to sickness as it spread to adjacent houses and streets.

Serious investigations, promoted largely by Edwin Chadwick, resulted in the important *Report of the Select Committee on the Health of Towns* (1840) and the *Supplementary Report on the Results of a Special Inquiry into the Practice of Interment in Towns* (1843), both of which considered metropolitan interment in the larger context of the sanitary movement (see note to chapter 46, pp. 250–2). Years passed with no reform until an outbreak of cholera in 1849 stirred up alarm and initiated widespread criticism of the complacency of the vested interests opposed to reform. The publicity and public pressure resulted in a Bill 'to make better Provision for the Interment of the Dead in and near the Metropolis', which passed into law in 1850 as the Metropolitan Interments Act.

Dickens's keen involvement in the general movement for sanitary reform during the 1840s and 1850s is evidenced by his relations with Chadwick, with Henry Austin (Secretary to the General Board of Health and his brother-in-law) and with Miss Coutts. He gave a speech at the Freemasons' Tavern in February 1850 when the Metropolitan Sanitary Association was founded (*Speeches* 104–10). The same month, Austin sent him a copy of the newly published *Report on a General Scheme for Extra-mural Sepulture*. Dickens replied immediately: 'Many thanks for the Report, which is extraordinarily interesting. I began to read it last night, in bed – and dreamed of putrefaction generally' (*Speeches* 131, n. 2). Further examples of his involvement are the articles he wrote collaboratively with Austin for the *Examiner* (see Fielding and Brice, 1970, 117–28).

His interest in the abuses of metropolitan interment is displayed as early as 1839 in a passage in chapter 62 of *NN* which anticipates the description of Nemo's burying-ground. Moreover, several articles on the subject appeared in *HW* whilst the Metropolitan Interments Bill was before Parliament: 'Heathen and Christian Burial', 1.43–8 (George Hogarth and W. H. Wills); 'Address from an Undertaker to the Trade', 1.301–4 (Percival Leigh); 'Trading in Death', 6.241–5 (Dickens). A poem, 'City Graves' (2.277), contains interesting verbal similarities to the present passage and to the scene in chapter 16 in which Jo shows Lady Dedlock the 'consecrated ground'. The *Household Narrative of Current Events* also carried articles on the subject throughout this period. Different types of city graveyard are described in the *UT* essay, 'The City of the Absent'. (See: 'The Dead *versus* the Living', *Westminster Review* 37, 1842, 201–16; 'London Churchyards', *Westminster Review* 40, 1843, 149–82; review of the *Supplementary Report on the Results of a Special Inquiry into the Practice of Interment in Towns*, and books on cemeteries by J. C. Loudon, G. A. Walker and F. E. Pajet in *Quarterly Review*, no. 146, 1844, 438–77; Fielding and Brice, 1970; Morley, 1971, *passim*; Sheppard, 1971, 259–60, 268, 273–4.)

a beastly scrap of ground which a Turk would reject as a savage abomination, and a Caffre would shudder at]   The comparison derives from the *HW* article, 'Heathen and Christian Burial', which describes the burial customs of such heathens as the 'Mahommedans' and 'the Caffres, Hottentots, and other savage tribes of Southern Africa' (1.43–8). The name 'Caffre', which applies to the members of the Bantu tribe, was familiar to the public on account of the Caffre War in 1848, in which British soldiers fought.

With houses looking on

sow him in corruption, to be raised in corruption]   The Burial Service reads: 'So also is the resurrection of the dead: It is sown in corruption; it is raised in incorruption' (1 Corinthians 15.42).

Come night, come darkness,

Come night, come darkness,]   Compare *Macbeth* 3.2.46–7: 'Come, seeling night,/Scarf up the tender eye of pitiful day' (Smith, 1974, 60–1); and also *Romeo and Juliet* 3.2.17: 'Come, night; come, Romeo; come, thou day in night.'

Jo, is it thou?

thou art not quite in outer darkness.]   Compare Matthew 22.13: 'cast him into outer darkness' (*Norton*).

Chapter 12

ON THE WATCH.

It has left off raining

communicates the glad tidings]   As in Acts 13.32, 'And we declare unto you glad tidings', and elsewhere in the New Testament.

the *élite* of the *beau monde*]

The slang of the fashionable world is mostly imported from France; an unmeaning gibberish of Gallicisms runs through English fashionable conversation, and fashionable novels, and accounts of fashionable parties in the fashionable newspapers . . . If you were to tell a well-bred Frenchman . . . of the *beau monde*, he would imagine you meant the world which God made, not half-a-dozen streets and squares between Hyde Park Corner and Chelsea Bun House. ('Slang', *HW* 8.76)

115

a giant refreshed] Psalms 78.66: 'So the Lord awaked as one out of sleep: and like a giant refreshed with wine.'

For the greater honour

The clear cold sunshine . . . Athwart the picture of my Lady . . . throws a broad bend-sinister] In heraldry the bend-sinister extends from top right to bottom left on the coat of arms and is an indication of illegitimacy.

Through the same cold sunshine

my Lady and Sir Leicester, in their travelling chariot . . . start for home.] Only the rich could afford to take their private carriages to the Continent, as Mayhew remarked: 'This was the aristocratic style of travelling, and its indulgence was costly' (3.321). The practice was discouraged by the 'Roving Englishman' (Grenville Murray) in his 'Hints to Travellers':

> A carriage has now [1852] become almost a useless incumbrance; neverthe-less, where one is still necessary, it is a silly increase of expense to drag one from England to the place where it is wanted . . . good travelling carriages may be hired anywhere. (*HW* 6.212)

Instead of being driven four-in-hand, as in Britain, the horses of private carriages in France were ridden by two postilions, whose curious costume – glazed hats (to ward off rain) and large, heavy boots which came above the knee – was often remarked upon by English travellers (Maxwell, 1932, 216 n.).

The most direct route from Paris to London in the early 1840s was by *diligence* (or private carriage) to Calais or Boulogne, and thence by steam-packet to London (coach from port). Steam-packets also operated from Le Havre, and other destina-tions were Dover, Margate, Ramsgate, Brighton and Southampton. The descrip-tion of the Dedlocks' arduous three-day journey home by road contrasts with the eleven-hour journey by rail which was possible after 1847. Dickens described a journey by rail between London and Paris in 'A Flight' (*HW* 3.529–33), an article written shortly before he began *BH* and one which he obviously had in mind as he composed the present scene. For instance, as he sits in his speeding railway carriage, he recalls what it was like to make the journey by road:

> What has the South Eastern done with all the horrible little villages we used to pass through, in the *Diligence*? What have they done . . . with all the long-tailed horses who were always biting one another, with all the big postilions in jack-boots . . . (532)

France began to be popular and fashionable with the British in the late eighteenth century, particularly because French literature, manners and culture then began to set the standard for the rest of Europe. The vogue for French fashions which started at the beginning of the nineteenth century further established the country as a favourite destination of British travellers, for whom a visit to Paris was the chief attraction (Maxwell, 1932, 1–45 *passim*). In the present passage, the incidental references to the famous sights of Paris evoke what visitors most admired about the city – its gay and aristocratic ambience, the general magnificence of its architecture and gardens, and the Parisians' taste for the fine arts and elegant amusements. Dickens himself knew Paris well, having first visited it in 1844 on his way to Italy. Whilst writing *DS*, he lived with his family for three months in 1846–7 in the Faubourg Saint-Honoré, and throughout the rest of his life he made frequent excursions there with one or another of his friends, always seeming to find stimulation in the excitement and bustle of the city.

the Hotel Bristol in the Place Vendôme . . . the Rue de Rivoli] The Hôtel Bristol is listed in *Galignani's New Paris Guide* (1842) as one of the 'principal furnished hotels' in the city. Dickens stayed there in November 1844 and wrote to his wife that he considered the hotel 'the best I ever was in' (*Letters* 4.230). In 'A Flight' he describes how he would 'stroll down to the sparkling Palais Royal, up the Rue de Rivoli, to the Place Vendôme' (533). By 1842 the handsome and commodious houses in the Rue de Rivoli, opposite the Tuileries, were entirely occupied by foreigners or hotel-keepers. Carlyle mentions this important street and other places in his *Excursion (Futile Enough) to Paris; Autumn 1851*, in which he remarks on how Paris has changed since his last visit in 1824:

> Rue de Rivoli had been mainly built since my former visit to Paris; a very fine-looking straight street, of five or six storey houses, with piazza . . . Tuileries Garden (close on my left) seemed to have grown *bushier* since my visit . . . Place de la Révolution (Place Louis Quinze) is *altogether* altered . . . Louvre getting itself new-faced . . . Carrousel, Tuileries, Jardin des Tuileries, Palais Royal, &c., all looked *dirty*, or insufficiently swept.

the garden of the ill-fated palace of a headless king and queen] Louis XVI and Marie-Antoinette were beheaded in the garden of the Tuileries in 1793. Dickens would have been unfamiliar with Carlyle's notable description of the heroic attempt of the Swiss guards to defend the Tuileries ('The Swiss', *The French Revolution* 3.6.7).

the Place of Concord, and the Elysian Fields, and the Gate of the Star] As Carlyle mentions in his *Excursion . . . to Paris*, these sights had been either recently improved and altered (Place de la Concorde, called Place de la Révolution until 1800, in 1836; les Champs Elysées, in 1820), or recently constructed (the Barrière de l'Etoile, otherwise the Arc de Triomphe de l'Etoile, was begun in 1806 and completed in 1836).

Sooth to say, they cannot go away

nothing is new to my Lady, under the worn-out heavens.] A variation on the commonplace of biblical origin, 'there is no new thing under the sun' (Ecclesiastes 1.9).

Only last Sunday, when poor wretches were gay . . . performing dogs and wooden horses . . . dancing, love-making, wine-drinking, tobacco-smoking, tomb-visiting, billiard₍ᵧ₎ card and domino playing, quack-doctoring]

> I walk up to the Barrière de l'Etoile, sufficiently dazed by my flight to have a pleasant doubt of the reality of everything about me; of the lively crowd, the overhanging trees, the performing dogs, the hobby-horses. ('A Flight', 533)

Many of the pastimes are mentioned in another *HW* article, 'Deadly Lively', which describes how to spend a holiday, particularly a Sunday, in Paris:

> There are the Tuileries and Luxembourg Gardens, the Musée, the Louvre, and reading rooms . . . then the open-air concerts, and dancing-dogs, and Fantoccini . . . of the Champs Elysées, are tempting. But all these are sports or pastimes adapted to the afternoon or evening . . . Therefore, for early morning holiday amusement, the Parisian has no great variety of attractions. He cannot then play at dominoes or piquet; even billiards before noon are wearisome. Thus . . . excursionists, in hundreds and thousands, flock every Sunday to the great metropolitan cemeteries. (9.138)

'Quack-doctoring' was practised in public by charlatans and mountebanks, who sold remedies and cure-alls and sometimes performed mesmerism.

the clipped trees and the statues in the Palace Garden]

> There is a great deal of good sculpture in the garden of the Tuileries that deserves examination . . . From the great size of this garden [67 acres], the white marble of the statues produces a light and pleasing effect contrasted with the flowers or the foliage of the trees.   (*Galignani's New Paris Guide,* 1842, 166)

the gloomy Cathedral of our Lady]   The Cathedral Church of Notre-Dame. As expressed in *PI*, Dickens's inevitable general impression of Continental Roman Catholic churches was that they were gloomy and oppressive.

the clutch of Giant Despair]   This giant owns Doubting Castle and captures Christian and Hope in John Bunyan's *The Pilgrim's Progress* (1678).

She cannot, therefore, go too fast

her Ariel has put a girdle of it round the whole earth]   Dickens confuses Ariel (in *The Tempest*) with Puck (in *A Midsummer Night's Dream*), who 'put a girdle round about the earth/In forty minutes' (2.1.174).

endless avenues and cross-avenues of wintry trees!]　In 'A Flight' Dickens suggests that the advent of railways has made such vistas of the French countryside less tedious: 'What have they done with all the summer dust, with all the winter mud, with all the dreary avenues of little trees' (532).

like the angels in Jacob's dream!]　Genesis 28.12: 'And he dreamed, and behold a ladder set upon the earth, and the top of it reached to heaven: and behold the angels of God ascending and descending on it.'

The rattle and clatter

the Golden Ape]　Apparently Dickens's invention (on the model of Hôtel Lion d'Or, Hôtel de la Porte d'Or, Hôtel de la Clef d'Or, for example); the English have traditionally caricatured the French as chattering monkeys.

My Lady's maid is a Frenchwoman

My Lady's maid is a Frenchwoman]　The corrected proofs of chapter 2 show that Dickens initially intended to call her 'Marie', the name of the woman she is modelled on, Maria Manning, née Marie de Roux (Plate 10). A Swiss, married to a former English railway guard and publican, Maria Manning had been lady's maid to several aristocrats. In November 1849, following a sensational trial, Mr and Mrs Manning were hanged at Horsemonger Lane Gaol for the murder of her lover. Details of the case, including descriptions of Mrs Manning, were widely published. She was an attractive woman with dark eyes and hair, and her features, 'though they were neither regular nor feminine, were rather pleasing than otherwise' (*Annual Register* 431). Her speech was deliberate, distinct and marked with a slight foreign accent. The *Annual Register* remarked on her calmness and self-possession throughout the trial, but *The Times* reported that her conduct grew violent, and that in prison before her execution she grew and sharpened her nails and attempted to strangle herself (13 November, cited in *Letters* 5.642 n.). Her concern for her clothes was also noticed: she always appeared in satin dresses and bonnets, and 'her thoughts in prison appeared to be wholly devoted to dress'. At her execution, moreover, 'she was attired in a manner that evinced the greatest attention to her personal appearance' (*Annual Register* 435, 447).

　　Dickens and Forster were among the crowd of 30,000 who attended the public hanging of the Mannings on 13 November, and Dickens afterwards wrote two letters to *The Times* (published on 14 and 19 November) in which he condemned public executions for their 'demoralizing nature' and their 'hardening influence' on 'coarse minds', (*Letters* 5.644–5, 651–4). Four months after the publication of the present number, he described in 'Lying Awake' (*HW* 6.145–8) how his memories of the Mannings' execution had kept him awake long after the event.

　　The characterization of Hortense is also partly indebted to Carlyle's depiction of the fierce women, 'of violent speech and gesture' who played a prominent role in the French Revolution (see especially 'The Insurrection of Women', book 7 in

Volume 2 of *The French Revolution*). In chapter 23, Esther likens Hortense to 'some woman from the streets of Paris in the reign of terror'.

Ha, ha, ha! She, Hortense,

She, Hortense, been in my Lady's service since five years . . . It is the *best* thing altogether.]   Throughout the novel, the 'Frenchness' of the reported speech and dialogue of Hortense is conveyed by her imperfect command and pronunciation of English; her use of literal English translations of French words and expressions (' "since five years" ', ' "You are right there!" ', ' "I come from arriving" '); her use of words which are common to both English and French (' "droll" '); and her use of superlatives (' "It is the *best* thing altogether" ') and of actual French words (' "Mademoiselle" ', ' "spirituel" ' – spelt 'spiritual' in chapter 54). For these and other devices by which Dickens represents foreign speech in his works (especially French in *TTC*), see Monod, 1970; Page, 1973, 74–7; Haig, 1983.

All the mirrors in the house

a mighty hunter before the Lord,]   Nimrod, in Genesis 10.9, is the 'mighty hunter before the Lord'.

the Court of St. James's]   To be presented to the monarch at Court, as Becky Sharp is in *Vanity Fair* (1847–8), was considered the launch of a person in society.

Dandyism? There is no King George

Dandyism? There is no King George the Fourth now . . . to set the dandy fashion]   The observations on dandies in the present and subsequent paragraphs are partly informed by two chapters by Carlyle: 'The Dandiacal Body' in *Sartor Resartus* (1833–4; 1838), and 'Gospel of Dilettantism' in *Past and Present* (1843). 'The Dandiacal Body' begins with a description of a dandy: 'A Dandy is a Clothes-wearing Man, a Man whose trade, office, and existence consists in the wearing of Clothes . . . wisely and well: so that as others dress to live, he lives to dress.'
,   Around 1813–16 the word 'dandy' became a London colloquialism for an exquisite of the period. George IV, first as Prince of Wales and later as Prince Regent, established a reputation for fastidious, elaborate dressing. Although his opinions on taste were adopted by men of fashion, rank and wealth, the ultimate dictator in matters of men's dress was Beau Brummell (1778–1840), who held sway even over the Prince himself. For other reflections in the novel of Dickens's dislike of George IV, see notes to chapter 14 pp. 131, 134, 135–6.

there are no clear-starched, jack-towel neckcloths, no short-waisted coats, no false calves, no stays.]   Colourless starch was used to stiffen and dress

10   Maria Manning, as she appeared at Union Hall Police Court in 1849. From a verbatim report of the trial, in the British Library

linen. Its use on neckcloths, the length of which is likened to that of long towels on rollers, was introduced by Beau Brummell. A faultlessly tied cravat was the essential element in the dandy's wardrobe. Coats during the Regency were cut away at the front just below the waist, with the coat-tails almost touching the heels. The slim lines of the coats required many dandies to wear corsets. Calves were padded to give stockinged legs a good shape.

There are no caricatures, now, of effeminate Exquisites so arrayed]   As in one of Dickens's childhood picture-books, *The Dandies' Ball; or, High Life in the City* (1819), illustrated with coloured engravings. Dickens recollected it in 'First Fruits', a *HW* article published the month before the present number:

> The first picture-book! We date from the time of the Prince Regent, and remember picture-books about dandies – satires upon that eminent personage himself, possibly – but *we* never knew it . . .
>   The pictures represented male dandies in every stage of preparation for this festival [a supper and ball]; holding on to bed-posts to have their stays laced; embellishing themselves with artificial personal graces of many kinds; and enduring various humiliations in remote garrets. (5.190)

Four illustrations from *The Dandies' Ball* are reproduced in Stone, 1968, 2.414.

swooning in opera-boxes with excess of delight]   Dandies affected delicacy and effeminacy as an aspect of their refinement. However, it was not uncommon for ordinary people to swoon at the opera, for English opera and theatre had long enjoyed a reputation for scenes of exaggerated horror and terrifying effects (see Addison's remarks in *The Spectator*, 44, 20 April 1711).

buckskins]   Skin-tight leather knee-breeches.

or who goes to see all the executions]   This was George Augustus Selwyn (1719–91), one of the most conspicuous figures of society under George III. Morbidly attracted to sights of human suffering, particularly criminal executions, Selwyn constantly frequented such scenes and interested himself in all the particulars of the crime and the history of the criminal. He also relished the most dreadful details of suicide and murder, the investigation of disfigured corpses, and the sight of a friend in his shroud. His preoccupation occasioned numerous jokes and anecdotes, the best of which are related by Horace Walpole. A four-volume biography by John Heneage Jesse was published in 1843–4, *George Selwyn and His Contemporaries*, and reviewed by Leigh Hunt in the *Edinburgh Review* 80 (1844), 1–42.

the self-reproach of having once consumed a pea.]   Beau Brummell protested that some foods were too coarse for his delicate palate. When he was asked if he ever ate vegetables, he replied: 'Madam, I once ate a pea' (Moers, 1960, 21).

Why, yes. It cannot be disguised.

a Dandyism – in Religion . . . cancelling a few hundred years of history.]

'In these distracted times,' writes he [Professor Teufelsdröckh], 'when the Religious Principle, driven out of most Churches, either lies unseen in the hearts of good men . . . or else wanders homeless over the world, like a disembodied soul seeking its terrestrial organisation, – into how many strange shapes, of Superstition and Fanaticism, does it not tentatively and errantly cast itself! . . . thus Sect after Sect, and Church after Church, bodies itself forth, and melts again into new metamorphosis.

'Chiefly is this observable in England . . . Among the newer Sects of that country, one of the most notable . . . is that of the *Dandies* . . . it appears as if this Dandiacal Sect were but a new modification, adapted to the new time, of that primeval Superstition, *Self-Worship*. ('The Dandiacal Body')

'Cancelling a few hundred years of history' alludes to the Oxford Movement and the allied Young England party, which encouraged an interest in the revival of the past and of old ideals of church and state. Reacting against the contemporary trend promoted by the Protestants towards individualism and liberalism in religion and politics, high-church Anglicans sought a return to the medieval era when the church, the monarch and the nobility governed England. Disraeli's Young England party became a joke in Parliament and was frequently caricatured in *Punch*.

There are also ladies and gentlemen

who have agreed to put a smooth glaze on the world, and to keep down all its realities . . . not to be disturbed by ideas.] Criticized here are some widespread reactions among many people who were made nervous, anxious and insecure when forced to confront the harsh realities of economic and social life, the attacks on the moral stability of society posed by French novels, prostitution and theories of free love, and the undermining of religious orthodoxy by biblical criticism and new scientific discoveries. The present passage echoes the preface to the third edition of *OT* (1841), where Dickens defended his portrayal of criminals and prostitutes against objections 'on some very high moral grounds in some very high moral quarters'. Moreover, it anticipates Mr Podsnap in *OMF* (' "I don't want to know about it; I don't choose to discuss it; I don't admit it!" '), and Mrs General, who obliterates impropriety by 'varnish[ing] the surface of every object that came under consideration. The more cracked it was, the more Mrs General varnished it' (*LD* 2.2).

the Fine Arts . . . walking backward like the Lord Chamberlain, must array themselves in the milliners' and tailors' patterns of past generations] The Lord Great Chamberlain of England (a different official from the Lord Chamberlain of the Household) walks backwards when leaving the presence of those on whom he attends, the monarch at coronations and peers and bishops at their creation or doing of homage. The romantic neo-Gothic movement manifested itself in contemporary painting in pictures with antiquarian themes derived from the classics, the Bible, the drama, history and literature. The subjects were appropriately costumed. In chapter 29 this antiquarian tendency is described as 'the Fancy Ball School'.

Then there is my Lord Boodle

Boodle ... Coodle ... Doodle ... Foodle ... Noodle?]   In *Tom Thumb* (1730) Fielding gave the names Noodle and Doodle to courtiers 'in place' and the name of Foodle to a courtier in the opposition party. The next year, William Rufus Chetwood named two booby squires Noodle and Doodle in *The Generous Free-mason*, a play satirizing Sir Robert Walpole. The use of 'noodle' in nineteenth-century political vocabulary has been traced by McLean (1970). The *Edinburgh Review*, the *Examiner*, *Fraser's* and *Blackwood's* used 'noodle' to describe a stupid person. The term's particular use by Whigs to disparage Tories was influenced by Sidney Smith's satire on an obstructionist old Tory, 'Noodle's Oration', which was part of his review of Bentham's *Book of Fallacies* in the *Edinburgh Review* 42 (1825), 367–89. Dickens alluded to 'Noodle's Oration' in 1849 in his *Examiner* article on the Tooting baby farm, 'A Recorder's Charge' (Brice and Fielding, 1968, 237 n.). The oration is delivered by a fictitious Tory MP who opposes all innovations and insists that Parliament should be guided entirely by precedent and never be precipitate. The nickname 'Lord Doodle' was given to Lord Dudley, the Tory secretary of state for foreign affairs under the Duke of Wellington in 1828.

supposing the present Government to be overthrown]   For the ministerial crisis of 1851, to which this alludes and which inspired Dickens's description of the resignation of the government in chapter 40, 'National and Domestic', see note to that chapter, pp. 236–7). The political chatter between Boodle and Buffy has been noticed by Kathleen Tillotson to be a burlesque of the fashionable novel (1954; 1983, 88, n. 2).

You can't put him in the Woods and Forests]   In the March and April prior to the publication of the present number, *Punch* was mocking both the outgoing Commissioner of Woods and Forests and Land Revenues (responsible for the administration of Crown lands), Lord Seymour, and the new Commissioner, Lord John Manners, a well-known Young Englander. Manners was ridiculed in particular for having composed the lines, 'Let laws and learning, wealth and commerce, die,/But leave us still our old nobility':

> Now, woodcraft and forestcraft are especially the learning and accomplish-
> ments of our old nobility. The Forest Laws were animated by the humanising
> spirit of that old nobility, that made man's life very much cheaper than beasts' . . .
> there lingers about our Woods and Forests . . . a pleasant, wild romance, that
> [owes] its prettiness to the milk-diet taste of Young England.   (22.101; see also
> 22.133, 156, 163)

As to this point, and as to

A People there are, no doubt . . . but Boodle and Buffy, their followers and families . . . are the born first-actors]   During the ministerial crisis of 1851 *The Times* continuously attacked both Parliament and government for failing to perform their duties. Butt and Tillotson note the influence of the paper's attitude on the present passage and also quote a leading article for 5 March:

> It is an insult to a free people and a constitutional State to allege that the faculty of government is confined among us just to a score or two hands. What becomes of all our numerous institutions for self-government . . . if, with all this apparatus of political training, the sacred gift of government, is after all, an heirloom in two or three families. (1957, 187–8)

During the period 1850–2, Dickens published articles disparaging representative government and expressing a lack of confidence in it in *Household Narrative of Current Events* (1.51, an attack on the property requirement for the franchise), and in *HW*: 'The Royal Rotton Row Commission', 1.274–6 (W. T. Haly and W. H. Wills); 'Red Tape', 2.481–4 (Dickens) (see Engel, 1956, 947–8).

In this, too, there is perhaps

the circle the necromancer draws around him]   The necromancer stands within a protective circle when he summons the dead from their graves to reveal the secrets of the future.

Chesney Wold is quite full

He sleeps in his turret with a complaining flag-staff over his head] Tulkinghorn's room is modelled on the small chamber halfway up the flag-tower at Rockingham Castle. The tower was added to the castle in 1838.

During the utterance of every

a begging-letter writer]   Many paupers and pretended paupers would write letters to famous and wealthy people describing their sorrows and hardships (usually fictitious), in the hope of receiving money. In 'The Begging-Letter Writer' (*HW* 1.169–72), Dickens himself admitted that such persons had plagued him for fourteen years, and he condemned them as 'public robbers' and 'the scum of the earth'.

Chapter 13

ESTHER'S NARRATIVE.

"How much of this indecision

The character of much older and steadier people may be even changed by the circumstances surrounding them. It would be too much to expect that a boy's, in its formation, should . . . escape them."]   Dickens expressed the same sentiments about his original conception of the character and fate of Walter Gay when he sent Forster the manuscript of the first four chapters of *DS* in July 1846:

> I think it would be a good thing to disappoint all . . . expectations . . . and to show him gradually and naturally trailing away, from that love of adventure and boyish light-heartedness, into negligence, idleness, dissipation, dishonesty, and ruin. To show, in short, that common, every-day, miserable declension of which we know so much in our ordinary life; to exhibit something of the philosophy of it, in great temptations and an easy nature; and to show how the good turns into bad, by degrees.   (*Letters* 4.593)

Forster remarks that this rejected idea 'took subsequent shape, amid circumstances better suited to its excellent capabilities, in the striking character of Richard Carstone' (2.313).

I felt this to be true

He had been eight years at a public school, and had learnt . . . to make Latin Verses]   Richard's school, Winchester (mentioned in chapter 4), had a curriculum which was almost exclusively classical and for this reason had been attacked by Brougham, Cobbett and the Public School Commissioners. At a time when public schools in general emphasized the classics, Dickens's own attitude towards the education of boys was strictly practical. For example, when his son Plorn was 15, Dickens expressed approval that the boy should discontinue Latin in favour of learning useful subjects which would help prepare him for his intended emigration to Australia. And in *DS* the exclusive and excessive teaching of the classics (Miss Blimber is 'dry and sandy with working in the graves of deceased languages') is one of the minor indictments against the Blimber system (see Collins, 1963, *passim*).

"I don't know that, sir!"

Articled clerks go a good deal on the water.]   When the courts were in session, lawyers in the Temple and the other legal Inns made their way to Westminster via the Thames – by rowing-boat before the introduction of steam, and later by steamboat.

"That's the thing, sir!"

M.R.C.S.] Member of the Royal College of Surgeons, a qualification which could be earned by examination following a five-year apprenticeship to a surgeon and a sixth year of clinical experience in hospital.

"By Heaven!" cried Mr. Boythorn

"the treatment of Surgeons aboard ship] The unequal treatment accorded naval surgeons as compared to that given army surgeons had been topical since the late 1830s and during the next twenty years became one of the important issues in the medical reform movement (see note to chapter 11, p. 106). Since at least the turn of the century, the anomaly had existed that surgeons in the Navy ranked lower than their army equivalents, were promoted less often, paid less, and were generally not given the privileges due to an officer and a gentleman aboard ship. In the late 1840s the correspondence on the subject in the *Lancet* became so heavy that the editor made a plea for no more letters until further notice. In 1850 a parliamentary resolution granted assistant surgeons improved accommodation, but this had not been enforced by the spring of 1851, when the plight of naval surgeons became an issue in the debate on official salaries in the House of Commons and *The Times* took up the cause (see *Lancet* 1, 13 April 1850, 449–50; 1, 10 May 1851, 535, 537). The inequalities were still unresolved three years later, by which time the events of the Crimean War helped to keep the issue in front of the public.

a transportable offence] The transportation of convicted prisoners to Australia was a sentence still in effect in the mid-nineteenth century but ceased in 1868.

"No!" cried Mr. Boythorn

they ought to be worked in quicksilver mines] This was a sentence 'worse than death', according to *100 Wonders of the World* (1821; 12th edn), which describes conditions in the quicksilver mines of Austria:

> In some of the subterraneous passages the heat is so intense, as to occasion a profuse sweat; and in several of the shafts the air was formerly so confined, that several miners were suffocated by an igneous vapour, or gaseous exhalation, called the fire-damp . . . To these pernicious and deadly caverns criminals are occasionally banished by the Austrian government; and it has sometimes happened that the punishment has been allotted to persons of considerable rank and family. (271–3)

their skulls arranged in Surgeons' Hall] The hall of the Royal College of

Surgeons, in Lincoln's Inn Fields, contains the Hunterian Museum, a vast collection of anatomical specimens and curiosities. It is described in a *HW* article of 1850, 'The Hunterian Museum', 2.277–82.

"Truly," said Mr. Kenge.

the classic shades]   An adaptation of the familiar phrase for a secluded life of study, deriving from 'vita umbratilis' (Cicero), or 'vita umbratica' (Quintilian), or 'studia in umbra educata' (Tacitus).

a poet was said (unless I mistake) to be born, not made]   The Latin tag, 'Poeta nascitur, non fit'.

"Very requisite, no doubt," returned Mr. Kenge.

We have only . . . to discover a sufficiently eligible practitioner; and . . . to pay a premium?]   A qualified surgeon who had been elected to a hospital post (as Mr Bayham Badger had) could also practise privately and take on pupils for instruction, charging an annual premium of about £100.

Mr. Boythorn leaving us within a week

the principal theatres]   The Princess's, the Olympic, the Lyceum, Covent Garden, Drury Lane and Sadler's Wells.

I really cannot express how uneasy

the dreadful expense to which this young man was putting himself] His seat in the pit would cost two shillings, and Jarndyce would pay sixteen shillings for a box in a theatre such as Drury Lane. Assuming Esther might attend the theatre three times a week, Guppy would be spending a good portion of his salary of 'two pound a week'.

Sometimes, I thought of telling Mr. Jarndyce.

spikes]   These were placed along the rear axle of vehicles to prevent boys from catching hold and enjoying a free ride.

While we were making this round

Mr. Bayham Badger]   Perhaps his first name was suggested by number 16 Bayham Street, Camden Town, where the young Dickens lodged with his family in 1822–3.

Chelsea]   Formerly a rustic and retired village, by the middle of the nineteenth century Chelsea had become built-up and encompassed by London, but it was still considered picturesque and pleasantly old-fashioned.

a large public Institution]   There were about 125 general medical hospitals, medical charities and dispensaries in London supported by private charities. Among the largest general hospitals were Charing Cross, Guy's, King's College, the Royal Free, St Bartholomew's, St George's, St Thomas's and Westminster.

"So that Mrs. Badger has been married

the twenty-first of March]   The date of the vernal equinox, a time traditionally appropriate to Mrs Badger's youthful pretensions and passionate nature.

"And, my dear," said Mr. Badger

the African Station, where he had suffered from the fever of the country.] His fate was doubtless suggested by the Niger Expedition, which failed when forty-one of its members died of the African fever (see note to chapter 4, p. 55).

"The dear old Crippler!"

all a taunto]   With all sails set.

"It was a great change from Captain Swosser

his botanical excursions]   Like geology, botany was one of the sciences which gained a wide popularity in the nineteenth century, when amateur naturalists and field-botanists travelled widely, bringing home specimens from abroad and so introducing to Britain a vast number of new species.

We then passed into a narrative of the deaths

Laura]   The romantic associations of the name originate with Petrarch. Byron named the heroine in *Beppo* (1818) Laura, and Laura Bell is Arthur's ideal mate in Thackeray's *Pendennis* (1848). Skimpole's 'sentiment daughter' is also called Laura (chapter 43).

"Come!" said Mr. Jarndyce.

Trust in nothing but in Providence and your own efforts. Never separate the two, like the heathen waggoner.]   The story of Phaethon, who was allowed to drive the chariot of the sun but gave up the effort to control it, is told by Ovid in *Metamorphoses* 2.140–1. Dickens seems to have been recalling Addison's translation of the advice of Apollo to his son: 'the rest let Fortune guide,/And better for thee than thyself provide!' The use of 'waggoner' is probably a memory of *Romeo and Juliet* 3.2.2–3: 'such a waggoner/As Phaethon would whip you to the west'. (The note in *Norton* referring to Aesop's *Fables* is misleading.)

Chapter 14

Fifth monthly number
July 1852

DEPORTMENT.

So Richard said there was an end of it

the great wall of China]   China became a subject of popular knowledge in Britain in 1839, when the Opium War made all aspects of the country a topic of great interest in books and periodicals. In 1841 the magnificent Chinese Exhibition, the collection of a rich American resident of China, opened at Hyde Park Corner, housed in a two-storey pagoda, and in 1847 a mainly pictorial Chinese Collection opened briefly in the East End. Then in March 1848 the celebrated Chinese Junk which had set sail from Hong Kong in 1846 arrived at the East India Docks. Crowds of people visited the ship, and although Dickens dismissed it in the *Examiner* as a symbol of ignorance and superstition, he nevertheless described it as a 'remarkable sight (which all who can, should see)' (*MP*; Altick, 1978, 292–7).

It being, now, beyond the time

Mile End]   Mile End Road, situated to the east of the Tower of London, in Whitechapel, was so called because it began one mile from the old city wall at Aldgate. In Whitechapel and Bethnal Green lived the majority of London's working class, so the district was one of notable impoverishment.

the dustman's cart]   The dustman collected from private dwellings the refuse of fires: the white ash and cinders and small fragments of unconsumed coke. With his cart, horse, basket and shovel, he walked the streets shouting for the dust as he went, 'Dust-ho!', and then emptied his cart on plots of waste ground (Mayhew 2.166, 169; for the other constituents of dust-heaps, see Cotsell, 1986, 33–4).

"The sheep?"... on market days he sometimes followed them quite out of town]   They would have been purchased at the cattle market at Smithfield, north-east of Holborn. Smithfield was much in the news during the early 1850s: in 1851, as the result of a public campaign supported by articles in *HW*, a Bill came before the House to abolish and relocate the market on the grounds of its being a public nuisance and its methods of slaughter cruel to animals. Old Smithfield was finally closed for the sale of cattle, horses and sheep in June 1855 (see 'The Cattle-Road to Ruin', 1.325–30; 'Chips: From Mr Thomas Bovington', 1.377; 'Nice White Veal', 1.467–8; 'Chip: Torture in the Way of Business', 1.587–8; 'A Monument of French Folly', 2.553–8; 'Chip: The Smithfield Model of the Model Smithfield', 2.572–3; 'The Last Days of Smithfield', *Punch* 21.16). Allusions in *BH* to the abuses associated with Smithfield are the mentions of the 'blinded oxen, over-goaded, over-driven, never guided' which run amok in the streets on market day in chapter 16, and 'the unwholesome trades' (connected with the slaughter-houses) which taint the air of the hot night in chapter 32.

"We are going on just as bad

Talk of Africa! I couldn't be worse off if I was a what's-his-name – man and a brother!"]   The seal of the Anti-Slavery Society derived from a Wedgwood cameo modelled in 1786 showing a negro in chains kneeling in supplication and uttering 'Am I not a man and a brother?' – the words of the title of a pamphlet published anonymously in 1778 by Peter Peckard.

"I felt I was so awkward," she replied

Mr. Turveydrop's Academy in Newman Street."]   'The Dancing Academy' (*SB*) describes Signor Billsmethi's establishment, which

> was not in Spring Gardens, or Newman Street, or Berners Street, or Gower Street, or Charlotte Street, or Percy Street, or any other of the numerous streets which have been devoted time out of mind to professional people, dispensaries, and boarding houses.

Newman Street, which intersects Oxford Street from the north, was built between 1750 and 1770 and was originally inhabited by celebrated artists.

"I don't know why you should

Old Mr. Turveydrop is a very gentlemanly man indeed – very gentle-manly."]   The depiction of Turveydrop is a composite of three men: George IV (known as 'the first gentleman in Europe'); Lord Chesterfield; and John Henry Skelton. According to John Camden Hotten in 1874, the caricature of George IV had long been recognized (214). The direct references to Turveydrop's admiration of the Prince Regent, as well as Esther's description of Turveydrop and Browne's illustrations, modelled on portraits of the king (see below), make the caricature less than subtle. Dickens's well-known detestation of George IV and the values he represented is epitomized in the way the king is virtually effaced from history in the last chapter of *CHE*, which mentions him only in passing: 'William the Fourth succeeded George the Fourth in the year one thousand eight hundred and thirty.' (For the king's association with dandyism, see notes to chapter 12, p. 120.)

Dickens had already caricatured Lord Chesterfield, the fourth earl (1694–1773), in *BR*. Sir John Chester is in fact depicted as devoted to Lord Chesterfield's *Letters* to his natural son (published 1774): ' "upon my honour, the most masterly composition, the most delicate thoughts, the finest code of morality, and the most gentlemanly sentiments in the universe!" ' (23). Whereas Chesterfield's son was awkward and ungraceful, Dickens makes Turveydrop's son a dancing-master.

Richard. No.

Miss Jellyby? Yes.   Dancing Master's son

Joe Jo? Yes

Snagsby? No

The Brickmaker's Family? No

                                    Allan Woodcourt.
                                    John
                              .   George
Coavinses? Yes.   Miles
                                    Edmund
                                    Leonard

Skimpole and Boythorn brought together? Next time

Miss Flite's friends? — Her birds? Yes slightly. The
                                        birds. Not the
                                        friends

Old Turveydrop — Pathetic too — blesses people — My son! etc
"I have forgotten to mention again — at least, I have not
mentioned —"

(Bleak House ———— No. V.)

Chapter XIV.

Deportment.

Mr Turveydrop – Prince Turveydrop

George the Fourth   Old Turveydrop's
model of ————
                    Deportment.

Chapter XV.

Bell Yard

Skimpole – Coavinses –

Charley, working for the rest
"only a follerer"

Gridley, the man from Shropshire
Skimpole delighted. Employed Coavinses.

Chapter XVI.

Tom-all-Alone's

Tom-all-Alone's the ruined property in Jarndyce & Jarndyce,
already described by Mr Jarndyce.

The Dedlock Gout – family gout

Jo – Shadowing forth of Lady Dedlock at the churchyard.
Pointing hand of allegory – Consecrated ground
"Is it Blessed?"

Dickens would have known Dr Johnson's comment on the *Letters*: 'they teach the morals of a whore, and the manners of a dancing master' (Boswell's *Life of Johnson*, 1791, entry for 1751–4).

The third original for Turveydrop has been identified as John Henry Skelton, an ageing dandy well known in London during the first half of the nineteenth century (Stevenson, 1948). Skelton was described by John Camden Hotten ('Theodore Taylor') in 1864, but the resemblance to Turveydrop is not remarked on:

> [He] had been a woollen-draper in the neighbourhood of Regent-street. He had become possessed of the fixed idea that he was destined to become the instructor of mankind in the true art of etiquette . . . He husbanded his small resources, limiting himself to an humble dinner daily at a coffee-house in the neighbourhood of his old home, where his perfectly-fitting dress-coat . . . his brown wig and dyed whiskers, his ample white cravat of the style of the Prince Regent's days, and his well polished boots, were long destined to raise the character of the house on which he bestowed his patronage. (55–6)

It has been suggested that Turveydrop's name may derive from a children's marching game called 'Turvey', in which the song rungs: 'Turvey, turvey, clothed in black,/With silver buttons upon your back;/One by one, and two by two,/Turn about, and that will do' (Ser, 1969). There is a town near Bedford, *en route* to Northampton, named Turvey.

"Old Mr. Turveydrop's wife

"There's no such person. He is a widower."]　　George IV became a widower in 1821. As Prince of Wales, he had married his cousin, Princess Caroline of Brunswick-Wolfenbüttel, in 1795, but they were estranged from the beginning: she was excluded from Court and went to live abroad, and he publicly maligned her character. When he succeeded to the throne in 1820, he refused to allow her to take the title of Queen of England and attempted to divorce her, and she died a few weeks after being prohibited to attend the coronation. Queen Caroline was beloved by the public, who supported her loyally against the accusations of her husband and welcomed her enthusiastically on her return to England in 1820 (*DNB*). Esther notices a token of the public's sympathy for the queen in the 'coloured print of Queen Caroline' which decorates the inn she visits in chapter 37.

Caddy went on to say

Old Mr. Turveydrop had him christened Prince, in remembrance of the Prince Regent.]　　Prince was in fact sometimes used as a Christian name; for example, Prince Hoare (1755–1834), the dramatist and artist.

He was a fat old gentleman

He was a fat old gentleman . . . a model of Deportment.]　　The physical

11   George IV in 1822, by Sir Thomas Lawrence

condition of Turveydrop is that of George IV in later life. The details of Turvey-drop's costume and physiognomy are borrowed from Lawrence's portrait of George IV in private dress (Plate 11), to which Esther makes two allusions. The king, who was 60 years old when the portrait was painted in 1822, is shown wearing the Order of the Garter. The painting was engraved many times: by C. Turner in 1824, Finden in 1829 and P. Thomas in 1841. In Browne's illustration to the eighth number, 'A Model of Parental Deportment' (Plate 12), the painting is depicted hanging on the wall and imitated in Turveydrop's pose. For Browne's also incorporating elements of Gillray's 'A Voluptuary Under the Horrors of Digestion', see note to chapter 23, p. 186.

"Go on, Prince! Go on!"

Mr. Turveydrop, standing with his back to the fire]   The scene is depicted in Browne's illustration to the present number, 'The Dancing School'. Browne modelled Turveydrop's pose on the famous depiction by Cruikshank, a serious portrait executed after the coronation in 1821, showing George IV with the Royal Pavilion in the background (Steig, 1972, 59).

He had married a meek dancing-mistress

to be seen at Brighton]   Brighton was already a fashionable resort when the then Prince of Wales was introduced to it by his uncle. The Prince liked the town, commissioned the fantastic Pavilion by Holland and Nash, and visited the resort often. His attraction to Brighton confirmed it as the watering-place of the upper class until about 1870.

He replied with the high-shouldered bow.

England – alas, my country!]   An echo of the last words of Pitt: ' "Oh, my country! how I leave my country!" '

a race of weavers."]   He alludes to the series of inventions in the textile industry during the 1770s which initiated the Industrial Revolution. Richard Arkwright's spinning mills transformed the manufacture of cotton in the north of England, and his spinning machines were later adopted for the woollen and worsted trade.

"It is my reward," said Mr. Turveydrop

But Wooman, lovely Wooman . . . what a sex you are!"]   He echoes Byron's 'I would I were a careless child' (1807): 'And woman, lovely woman! thou,/My hope, my comforter, my all!'

"My son," said he, "It's two o'clock.

Kensington]   The parish of Kensington, a mile and a half west of Hyde Park

12 'A Model of Parental Deportment', by H. K. Browne, in the eighth monthly number of
Bleak House

Corner, comprised the hamlets of Brompton, Earl's Court, the Gravelpits and parts of Little Chelsea. The tone of Kensington village was considerably more elevated than that of Newman Street on account of the presence of Kensington Palace and the important houses and costly mansions associated with it.

"My dear child, I intend to.

the French house, in the Opera Colonnade."]   The Opera Colonnade, in the Haymarket, contained shops, coffee-houses and restaurants which basked in the elegance associated with the aristocratic patrons of the Opera House, the name generally given to Her Majesty's Theatre (reconstructed from an earlier building by Nash and Repton in 1818). Turveydrop's 'French house' may be the notable French restaurant in the Colonnade, the Café de l'Europe:

> Despite of its French title, the admirers of our national fare – fresh fish, well-dressed joints, tender steaks, sound sherry, and good old port – will find all that they can require at a reasonable rate; as will those whose palates and pockets aspire to the more refined luxuries of turtle, entrées, venison, and vin de Bourdeaux.   (*London at Table*, 1851; 1858 edn, 9)

The guide advises: 'If the digestive organs are somewhat impaired, a light French dinner is preferable to a substantial English one.'

"Honoured, indeed," said she

"Fitz-Jarndyce, my dear"; she had bestowed that name on Caddy]   'Fitz' was the Anglo-Norman word for 'son' and was followed by the name of the parent. In later times new surnames of the kind were given to the illegitimate children of royal princes. Miss Flite's usage was surely suggested to Dickens by the ironic interpretation given the name in chapter 7 of Mrs Gaskell's *Cranford*, which, as 'Visiting at Cranford', was serialized in *HW* three months before the publication of the present number:

> 'She had always understood that Fitz meant something aristocratic; there was Fitz-Roy – she thought that some of the Kings' children had been called Fitz-Roy: and there was Fitz-Clarence now – they were the children of dear good King William the Fourth.' (5.56–7)

"Would you though?" returned Krook

The burnt child, sir!]   The proverb, 'The burnt child dreads the fire'.

"Hope, Joy, Youth, Peace

Gammon, and Spinach]   The expression 'gammon and spinach' means 'ridiculous nonsense suited to deceive simple persons only' (*OED*). *Norton* suggests the influence of the refrain in the nursery rhyme, 'A Frog He Would a-Wooing Go' – 'With a rowley, powley, gammon and spinach' – but the expression was so commonplace that Dickens surely needed no particular influence.

Chapter 15

BELL YARD.

While we were in London

those two shining knobs of temples of his]   They identify Quale as an adherent of phrenology, the short-lived pseudoscience made popular by Franz Joseph Gall (1758–1828) and his disciple, Johann Gaspar Spurzheim (1776–1832). Gall originated the theory, partly derived from the physiognomist Lavater, that the size and contours of the cranium indicate the development of the corresponding regions of the brain (called 'organs'), which he identified with thirty-seven different aptitudes or propensities. A well-developed region of the skull would indicate a correspondingly well-developed aptitude, and as the aptitudes could be enhanced through exercise, a person could consciously cultivate his virtues ('Mirthfulness', 'Agreeableness') and suppress his undesirable qualities ('Destructiveness', 'Acquisitiveness'). Mr Quayle's protuberant temples, for example, indicate a highly developed organ of 'Ideality' (imaginativeness) – an aptitude he fails to demonstrate. The adherents of phrenology believed it to be more than an esoteric science: they considered it a social philosophy relevant to education, penology and religion because it taught that people's minds were in their own control (Davies, 1955, *passim*).

Spurzheim's Scottish disciple, George Combe, was responsible for the popularity of the subject in Britain, and Dickens himself confessed to 'believe in it, in the main and broadly, as as essential part of the truth of physiognomy' (21 February 1860, *Nonesuch* 3.152).

organ-blower]   The person who manually pumped the bellows of church organs before the invention of mechanical air-pumps.

Mr. Jarndyce had fallen into this company

he felt it to be too often an unsatisfactory company]   For Dickens's own attitude towards philanthropy, see note to chapter 8, pp. 83–4. The ideas in the present paragraph are reiterated and expanded in chapter 17 of *MED*, 'Philanthropy, Professional and Unprofessional'.

the widow's mite]   Mark 12.42–4, quoted in note to chapter 8, p. 90.

"There was a follower

a follower]   A sherriff's officer followed the person to be arrested for debt, waiting for an opportunity to take him into custody.

"Bell Yard," said the boy"

Bell Yard]   This was a narrow lane running from Fleet Street to Carey Street. Dickens rented an office at 5 Bell Yard when he worked as a shorthand writer in Doctors' Commons. The lane was altered entirely in 1874 when the Royal Courts of Justice were constructed.

"Well, well!" said my Guardian

forasmuch as she did it unto the least of these—!]   Jesus said to the righteous men who had fed and cared for the sick and helpless: 'Inasmuch as ye have done it unto one of the least of these my brethren, ye have done it unto me' (Matthew 25.40).

Upon that, Mr. Skimpole began to talk

inharmonious blacksmith]   A play on the 'Harmonious Blacksmith', the familiar harpsichord air by Handel.

Young Love among the thorns]   The source of the allusion cannot be identified with certainty. In *BR* Edward Chester is described as looking 'like love among the roses' (19), an image which Hill suggests derives from a song composed by J. C. Doyle (1955, 139), but a more probable source for Skimpole's allusion is proposed by *Norton*: a song in Thomas Moore's 'M.P; or, The Blue-Stocking':

> Young Love lived once in an humble shed,
>   Where roses breathing
>   And woodbines wreathing,
> Around the lattice their tendrils spread,
> As wild and sweet as the life he led. (1–5)

Dickens quoted Moore's poem in a letter of 1849: 'our Cottage (I believe it is the identical "humble shed" that Young Love lived in, in the song)' (21 July, *Letters* 5.579).

a Sultan, and his Grand Vizier]   Such figures appear frequently in the *Arabian Nights*.

Chapter 16

TOM-ALL-ALONE'S.

Dickens's MS sheets of alternative titles (Appendix) show 'Tom-All-Alone's' to have been preferred up until he settled on 'Bleak House'; his choice of title and the origin of the name 'Tom-all-Alone's' are discussed on p. 13. Forster recorded that Dickens's first intention was 'to have made Jo more prominent in the story, and its earliest title was taken from the tumbling tenements in Chancery, "Tom-all-Alone's", where he finds his wretched habitation; but this was abandoned' (3.29).

Sir Leicester receives the gout

the gout . . . a demon of the patrician order.]   See note to chapter 2, p. 40.

the memory of man goeth not to the contrary]   A quotation from Blackstone's *Commentaries* (1.18): 'Time whereof the memory of man runneth not to the contrary.'

What connexion can there be

What connexion can there be . . . very curiously brought together!]   For the development of this idea and Carlyle's influence on it ('[the poor] claim relationship by conveying to us in a fatal brotherly way their diseases and their mortality'), see note to chapter 46, pp. 253–4.

Jo lives – that is to say

a ruinous place, known . . . by the name of Tom-all-Alone's.]   In 1851, Dickens accompanied Inspector Charles Field (the original of Mr Bucket) and a group of detectives to the rookery of St. Giles's, near Oxford Street. He subsequently described the area in one of a series of *HW* articles on the Detective Police (see notes to chapter 22, pp. 177, 179), 'On Duty With Inspector Field':

> How many people may there be in London, who, if we had brought them deviously and blindfold, to this street, fifty paces from the Station House, and within call of Saint Giles's church, would know it for a not remote part of the city in which their lives are passed? How many, who amidst this compound of sickening smells, these heaps of filth, these tumbling houses, with all their vile contents, animate and inanimate, slimily overflowing into the black road, would believe that they breathe *this* air? (3.265)

St Giles's rookery was for the most part demolished in the course of the construction of New Oxford Street, opened in 1847 (see Timbs below), so Dickens did not see the area when it was most extensive. His account nevertheless agrees with one written before demolition had begun, the account of Friedrich Engels in his *The Condition of the Working Class in England* (published in German in 1845; first translated into English in an American edition, 1886; first translated and published in England, 1892):

> St Giles is situated in the most densely-populated part of London and is surrounded by splendid wide streets which are used by the fashionable world . . . The narrow, dirty streets are just as crowded as the main thoroughfares, but in St Giles one sees only members of the working classes . . . Here live the poorest of the poor. Here the worst-paid workers rub shoulders with thieves, rogues and prostitutes. Most of them have come from Ireland or are of Irish extraction. Those who have not yet been entirely engulfed in the morass of iniquity by which they are surrounded are daily losing the power to resist the demoralising influences of poverty, dirt and low environment.   ('The Great Towns')

By 1855 the slum known to Dickens and Engels had 'almost entirely disappeared', according to Timbs, 'and in its place stands a block of "Model Houses for Families," with perfect ventilation and drainage, and rents lower than the average paid for the airless, dark and fetid rooms of the old "Rookery" ' (331).

This desirable property

This desirable property]   The usual phrase of house-sale advertisements. G. A. Sala remarked on the style in *Gaslight and Daylight* (1859):

> A House to Let may be a mansion, a noble mansion, a family mansion, a residence, a desirable residence, a genteel residence . . . a desirable villa . . . Rarely do the advertisements bear reference only to a house, a villa, or a cottage. ('Houses to Let', 219)

It must be a strange state

It must be a strange state to be like Jo!]   This paragraph and the following five depicting Jo's activities show the influence of ideas, images and scenes in G. A. Sala's essay on vagrants in London, 'The Key of the Street', published in *HW* in 1851 (3.565–72).

that inestimable jewel to him (if he only knew it) the Constitution]   The belief in the superiority over Continental systems of government of the unwritten British constitution, embodied in the parliamentary system, was an aspect of the national conceit which Dickens repeatedly lampooned. For example, Mr Podsnap explains to his French guest: ' "We Englishmen are Very Proud of Our Constitution, Sir" '(*OMF* 1.11) (see Cotsell, 1986, 97).

Jo comes out of Tom-all-Alone's

the Society for the Propagation of the Gospel in Foreign Parts] The
Society, founded in 1701, was located in the 1850s in Pall Mall. Its principal
interest was in British settlers abroad and in preaching the gospel to the natives in
British possessions. For charities which gave aid to foreign countries, see note to
chapter 4, pp. 54–5. The scene of Jo on the doorstep of the SPG prompted an angry
letter to Dickens from a clergyman, the Reverend Henry Christopherson, who
accused him of making an undeserved attack on the good works of such groups.
Dickens replied:

> If you think the balance between the home mission and the foreign mission
> justly held in the present time, I do not. . . I am decidedly of opinion that the two
> works, the home and the foreign, are *not* conducted with an equal hand, and that
> the home claim is by far the stronger and the more pressing of the two.
> Indeed, I have very grave doubts whether a great commercial country, holding
> communication with all parts of the world, can better Christianise the benighted
> portions of it than by the bestowal of its wealth and energy on the making of good
> Christians at home, and on the utter removal of neglected and untaught child-
> hood from its streets, before it wanders elsewhere. (9 July 1852, *Nonesuch*
> 2.400–1)

He goes to his crossing

tee-totum] This children's toy was a four-sided top with an initial letter
inscribed on each side. When it fell after spinning, the uppermost letter decided
the fortune of the player.

It is market-day. The blinded oxen] For the abuses associated with the
nearby Smithfield market and the campaign for its abolition, see note to chapter 14,
pp. 130–31.

A band of music comes

A band of music comes and plays.] A street-musician interviewed by
Mayhew estimated that there were almost 250 street-bands in London, averaging
four members, but usually larger. The bands were predominantly of German
origin, and German bands played for half of what the English bands asked. So-
called 'Ethiopian' bands were more common in the latter half of the century. Some
street-bands played to a high standard and were appreciated (see *HW* 2.96), but
others intentionally played off key or tuned their instruments differently in order to
extract money by blackmail. Street-music in general was considered one of the
greatest nuisances of city life, particularly in the middle years of the century, and
was complained of vociferously. The variety of street-musicians was enormous:
Dickens mentioned a few types when telling Forster of the noise around his house
at Broadstairs in 1847:

Unless it pours of rain, I cannot write half-an-hour without the most excruciating organs, fiddles, bells, or glee-singers. There is a violin of the most torturing kind under the window now (time, ten in the morning) and an Italian box of music on the steps – both in full blast.   (*Letters* 5.162–3)

Along with other periodicals (notably *Punch*), *HW* supported the campaign which resulted in an MP named Bass sponsoring legislation for the better regulation of street-music. The incongruously named Bass's Bill passed into law in 1864 as the Street Music (Metropolis) Act, but it had little effect, for the chorus of complaints continued down to the end of the century (Mayhew 3.163–4; 'The Monster Promenade Concerts', *HW* 2.95–6; 'Chip: A Voice from a "Quiet" Street', 2.143–4; Stock, 1982).

a dog – a drover's dog . . . how far above the human listener is the brute!] The comparison derives from that of G. A. Sala in 'The Key of the Street':

Safe at the corner . . . where a mongrel dog joins company. I know he is a dog without a bed, like I am, for he has not that grave trot, so full of purpose, which the dog on business has. This dog wanders irresolutely, and makes feigned turnings up by-streets . . . But even that dog is happier than I am, for he can lie down on any doorstep, and take his rest, and no policeman shall say him nay; but the New Police Act won't let me do so, and says sternly that I must "move on." (3.569)

The day changes as it wears itself away

the lamplighter, with his ladder]   Gas street-lamps still required lighting by hand. The lamplighter used a pole having a small oil-lamp in the head surrounded by a perforated cylinder to render the flame draught-proof. The lantern on the lamp-standard had a small glass panel which the man pushed open and then, with his pole, turned on the gas-tap (Brumleigh, 1942, 212). The process is alluded to in chapter 58 ('the bright gas springs up in the street . . . ').

In his chambers, Mr. Tulkinghorn sits

foreshortened Allegory . . . points with the arm of Samson (out of joint, and an odd one)]   Samson is the strong man in Judges who pulls down the pillars of the Philistines' temple, killing himself and the thousands who gathered inside. The allusion is to bad anatomical drawing.

"I am fly," says Jo.

"I am fly," says Jo. "But fen larks, you know! Stow hooking it!"]   That is, ' "I'm knowing, but no mischief, no running away!" '

"Him wot give him his writing

half a bull]   Half a crown.

His first proceeding is

to put it in his mouth for safety] A boy crossing-sweeper interviewed by Mayhew told him: ' "We never carries no pockets, for if the policemen find us we generally pass the money to our mates, for if money's found on us we have fourteen days in prison" ' (2.496).

Chapter 17   Sixth monthly number
August 1852

ESTHER'S NARRATIVE.

"Why, Mr. Carstone," said Mrs. Badger

junk] Salt-meat used on long voyages.

earings] The small ropes used to fasten the upper corner of a sail to the yard.

"My dears, though still young

pipe-claying their weekly accounts] Pipe-clay was a fine white clay used to make tobacco-pipes and also used by soldiers and sailors to clean white trousers. Figuratively, 'pipe-claying' means 'to put in spick and span order'.

"When I lost my dear first

speaking of her former husbands as if they were parts of a charade] In charades, each syllable of the word to be guessed, and sometimes the word itself (what is alluded to here), is enigmatically described.

a kind of Scientific Exchange] On the model of the Royal Exchange, the building in which merchants and stockbrokers met to transact business.

"People objected to Professor Dingo

the North of Devon] The West Country in general was a favourite haunt of fossil-hunters.

"Precisely the same," said Mr. Badger.

The ruling passion!"] An eighteenth-century notion, expressed by Pope in his Epistle to Bathurst: 'The ruling Passion, be it what it will,/The ruling Passion conquers Reason still' (155–6).

Bayham Badger?   <u>Yes.</u>   To introduce Richard's
                               <u>unreliability</u>

Richard?   <u>Yes.</u>   Carry through, his character – developing
                         itself.

Boythorn and Skimpole.   <u>Yes.</u>   Not much

Rosa <& Ir> and Watt?   Slightly

Mrs Rouncewell?   No

My lady's maid?   Slightly

Mr Guppy?   Yes.

Snagsby?   Yes.   Carry through

Chapter XVII.

Esther's Narrative.

Captain Swosser of the Royal Navy, & Professor Dingo
Geological hammer

Richard. "O! It's all right enough. Let us talk about
something else"

Allan Woodcourt

Esther

The flowers "Does it look like that sort of thing?"
"Why, rather like"
my dear

Chapter XVIII.

Lady Dedlock
Down at Boythorn's in the high summer time

Old garden wall

The little church in the Park – Lady Dedlock & Esther.

Storm. Esther supposed to speak – but Lady Dedlock
Hortense.   walking barefoot home

Chapter XIX.

Moving on.

The great remedy for Jo, and all such as he.   Move on!

Mr and Mrs Chadband (Mistress Rachael).   Can we
fly my friends?   We cannot.   And why can we not fly my friends?" &c &c

a man with a good deal of train oil in his composition

Closing picture on the bridge Golden Cross of St Paul's
– so high up ·· so far off –

"If I went into Kenge's office," said Richard

Blackstone]   Sir William Blackstone (1723–80), the eminent legal writer and judge best known for his *Commentaries on the Laws of England* (1765–9), which was read by students of the law.

So quietly and honestly she said it

looking up into his face, like the picture of Truth!]   Truth was a familiar emblem and allegorical figure, but the recollection here may be of the life-sized statue of Truth in the south wall of the nave of Rochester Cathedral. Atop the monument to Dame Ann Henniker, erected in 1793, stands a winged female figure whose left arm is extended upwards, and her face looks upwards as well.

"I think," said my guardian

the virtues of the mothers shall . . . be visited on the children, as well as the sins of the fathers.]   The third Commandment, Exodus 20.5: 'I the Lord thy God am a jealous God, visiting the iniquity of the fathers upon the children unto the third and fourth generation of them that hate me.'

We had a visitor next day.

a surgeon on board ship.]   For this topical issue, see note to chapter 13, p. 127.

I think – I mean, he told us

he had no fortune or private means, and so he was going away.]   The opportunity to get rich quickly and easily was a major incentive for young men to go out to India as officers or as civil servants, particularly at the end of the eighteenth century and at the turn of the century, but with the decline of the East India Company the certainty of making a fortune decreased.

When he came to bid us good-bye

She came from Wales; and had had . . . an eminent person for an ancestor, of the name of Morgan ap-Kerrig . . . all of whose relations were a sort of Royal Family.]   The Welsh have traditionally displayed a great respect for genealogies: the desire for a good pedigree was remarked upon by many observers of the Welsh scene in the Tudor period and was satirized by Welsh writers from the sixteenth century onwards. It is one of the social pretensions ridiculed by Thackeray in the *Book of Snobs* (1847), chapter 7 of which gives the genealogy of the Muggins family, who become the Mogyns Smyths. 'Morgan ap-Kerrig' could be an accidental corruption of a genuine Welsh form, possibly 'ap Cynwrig', but it is likelier that Dickens invented the name (the noun *cerrig* is the plural form of *carreg*, 'stone') on the model of names of actual Welsh princes and sovereigns from the ninth century, for instance, Bleddyn ap Cynvyn, Gryffydh ap Cynan and Llewelyn ap Jorwerth. 'Gimlet' (derived from 'hamlet'?) is almost certainly an imagined place-name.

a Bard whose name sounded like Crumlinwallinwer had sung his praises, in a piece which was called. . . Mewlinnwillinwodd.] Examples of genuine bardic names include Cynddelw and Brydydd-Mawr, and the invented title 'Mewlinnwillinwodd' is not dissimilar to the titles of actual works, for example, 'Gorhoffedd' and 'Llewellin' (see Warrington, 1786, 9.526–39; Hotten, 1863, 248). The celebrated collection of Welsh tales, the *Mabinogion*, had recently been published in English (1838–49) in a translation by Lady Charlotte Guest which was widely reviewed.

Mrs. Woodcourt, after expatiating

there were many handsome English ladies in India who went out on speculation] The eligible young officers stationed in India and the civil servants of the East India Company customarily found wives from among the sisters and daughters of their colleagues who travelled out to India for the purpose of finding husbands. Thackeray (whose own aunts were sent to Calcutta to find husbands) refers to the practice in *Vanity Fair* (1847–8), where the Indian matron Mrs Hardyman 'had out her thirteen sisters, daughters of a country curate, the Rev. Felix Rabbits, and married eleven of them, seven high up in the service' (60). The practice is mentioned in a *HW* article which explains how seamstresses were assisted to emigrate to Australia and become wives:

> Some very delicate people were shocked to think that wives should be exported like so many bales of printed cotton: though the same very delicate people were not found to object to the genteel custom of sending moneyless young ladies out to India, to shed the brightness of domestic life around the persons of many and divers wealthy gentlemen with a considerable derangement of the liver. ('The Iron Seamstress', 8.575)

Chapter 18

LADY DEDLOCK.

All this time he was

Fortunatus's purse]   Fortunatus is the beggar in a European fifteenth-century romance who meets Fortune and is asked to choose from among various virtues, long life and wealth. Choosing wealth, he receives a purse with an unlimited amount of money in it and enjoys numerous adventures, but at the height of his success Fortune intervenes and ends his life.

It was a question much discussed

Queen Square]   In Bloomsbury; a square of eighteenth-century houses which was in decline by the 1850s as a place of fashionable residence.

It was delightful weather.

the market-town . . . a dull little town]   Several places in Lincolnshire suit Esther's description – for example, Grantham, Gainsborough and Sleaford. Tennyson, a Lincolnshire man, considered the county in general dull. Alternatively, Philip Collins suggests that Dickens may have had in mind Kettering, Northamptonshire, which lies on the most probable route for him to have travelled when visiting Rockingham Castle, the model for Chesney Wold (personal communication).

"I can lay no prohibition

eight-day clocks in gorgeous cases that never go and never went]   Long-case clocks requiring winding once a week have no special reputation for not working (as *Norton* notes). Perhaps the image was a private joke with someone?

"Well, said Mr. Boythorn

Ajax defying the lightning]   Ajax, called the lesser Ajax, was punished by Minerva for the violation of her priestess Cassandra during the sack of Troy. He was smitten by a thunderbolt which Minerva borrowed from Jove. The episode is vividly described by Quintus Smyrnaeus (*The Fall of Troy* 14.502–89) and briefly referred to by Horace (*Epodes* 10) and by Ovid (*Metamorphoses* 14.468). (A different account of the death of Ajax is related by Homer.) The image of Ajax defying the lightning became a commonplace, and the origin of the phrase for Dickens was doubtless schoolboy learning or an illustration of the subject. In 1844 he described to Forster the gesture of a marquis he met at Albaro who 'stretches out his arm like the living statue defying the lightning at Astley's' (2.106).

It was a picturesque old house

chimney, and tower, and]   Added in MS. Further MS revisions of the description of Boythorn's house in this paragraph and those following enhance the mood of antiquity, maturity and completeness.

The house, though a little disorderly

"Man-traps and spring-guns]   The devices were used by landowners to deter trespassers who were not poachers. Boythorn's man-traps might have been the modern 'humane man-traps', so called because they snapped the bone of a man's leg smoothly rather than making a compound fracture like the old ones (see 'Market Gardens', *HW* 7.414).

The congregation was extremely small

all the pomps and vanities]   Alluding to the third answer of the catechumen in the Prayer Book: 'I should renounce the devil and all his works, the pomps and vanity of this wicked world' (*Norton*).

" 'Enter not into judgment

" 'Enter not into judgment with thy servant, O Lord, for in thy sight—' "] From one of the verses to be read at the opening of Morning Prayer: 'Enter not into judgment with thy servant, O Lord; for in thy sight shall no man living be justified' (Psalms 143.2).

"Do you really?" returned Mr. Skimpole

I turn my silver lining outward like Milton's cloud]   *Comus* 221.2: 'Was I deceived, or did a sable cloud/Turn forth her silver lining on the night?'

speaking as a child!"]   From 1 Corinthians 13.11: 'When I was a child, I spake as a child, I understood as a child, I thought as a child.'

"Enterprise and effort," he would say

adventurous spirits going to the North Pole, or penetrating to the heart of the Torrid Zone]   The Franklin polar expedition, which set out in 1845 under the command of the eminent Arctic explorer Sir John Franklin (1786–1847), was a subject of national interest during the next fifteen years. Public anxiety was aroused after the first winter, when no letters were received from the two ships. A series of relief and search expeditions began in 1847, and by 1852 thirty groups had set off, but not until 1859 were traces of the lost expedition discovered, revealing that Franklin had died in 1847 and his crew some time later.

'Torrid' is Dickens's MS revision of 'African'. The 'heart' of Africa featured prominently in the news during the 1840s and 1850s on account of the exploits of two Scotsmen, the medical missionary and explorer David Livingstone (1813–73), who began his thirty-year series of journeys into the interior of Africa in 1841, and the lion-hunter Roualeyn George Gordon-Cumming (1820-66). He returned to England in 1848 and published in 1850 his *Five Years of a Hunter's Life in the Far Interior of South Africa*, a book which, according to the *DNB*, 'had an immediate success, and made him the lion of the season'. It was reviewed in *HW* 1.399–402. To coincide with the publication, Gordon-Cumming opened an exhibition of his trophies and other African material at St George's Gallery, Hyde Park Corner (*DNB*; Altick, 1978, 290–2).

Take an extreme case. Take the case of the Slaves on American plantations . . . they people the landscape for me, they give it a poetry for me]   The remark reflects the controversy about the advantage of slavery compared to freedom from slavery (which might lead to idleness) which is partly illustrated by Carlyle's 'The Nigger Question' (1849):

> A poor Negro overworked on the Cuba sugar-grounds, he is sad to look upon; yet he inspires me with sacred pity, and a kind of human respect is not denied him; him, the hapless brother mortal, performing something useful in his day, and only suffering inhumanity, not doing it or being it.

Dickens's abhorrence of slavery is well known: he had observed its 'atrocities' during his visit to the South in 1842 and had personally experienced the hostility his Southern hosts felt towards the abolitionist sympathies of the British. His letters written from Washington, Baltimore and Richmond at this time give vent to his passionate outbursts, describing anecdotes of ugly scenes and accounts of angry confrontations with upholders of the system (see *Letters* 3.131–60). He reiterated the sentiments expressed to his friends in 'Slavery', a vitriolic chapter in *AN*.

The lodge was so dark

now the sky was overcast]   Added in MS. From this point down to the end of the chapter, four further MS additions to the description of the meeting with Lady Dedlock serve to enhance the aura of mystery and composure which surrounds the keeper's lodge and Chesney Wold.

"You will lose the disinterested

your Don Quixote character]   The kindly and dignified hero of Cervantes' novel set off to avenge the oppressed of the whole world. Dickens recalled his fondness for this book from his childhood in 'Nurse's Stories':

I was never in Don Quixote's study . . . yet you couldn't move a book in it without my knowledge, or with my consent. So with . . . many hundreds of places – I was never at them, yet it is an affair of my life to keep them intact, and I am always going back to them. (*UT*)

I supposed there is nothing

She . . . slipped off her shoes . . . and walked deliberately . . . through the wettest of the wet grass.] Hortense's action has been strangely interpreted as an instance of the 'reckless independent motion out-of-doors' which was a persistent fictional metaphor of feminism and female heroism (Moers, 1973, 22); but, as K. J. Fielding has remarked, the maid's short walk seems unrelated to the 'voyagings toward liberty and experience' of the heroines – Hortense is, after all, a villainess – whom Moers sees as fictional analogues (personal communication).

Chapter 19

MOVING ON.

The images and diction in the first, fourth and fifth paragraphs derive from the visit of Aeneas to the mournful fields of Hades in the sixth book of the *Aeneid* (Dryden's translation). The mournful fields are

> So call'd, from Lovers that inhabit there.
> The Souls, whom that unhappy Flame invades,
> In secret Solitude, and Myrtle Shades. (597–9)

This passage is the origin of the description of Westminster Hall: 'Westminster Hall itself is a shady solitude where nightingales might sing, and a tenderer class of suitors than is usually found there, walk.' The lovers who inhabit the mournful fields 'Make endless Moans, and pining with Desire,/Lament too late, their unextinguish'd Fire' (600–1). Similarly, 'All the young clerks are madly in love, and . . . pine for bliss with the beloved object'.

The encounter between the lawyer and the suitor in Chancery Lane ('If such a lonely member of the bar do flit across the waste . . . and retreat into opposite shades') derives from the encounter between Aeneas and Dido: she disdained him and 'whirl'd away, to shun his hateful sight,/Hid in the Forest, and the Shades of Night' (637–8). Aeneas 'follow'd with his Eyes the flitting Shade' and went in the opposite direction: 'Then took the forward Way, by Fate ordain'd,/And, with his Guide, the farther Fields attain'd' (642–4).

It is the long vacation

long vacation]   Summer vacation in the law courts (and universities), so called to distinguish it from the Christmas and Easter vacations.

teak-built, copper-bottomed, iron-fastened, brazened-faced, and not by any means fast-sailing Clippers]   African teak from Sierra Leone began to be used for shipbuilding in the 1820s on account of diminishing supplies of oak in Britain. Copper-plate was used to sheathe the underwater planking of ships from the 1760s until the 1820s, when cast iron was placed over the copper to reduce oxidation. Diagonal strips of iron were fixed to the sides of ships to strengthen them. A ship might look 'brazen-faced' because the figurehead attached to the bow was usually a brightly painted carving of the scantily clad upper half of a voluptuous woman. Clipper ships were developed by the Americans in the 1840s: their long, slender dimensions made them faster than the conventional sailing ships.

The Flying Dutchman]   A legendary spectral ship which superstitious seamen believed haunted the southern seas around the Cape of Good Hope. Condemned to sail for ever without rest or anchorage because its captain had blasphemed against God, the ship was to be seen only in stormy weather and was believed responsible for a variety of misfortunes at sea.

Westminster Hall]   The hall of the Palace of Westminster, erected in the fourteenth century. Early Parliaments were often held here, and the chief courts of English law sat here from medieval times, so 'Westminster Hall' became synonymous for the law itself (Wheatley and Cunningham 3.483). In 1825 the courts moved to Sir John Soane's new Law Courts, erected nearby. These are visited by Esther and Richard in chapter 24: 'we walked down to Westminster, where the Court was then sitting'. The reason for the Court of Chancery moving its sittings from Westminster to Lincoln's Inn out of term was solely traditional and caused loss of time to the counsel and expense to the client. Abolition of the practice was among the proposed reforms of the Chancery system (see *Westminster Review*, 34, 1840, 246–7).

The Temple, Chancery Lane

The Temple, Chancery Lane . . . eat it thoughtfully.]   This paragraph echoes a *HW* essay by Dickens which was published shortly before he began to compose *BH*, 'Our Watering Place':

> It is dead low-water . . . the fishing-boats in the tiny harbour are all stranded in the mud – our two colliers (our Watering Place has a maritime trade employing that amount of shipping) have not an inch of water within a quarter of a mile of them, and turn, exhausted, on their sides, like faint fish of an antediluvian species. (3.433)

The paragraph is also reminiscent of the description in *BR* of the Temple as a refuge during hot weather (15). *Norton* notes the allusion in the opening phrase ('The Temple . . . even unto the Fields') to Wordsworth's sonnet, 'Composed Upon Westminster Bridge, Sept. 2, 1802': 'Ships, towers, domes, theatres, and temples lie/Open unto the fields.'

Serjeants' Inn]   In Chancery Lane. One of the ten Inns of Chancery, it was originally established for serjeants-at-law, one of the orders of barristers. The Inn was demolished in 1877.

ticket-porters . . . with their white aprons]   These men were members of a body of porters in the City who were licensed by the Corporation and had the exclusive right of porterage of every description within the precincts of the City. To show that they were licensed, they displayed a document (or ticket) as a badge, and they also usually wore white aprons (Mayhew 3.364–7). Trotty Veck in *The Chimes* is a ticket-porter.

There is only one Judge in town.

no javelin-men, no white wands.]   Judges at assize courts were attended by men (originally yeomen retained by the sheriff) who carried pikes to protect them. On ceremonial occasions, the practice still survives for the officer of a court to carry a wooden rod and walk before the judges.

the shell-fish shop . . . iced ginger-beer!]   In the summer, shellfish and ginger beer were usually sold by the same vendor, as both were 'open-air' articles. 'Iced' meant only that the ginger beer was kept cool over a container of water (Mayhew 1.186–7).

The bar of England is scattered

The bar of England is scattered over the face of the earth . . . into opposite shades.]   The variety of Continental and eastern destinations to which the members of the Bar scatter is a reflection of the mid-nineteenth century as the great age of British travel, made possible by a Continent relatively free from wars and disturbances, by the expansion of the railways, by the opening of the Overland Route to India and by comparative low cost:

> the cost in money of a journey has diminished with its cost of time. The cash which a few years ago was required to go to York, will now take the tourist to Cologne . . . the excellent tendency is, that the summer holiday folks will extend their notions of an excursion beyond the Channel.
> ('How to Spend a Summer Holiday', *HW* 1.356)

that shield and buckler of Britannia]   The biblical expression 'shield and buckler' is applied to the seated figure of Britannia with helmet, spear and shield which appeared on the copper coinage of the realm from the reign of Charles II.

as merry as a grig]   'A merry (or mad) grig' (cricket) is an extravagantly lively person. The origin of the phrase is obscure, but 'a merry Greek' is probably a perversion (*OED*).

legal "chaff"]   Colloquial for 'banter'. The word or sense 'probably arose as cadgers' slang, and is still considered slangy, and usually apologized for by inverted commas' (*OED*).

Constantinople]   The chief sights for the tourist were the bazaars, mosques, tombs, the Seraglio and the offices of the Sublime Porte, all of which could be examined in two days, but six days were better, according to Murray's *Handbook for Travellers in Turkey* (3rd edn, 1854). Constantinople was the only part of Turkey commonly visited by Europeans other than hardened tourists and travel writers on account of the dangers of fever and the difficulties of journeying into the interior. The shortest route from London was via the Danube (five days, but inconvenient for ladies and invalids); the next shortest was through France to Marseilles and thence by direct steamer to Constantinople (ten days).

Palladium]   The image of the goddess Pallas Athene at Troy, on which the safety of the city was supposed to depend.

the second cataract of the Nile]   The British began to travel to Egypt in significant numbers during the 1830s. Aside from the general fascination which Egypt exerted on the European imagination throughout the century, reasons for visiting the country included a widespread interest in the discoveries being made by Egyptologists and an interest in the reputed sites of biblical events. The usual routes from England were via Gibraltar and Malta, or through France by Paris and Marseilles, and thence by steamer to Malta and Alexandria. Murray's *Handbook for Travellers in Egypt* (1847) estimated the expense of a journey was £60 for three months if travelling with a companion, and £80 if by oneself.

the baths of Germany]   The German spas were preferred by the British to Bath, Cheltenham, Leamington and Malvern and were also cheaper. British visitors predominated at Baden-Baden in the first half of the nineteenth century and frequented the other spas renowned for their gambling casinos as much as for their water-cures. In the chapter 'Am Rhein' in *Vanity Fair*, Thackeray remarks on some of the summertime steamboat passengers leaving London for 'their annual tour in search of pleasure or health': 'there were old Pall Mall loungers bound for Ems and Wiesbaden, and a course of waters to clear off the dinners of the season, and a little roulette and *trente-et-quarante* to keep the excitement going' (62).

It is the hottest long vacation

All the young clerks . . . according to their various degrees]   The well-to-do articled clerk (as represented by Richard), the 'swell' salaried clerk (Guppy), the shabby and middle-aged copying clerk, and 'varieties of the genus, too numerous to recapitulate' are described in *PP* (31).

Margate, Ramsgate, or Gravesend.]   Each English resort had its particular ambience. In 1850 trains and steamers (five shillings cheaper than trains) took the middle class to Margate. Ramsgate was frequented by the working class – for example, the Tuggs family in *SB*. The same clientele descended in hordes upon Gravesend with the introduction of the steam-packet in 1815–16 and later the railway (Thorne, 1876, 1.239; Hern, 1967, *passim*).

There are offices about the Inns of Court

Little Swills is engaged at the Pastoral Gardens down the river]   Vauxhall Gardens, on the south side of the Thames, were a place of fashionable resort from the late seventeenth century (when they were laid out) until near the end of the reign of George III. Ceasing to be fashionable, they became popular, continuing to be celebrated for their walks, thousands of lights, musical and other performances, suppers and fireworks. They are described in 'Vauxhall Gardens by Day' (*SB*), which mentions that 'the comic singer . . . was the especial favourite'.

Guster is busy in the little drawing-room

Mr. and Mrs. Chadband]   The surname is peculiar to Warwickshire, where Dickens discovered it. He related the story to an acquaintance, Howard Paul, who left an account:

> I once had a conversation with Mr. Charles Dickens on the subject of the names he bestowed on his characters. I may say, *en passant*, I enjoyed two charming walks with him. One was from Stratford-on-Avon to Warwick, when we passed on the road the sign of a draper named Chadband. I pointed it out with the observation, "I thought, sir, you invented that name. It so precisely suited the character that I imagined it must have come from your own fertile brain."
>
> "No," he replied; "I took it from that very sign, and you are one of the few people who has noted the discovery. I saw it a year or more before I used it, popped it down in my notebook, and when I was thinking over a name for the character I was then engaged on Chadband seemed to fit it; and it was a telling stroke, for people seem to remember both the character and the name." ([1896], 36–7)

(I am very grateful to Philip Collins for the information.)

Mr. Chadband's being much given to describe himself . . . as a vessel]   As St Paul is described in Acts 9.15: 'But the Lord said unto him, Go thy way: for he is a chosen vessel unto me, to bear my name before the Gentiles, and kings, and the children of Israel.' The term owed its currency to dissenting ministers (Yamamoto, 1952, 255); in *PP*, for example, Mr Weller complains to his son that the Reverend

Stiggins ' "called me a wessel, Sammy – a wessel of wrath – and all sorts o' names" ' (22).

Chadband is one of many examples of Dickens's distaste for displays of religiosity, particularly the evangelical cant characteristic of nonconformists. In *Sunday Under Three Heads* (1836), his political pamphlet opposing a proposed Bill to prohibit all recreation on Sundays, he criticized a representative chapel for its intolerant zeal and lampooned its preacher for his blasphemy, ranting and egoism. Other unlikeable lay preachers are mocked in *PP* (Mr Stiggins), *OCS* (the clergy-man of Little Bethel chapel is 'by trade a Shoemaker, and by calling a Divine') and *DS* (Rev. Melchisedech Howler). Chadband's appearance and oratorical habits are modelled on the itinerant preacher in *PP*, the Rev. Anthony Humm ('a sleek, white-faced man, in a perpetual perspiration') (33).

his persecutors]   Chadband's speech mixes actual biblical expressions and archaisms ('persecutors', 'handmaid') with mock-biblical (' "you are not a stick, or a staff, or a stock, or a stone, or a post, or a pillar" ') and inappropriate scriptural quotations (' "For what are you, my young friend? Are you a beast of the field? No. A bird of the air? No. A fish of the sea or river? No. You are a human boy" ') (Brook, 1970, 81, 82). The use of 'persecutors' prepares for the presentation of Chadband as 'a fighter': the language and gestures of pugilism which Dickens associates with him (and with the pugnacious evangelical philanthropist Honeythunder in *MED*) are in part a satiric comment on the divisiveness and squabbling among sectarian creeds.

Bark A1]   'A1' is a marine insurance term applied to ships in first-class condition: 'This "A1" is an important matter to a ship-owner; for it affects the reputation of his ship, the facility with which he can obtain freights, and the rate at which he can have it insured' (Dodd, 1852, 3).

"To come up to it!"

"To come up to it!"]   'To come up to the scratch', a pugilistic term, is what the contestants were required to do at the beginning of a fight and at the start of each new round; the 'scratch' was a line drawn across the centre of the ring.

Here Guster, who has been looking out

comes rustling and scratching down the little staircase like a popular ghost] The 'popular ghost' has not been identified; the source seems also to have inspired the description in *MED* of Mrs Tisher, who comes 'rustling through the room like the legendary ghost of a Dowager in silken skirts' (3).

Mr. Chadband is a large yellow man

Mr. Chadband is a large yellow man]   Revisions in MS and proof which begin in this paragraph heighten Chadband's unctuousness, oratorical style and large flabby body. Further revisions enhance Mrs Chadband's humourlessness and the general comic solemnity of the occasion.

train oil] Boiled blubber used in lamps. 'Train' derives from the Dutch term for whale oil, *walvisch traan*. According to the *National Encyclopedia* (1873) as quoted by *Norton*, train oil 'is of a brownish colour, rather viscid, and has a disagreeable smell and taste'.

While Mrs. Snagsby, drawing her breath

the head and front of his pretensions] *Othello* 1.3.80–1: 'The very head and front of my offending/Hath this extent, no more.'

With which remark, which appears

which appears from its sound to be an extract in verse] In fact it is an echo of Psalms, where the expression 'to be joyful' occurs frequently.

The persecutors denied that

Mr. Chadband's piling verbose flights of stairs, one upon another] A pun on 'climax', the rhetorical term for 'mounting by degrees through words or sentences of increasing weight and in parallel construction'. His speech is similarly referred to as 'this flight of oratory' in chapter 25.

"This boy," says the constable

"This boy," says the constable, "although he's repeatedly told to, won't move on—"] If a crossing-sweeper had not been given 'liberty to stop' at his crossing by the policeman on the beat, he was moved on (Mayhew 2.472). 'Move on' became a commonplace as a result of the Metropolitan Police Act (1829), which empowered a policeman to apprehend all persons whom he found 'loitering . . . and not giving a satisfactory Account of themselves'. *Punch* commented in 1850 on the establishment of a contingent of British police in Constantinople: 'It seems to be the destiny of the Police force to keep perpetually "Moving on." They are themselves the pioneers in obeying the directions they are always giving to others' ('Policemen in the East', 19.82).

"I'm always a-moving on

wiping away his grimy tears with his arm.] Added in MS. From this paragraph to the end of the chapter, further additions in MS and proof enhance the pathos and alienation of Jo's plight.

"He won't move on," says the constable

gonoph] From the Hebrew *ganov* ('thief'): According to Mayhew, the word

159

was probably made current by Jewish 'fences', and it generally applied to young boys. Even among other criminals, gonophs had a reputation for being shady and untrustworthy:

> my informant has known a housebreaker to say with a sneer, when requested to sit down with the "gonaffs", "No, no! I may be a thief, sir; but, thank God, at least I'm a respectable one." (3.315)

Do you hear, Jo?

the be-all and the end-all]   *Macbeth* 1.7.4–5: 'that but this blow/Might be the be-all and the end-all here—'.

You are by no means to move off, Jo, for the great lights can't at all agree about that.]   A debate on the punishment of attempted suicides was initiated in 1841 by the campaign of Sir Peter Laurie to end the numerous attempted suicides among the poor by sentencing offenders to prison and hard labour. He was criticized on humanitarian grounds and satirized by Dickens in *The Chimes* in the person of Alderman Cute, who declares that he has made up his mind to ' "Put all suicide down" ' (First Quarter). Behind the satire lay the death sentence imposed in April 1844 on Mary Furley for her attempted suicide and the death of her youngest child. The case aroused a public outcry which was supported by *The Times* (26 March, 1, 17, 19, 20, 27 and 29 April, 2 and 15 May). The campaign effected the postponement of her execution and eventually the commutation of her sentence to transportation for seven years. Dickens alluded to the case of Mary Furley in his ironic 'Threatening Letter to Thomas Hood from an Ancient Gentleman' which preceded Hood's poem on the subject, 'The Bridge of Sighs', when it was published in May 1844 (Clubbe, 1970, 392).

"They're wot's left, Mr. Snagsby," says Jo

drains]   Slang for 'drinks'.

Now, Jo's improbable story

patting him into this shape, that shape . . . like a butter-man dealing with so much butter]   Butter used to be cut off the lump in shops and patted dexterously into various shapes with a pair of wooden paddles.

"Well!" says Mr. Guppy

cobbler's-wax]   A resin used by shoemakers to rub thread.

"My young friend," says Chadband

O running stream of sparkling joy/To be a soaring human boy!]   MS revisions show these lines to be Dickens's own composition.

160

"My friends," says Mr. Chadband, with his persecuted chin

my three hours' improving] 'Improving', meaning 'preaching with a view to spiritual edification', was a term especially used by nonconformists. The usual expression (appearing in one of the running titles to the chapter in CD) was 'to improve the occasion' (*OED*).

So Mr. Chadband – of whom the persecutors say

Blackfriars Bridge] Designed by the Edinburgh architect Robert Mylne, the bridge, of Portland stone, was opened in 1769 under the name of Pitt Bridge, but the usage soon dropped off, as Thornbury and Walford punningly explain, because 'the monastic locality asserted its prior right' (1.207).

And there he sits, munching and gnawing

looking up at the great Cross on the summit of St. Paul's Cathedral . . . so golden, so high up, so far out of his reach. There he sits, the sun going down, the river running fast, the crowd flowing by him in two streams – everything moving on to some purpose and to one end] The passage is a reminiscence of Hood's 'Moral Reflections on the Cross of St Paul's' (1826):

> The man that pays his pence, and goes
> > Up to thy lofty cross, St Paul,
> Looks over London's naked nose,
> > Women and men:
> > > The world is all beneath his ken,
> > He sits above the *Ball*
> He seems on Mount Olympus' top,
> Among the Gods, by Jupiter! and lets drop
> > His eyes from the empyreal clouds
> > On mortal crowds . . .
>
> What is this world with London in its lap?
> > Mogg's Map.
> The Thames, that ebbs and flows in its broad channel?
> > A *tidy* kennel.
> The bridges stretching from its banks?
> > Stone planks.
> Oh me! hence could I read an admonition
> > To mad Ambition!
> But that he would not listen to my call,
> > Though I should stand upon the cross, and *ball*!
> > > > > (1, 2, 4)

As rebuilt by Wren after the Great Fire of London, the cathedral is surmounted by a dome ringed with a gallery and crowned with a golden ball and cross. The height from the pavement of the nave to the top of the cross is 365 feet.

Chapter 20

Seventh monthly number
September 1852

A NEW LODGER.

Kenge and Carboy are out of town

the articled clerk has taken out a shooting license, and gone down to his father's]

> There are several grades of Lawyers' Clerks. There is the Articled Clerk, who has paid a premium, and is an attorney in perspective, who runs a tailor's bill, receives invitations to parties, knows a family in Gower Street, and another in Tavistock Square: who goes out of town every Long Vacation to see his father, who keeps live horses innumerable; and who is, in short, the very aristocrat of clerks. (*PP* 31)

Whether Young Smallweed

limb of the law]   The *Dictionary of Modern Slang* (1860) gives 'land-shark' as one of the derisive synonyms for lawyer, defining 'limb of the law' as 'a milder term'.

his very tall hat]   Browne's illustration, 'Mr. Guppy's Entertainment', depicts some of the various styles of tall hat which were fashionable from the 1830s into the 1850s.

He dresses at that gentleman]   That is, he endeavours to dress like Guppy. In *MED* 'Mr Sapsea "dresses at" the Dean; has been bowed to for the Dean, in mistake' (4).

Mr. Guppy has been lolling

effervescent drinks]   Such as soda-water, lemonade, 'sherbert' 'raspberry', 'lemonjuice' and 'nectar'. In the summertime these 'effervescing draughts' were sold by street-vendors in powdered form (a spoonful cost a penny or a halfpenny) as well as in bottles or by the glass (Mayhew 1.186–8). Smallweed buys the soda-powder, for he mixes the drinks in the tumblers.

the ruler]   A heavy rod of ebony about twelve inches long and nearly an inch in diameter. Parallel lines could be ruled as the rod rolled smoothly down the paper. In *CC* Bob Cratchit thinks about knocking down Scrooge with such a ruler (5), and in *DC* Mr Micawber uses one, 'apparently as a defensive weapon', to protect himself from Uriah Heep (52).

While thus looking out

a manly whisker]   Although beards and moustaches had been widely worn on the Continent from the 1830s, in Britain up until 1853–4 they were acceptable only on cavalry officers: the few civilians who dared to sport them were considered swells, or sham foreign counts. A beard, in particular, was 'an abomination in English eyes, and was never seen, unless occasionally in aged eccentrics ripe for Bedlam, or on the chins of ancient Hebrews' ('The Beard and Moustache Movement', *Illustrated London News* 24, 4 February 1854, 95). But the increase of foreign travel and the advent of the Crimean War caused whiskers to become the vogue among civilians, and a *HW* article of 1853, 'Why Shave?', urges men to adopt the fashion (7.560-3). As depicted in Browne's plate, 'Mr. Guppy's Entertainment', Jobling wears the style of whisker vulgarly known as the 'Newgate frill'.

"Why, you don't mean it?"

Jobling]   In *MC* John Jobling is the name of the medical officer of the Anglo-Bengalee Disinterested Loan and Life Insurance Company.

"From the market-gardens

the market-gardens down by Deptford.]   Deptford, on the Thames immediately west of Greenwich, was part of the market-garden region on the south bank which also comprises Bermondsey and Rotherhithe. 'Market Gardens' (*HW* 7.409–14) mentions Deptford as the home of the celebrated Mr Myatt, the first gardener to cultivate rhubarb for commercial sale.

I must enlist.]   Unemployment was one of the principal causes of enlistment.

Smallweed suggests the Law List.

the Law List]   A quasi-official annual directory containing information about the legal profession.

Mr. Guppy replying that he is not much to boast of

there *are* chords in the human mind—"]   Guppy employs a slightly confused variant of the usual cliché of lovers – as spoken by Sim Tappertit, ' "There are strings . . . in the human heart that had better not be wibrated" ' (*BR* 22), and by Mr Venus: ' "There are strings that must not be played upon" ' (*OMF* 4.14).

Accordingly they betake themselves

Slap-Bang]   In the eighteenth century, slap-bangs were eating-houses or petty cook's shops where no credit was given and the customer was required to pay 'slap-bang', that is, immediately. In the next century the term came to be applied to places

Mems:

Mr Guppy – His mother? Not yet

Mr Krook Yes

The Turveydrops. No. Next time

Tom-all-Alone's. D°. Yes.

Miss Flite – Her friend? Not yet

The Brickmaker's family? Slightly

Gridley? Very slightly

Mr Tulkinghorn? Carry on

Mems: for future

Mr Tulkinghorn finds Joe – hearing from Mr Snagsby what
he said there – and gets him to identify Lady Dedlock

Tony Jobling in his lodging, mistaken for the dead lodger.
Has Lady Dedlock's picture among the Galaxy Gallery

Chapter XX.

A New Lodger.

Mr Guppy's friend who went over Chesney Wold with him, gets established at Krook's.

Tony Jobling – assumed name   Owen
Weevle.

Mr Smallweed (ancient office lad)

Slap-Bang Dinner – "There are chords—"

Thank you Guppy, I dont know but what I will take a—" &c

Krook getting on   Chapter XXI.

The Smallweed Family.

No childhood – no amusements.

old man – old woman – old grandchildren

/ Cushion. You're a brimstone chatterer.

/ Trooper. Shooting Gallery

Phil Squod

Chapter XXII.

Mr Bucket.

Mr Snagsby – Detective officer

/ Frenchwoman / Jo.

"That there's the wale, the bonnet, and the gownd"

where the food was served carelessly and with haste, as is indicated by Henry Mayhew in *The Upper Rhine* (1858): 'the tables are unpolished, the boards uncarpeted, and the refreshments served with no more style than at what we term a "slap-bang"' (3.106).

John Doe . . . the Roe family]   John Doe and Richard Roe were legal fictions used to denote the plaintiff and the defendant in an action of ejectment. The usage was abolished in 1852 along with other unnecessary forms on the recommendation of the Common Law Commissioners, who considered that the names tended to complicate and delay proceedings. In February *Punch* joked about the impending abolition in 'Alarming Illness of Two Eminent Legal Characters':

> All who have any reverence for time-honoured names in connection with our venerable system of English law, will learn, with regret, that two celebrated personages, who have long figured in professional antagonism in the courts of *Nisi Prius*, have been attacked with symptoms giving occasion for the most serious apprehension on the part of their friends. (22.60)

(For Dickens's passing allusions to the topical subject of legal fictions, see Stone, 1985.)

Into the dining-house, unaffected

he bespeaks all the papers]   Because daily newspapers were relatively expensive for the average reader to buy, eating-houses and public houses provided copies for their patrons.

a full-sized "bread,"]   Colloquial for an individual portion of bread.

"Will you take any other vegetables?

Grass?]   'Sparrowgrass', a vulgar name for asparagus.

"Marrow puddings," says Mr. Smallweed

Marrow puddings]   Mrs Beeton's recipe for baked or boiled marrow pudding comprises breadcrumbs, milk, eggs, grated marrow, sugar, raisins or currants and nutmeg. If to be boiled, it was put in a buttered mould; if baked, into a pie-dish edged with puff-paste.

"Why, what I may think

"Ill fo manger. That's the French saying]   From Molière, *L'Avare* 3.1: 'il faut manger pour vivre, et non pas vivre pour manger' ('one must eat to live, and not live to eat').

"Still, Tony, you were on the wrong

you were on the wrong side of the post]   'To bet on the wrong side of the post'
is to bet on a losing horse.

"I had confident expectations

sew me up]   Slang for 'bring me to a standstill'.

"Jobling," says Mr. Guppy

our mutual friend]   This expression was generally used by Dickens as a
somewhat pompous cliché (see Cotsell, 1986, 15).

Mr. Jobling is about to interrupt

"Hem! Shakespeare!"]   This seems to have been a cue to be silent; it is
similarly used in *PP* in the scene in which Pickwick wakes up amidst a group of
carousing Fleet prisoners:

> This figure was the first to perceive that Mr Pickwick was looking on; upon
> which he winked to the Zephyr, and entreated him, with mock gravity, not to
> wake the gentleman.
> 'Why, bless the gentleman's honest heart and soul!' said the Zephyr, turning
> round and affecting the extremity of surprise; 'the gentleman *is* awake. Hem.
> Shakespeare! How do you do, sir?' (41)

However, the compact being virtually made

the trusty Smallweed]   Smallweed is likened to Achates, the companion of
Aeneas who is frequently sent on errands and thus referred to as 'fidus Achates'.

"like one o'clock."]   Colloquial for 'rapidly'.

Mr. Smallweed, compelling the attendance

"Four veals and hams ... eighteenpence out!"]   He correctly sums up
the bill:

Veal and ham, French beans, stuffing	$4 \times 9d = 3s$
Potatoes	$4 \times 1d = 4d$
Summer cabbage	$1 \times 2d = 2d$
Marrow pudding	$3 \times 4d = 1s$
Bread (twice)	$3 \times 2d = 6d$
Cheshire cheese	$3 \times 1d = 3d$
½ pint half-and-half	$4 \times 3d = 1s$
Rum (small)	$4 \times 6d = 2s$

Tip for Polly	$3 \times 1d =$	$3d$
Total		$8s6d$
Paid ('half a sovereign')		$10s$
Change ('eighteenpence out')		$1s6d$

"I say!" he cries, like the Hobgoblin

"I say!" he cries, like the Hobgoblin in the story. "Somebody's been making free here!"]   This alludes to 'The Three Bears', an old tale (sometimes featuring hobgoblins instead of bears) popularized by Robert Southey in his miscellany, *The Doctor* (1834–47). Dickens refers to the story again in *OMF* in the chapter entitled 'The Feast of the Three Hobgoblins' (3.16): 'It was, as Bella gaily said, like the supper provided for the three nursery hobgoblins at their house in the forest, without their thunderous low growlings of the alarming discovery, "Somebody's been drinking *my* milk!"'

But what Mr. Weevle prizes most

The Divinities of Albion, or Galaxy Gallery of British Beauty, representing ladies of title and fashion in every variety of smirk]   Sir Peter Lely's series of paintings of the beauties of the court of Charles II, known as the 'Hampton Court Beauties', established the tradition for subsequent series of idealized female portraiture by such artists as Reynolds, Romney and Landseer. The paintings were engraved in large numbers for popular distribution and published in volumes. Typical of the style was elegance rather than characterization, and in contrast to the serious expression given to eighteenth-century female portraits, Regency portraiture in particular tended to depict women smiling. The miniatures painted by Miss La Creevy in *NN* are an example, for in her opinion ' "there are only two styles of portrait painting, the serious and the smirk; and we always use the serious for professional people . . . and the smirk for private ladies and gentlemen who don't care so much about looking clever" ' (10.)

But fashion is Mr. Weevle's

on the tapis]   The expression was ridiculed in the *HW* article, 'Slang':

> The slang of the fashionable world is mostly imported from France . . . Yet, ludicrously enough, immediately the fashionable magnates of England seize on any French idiom, the French themselves not only universally abandon it to us, but positively repudiate it altogether from their idiomatic vocabulary. If you were to tell a well-bred Frenchman that such and such an aristocratic marriage was on the *tapis*, he would stare with astonishment, and look down on the carpet in the startled endeavour to find a marriage in so unusual a place. (8.76)

Chapter 21

THE SMALLWEED FAMILY.

In a rather ill-favoured

Mount Pleasant]   The euphemistic name derived from the dust-heap established in the 1640s for use by the fort built to command Gray's Inn Road. The region, near King's Cross and Battle Bridge, comprised the great dust-heaps of London: 'The mountains of cinders and filth were the *débris* of years, and were the haunts of innumerable pigs' (Thornbury and Walford 2.278). The dust-heaps in *OMF* are situated at Belle Isle, near Battle Bridge (see Cotsell, 1986, 45–6).

Mr. Smallweed's grandfather

Mr. Smallweed's grandfather]   The poet Samuel Rogers (1763–1855) has been identified as the original of Grandfather Smallweed, and Rogers's sister, Sarah, as the original of Grandmother Smallweed (Alexander, 1984 – to which the present note is almost entirely indebted). Rogers was aged 89 in 1852 and had been lamed by an accident in 1850. Acquaintances recorded how he would habitually slip down into his armchair whilst talking and need a servant to pull him up by the collar. Four months before the publication of the present number, Dickens described for a friend how Rogers was transported about town in his chair (just as Smallweed is carried about in chapters 26, 54, 62): Rogers had his chair 'lifted in and out of his carriage, wheeled to his table, carried upstairs with him in it . . . and put to bed with him I suppose' (*Nonesuch* 2.394). A banker descended from a family of bankers (Smallweed descends from bill-discounters), Rogers was rich, highly cultivated and a generous benefactor, but he was also notorious for his spiteful, malicious tongue and, in later life, for his terrible fits of rage.

He wore a black skull-cap to cover his baldness and was also deaf, an infirmity which Dickens gives to both Grandfather and Grandmother Smallweed. Alexander suggests that the description of them as seated facing each other 'like a couple of sentinels' was inspired by Dickens's seeing Rogers together with his sister, who had been confined to a chair two years before her brother as the result of a paralytic stroke which also rendered her speechless. The cadaverous decrepitude attributed to both the Smallweeds had been a notable feature of Rogers for many years: Byron remarked on it in his cruel poem 'On Sam Rogers', for example, and it is the principal subject in the witty biographical and critical essay on Rogers published in *Fraser's* in 1830 ('. . . Independently of the persecution Sam suffers from being dead, a grievance which he has in a great measure outlived. . .') (2.237). Accompanying the essay was a caricature by Maclise which not unfaithfully depicts Rogers's mean, wizened, pinched features and on which Browne modelled his illustrations of Smallweed in his porter's chair (Plate 13).

Saml Rogers

13   Samuel Rogers, by Daniel Maclise. From *Fraser's Magazine*, 1830

As Alexander comments, 'One would never expect to find in this "ghastly spectacle" the poet of whom Dickens had spoken (in a letter of 9 September 1839) as "Rogers (bless his heart)" '. Dickens warmly dedicated *OCS* to Rogers and during the next few years often expressed his admiration of him. As to why Dickens's attitude towards Rogers radically changed between 1839 and 1852, Alexander concludes, 'For one thing, Rogers's negative characteristics strengthened as his body weakened,' and she traces Dickens's growing awareness that Rogers was bad-tempered, spiteful and revengeful. Wickedly, Dickens also gives to Grandfather Smallweed some of Rogers's endearing mannerisms, such as his referring to people as 'my dear friend' and his habit of taking people affectionately by both hands. Additions and revisions in MS and proofs of the present chapter and of chapter 26 heighten the ugliness, viciousness and selfishness of the entire Smallweed family.

phrenological attributes]   See note to chapter 15, p. 139.

The father of this pleasant

a Charity School]   Charity schools were supported by subscription for children of the poor. The teaching at the schools was generally inadequate, and the pupils were humiliated by having to wear charity uniforms and march to church under the care of the parish beadle (Collins, 1963, 78). The products of charity schools in Dickens (Smallweed, Rob the Grinder in *DS*, and Uriah Heep in *DC*) are invariably little hypocrites who have learnt cunning humility and calculated selfishness.

a complete course, according to question and answer, of those ancient people the Amorites and Hittites]   The Amorites, one of the tribes in the Bible (with the Hittites), are mentioned in *OMF* (4.11) as an example of useless knowledge. Learning by rote was the prevailing method of education in the nineteenth century. Many different sets of questions and answers were published, but the best-known is the one most likely alluded to here: Richmal Mangnall's *Historical and Miscellaneous Questions for the Use of Young People*, a volume first published in 1800 and issued in numerous editions down to the end of the century. In 500 pages, Mangnall's *Questions* presents world history, biblical history, brief biographies, foreign phrases, Latin proverbs, astronomy, the planetary system and an 'abstract of the heathen mythology', and although there is no specific reference to the Amorites and Hittites, the volume begins in an intimidating way with questions about other ancient kingdoms (see Shatto, 1974).

His spirit shone through

his mind, which was of a lean and anxious character]   An echo of Caesar's remark, 'Yond Cassius has a lean and hungry look;/He thinks too much. Such men are dangerous' (*Julius Caesar* 1.2.194–5).

the discounting profession]   Bill-discounters charged interest as a deduction when advancing the value of a bill in cash before the due date. Although money-lenders were traditionally Jews, there is no indication that Smallweed is one – presumably because he is modelled on Samuel Rogers. Three articles in *AYR* describe the way bill-discounting worked and the kind of people who became its victims: 'Wanted to Borrow, One Hundred Pounds', 'Accommodation' and 'How I Discounted My Bill' (13.164–8, 260–4, 557–61).

has discarded all amusements, discountenanced all story-books, fairy tales, fictions, and fables]   The importance to Dickens of both recreation of all kinds and of fairy-tales and fiction in general is well known. In 1836 he expressed his opposition to a Bill intended to prohibit all recreation on Sundays by publishing a political pamphlet denouncing the measure's repressive, puritanical and discriminatory sympathies, *Sunday under Three Heads: As It Is; As Sabbath Bills Would Make It; As It Might Be Made*. In *HT* he interwove his views on the subjects of popular amusement and the exercise of imagination in children, making them a major theme of the novel. A further notable statement of his frequently expressed belief in the benefits and lifelong influences of children's literature is his *HW* essay, 'Frauds on the Fairies' (8.97–100).

At the present time

porter's chairs]   These were hooded to shelter from draughts the porters who sat in them.

a sort of brass gallows for roasting]   The clockwork bottle-jack was a brass spit the size and shape of a bottle which hung neck upwards close to the fire. Meat was hung on a hook at the base and was slowly rotated by a clockwork motor (Wright, 1964, 50–2).

The effect of this act

the sharer of his life's evening]   'Life's evening' was a poetical cliché, like 'the autumn of life'. It was used by Pope ('The First Epistle of the First Book of Horace Imitated', 7–9) and, in ridicule, by Johnson (Boswell, *Life of Johnson*, 18 September 1777).

the Black Serjeant, Death]   An adaptation of Hamlet's 'this fell sergeant Death' (5.2.328).

Judy the twin is worthy company

attired in a spangled robe and cap, she might walk about . . . on the top of a barrel-organ]   The costume of organ grinders' monkeys is mentioned in *The Mudfog and Other Sketches*: 'many children of great abilities had been induced to believe, from what they had observed in the streets . . . that all monkeys were born in red coats and spangles, and that their hats and feathers also came by nature' (Report of the Second Meeting). The organ-grinders who plied the streets of London were predominantly Italian immigrants, although a great many Savoyards also operated, as well as some Tyroleans. The southern European grinders, dressed in their native costumes, customarily kept a monkey or marmoset on top of their portable barrel-organs, and some of them would also play the tabor, work knee-puppets, or blow a tin whistle whilst the monkey ground the organ for them (Stock, 1982, 4.47).

And her twin-brother couldn't wind up a top

Jack the Giant Killer, or . . . Sinbad the Sailor]   The first story is the familiar old English fairy-tale set in Cornwall during the reign of King Arthur. Sinbad is the hero of a story in the *Arabian Nights*.

This touches a spring in Grandmother Smallweed

"Over the water! Charley over the water]   'Charlie over the water' was the facetious name of the Jacobite toast, 'The King over the water', which the followers of Charles Edward Stuart drank during his exile in France and Italy. By holding the wine-glass over a bowl or glass of water, the Jacobite could drink a toast to 'the King' and not seem to be disloyal in public. 'Over the Water to Charlie' was a popular Jacobite song:

> We'll o'er the water, we'll o'er the sea,
>   We'll o'er the water to Charlie.
> Come weal, come woe, we'll gather and go,
>   And live or die wi' Charlie. (st. 2)

His grandson, without receiving this good counsel

The four old faces then hover over teacups, like a company of ghastly cherubim]   An allusion to pictorial representations of cherubim, based on Ezekiel 10: the four cherubim who hover over the fire have 'one likeness' (10.10).

black draught]   A purgative medicine of senna, sulphate of magnesia and extract of liquorice.

One might infer, from Judy's appearance

artificial flower-making]   The finest and most beautiful artificial flowers were made in France, but even in England their manufacture was a considerable industry. In 1847, for example, English workwomen produced artificial flowers worth £12,000. Constructed with great care and fidelity to nature, the flowers were made mostly from cambric, silk and other fabrics, but ribbon, feathers, wax, seashells and thin whalebone were also used. Simple arrangements could be

173

bought for a shilling and bouquets were customarily displayed under glass domes (*HW* 8.230–3).

Charley is accordingly introduced

a Druidical ruin of bread-and-butter.]   The basketful of fragments and worn-down heels of loaves is likened to Stonehenge and the other stone circles (now mostly in ruins) constructed by the Druids.

It is one "Mr. George,"

Mr. George]   The characterization of Mr George, the former cavalry soldier, reflects the contemporary national admiration of professional military activity in general and of the soldier in particular. Such admiration was in part inherited from the widespread approval of military prowess and glory which developed through-out Europe during the years leading up to the defeat of Napoleon at Waterloo. The 'cult of the Revolutionary and Napoleonic soldier' is discussed by Best (1982), who describes why and how the common soldier became an object of public esteem and affection (198–200).

Another factor influencing the depiction of Mr George, as well as of his friend Bagnet, the ex-artilleryman introduced in chapter 27, was the level of popular emotion aroused by the death of the Duke of Wellington on 14 September 1852 and sustained for a considerable period even after his state funeral in November. The present number of *BH* was published in the month of the Duke's death. A further influence was the tenor of the early 1850s, years of anxiety and nationalistic fervour in Britain on account of the belief in an immanent invasion from France. During 1852 and 1853, Russia became the object of these militaristic emotions as its dispute with Turkey developed into the Crimean War. Britain and France both perceived the Russian aggrandizement as a threat to the balance of power in Europe, and war fever had begun to sweep Britain by the time the last double number of *BH* was published.

The qualities characteristic of the common soldier are admired in a series of *HW* articles published in 1851, 'The Modern Soldier's Progress' (2.391–5, 427–31, 451–5), and in a later article, 'The Horse Guards Rampant' (8.428–31). The traditional conception of the soldier as being a serious man (like Mr George and Mr Bagnet) is described by R. H. Horne in 'The British Soldier', an essay in *Heads of the People* (1841 supplement) which celebrates the soldier's heroism, courage and fortitude (quoted in note to chapter 27, p. 198).

Mr George's personal heroism is enhanced by the fact that Dickens makes him a veteran of the Dragoon Guards who has seen service in North America (that is, British North America, comprising Quebec, Ontario and Nova Scotia). The King's Dragoon Guards were the senior cavalry regiment after the Household Brigade; they were sent with the 7th Hussars to help put down the French Canadian rising of 1837. George has also been 'one of the Roughs' (chapters 24, 26), that is, a 'Rough Rider', one of the expert horsemen who assisted the riding masters in cavalry regiments (Sullivan, 1950, 142).

"However," Mr. George resumes

a devil-and-all of a scrape]   The proverb is 'The devil and all to pay', a reference to the alleged bargains made by wizards with Satan and the inevitable payment to be made in the end.

"My dear friend!" cries Grandfather Smallweed

my friend in the city that I got to lend you the money]   That the person arranging the loan was not the principal was a conventional fiction (Cotsell, 1986, 158).

"My dear friend, he is not to be depended on.

He will have his bond]   An echo of Shylock's reiterated demand in *The Merchant of Venice*, 'I'll have my bond!' (3.3.4–17).

Mr. George, who has been looking

to make his head roll like a harlequin's]   Harlequin is the ludicrous mute character in pantomime with clownish attributes. In Thackeray, *Pendennis* (1850), Mr Foker 'began twirling his head round and round with immense rapidity, like Harlequin in the Pantomime when he first issues from the cocoon or envelope' (13).

Grandfather Smallweed has been gradually

Houri]   A nymph of the Mohammedan paradise whose presence gives great happiness. Houris feature frequently in the *Arabian Nights* (where the term is applied allusively to any voluptuously beautiful woman) and in Thomas Moore's *Lalla Rookh* (1817).

"In the first place," returns Mr. George

to hear of something to his advantage."]   A cliché used in the personal columns of newspapers and in lawyers' advertisements.

"That's the Dead March in Saul.

the Dead March in Saul.]   From Handel's oratorio. It was played at military funerals.

While the twain are faithful to their post,

Astley's Theatre]   Astley's Royal Equestrian Amphitheatre was a popular place of entertainment located on the south side of the river in Westminster Bridge Road. The performances featured melodramatic spectacles employing horses, riders, carriages and chariots; realistic battle scenes were very popular. Horse-manship was originally the only entertainment, but gradually the theatre began to offer fireworks, slack-rope vaulting and acrobatics. Admission prices ranged from sixpence to four shillings.

The theatre over, Mr. George comes across

that curious region lying about the Haymarket and Leicester Square . . . a large medley of shabbiness and shrinking out of sight.]   This is Soho, the square mile which became London's chief foreign quarter in the early seventeenth century. Up until the end of the century the centre of Soho, Leicester Square, was composed of rustic hedgerows and lanes. Then streets were laid out and the square railed round, so providing a venue for all the important duels of the day. Leicester Square was long associated with a variety of popular entertainments, including shows, exhibitions, circuses, theatres and panoramas. By the middle of the nineteenth century it had become squalid and shabby, the haunt of all kinds of ne'er-do-wells (as described in the opening paragraph of chapter 26).

GEORGE'S SHOOTING GALLERY, &c.]   Shooting galleries, where men could practise or challenge each other to contests by firing at targets, flourished before the virtual extinction of the duel of honour in the late 1840s. That Mr George is able both to make use in civilian life of the skills learnt in the Army and to run a business as well (just as Mr Bagnet keeps a musical instrument shop) is a reflection of the contemporary improvements in the system of training enlisted men which were first suggested by Edwin Chadwick in 1833, when he was chief commissioner in the Poor Law Commission. The improvements are praised in a *Quarterly Review* article of 1846, 'Education and Lodging of A Soldier' (77.540–1) and described in 'The Modern Soldier's Progress' (apropos of the provisions of the Limited Enlistment Bill):

> education in the army is not confined at present, as it was of yore, to the mere rudiments . . . on returning to "civil life," the soldier is not compelled to fall back on the little mechanical knowledge which, peradventure, he owned before he exchanged the cobbler's awl, or the tailor's needle, for the musket and bayonet, but may earn an honourable existence by teaching those sciences which he has acquired in his military capacity. (2.452)

Into George's Shooting Gallery, &c.

the British art of boxing]   Although the 'noble art' retained its popularity throughout the nineteenth century, its heyday was the Regency.

"Flat as ever so much swipes," says Phil.

swipes]   Small beer.

"Five dozen rifle and a dozen pistol.]   That is, the few clients have used only sixty shots from the rifles and twelve from the pistols.

Chapter 22

MR. BUCKET.

Plenty of dust comes in

it flings as much dust in the eyes of Allegory] The proverb is 'to cast dust in a man's eyes'.

In his lowering magazine of dust,

dust, the universal article into which ... all things of earth ... are resolving] The allusion is to the passage in the Prayer Book from the Burial of the Dead: 'we therefore commit his body to the ground: earth to earth, ashes to ashes, dust to dust'.

a radiant nectar ... that blushes ... to find itself so famous] An echo of the familiar remark in Byron's Memoranda on the publication of the first two cantos of *Childe Harold* in March 1812: 'I awoke one morning and found myself famous' (Thomas Moore, *Letters and Journals of Lord Byron*, 1830, 1.347).

"Yes, sir, and to-night, too.

the Evening Exertions] 'Exertions' was frequently used in a religious context from the seventeenth century onwards.

Mr. Snagsby is dismayed to see

he looks at Mr. Snagsby as if he were going to take his portrait] 'Sitting for your portrait' was the facetious expression given to the practice of prison turnkeys carefully scrutinizing the features of new prisoners so as to be able to distinguish them from visitors. Mr Pickwick is subjected to the procedure on entering the Fleet (40), a scene illustrated by Hablot K. Browne. For Dickens's own experience, see the following.

"Don't mind this gentleman," says Mr. Tulkinghorn

Mr. Bucket] The character of Bucket, and the depiction of him by Browne in the illustration 'Friendly Behaviour of Mr. Bucket', are modelled on Inspector Charles Field (Plates 14, 15), the detective officer whom Dickens met when he invited a group of detective policemen to the office of *HW* in July 1850. This meet-

INSPECTOR FIELD, THE DETECTIVE OFFICER.

14　Inspector Charles Field in 1856

ing and those which followed provided him with material for a series of articles: 'A Detective Police Party' (1.409–14, 457–60); 'Three "Detective" Anecdotes' (1.577–80); and 'On Duty with Inspector Field' (3.265–70); and W. H. Wills, sub-editor of *HW*, contributed 'The Modern Science of Thief-Taking' (1.368–72). (See Collins, 1962, 206–11, 344.) The tone of all the articles is pride in the increased professionalization of the police which had resulted from the reforms instigated by Edwin Chadwick. In Dickens's articles, Inspector Field is described as

> a middle-aged man of a portly presence, with a large, moist, knowing eye, a husky voice, and a habit of emphasising his conversation by the aid of a corpulent fore-finger, which is constantly in juxta-position with his eyes or nose. (1.409)

On first meeting Dickens, Field and his fellow-detectives are described 'taking his portrait' in the same way that Bucket studies Snagsby:

> Every man of them, in a glance, immediately takes an inventory of the furniture and an accurate sketch of the editorial presence. The Editor feels that any gentleman in company could take him up, if need should be, without the smallest hesitation, twenty years hence. (1.409–10)

In 1851, Dickens accompanied Field and a group of detectives to a rookery in St Giles's, an expedition recorded in 'On Duty with Inspector Field'. Many of Field's personal traits are given to Bucket, and sometimes the passages in the present chapter are borrowed with little significant change from the *HW* articles. A police superintendent resembling Bucket is described in the *UT* essay, 'Poor Mercantile Jack'. G. A. Sala remembered Field as 'a clean-shaven, farmer-like, elderly individual . . . There was something, but not much, of Dickens's Inspector Bucket about Inspector Field' (*Things I Have Known*, 1894, cited in Collins, 1981, 2.202). For Field's conducting tours of the East End opium dens depicted in *MED*, see Collins, 1964.

"It's very plain, sir.

he's not to be found on his old lay]   'Lay' is slang for 'occupation'; 'on (a certain) lay' means 'at a particular job'.

As they walk along, Mr. Snagsby observes

some undersized young man with a shining hat on, and his sleek hair twisted into one flat curl on each side of his head]   He resembles 'the sulky gentleman with the damp flat side-curls' encountered by Inspector Field during a visit to a low lodging-house (*HW* 3.267). The heavily greased side-whiskers were known as 'Newgate knockers'.

mourning ring]   Mourning rings were the most important article of mourning jewellery, worn in memory of the recently deceased. The money for the purchase

179

15 'Friendly Behaviour of Mr. Bucket', by H. K. Browne, in the sixteenth monthly
number of *Bleak House*

of the rings by relatives and close friends was usually provided for in the will of the deceased. Field may in fact have worn such a ring (and such a brooch) but, if not, perhaps the jewellery is intended to enhance the depiction of Bucket as a man of feeling and sentiment, as in R. H. Horne's description of 'The Fashionable Physician', who 'wears an ostentatious mourning-ring – the gift of a dear, deceased patient, who died under his hands' (*Heads of the People*, 1840, 58).

When they come at last

a lighted bull's-eye]   An oil-lantern carried by metropolitan policemen which shed a particularly penetrating light, even in thick fog.

Mr. Snagsby sickens in body and mind]   This was no doubt a common occurrence on such visits, but it is reminiscent nevertheless of Dickens's expedition to a notorious London thieves' den in 1842, accompanied by Forster, Maclise and the American poet Longfellow; they were guided by 'the most trusted officers of the two great metropolitan prisons'. According to Forster, on entering a low lodging-house, Maclise 'was struck with such sickness' that he had to remain outside under police protection while his companions made their tour (2.3).

as if he were going, every moment deeper down, into the infernal gulf.] The imagery of Snagsby's visit to Tom-all-Alone's is drawn from the descent of Aeneas into hell in the sixth book of the *Aeneid* (Dryden's translation is quoted here.) Compare, for instance: 'Such deadly Stenches from the depth arise, And steaming Sulphur, that infects the Skies' (344–5). The undrained, unventilated street in Tom-all-Alone's, 'deep in black mud and corrupt water', is like deep Acheron's 'troubled Eddies': 'thick with Ooze and Clay' (410–11). On entering the jaws of hell, Aeneas found that here

> Revengeful Cares, and sullen Sorrows dwell;
> And pale Diseases, and repining Age;
> Want, Fear, and Famine's unresisted rage.
> Here Toils, and Death, and Death's half-brother, Sleep,
> Forms terrible to view, their Centry keep . . .
> Of various Forms unnumber'd Specters more;
> Centaurs, and double Shapes, beseige the Door. (385–9, 398–9)

The image of the surging crowd around Snagsby parallels the scene in which Aeneas was besieged by 'the thronging people' pressing for passage in Charon's boat:

> An Airy Crowd came rushing where he stood;
> Which fill'd the Margin of the fatal Flood . . .
> With hollow Groans, and Shrieks, and feeble Cries . . .
> Such, and so thick, the shiv'ring Army stands:
> And press for passage with extended hands. (422–32)

(Shatto, 1974 diss., and 1975. Some further parallels are noticed by Beckwith, 1984.)

"Draw off a bit here, Mr. Snagsby," says Bucket

"Here's the fever coming up the street!"]   Typhus fever, also known as Irish fever, gaol fever, ship fever, putrid fever, camp fever and tramp fever, was widespread throughout Britain up to 1870, when the epidemics began to decline. The mortality was high, about a third of all the notified cases resulting in death. The epidemic of 1848 killed 3,569 people, and a *HW* article of 1850, 'Health by Act of Parliament', observed that cholera did not kill a tenth of the victims killed by fever, consumption and other preventable diseases (1.461). A rickettsial disease spread mainly by the faeces of the body louse, typhus was most prevalent in the densely packed courts of large cities, but its association with uncovered sewers, stagnant ditches and nightmen's yards and privies was not recognized until the publication in 1839 of the report of the first Sanitary Commission, instigated by Edwin Chadwick following the epidemic in Whitechapel the previous year. The shocking facts of the report, together with its conclusions and remedial suggestions, made it a textbook of sanitation throughout the country and initiated public sanitary reform. Moreover, the adoption of the report's suggestions, including the removal of sources of pollution and the provision of sewers and other sanitary improvements, contributed to the dramatic decline in typhus deaths in the second half of the century (Mayhew 3.376; *DNB*; Shepherd, 1971, 251–3; Wohl, 1983, 125–7).

"Are those the fever-houses,

Darby]   'Darbies' is slang for 'handcuffs' (*Norton*).

At last there is a lair

a lair]   In the common lodging-houses of London, lodgers paid a few pence a night for a bunk and access to a fire to cook their own food; but, as Mayhew describes, amenities were inadequate and the accommodation and clientele were filthy and infested with vermin (3.315). The lodging-house where Jo and the Irish brickmakers stay in chapter 46 would have been of the worst sort; 'On Duty with Inspector Field' records Dickens's visit to several places in St Giles's: 'we enter other lodging houses, public-houses, many lairs and holes; all noisome and offensive; none so filthy and so crowded as where Irish are' (3.267).

Toughy, or the Tough Subject]   'Tough subject' is pugilist slang.

Toughy has gone to the Doctor's to get a bottle of stuff for a sick woman]   In fact, the drunken speaker means he has gone to an apothecary's shop, like the one sought for by Woodcourt in chapter 47. In London drugs were dispensed not by surgeons and physicians, as in the country, but by chemists and druggists (the terms were synonymous), who, under the Apothecaries Act of 1815, could supply medicines wholesale and retail. They had no qualification, as physicians had, and no prescribed training or apprenticeship, as surgeons had, so there was no real standard by which to regulate their goods or their dispensing. In 1841 chemists and druggists united to oppose the introduction of a Bill which would have obliged them to be examined and licensed, and in the same year the Pharmaceutical Society was founded and provided examinations for the qualification of pharmaceutical chemist. The efforts made during the 1840s to protect the public from untrained and unqualified practitioners culminated in the Pharmacy Act of 1852, which provided for a register of chemists and druggists (Matthews, 1962, 114–32).

"Why, what age do you call that little creature?"

Mr. Snagsby is strangely reminded of another infant, encircled with light, that he has seen in pictures.]   This kind of illumination of a Nativity scene was of course very common, having been often imitated since its invention by seventeenth-century painters. Among the more famous of such pictures which Dickens may have known was Domenichino's 'The Adoration of the Shepherds', then owned by the Dulwich College Picture Gallery.

"A word from Mr. Tulkinghorn is so powerful."

Mr. Bucket . . . shows her down-stairs, not without gallantry.]   'Inspector Field is polite and soothing – knows his woman and the sex' ('On Duty with Inspector Field', 1.268).

Chapter 23

Eighth monthly number
October 1852

ESTHER'S NARRATIVE.

There was a lowering energy in her face

some woman from the streets of Paris in the reign of terror.]   For the influence of Carlyle's *The French Revolution* on the depiction of Hortense, see note to chapter 12, pp. 119–20.

"Yes," said Richard, "I am a little so

Now the murder's out]   The proverb, recurrent in Shakespeare, is 'Murder will out'.

[Dickens left this side blank]

Chapter XXIII.

Esther's Narrative

French maid – <Ca>

Richard. Downward progress.   Jarndyce & Jarndyce.

The army
Caddy Jellyby's engagement – Mr Turveydrop – "My children you shall
always live with me" – meaning, I will always live with you
Mrs Jellyby.
Charley – Esther's maid —————————

Chapter XXIV.

An Appeal Case.

Richard. Engagement off.

Gridley taken refuge with the trooper.

Bucket

Gridley's Death

The Shadow of Miss Flite on Richard

Chapter XXV.

Mrs Snagsby sees it all.

Mrs Snagsby becomes jealous – Mr Snagsby must be
that boy's father.

Sets herself to watch him at all times

Let all concerned in any secresy, Beware!

(Guster pities Jo – so like him in the first part of
her fortunes)

"I have looked well into

it's on the paper]   The paper of causes is the list of causes or cases intended for argument.

At last, we came to Soho Square

Soho Square]   Originally called King's Square, Soho Square was begun in the reign of Charles II. A statue of the king stands in the garden. The handsome houses in the square and the surrounding streets were originally tenanted by the nobility and gentry until the region began its decline, as described in the note to chapter 21, p. 176).

Prince was teaching, of course.

Mr. Turveydrop . . . grouped with his hat and gloves . . . on the sofa . . . his dressing-case, brushes, and so forth . . . lay about.]   Browne's illustration of this scene, 'A Model of Parental Deportment' (Plate 12), has a complex pictorial inheritance. There is an obvious allusion to the Lawrence portrait of George IV seated on a sofa (Plate 11; see note to chapter 14, p. 134–6), a copy of which is itself depicted at the top centre of Browne's illustration. It has also been noticed that another influence was the caricature of the Prince Regent in the pamphlet by William Hone and George Cruikshank, *The Queen's Matrimonial Ladder* (1820), a caricature which itself derives from Gillray's depiction of the prince in 1792, 'A Voluptuary Under the Horrors of Digestion' (Steig, 1972, 61–5).

"Boy," said Mr. Turveydrop

Strike deep, and spare not.]   An echo of the instructions of God to Saul in 1 Samuel 15.3: 'Now go and smite Amalek . . . and spare them not' (*Norton*).

"For myself, my children," said Mr. Turveydrop

"I am falling into the sear and yellow leaf]   The words of Macbeth on realizing that his hopes are frustrated and he is soon to die: 'My way of life/Is fall'n into the sear, the yellow leaf' (5.3.22–3).

The house in Thavies Inn

the list of Bankrupts]   The *London Gazette*, an official journal issued twice weekly, contained the names of bankrupts, lists of government appointments and promotions, and other public notices.

Chapter 24

AN APPEAL CASE.

We learnt, however, as the time went on

His name was entered at the Horse Guards . . . the purchase-money was deposited . . . and Richard . . . plunged into a violent course of military study] The Horse Guards, in Whitehall, housed the offices of the Secretary of War, the Commander-in-Chief, the Adjutant-General and the Quartermaster-General. The purchase of a commission in a fashionable regiment in 1850 cost £450, according to a series of *HW* articles tracing the profligate and dissipated military career of an impoverished young aristocrat who exemplifies the type of officer who had begun to be outdated by the mid-nineteenth century ('The Modern "Officer's" Progress', 1.304–7, 317–20, 353–6). The abolition of the purchase system in 1871 was one of a series of reforms which began to be made in the years prior to the Crimean War partly in order to engender a professional competence in military life which would equal the increasing professionalism in civilian occupations and partly to imitate the example set by the Prussian army (Trustram, 1984, 15–16). The initiation of reforms in the system of officer training is reflected in Richard's 'course of military study' under the instruction of Mr George and the London professor. Such preparation was a move towards the type of military education proposed by the commission of inquiry into the subject which is alluded to in the *HW* articles.

Thus vacation succeeded term

a regiment in Ireland] The destination may reflect the contemporary state of civil unrest among the Irish. Fomented by the public preaching of sedition and the gathering of revolutionary forces, there was a growing movement for a rebellion against English rule which caused Westminster to begin to dispatch additional troops to Ireland during 1848 and 1849.

He reddened a little through his brown

I am one of the Roughs."] 'Rough riders' was the name given the expert horsemen who assisted the riding masters in cavalry regiments (Sullivan, 1950, 142; see note to chapter 21, p. 174).

This was the morning of the day

Liverpool for Holyhead] Liverpool was the main transatlantic port as well as the point of departure for Ireland, the traveller sailing first to Holyhead and thence by packet-boat to Dublin or Belfast.

To see everything going on

the sickness of hope deferred]   Proverbs 13.12: 'Hope deferred maketh the heart sick.'

I think it came on

"for further directions,"]   The court has given further instructions to the solicitors in the cause on submitting the bill of costs, the statement of the charges of disbursements of a solicitor incurred in the conduct of his client's business.

"referred back for the present,"]   The whole case, or some part of it, has been referred to the decision of an auditor or referee because of intricate details which require minute examination.

Poor Miss Flite deemed it necessary

sealed it at a coffee-house]   If intercepted by the police and interrogated, the ticket-porter would not be able to identify the sender by a private residence.

We then took a hackney-coach

hackney-coach]   The hackney-coach plied for hire (a shilling a mile) at an appointed stand and carried no one but the party hiring it. The vehicles were the disused family coaches of noblemen and gentlemen. During the 1830s the coaches were superseded by hackney cabriolets, so by 1840 there only remained a few old men with old horses and old coaches. By 1850, according to Mayhew, not one hackney-coach was to be seen in the streets of London (3.347–9). In *SB*, 'Hackney-coach Stands' gives a picturesque description, lamenting the advent of cabs.

a very respectable old gentleman . . . carrying a large gold-headed cane]   Bucket wears the costume characteristic of a physician of the period, as described by R. H. Horne in 'The Fashionable Physician' (*Heads of the People*, 1840, 57–8). The spencer was a short double-breasted overcoat without tails which was introduced by the second Earl Spencer (1758–1834); it was considered old-fashioned in the 1850s. Accounts of Inspector Field record his propensity for adopting disguises and assuming various characters (personal communciation from Philip Collins).

"Gammon, George!

"Gammon]   See note to chapter 14, pp. 138–9.

Old William Tell, Old Shaw, the Life Guardsman!]   William Tell (d.1350) was the hero of the Swiss struggle for freedom from Austrian domination in the early fourteenth century. Of his legendary exploits, the most famous is his successful attempt, when ordered by his Austrian oppressor, to shoot an apple from atop his son's head with a bow and arrow. John Shaw (1789–1815), corporal in the Second Life Guards, gained a national reputation at an early age as a boxer and, being of massive physique, he served as model to painters and sculptors. An expert with the sword and other weapons, he performed amazing deeds of courage and strength at Waterloo, even after being wounded. He died in consequence of a carbine shot. Volumnia admiringly compares Mr George to Shaw ('her favourite Life Guardsman') in chapter 58.

He had been still writing

He had been still writing . . . still dwelling on his grievances] The description is indebted to that of the prisoner whom Mr Pickwick encounters in the Fleet Prison in *PP* (41).

"Don't shake your head," said Mr. Bucket.

the Fleet] The debtors' prison, in Farringdon Street. The outer walls were removed in 1846 and the prison abolished under an Act consolidating it with the Queen's Bench and the Marshalsea into one prison called the Queen's Prison.

"Worn out, Mr. Gridley?

backed into half-a-dozen counties] That is, the warrant issued by a justice of the peace has been signed by justices of the peace in six counties so that it can be executed in any of them, if necessary.

Chapter 25

MRS. SNAGSBY SEES IT ALL.

For Tom-all-Alone's

a pair of ungovernable coursers . . . the chariot of Mrs. Snagsby's imagination] The passions as rampant horses, derived from Plato's *Republic*, is an image frequently depicted in emblem-books.

Mr. Snagsby cannot make out

the stars and garters] The star and garter is the insignia of the Knights of the Bath; it is worn by George IV in the portrait by Lawrence (Plate 11).

Mrs. Snagsby is so perpetually on the alert

he said the Lord's Prayer backwards.]   A popular superstition was that witches and possessed persons said the Lord's Prayer backwards for evil purposes.

He has no respect for Mr. Chadband.

contagious]   A malapropism for 'contingent'.

Mrs. Snagsby sounds no timbrel

Mrs. Snagsby sounds no timbrel in anybody's ears]   Exodus 15.20: 'And Miriam the prophetess, the sister of Aaron, took a timbrel in her hand; and all the women went out after her with timbrels and with dances.' *Norton* compares the song by Thomas Moore which derives from Exodus, 'Sound the Loud Timbrel', in *Sacred Songs* (1819), but the comparison does not seem close.

"Peace, my friends," says Chadband

comes home untoe us like the dove.]   The dove which Noah twice sent out from the ark to see if the waters had abated (Genesis 8, 9, 11).

When he is at last adjusted

lay-figure]   A jointed wooden figure of the human body used by artists as a model for poses and the arrangement of draperies.

Mr. Chadband, retiring behind the table]   The similarities in composition and iconography between Browne's plate for this scene, 'Mr. Chadband "Improving" a Tough Subject', and the other plate for the number, 'A Model of Parental Deportment', are discussed by Steig (1972, 60, 61, 65).

It happens that Mr. Chadband has

other audible expression of inward working . . . echoed . . . and so communicated]   An allusion to the doctrine of inner light (described by Chadband as 'the light that shines in upon some of us'), the belief, held primarily by Methodists and other dissenters, that the individual's perception of Christ in his soul is an illumination which can take the form of a religious frenzy communicable to other believers.

forfeits]   A game in which the same sound is repeated at the beginning of each word in a fixed pattern of speech. It is played by Miss Mowcher in *DC* (22).

"We have here among us

" a Gentile and a Heathen, a dweller in the tents]   'Gentile' was a synonym for 'heathen' which was obsolete in Dickens's time (*OED*). 'Dweller in the tents' and many other images with which Chadband laces his discourse (for example, 'flocks and herds', 'gold and silver', 'the ray of rays, the sun of suns') are recurrent biblical phrases or stylistic imitations.

"I hear a voice," says Chadband

a still small voice]   1 Kings 19.12: 'And after the earthquake a fire; but the Lord was not in the fire: and after the fire a still small voice.'

'Of Terewth," says Mr. Chadband

you shall be bruised, you shall be battered, you shall be flawed, you shall be smashed."]   In a letter to Forster on 18 January 1844, Dickens referred to his success in a legal case over the pirating of his works: 'The pirates are beaten flat. They are bruised, bloody, battered, smashed, squelched, and utterly undone' (*Letters* 4.24).

The present effect of this flight

a forehead of brass and a heart of adamant]   Isaiah 48.4: 'Because I knew that thou art obstinate, and thy neck is an iron sinew, and thy brow brass'; and Zechariah 7.12: 'Yea, they made their hearts as an adamant stone, lest they should hear the law.'

"No, my friends, it is neither

a story of a Cock, and of a Bull]   'Cock and bull story', the slang expression for a fictitious narrative, derives from the old fables in which cocks, bulls and other animals discourse in human language on various topics. The *OED* cites Mayhew's *London Labour and the London Poor* as the earliest published example of the expression, but it appears in the closing words of Sterne's *Tristram Shandy* (1760–7).

"Or, my juvenile friends," says Chadband

Sarah]   According to the affectations of religious discourse, Chadband applies the name of Abraham's wife as a type of the mistress of the house and of conjugal obedience, a usage deriving from the passage in the Solemnization of Matrimony which sets forth the duties of the wife to her husband: 'even as Sarah obeyed Abraham, calling him lord: whose daughters ye are as long as ye do well'.

All this time, Jo has been standing

a history so interesting and affecting even to minds as near the brutes as thine . . . thou might learn from it yet!]   Dickens's belief in the benefit of teaching poor children the lessons of the New Testament, as opposed to doctrine and sectarianism, is expressed in a letter to Miss Coutts in which he describes his visit to a class of boys in a ragged school:

> To impress them, even with the idea of a God, when their own condition is so desolate, becomes a monstrous task. To find anything within them – who know nothing of affection, care, love, or kindness of any sort – to which it is possible to appeal, is, at first, like a search for the philosopher's stone. And here it is that the viciousness of insisting on creeds and forms in educating such miserable beings, is most apparent. To talk of Catechisms, outward and visible signs, and inward and spiritual graces, to these children, is a thing no Bedlamite would do, who saw them. To get them, whose whole lives from the moment of their birth, are one continued punishment, to believe in the judgment of the Dead and a future state of punishment for their sins, requires a System in itself. (16 September 1843, *Letters* 3.563)

A ghostly shade, frilled and night-capped

bone of his bone, flesh of his flesh]   Genesis 2.23: 'And Adam said, this is now bone of my bones, and flesh of my flesh', a passage quoted in the Solemnization of Matrimony.

Chapter 26   Ninth monthly number
                                                            November 1852

SHARPSHOOTERS.

Wintry morning

Leicester Square]   See note to chapter 21, p. 176.

home treadmills]   The treadmill was invented around 1818 by the civil engineer, William Cubitt (1785–1861), whose initial intention was to utilize the labour of convicts, not to find a new means of punishment. Immediately adopted by the major British prisons, treadmills were used for such purposes as grinding flour, drawing water and operating ventilation fans. Millbank, Pentonville, Holloway and Brixton prisons put inmates to the treadmill as a form of hard labour; Tulkinghorn threatens Hortense with such punishment in chapter 42 (see note, p. 242).

branding-iron]   Branding with a hot iron was abolished as a form of punishment in 1829.

more cruelty in them than was in Nero, and more crime than is in Newgate]
Nero was the Roman emperor (AD 54–68) proverbial for his brutality. Newgate

Prison, in the Old Bailey, came to be synonymous with crime on account of *The Newgate Calendar, or Malefactors' Bloody Register*, a series published from around 1774 which dealt with notorious crimes from 1700 onwards. Later series were issued around 1826.

But the wintry morning wants him not

They arise, roll up and stow away their mattresses.] The military practice is described in 'The Modern Soldier's Progress' (*HW* 2.392): 'each man made his bed after the military fashion, rolling up his paillasse, folding the bed-clothes separately and laying them on the top, with a prescribed neatness, which soon became habit'.

"The *marshes, commander,"* returns Phil.

"*The* marshes] The Kentish marshes, comprising the low-lying peninsula between the Thames estuary and the mouth of the Medway, near Rochester; they feature in *GE*.

"*I was just eight,"* says Phil

"agreeable to the parish calculation] He was born in a workhouse, or left in one when a baby.

Clerkenwell] A working-class district extending north from St Andrew's, Holborn, and Smithfield, to the Pentonville Road.

"*Drink put him in the hospital*

the hospital put him – in a glass case] The bodies of persons who died without known relatives were used by the medical schools as cadavers and ultimately as skeletons.

"*Yes, commander, I took the business.*

Saffron Hill, Hatton Garden, Clerkenwell, Smiffeld] Saffron Hill was a densely inhabited low neighbourhood between Holborn and Clerkenwell; it is described in *OT* (8). Hatton Garden, near Holborn Circus, was occupied by tradesmen; the Jellyby family take lodgings there in chapter 30. Smithfield, for centuries a cattle and hay market, had become morally and physically repugnant by the early nineteenth century; its disgusting atmosphere is described in *OT* (21) (see also note to chapter 14, pp. 130–31.

"*No, guv'ner,"* returns Phil

a accident at a gas-works] Such accidents were commonplace: *The Times*

Mems:

Boythorn?

Skimpole?

Hortense?

Sir Leicester?

Lady Dedlock?

Mr Guppy?

Mr Weevle?

The Smallweeds

Mrs Rouncewell's other son, or Watt, or Rosa? – Yes

(Bleak House ———— No. IX.)

Chapter XXVI

Sharpshooters

Shooting Gallery. George washing – and Phil

Visitors – Mr Smallweed and Judy / Your Brimstone Grandmother

For any writing of Captain Hawdon's
So to Mr Tulkinghorn's

Chapter XXVII.

More old soldiers than one.

Mr Tulkinghorn's room

George and the boxes. Strong box.

Matthew Bagnet. Mrs Bagnet, Quebec and Malta, and
Young Woolwich

Discipline was to be maintained / Tell him my opinion, old girl
a threatening, murderous, dangerous fellow.

Chapter XXVIII.

The Ironmaster

Chesney Wold and the cousins

Mrs Rouncewell's other son. Watt and Rosa.

Chapter XXIX.

The Young Man.

Mr Guppy waits on Lady Dedlock. She finds that Esther is her child.

Guppy to bring <Kro> Krook's papers from the old portmanteau

reported them regularly. Phil might have been employed in the large works of the London Gas Company, established in 1833, on the south side of the Thames near Vauxhall Bridge.

blowed out of winder, case-filling at the firework business]   Explosions of detonating powder causing injuries and deaths were also frequently reported in *The Times*. A *HW* article on the manufacture of fireworks describes the packing and securing of the paper or pasteboard cases and remarks that the processes are 'nice operations, requiring much care' (8.48).

"When you stops, you know," cries Phil

a light-weight, to be throwed for practice, Cornwall, Devonshire, or Lancashire]   This is perhaps a reference to the style used in fight promotion bills, in which the venues of fights were stated in general rather than specific terms in order to allow the magistrates no opportunity to intervene; magistrates for certain counties were known to be especially opposed to pugilism (Ford, 1971, 95). *Norton* notes that these are regional names of different sets of rules for wrestling matches, but boxing is the game in question.

Mr. George, after laughing cheerfully

the fifth of November ... to blow Old England up alive]   On this date, children carry around the streets a stuffed effigy, or 'guy', to commemorate Guy Fawkes' Day (see note to chapter 9, p. 94). The anonymous traditional 'popular verses' are: 'Please to remember the Fifth of November,/Gunpowder treason and plot.'

"I had no such thing.

Plague pestilence and famine ... making a curse out of one of his few remembrances of a prayer]   From the Litany: 'From lightning and tempest; from plague, pestilence, and famine; from battle and murder, and from sudden death, Good Lord, deliver us.'

Chapter 27

MORE OLD SOLDIERS THAN ONE.

"If I wasn't as weak as a Brimstone Baby

you crabbed image for the sign of a walking-stick shop]   The shop is alleged to have been that of Moore & Co., 90 St Martin's Lane, which displayed throughout the nineteenth century two walking-sticks with grotesquely carved heads of an old man and an old woman (Henderson, quoting C. F. Tufnell, 1924).

By the cloisterly Temple

Whitefriars ... Hanging-Sword Alley]   Whitefriars lies between Fleet Street and the Thames, the Temple walls and Water Lane. Hanging-Sword Alley is the first turning on the left in Water Lane (Whitefriars Street) from Fleet Street.

the far-famed Elephant who has lost his castle formed of a thousand four-horse coaches, to a stronger iron monster than he]   Before the coming of the railways to this part of London made stagecoaches redundant in the early 1840s, the Elephant and Castle was both a well-known locality and the name of a celebrated tavern at Walworth, where the Kennington, Walworth and New Kent Roads meet, about a mile and a half from Westminster, Waterloo and Blackfriars Bridges and leading from these bridges to important places in Kent and Surrey. The London and South-Western Railway extended across Lambeth from its terminus in the Waterloo Bridge Road, and from 1836 the London Bridge terminus served lines running to the south-east.

certain elongated scraps of music]   Not ballads, but military music, which was printed the long way on oblong sheets.

a soldierly-looking woman ... I never saw her, except upon a baggage-waggon, when she wasn't washing greens!"]   Before troops were transported by rail, the wives and children travelled free on the baggage-waggons. The joke about washing is that, as the wife of a soldier, Mrs Bagnet's usual employment whilst her husband was enlisted would have been washing not cabbages but laundry, for washing and sewing were the most common kind of work performed by soldiers' wives as an essential supplement to their husbands' low pay. Generally only about 6 per cent of a regiment were given permission to marry, the same as the proportion allowed to bring their wives into barracks, where married men and their families were accommodated alongside single men. Marriage was traditionally discouraged, for women and children were considered a liability and wives and daughters of soldiers held a slatternly reputation. But in the mid-nineteenth century the attitude of the army officials towards marriage began to change: aside from the usefulness of the women as a cheap and well-disciplined labour force, the presence of wives and children in the barracks proved to have a steadying, wholesome, humanizing influence on the traditionally irresponsible and licentious soldiery (Trustram, 1984, 29–45, 91, 105–11).

"I never," she says, "George

Bagnet]   A vulgar synonym for 'bayonet'.

These young ladies – not supposed to have been

always so called . . . from the places of their birth in barracks]   A British garrison had been established in Quebec since 1757, when the territory was captured from the French. The strategic location of Malta made it the most important station in Europe for a naval power. During the first half of the nineteenth century, the British Mediterranean squadron was deployed there to counter any intentions of France or Russia to establish routes which would endanger India.

"And how's young Woolwich?"

Woolwich]   A garrison town and the seat of the Royal Arsenal, situated on the south bank of the Thames eight miles from London. As an artilleryman, Bagnet would have lived with his family at the Royal Artillery Barracks, imposing buildings between the dockland and the common.

Mr. George is becoming thoughtful

an unbending, unyielding, brass-bound air, as if he were himself the bassoon of the human orchestra.]   The bassoon is of course a woodwind. Apparently with this in mind, soon after the publication of the present number a correspondent queried the possible ambiguity in the description. Dickens replied: 'I know a bassoon by sight pretty well and have some reason to, having had part of my childhood haunted by musical instruments of every description. "Brass boun[d]" applies to the man, not the instrument' (Ford, 1972, 104).

The characterization of Bagnet may be partly indebted to 'The Modern Soldier's Progress, Part II' (*HW* 2.427–31), which features a tender-hearted veteran who is a musician in the regimental band and experienced in foreign travel. The serious demeanour of both Bagnet and Mr George reflects the Victorian conception of a soldier, as described by R. H. Horne in 'The British Soldier':

> The British Soldier is not of a merry or joyous nature. He is generally a grave man. He possesses great energies, but they are only called forth by strong stimulants, and extraordinary occasions. He has little of what is called animal spirits.   (*Heads of the People*, 1841 supplement, 329–30)

"What college," pursues Bagnet

white lime ... fuller's earth ... sand]   Cleaning materials for scouring knives, iron pots and possibly military equipment. Fuller's earth is used for cleansing cloth.

Proceeding to converse on indifferent

like a military chaplain]   The influence of religious, family and domestic sentiments on military discipline and morale was increasingly recognized in the mid-nineteenth century. Prior to 1856, regimental chaplains were under the authority of the Church of England, but henceforward the Army took responsibility and recognized the Presbyterian and Roman Catholic churches as well, appointing chaplains in proportion to the denominational affiliations of each regiment (Trustram, 1984, 19–20).

Chapter 28

THE IRONMASTER.

Sir Leicester Dedlock

hot-water pipes]   Many country houses had water systems as early as the eighteenth century, but not until the first quarter of the next century was hot water available by means of a boiler built into the kitchen cooking range (Wright, 1960, 95, 188).

the listening earth]   From Addison's hymn, 'The Spacious Firmament on High' ('An Ode', *Spectator* 465):

> Soon as the evening shades prevail,
> The Moon takes up the wonderous tale;
> And nightly, to the listening Earth,
> Repeats the story of her birth:
> Whilst all the stars that round her burn,
> And all the planets, in their turn,
> Confirm the tidings as they roll,
> And spread the truth from pole to pole. (st. 2)

It is a melancholy truth

blood ... *will* cry aloud, and *will* be heard.]   An allusion to Genesis 4.10, in which the Lord rebukes Cain for murdering Abel: 'And he said, What hast thou done? the voice of thy brother's blood crieth unto me from the ground.'

are so many Murders . . . they "will out."]   The proverb cited in note to chapter 23, p. 183.

Of these, foremost in the front rank

Volumnia Dedlock]   Her name is that of the mother of Coriolanus in Shakespeare's play, the severe Roman matron who despises the plebeians, and her characterization is indebted to Hawthorne's depiction of Hepzibah Pyncheon in *The House of the Seven Gables*. As well as being the same age, the impoverished spinsters both have aristocratic airs and are mocked by their respective narrators; moreover, they both indulge in fantasies; in particular, the fantasy Volumnia entertains in chapter 58 after Sir Leicester falls ill is similar to Hepzibah's hope that a rich and aged uncle will marry her and leave her his fortune (4).

Bath . . . that dreary city.]   Bath began to decline as the watering-place of the aristocracy during the Regency and soon became known as a colony for half-pay and retired officers, for stately aged spinsters and for those with aristocratic lineage but limited incomes. Murray's *Handbook* comments:

> The whole city still bears the stamp of opulence in its aspect, although its baths and waters have lost much of their attraction, and its "season" no longer commands the *élite* of English society. It combines many of the advantages of the metropolis with those of a watering place; and education, a comfortable residence, amusements, and society, may be obtained here at a moderate expense. (1856, 139)

nankeen trousers]   Yellow cotton trousers worn in the early party of the nineteenth century, thus old-fashioned.

persistency in an obsolete pearl necklace like a rosary of little bird's-eggs.] Large pearls were generally unfashionable in the nineteenth century, when small pearls and seed pearls were preferred.

In any country in a wholesome state

the pension list]   That is, the Civil List, composed of persons of rank, royal favourites, public servants and any others who could gain influence and so receive an annual payment from the Treasury.

In this society, and where not

from pole to pole]   Another allusion to Addison's hymn, 'The Spacious Firmament on High', cited above, p. 199.

"And it is a remarkable example

Mrs. Rouncewell's son has been invited to go into Parliament."]　He later supports the candidate opposed to Sir Leicester's (chapter 40). The contest between them reflects the continuation into the 1850s of the parliamentary struggle begun by the Reform Bill of 1832 between the radical manufacturers and the Tory landed aristocracy, a point discussed by Sucksmith, 1975, 125–6.

"He is called, I believe – an – Ironmaster."

an – Ironmaster."]　The criticism of aristocratic arrogance towards manufacturers and inventors began in the early years of the Industrial Revolution; an example from the 1830s is Archibald Alison's 'Hints to the Aristocracy', quoted in the headnote to chapter 2, pp. 35–6. The admiration Dickens felt for the self-made successful industrialist is indicated in a letter written a few months before the publication of the present number; he wrote to Miss Coutts in praise of 'large ironmasters – of whom there are some notable cases – who have proceeded on the self-supporting principle, and have done wonders with their workpeople' (18 April 1852, *Letters: Coutts* 199).

The depictions of Rouncewell himself and of his relations with his men (chapter 63) are modelled on Carlyle's heroic figure, the 'Captain of Industry', and on his conception of the 'Chivalry of Labour', as expressed in *Past and Present* (1843):

> The Leaders of Industry, if Industry is ever to be led, are virtually the Captains of the World; if there be no nobleness in them, there will never be an Aristocracy more . . . Captains of Industry are the true Fighters, henceforth recognisable as the only true ones . . . and lead on Mankind in that great, and alone true, and universal warfare. (4.4)

Although published a decade after *BH*, Samuel Smiles's *Industrial Biography: Iron Workers and Tool Makers* (1863) illustrates a prevailing attitude towards industrialists in the mid-century, clearly an attitude which Dickens shared and reflected in Rouncewell. Smiles writes of their heroic stature, quoting the words of 'a distinguished living mechanic' in conversation with him:

> Kings, warriors, and statesmen have heretofore monopolized not only the pages of history, but almost those of biography. Surely some niche ought to be found for the Mechanic, without whose skill and labour society, as it is, could not exist. I do not begrudge destructive heroes their fame, but the constructive ones ought not to be forgotten; and there *is* a heroism of skill and toil belonging to the latter class . . . less perilous and romantic, it may be, than that of the other, but not less full of the results of human energy, bravery, and character. (iv)

Some fictional captains of industry in the Carlylean mould who share the pride and other personal qualities of Rouncewell are Disraeli's Millbank in *Coningsby; or, The New Generation* (1844), and Trafford in *Sybil* (1845), and John Thornton in

North and South, the novel by Mrs Gaskell serialized in *HW* in 1854–5. In that Rosa is presented as the protégée of Lady Dedlock, the alliance between Rouncewell's son and Rosa represents a theme found in other novels of the period: the marriage of the children of established and respectable manufacturers to the children of aristocratic families whose only objection to industrialists is lack of pedigree (see Melada, 1970, 34–5, 195). The closest analogue is in *Coningsby*, in which the hero, grandson of Lord Monmouth, is disinherited after falling in love with Edith Millbank, the daughter of a rich Lancashire manufacturer who is Monmouth's bitterest enemy and who also opposes the match. Eventually, Coningsby is elected to Parliament for Millbank's constituency, marries Edith and is restored to his inheritance.

That Dickens's original intention was to compensate for Sir Leicester's hostility to Mr Rouncewell by enhancing the depiction of Sir Leicester's deep affection for Rouncewell's brother and mother is evidenced in the dialogue in chapter 58 which was deleted in proof, evidently for lack of space, and also in notes for the chapter plan for the eighteenth number: '*Bring Sir Leicester and George together*' and 'George' (see note, p. 287).

Addressing her composed face

the strong Saxon face of the visitor, a picture of resolution and perseverance]   The attributes which Dickens associated with the Saxons (as opposed to the aristocratic Normans) had been described at length in his chapter on Alfred the Great in *CHE*, published in *HW* in 1851:

> The Saxons themselves were a handsome people. . . . the English-Saxon character . . . is the greatest character among the nations of the earth. Wherever the descendants of the Saxon race have gone . . . they have been patient, persevering, never to be broken in spirit, never to be turned aside from enter-prises on which they have resolved. (2.528)

From the village school of Chesney Wold

the whole framework of society]   A cliché in print from 1816 (*OED*). It is used by Montague Tigg in *MC*: ' "I do feel that there is a screw of such magnitude loose somewhere, that the whole framework of society is shaken" ' (7); and when Mr Sapsea uses it in *MED* he is 'confident that he invented that forcible figure' (12).

not minding their catechism, and getting out of the station unto which they are called]   One of the promises of the catechumen is to 'learn and labour truly to get mine own living, and to do my duty in that state of life, unto which it shall please God to call me'.

Volumnia is away next day

and the one wintry wind . . . shakes a shower from the trees . . . as if all the cousins had been changed into leaves]   An echo of the traditional simile found in the *Aeneid* and adopted by Dante (*Inferno* 3.112–14) and by Milton:

> An airy crowd came rushing where he stood . . .
> Thick as the leaves in autumn strew the woods . . .
> (Dryden's translation, 6.422)

> he stood and called
> His legions, angel forms, who lay entranced,
> Thick as autumnal leaves that strow the brooks
> In Vallombrosa.
> (*Paradise Lost* 1.300–3)

Chapter 29

THE YOUNG MAN.

But the house in town

seldom rejoicing when it rejoices, or mourning when it mourns]   Isaiah 66.10: 'Rejoice ye with Jerusalem, and be glad with her all ye that love her: rejoice for joy with her, all ye that mourn for her.'

a suit of armour containing Don Quixote."]   Owing to their amiable, humorous character, scenes from Cervantes were depicted by English painters more often than subjects from any other European source: from the late eighteenth century to the end of the nineteenth century, well over one hundred paintings of *Don Quixote* were exhibited at the Royal Academy and the British Institution alone (Altick, 1985, 118 n.)

"One stone terrace . . . and Othello."]   There were numerous pictorial representations of *Othello* painted from 1840 onwards. Several of these were influenced by Thomas Southard's highly romantic and heroic 'The Meeting of Othello and Desdemona', which was painted for Boydell's Shakespeare Gallery (1791–1805) and was subsequently engraved and frequently reproduced in editions of Shakespeare. Two important later treatments are William Frith's 'Othello and Desdemona' (exhibited at the British Institution, 1840), and James Clark Hook's depiction of Othello listening to Desdemona playing the lute (Royal Academy, 1852). Charles W. Cope's 'Othello Relating His Adventures' (Royal Academy, 1853) was exhibited after the composition of the present number (Altick, 1985, 45–9, 306–7).

"Now, it's a very singular circumstance

though not admitted, yet I have had a present of my articles made to me . . . on my mother's advancing . . . the money for the stamp]   Kenge and Carboy have waived the usual sum paid for articles of apprenticeship, and Guppy's mother has merely paid the stamp duty. A salaried clerk, he thus becomes articled, and in chapter 64 he tells Jarndyce that he has now come out of his articles and has been admitted to the roll of attorneys.

Mr. Guppy stares. Lady Dedlock sits before him.

the features of those long-preserved dead bodies sometimes opened up in tombs, which, struck by the air like lightning, vanish in a breath.]   This was a phenomenon to which Dickens often referred (*PP* 2, *TTC* 1.3, *GE* 8, *MED* 4). The many celebrated accounts of the opening of tombs are discussed by Jacobson (1986, 67–8). Of those which Dickens is likely to have known at the time of writing *BH*, she mentions that of Francis Lovell, the friend of Richard III, who went into hiding in a vault in his house upon the accession of Henry Tudor and apparently died of starvation. In 1708 the vault was opened to reveal the skeleton of a man seated at a table, everything crumbling to dust when the air was admitted (*DNB*). In addition, Dickens was familiar with Victor Hugo's *The Hunchback of Notre-Dame* (1831), in the last chapter of which the skeleton of a man is found clasping that of a young woman: 'When they strove to detach this skeleton from the one it was embracing, it fell to dust' (54).

So the young man makes his bow

Mercury does not . . . leave his Olympus]   From Olympus, the home of the Greek gods, Jupiter sent Mercury as a messenger.

No. Words, sobs, and cries

trumpet-tongued]   *Macbeth* 1.7.18–20: 'his virtues/Will plead like angels, trumpet-tongu'd, against/The deep damnation of his taking-off'.

Chapter 30

Tenth monthly number
December 1852

ESTHER'S NARRATIVE.

"Poor Mr. Woodcourt, my dear," she would say

an officer in the Royal Highlanders, and he died on the field.]   The Royal Highlanders (the Black Watch) are Scotland's oldest and favourite Highland corps; according to a saying, 'the best blood of the country has been shed in the ranks of the Royal Highlanders'. Mr Woodcourt would have died at Waterloo, where the regiment lost nearly 300 officers and men. The Duke of Wellington mentioned the Royal Highlanders as one of the regiments that particularly distinguished itself.

It seemed that Caddy's unfortunate papa

"gone through the Gazette,"]   The *London Gazette*, an official journal issued twice weekly, published the names of bankrupts, lists of government appointments and promotions, and other public notices.

he was a "Custom-House and General Agent," . . . when he wanted money more than usual he went to the Docks to look for it]   This description of Caddy's bankrupt father seems to conflate aspects of the histories of Dickens's own father, John Dickens, and John Dickens's father-in-law, Charles Barrow. John Dickens was a clerk in the Navy Pay Office at Portsmouth dockyard when Dickens was born and five years later was assigned to the government dockyard at Chatham. He was chronically insolvent and imprisoned for debt in 1824, when Dickens was aged 12. Charles Barrow, the Chief Conductor of Moneys in Town in the Navy Pay Office, confessed in 1810 to having embezzled the Navy Board for the previous seven years. He pleaded as an excuse the burdens of a large family and prolonged illness and absconded to the Continent, where he died in 1826.

As soon as her papa had tranquillised his mind

Hatton Garden]   An area near Holborn Circus occupied by tradesmen.

"Yes," said Caddy, "Wild Indians.

Wild Indians]   During the 1840s, a craze for Indians was created by the American painter and ethnologist George Catlin, who brought to London an exhibition of Indian artefacts in 1840 and in 1843 a group of Indians themselves, the Ojibbeways. Whilst touring the sights of London and the provinces, the

Richard? – No

Caddy Jellyby's marriage? <u>Yes.</u>

Brickmaker's family?

Charley's Illness   <u>Yes.</u>

<u>Dawn of Esther's?</u>

<u>Krook's death.</u>   Yes.

Miss Flite? <u>Yes.</u> Carry Allan Woodcourt through, by her
Connect Esther & Jo. <u>Yes.</u>

———————— Mrs Snagsby?

<u>Esther's love must be kept in view, to make the</u>
coming trial the greater and the victory
the more meritorious.

Chapter XXX.

Esther's Narrative.

Mrs Woodcourt.

Caddy Jellyby's marriage.

No East wind with the little Woman

Chapter XXXI.

Nurse and Patient.

JO – begin the illness from him. His disappearance

Then, Charley ill

Then, Esther

Ada

<Kee> "She will try to make her way into the room. Keep her out!"
"For I cannot see you Charley – I am blind"

Chapter XXXII.

The appointed time.

Weevle uneasiness

Snagsby.

Guppy and Weevle – Soot – oil from the window

All Injustice and wrong – "Spontaneous Combustion
and no other death." ————————————————

Ojibbeways developed an unfortunate reputation for getting drunk and causing disturbances, and by 1845, when Catlin took them to Paris, the British had tired of Indians. Dickens discussed the contemporary interest in American Indians, African tribesmen and other 'uncivilized' races in his *HW* essay of 1853, 'The Noble Savage', in which he debunks the romantic notion and comments that he considers the 'Noble Savage' 'a prodigious nuisance, and an enormous superstition' (7.337; Altick, 1978, 275–9).

Mr. and Mrs. Pardiggle were of the party

Miss Wisk's mission . . . was to show the world that woman's mission was man's mission; and that the only genuine mission, of both man and woman, was . . . at public meetings.] Three of Dickens's *HW* articles exemplify his contemptuous attitude towards feminism, a current vogue in certain intellectual circles: 'From the Raven in the Happy Family', 'Sucking Pigs' and 'Frauds on the Fairies' (1.156–8, 4.145–7, 8.97-100). 'From the Raven . . .' and 'Sucking Pigs' express his opposition to the woman who has pretensions to the rights of man and takes a role in public life, and 'Frauds on the Fairies' combines his detestation of the Exeter Hall style of oratory – promoting religious sectarianism, party politics and philanthropy – with his contempt for the idea of women's equality.

Chapter 31

NURSE AND PATIENT.

My little maid's countenance fell

the doctor's shop] In the country, drugs were dispensed by the physician and surgeon as well as by the chemist (see note to chapter 22, pp. 182–3).

The friend had been here and there

One official sent her to another] For the complex selection procedures governing admission to hospitals and workhouses, see notes to chapter 47, pp. 255, 258.

"This is a sorrowful case," said my guardian

Harold?"] The reading in MS-1853 is 'Leonard': Dickens corrected his oversight here and in three later instances in this chapter on an errata-slip in the final double number (see note to chapter 6, p. 70).

Ada being in our room with a cold

a little ballad . . . about a Peasant boy . . . bereft of a home."]   He sings the first two lines of 'The Peasant Boy' (1825) by John Parry. The score indicates the tone of the song as 'plaintive'; the stanza continues: 'A stranger to pleasure, to comfort and joy,/Behold little Edmund, the poor peasant boy.' Silas Wegg recites the ballad in *OMF* 1.15.

He was extremely gay

negus]   A mixture of wine, especially port or sherry, and hot water, sweetened with sugar and flavoured with lemon.

Charley fell ill.

Charley fell ill.]   She contracts smallpox from Jo, the carrier of the infection, who, although he suffers a high fever and dies from either terminal pneumonia or pulmonary tuberculosis (chapter 47), does not develop the disease himself. An epidemic of smallpox in 1837–40 caused almost 42,000 deaths in England and Wales, and less severe epidemics broke out again in 1844–5 and from 1848 to 1852. Although the Vaccination Extension Act of 1840 made vaccination at public expense available to everyone, it was not until 1853 that vaccination for newborn infants was made compulsory (Wohl, 1983, 132–3).

There were other times

that young man carried out to be buried . . . the only son of his mother]   A quotation from the account of one of the miracles performed by Christ: 'behold, there was a dead man carried out, the only son of his mother, and she was a widow' (Luke 7.12).

the ruler's daughter raised up]   As recorded in Matthew 9.25, Christ 'went in, and took her by the hand, and the maid arose'.

"I believe it, my dear Charley.

I am blind."]   Smallpox lesions may appear on the mucous membranes of the eyes, endangering the sight. The difficulty in speaking which Esther mentions would result from lesions in the mucous membranes of the mouth and throat.

Chapter 32

THE APPOINTED TIME.

The title derives from a reiterated expression in Job: 'Is there not an appointed time to man upon earth?' (7.1). The verse relevant to the present chapter is 20.29: 'This is the portion of a wicked man from God, and the heritage appointed unto him by God.' For an interpretation of the relevance of the book of Job to *BH*, see Larson, 1984.

It is night in Lincoln's Inn

valley of the shadow of the law]   Psalms 23.4: 'Yea, though I walk through the valley of the shadow of death, I will fear no evil: for thou art with me; thy rod and thy staff they comfort me.'

Argus]   In Greek mythology, Argus had a hundred eyes, of which only two were asleep at one time. He was appointed guardian of the cow into which Io had been changed but was lulled to sleep by the sweet notes of the lyre of Hermes.

bee-like industry . . . good account at last.]   From the song by Isaac Watts, 'Against Idleness and Mischief', cited in note to chapter 8, p. 79.

In the neighbouring court

scouring the plain]   A military image familiar from Pope, *An Essay on Criticism* 372–3: 'Not so, when swift Camilla scours the Plain,/Flies o'er th'unbending Corn, and skims along the Main.' The expression also appears frequently in Dryden ('The Medall', 'First Book of the *Georgics*', *Aeneis*, 4).

a roar like a very Yorick]   An allusion to Hamlet's address to the skull of the former court jester: 'Where be your gibes now, your gambols, your songs, your flashes of merriment that were wont to set the table on a roar?' (5.1.182–3).

the gruff line in a concerted piece]   A joking reference to his hoarse singing of the bass line in a piece arranged in parts for several voices or instruments.

Listen, listen, listen, Tew the wa-ter-Fall!]   The last line of the glee for four voices by the first Earl of Mornington (1735–81), 'Here, in cool grot':

> Here, in cool grot, and mossy cell,
> We rural fays and fairies dwell . . .
> Nor yet for artful strains we call,
> But listen to the waterfall.

"Sooner than which . . . I would get my living by selling lucifers."] Itinerant sellers of lucifer matches were often disdained because many of them used the matches as a mode of begging (Mayhew 1.431–3).

the potboy of the Sol's Arms appearing with her supper-pint] The practice for public houses to send their potboys to sell pints of beer around working-class districts in the evening is described in *SB*, 'The Streets – Night'.

It is a close night

the unwholesome trades] The bone-houses, cat-gut manufacturers and knackers' yards which surrounded the slaughterhouses at the nearby Smithfield Market (see note to chapter 14, pp. 130–1).

"Very true, sir. Don't you observe," says Mr. Snagsby

"don't you observe . . . that you're rather greasy here, sir?"] The offensive soot, grease and tainted air remarked on in this chapter, preparatory to the discovery of Krook's remains, agree with the details recorded in the accounts of spontaneous combustion which Dickens acknowledged as his sources in chapter 33, but it has been noticed that the polluted atmosphere is also similar to descriptions of the gaseous exhalations resulting from decomposing corpses in overcrowded burial-grounds. Such descriptions appeared in the parliamentary reports on metropolitan interment which were discussed in the *Westminster Review*, and elsewhere, in 1842 and 1843 (Wallins, 1974).

"William Guppy," replies the other

"I am in the Downs.] The stretch of breakwater between Deal and the Goodwin Sands (see note to chapter 45, pp. 248–9). Tony means 'down in spirits'.

"No! Dash it, Tony," says that gentleman

hover around one flower.] An allusion to Macheath's song, 'Pray, Fair One, Be Kind', in John Gay, *The Beggar's Opera* (1728):

> My heart was so free,
> It roved like the bee,
> Till Polly my passion requited;
> I sipped each flower,
> I changed ev'ry hour,
> But here ev'ry flower is united.   (1.13)

"Forgotten? Trust him for that.

Bibo, and old Charon, and Bibo being drunk when he died] Dialogues between Charon and either a mourner or the soul of the departed were parodied from the seventeenth century onwards. The allusion here is to an epigram of Matthew Prior which was set to music by John Travers in *Eighteen Canzonets* (1745?):

> When Bibo thought fit from the World to retreat,
> As full of Champaign as an Egg's full of Meat,
> He wak'd in the Boat, and to Charon he said,
> He wou'd be set back for he was not yet Dead:
> Trim the Boat and sit quiet, stern Charon reply'd,
> You may have forgot, You was Drunk when You Dy'd.

Mr. Guppy nods, and gives him a "lucky touch"

a "lucky touch"]   The superstition is explained in *LD* 1.18: '[Chivery] had . . . given his boy what he termed "a lucky touch", signifying that he considered such commendation of him to Good Fortune, preparatory to his that day declaring his passion and becoming triumphant.'

Chapter 33

Eleventh monthly number
January 1853

INTERLOPERS.

Now do those two gentlemen

tissue-paper]   Thin paper known as 'flimsy' which was backed with copying-paper and used by reporters to produce multiple copies (*Norton*).

pursuant to the Act of George the Second]   The Theatres Act of 1737: 2 George II., c.28 (1737). This conferred on the Lord Chamberlain a statutory power to license stage-plays and to prohibit the performance of any play. What is referred to here is an exception permitted by the Act: the performance of dancing and musical entertainments in public houses which would otherwise be deemed disorderly.

The whole court, adult as well as boy

The whole court . . . can do nothing but wrap up its many heads]   An allusion to *Coriolanus* 2.3.15: 'he himself stuck not to call us the many-headed multitude'.

the stomachic article of cloves]   Periphrasis for a cordial consisting of spirits strongly flavoured with cloves.

the Phoenix]   The Phoenix Fire Insurance Company was the second-largest of the fifteen which operated in London; the largest (calculated on the amount of stamp duty paid in 1842) was the Sun Insurance Company. Other companies included the Albion, Alliance, Globe, Guardian and Protector. Each firm maintained its own fire-engines and a company of firemen.

Mr. Snagsby's power of speech deserts him

For to see that injured female walk into the Sol's Arms . . . and stand . . . with her eyes fixed upon him like an accusing spirit, strikes him dumb.] The 'accusing spirit' is the ghost of Banquo when it appears at the banquet. On first seeing it, Macbeth's response is to feel accused: 'Thou canst not say I did it; never shake/Thy gory locks at me' (3.4.50–1).

"My dear," says Mr. Snagsby

shrub]   A drink made with orange or lemon juice, sugar, and rum or another spirit.

"My life," says the unhappy stationer

Wine Vaults]   A pretentious name for a public house (*OED*).

"My dear sir," cries Grandfather Smallweed

obleeging]   This was the polite pronunciation in the eighteenth century, but by the 1830s it had come to be considered by some either vulgar, or common to only a few octogenarians. Dickens seems to have considered it vulgar, for it is used by lower-class characters such as Tony Weller, Codlin, Mr Peggotty, Silas Wegg and Rogue Riderhood (Gerson, 1967, 127–8). But the usage by Grandfather Smallweed is surely intended to sound polite and to echo the pronunciation of his original, Samuel Rogers, aged 89 when *BH* was composed.

This little apostrophe to Mrs. Smallweed

she finds herself on her feet, to amble about, and "set" to inanimate objects]   To 'set', a term used in country-dancing, is to face and bow to one's partner; Dickens's remarks on parties at Rockingham Castle (*Letters* 5.662, 663) show that he was a keen country-dancer. (The reference in *Norton* to the action of a hunting dog pointing at game is misleading.)

"Mrs. Smallweed's brother, my dear friend

I shall take out letters of administration.]   Smallweed will claim his rights to administer Krook's estate in the absence of a will.

Richard – No.

Mrs Bucket   No.

Smallweed progress – Tulkinghorn – George & Bagnet.
                                                    Yes

Hortense and Tulkinghorn?   No

(Bleak House ——— No. XI.)

Chapter XXXIII.

Interlopers.

The Court, under the excitement

Krook Mrs Smallweed's brother. Smallweeds take possession

Lady Dedlock – the young man – and the old man.

Chapter XXXIV.

A Turn of the Screw

By old Smallweed & Mr Tulkinghorn

The Bagnets.

Mr George sees his mother.

Young Woolwich

Chapter XXXV.

Esther's Narrative.

Her illness and gradual recovery

Necklace and the beads—   Looking glass taken
                                         away.

<Chapter XXXVI.>

Work in Richard and the love

"And now I must tell the little secret."

The arrival of this unexpected heir

"The popular song of KING DEATH!]   At a harmonic meeting in Thackeray, *Pendennis* (1848–50), the bass singer reports that 'King Death' is part of his repertoire (30). The macabre words of the song are by B. W. Procter ('Barry Cornwall') (1787–1874), the music by S. Neukomm (1778–1858):

> King Death was a rare old fellow!
>   He sate where no sun could shine;
> And he lifted his hand so yellow,
>   And poured out his coal-black wine.
>   Hurrah! for the coal-black Wine! . . .
>
> All came to the royal old fellow,
>   Who laughed till his eyes dropped brine,
> As he gave them his hand so yellow,
>   And pledged them in Death's black wine.
>   Hurrah! – Hurrah!
>   Hurrah! for the coal-black Wine!   (sts 1, 4)

Out of the court, and a long way out of it

men of science and philosophy come to look . . . doctors . . . arrive with the same intent, and there is more learned talk about inflammable gases and phosphuretted hydrogen . . . an account of it]   Dickens's belief in spontaneous human combustion was widely shared and promulgated in the nineteenth century. Fictional descriptions of the phenomenon appeared in novels by Charles Brockden Brown (*Wieland*, 1798), Captain Marryat (*Jacob Faithful*, 1834) and Herman Melville (*Redburn*, 1849). Dickens may have known these, and he may have first encountered the theory while still a schoolboy, reading *The Terrific Register; or, Record of Crimes, Judgements, Providences, and Calamities* (2 vols, 1824–5). The penny weekly contained an article supplying evidence for the validity of spontaneous combustion and citing the case of the Countess Cornelia Bandi (or Baudi) of Casena (or Verona) and the testimony of Le Cat (2.340–3). The case of the countess was the most often printed occurrence, as the reference to it in the preface to *BH* implies, and Krook's death is modelled on an account of her death which was originally published in English in 1746 in *Philosophical Transactions* (no. 476). This account translated an Italian treatise of 1731 by J. Bianchini, of Verona.

Although Dickens professed to have read 'with great care' a number of books about spontaneous combustion, his depiction of Krook's death in chapter 32 has been shown to derive from only one source – a reprint of the account in *Philosophical Transactions*. Reprints appeared in both the *Gentleman's Magazine* of 1746 (16.368) and in the *Annual Register . . . for 1763* (91–5). Since he owned volumes of the *Annual Register* for the period 1758 to 1860, it is likely that this was the version he knew.

Bianchini relates that the countess, aged 62, had been well on the day prior to her death, but at night 'she began to be heavy':

In the morning, the maid going to call her, saw her corpse in this deplorable condition. Four feet distant . . . was a heap of ashes, two legs untouched . . . All the rest was ashes, which had this quality, that they left in the hand a greasy and stinking moisture. The air in the room had soot floating in it . . . This soot even got into a neighbouring kitchen, hung on its walls and utensils . . . In the room above, the said soot flew about, and from the windows trickled down a greasy, loathsome, yellowish liquor, with an unusual stink. The floor of the chamber was thick smeared with a gluish moisture, not easily got off, and the stink spread into other chambers. (*Annual Register*, 1763, 91)

Upon publication of chapter 32 in the tenth monthly number, G. H. Lewes, writing in the *Leader*, publicly challenged Dickens to supply scientific authorities to substantiate the phenomenon of spontaneous combustion (11 December 1852, 15 January, 5 and 12 February 1853). In the present passage, the long sentence beginning 'Some of these authorities . . .' was added in MS as a reply to Lewes's first challenge (referred to in the preface). Dickens had not read any of these authorities, but he found their names in a book from his own library, *The Anatomy of Drunkenness*, by Dr Robert MacNish (Glasgow, 1827; Dickens owned the 1840 edition. He also owned the author's *Philosophy of Sleep*: see note to chapter 35, p. 221). In his chapter on 'Spontaneous Combustion of Drunkards', MacNish cites the eighteenth-century and early nineteenth-century French physicians named Fodoré, Le Cat and Marc (his misspelling, 'Mere', is perpetuated by Dickens), and one of his own sources on spontaneous combustion, *Medical Jurisprudence*, by J. A. Paris and J. S. M. Fonblanque (3 vols, London, 1823), is referred to by Dickens as the 'book not quite unknown, on English Medical Jurisprudence'. MacNish himself seems to be alluded to in Dickens's mention in the preface of the 'distinguished medical professors, French, English, and Scotch, in more modern days'.

Like many scientists and temperance writers of his day, MacNish considered spontaneous combustion to be a complication of alcoholism. For example, Dr James Apjohn, the professor of chemistry who contributed the article on spontaneous combustion in the authoritative *Cyclopaedia of Practical Medicine* (4 vols, 1833), concluded that 'the human body admits of being reduced to a highly inflammable state'; that the condition is often promoted by the presence in the system of 'alcoholic vapours'; and that the process can result from the body coming into contact with an external fire or an electric spark, but that 'cases truly spontaneous, if any such have occurred, must be referred to the disengagement of phosphuretted hydrogen'. The subject is also considered in *Principles of General and Comparative Physiology* (1839), by the influential physiologist and supporter of the temperance movement, W. B. Carpenter, and it is mentioned in the *Temperance Encyclopaedia*, by W. Reid (1851). (See: Haight, 1955; Gaskell, 1973; Denman, 1986 – the definitive articles on Dickens and spontaneous combustion; see also Hayes, 1936; Howarth, 1937–8; McMaster, 1958; Wiley, 1962; Perkins, 1964.)

the artist of a picture newspaper … depicts that apartment as three-quarters of a mile long, by fifty yards high]   Sixpenny weekly newspapers such as the *Illustrated London News* and the *Pictorial Times* were profusely illustrated with full-page and half-page steel engravings which tended to portray scenes in a highly dramatic and larger-than-life manner.

Chapter 34

A TURN OF THE SCREW.

Phil Squod, with the aid of a brush

the girl he left behind him]   From the eighteenth-century song, 'The Girl I Left Behind Me':

> I'm lonesome since I cross'd the hills,
> And o'er the moor that's sedgy,
> Such heavy thoughts my mind doth fill,
> Since parting with my Betsy,
> Searching for one that's fine and gay,
> And sev'ral to remind me, °
> Blest be the hours I passed away
> With the girl I left behind me. (st. 1)

"Whitewashing."

"Whitewashing."]   The clearing of a bankrupt or insolvent by judicial process from liability for his debts.

"Now, George," says Mrs. Bagnet

Lignum Vitae]   A tough, hard and heavy wood, derived from a genus of trees and shrubs (*Guaiacum*) native to the West Indies and tropical America. Its resin was used in medicine and the wood itself was used, like ebony, in the manufacture of small, hard, durable objects. Bagnet's original nickname, cancelled in proof, was 'Number Seventy-Four, which is supposed to have been his old regimental number'.

Mr. Bagnet, otherwise as immoveable as a pump

puts his large right hand on the top of his bald head, as if to defend it from a shower-bath]   Dickens was an enthusiastic showerer: having praised a shower-bath at a hotel in Broadstairs in July 1849 (*Letters* 5.568), he created one later that month whilst renting a house at Bonchurch on the Isle of Wight (see *Letters* 5.574, 583, note). His shower-bath seems to have been modelled on the 'cold douche' administered at water-cure establishments, where the patient was instructed to hold his hands clasped above his head to protect it whilst the cascade of water hit the rest of his body, the experience being compared to standing beneath a load of falling gravel (Turner, 1967, 149–50).

"I do assure you both

the Mint]   The Royal Mint, then sited on Tower Hill, where the coins of the United Kingdom have been minted since 1810.

These encomiums bring them to Mount Pleasant

the perennial Judy . . . consults the oracle]   She is likened to the long-lived Sibyls who were themselves consulted as oracles.

"George," Mr. Bagnet gruffly whispers

'Why soldiers, why – should we be melancholly boys?']   From the early eighteenth-century song, 'How Stands the Glass Around?':

> Why, soldiers, why
> > Should we be melancholy, boys?
> Why, soldiers, why?
> > Whose business 'tis to die?
> What, sighing? fie!
> > Don't fear; drink on; be jolly, boys!

(Noted by *Norton*.) The song was parodied by Thomas Hood in 'Up the Rhine', which begins: 'Why, Tourist, why/With passports have to do . . .'

"I tell you, Serjeant, I have nothing to say

Melchisedech's in Clifford's Inn."]   Clifford's Inn, by the side of St Dunstan's Church in Fleet Street, was the oldest and most important of the Inns of Chancery. Money-lending was traditionally done by Jews; Douglas Jerrold sketched the type in 'The Money-Lender':

> Jew Money-Lenders . . . numerous as the hairs in Aaron's beard; and, for the most part, all alike. They have no variety of character, and have lost the

picturesque villainy of former centuries. We could feel a degree of sympathy for the outraged Hebrew . . . Persecution has ceased, and the Jew Money-Lender is merely a vulgar, ravenous, sordid thing – a horse-leech among leeches.

(*Heads of the People* 1841 supplement, 24)

Chapter 35

ESTHER'S NARRATIVE.

For the same reason I am almost afraid to hint

that time in my disorder – it seemed one long night . . . when I laboured up colossal staircases . . . piled up to the sky . . . it was such inexplicable agony and misery] The descriptions of Esther's illness and of her dreams of the staircase and flaming necklace derive from Thomas De Quincey, *Confessions of an English Opium-Eater* (1821; 1822). At the beginning of his section on 'The Pains of Opium', he states that his primary aim in writing the *Confessions* was to relate his dreams, and he attempts to describe the endlessness of his sufferings under the influence of opium:

> I seemed every night to descend, not metaphorically, but literally to descend, into chasms and sunless abysses, depths below depths, from which it seemed hopeless that I could ever reascend. Nor did I, by waking, feel that I *had* re-ascended. This I do not dwell upon; because the state of gloom which attended these gorgeous spectacles, amounting at least to utter darkness, as of some suicidal despondency, cannot be approached by words.
>
> The sense of space, and in the end, the sense of time, were both powerfully affected . . . Space swelled, and was amplified to an extent of unutterable infinity.   (1822 edn, 158)

He then compares the 'endless growth and self-reproduction' of the 'architecture' of his dreams with Piranesi's famous set of engravings which represent his own dreams, experienced 'during the delirium of a fever':

> Some of them . . . represented vast Gothic halls . . . Creeping along the sides of the walls, you perceived a staircase; and upon it, groping his way upwards, was Piranesi himself: follow the stairs a little further, and you perceive it come to a sudden abrupt termination, without any balustrade, and allowing no step onwards to him who had reached the extremity, except into the depths below. Whatever is to become of poor Piranesi, you suppose, at least, that his labours must in some way terminate here. But raise your eyes, and behold a second flight of stairs still higher: on which again Piranesi is perceived, but this time standing on the very brink of the abyss. Again elevate your eye[s] . . . and again is poor

Piranesi busy on his aspiring labours: and so on, until the unfinished stairs and
Piranesi both are lost in the upper glooms of the hall. (163–4)

At this point De Quincey quotes a passage from Wordsworth's *The Excursion*
(1814) to illustrate one of the images he saw frequently in sleep. The passage seems
to have suggested to Dickens Esther's dream of the 'flaming necklace, or ring, or
starry circle':

> The appearance, instantaneously disclosed,
> Was of a mighty city . . .
> Fabric it seem'd of diamond, and of gold,
> With alabaster domes, and silver spires,
> And blazing terrace upon terrace, high
> Uplifted . . .
>   there, towers begirt
> With battlements that on their restless fronts
> Bore stars – illumination of all gems!   (2.834–5, 839–45)

Perhaps the less I say of these sick experiences

**It may be that if we knew more of such strange afflictions, we might be
better able to alleviate their intensity.]**   This speculation reflects Dickens's
longstanding fascination with his own dreams and with contemporary dream
theories. His treatment of the subject in the present chapter seems to have been
particularly influenced by a *HW* article of 1851 entitled 'Dreams' (2.566–72). The
author was a doctor named Thomas Stone, but the article embodies many of
Dickens's own ideas as communicated to Stone in a long letter in which Dickens
claimed 'I have read something on the subject, and have long observed it with the
greatest attention and interest'. His criticism of the article first submitted by Stone
was that it might be made 'a little more original, and a little less recapitulative of the
usual stories in the books' (2 February 1851, *Nonesuch* 2.267).

Some of the books he had in mind were doubtless those in his own library: Dr
John Abercrombie, *Inquiries Concerning the Intellectual Powers and the Investigation of
Truth* (10th edn, 1840), and Dr Robert MacNish, *Philosophy of Sleep* (1840), both of
which are cited in the article by Stone. He also owned Dugald Stewart, *Elements of
the Philosophy of the Human Mind* (1843), and he seems to have been familiar with
the section on 'Dreaming' in chapter 27 of *Human Physiology* (1840), by his friend
Dr John Elliotson. An excellent survey of Victorian dream theories and of
Dickens's interest in them is given by Bernard (1981), who shows how Dickens's
ideas reflected the general shift in dream research towards scientific and
mechanistic interpretations, as opposed to religious and spiritualistic ones.

"Oh yes, it has, my dear," he said

broken . . . upon the wheel of Chancery]   Prior to the nineteenth century,
breaking on the wheel was a common form of execution for criminals in Europe.

The victim was laid on his back upon a cartwheel and bound to the spokes; his limbs were then smashed with a sledgehammer or heavy club, and the death-blow was delivered in the stomach.

"Let me see," said she.

Tambour work]   A type of embroidery done with the aid of a hook on a fabric stretched across a circular frame. Tambouring became commercialized in the 1780s, but by the early nineteenth century, when the stitch could be produced by mechanical means, tambour work lost its popularity. Ralph Nickleby suggests tambouring to Kate as an alternative to governessing, and Madeline Bray does it after being a governess (*NN* 3, 46).

"True! My dear, for the moment – true.

a terrible shipwreck over in those East-Indian seas.]   The shipwreck of East Indiamen was a common occurrence; for example, the *Annual Register* for 1850 records the wreck of two ships at Madras in May, and the loss of three in October.

And I did read all the noble history

the long account she had cut out of the newspaper.]

> Every fortnight, or thereabouts . . . the newspapers present their readers with two or three columns of closely-printed intelligence just conveyed to them from China and India by the Overland Mail . . . the numbers are comparatively small that take a direct interest in the news . . . with an anxious glance at the deaths and promotions, the marriages and sick-lists, the arrivals and departures . . . destinies that are sometimes shadowed out in dim little paragraphs from nooks and corners of the great frontier regions.   ('The Overland Mail Bag', *HW* 4.229)

I felt so triumphant ever to have known the man who had done such generous and gallant deeds . . . I so admired and loved what he had done] A reminiscence of Othello's account of how Desdemona fell in love with him whilst listening to the story of 'the battles, sieges, fortunes' of his life: 'She lov'd me for the dangers I had pass'd;/And I lov'd her that did pity them' (1.3.167–8).

I said it was not the custom in England

it was not the custom in England to confer titles on men distinguished by peaceful services, however good and great; unless occasionally, when they consisted of the accumulation of some very large amount of money.] The failure of the government to bestow titles and appointments on the 'good and great' in daily life was a topical subject. *Punch* conducted a campaign during the early 1850s on behalf of men such as Dr Walker, who promoted the Metropolitan Interments Act of 1850, George Stephenson, the engineer, and Rowland Hill, the inventor of penny postage. The article on Stephenson observes:

> We have a singular scale of rewards in England. Lord Mayors are made baronets by the dozen. Generals . . . are made lords and marquesses. A peerage is given to a banker, from the overpowering merit which a million sterling was supposed to confer on him. And yet to an Engineer, who occupies the first rank in his noble profession in England, perhaps in the world . . . the offer of a Knighthood is made! . . . We are glad that he sent back the insulting offer.   (19, 14 September 1850, 113)

Eighteen months later, however, *Punch* applauded the appointment of Rowland Hill as Postmaster-General, announcing the news as

> the most gratifying intelligence illustrative of the new and enlightened determination of the British Cabinet. It has too long been the reproach of the Ministry, that the bigger fishes and the whiter loaves have ever been bestowed upon the born aristocracy, the plebeian projectors being set aside, or at best rewarded with the smallest of sprats, and the coarsest of penny rolls.   (22, 7 February 1852, 61)

(See also 'English Gratitude', 19, 24 August 1850, 89.)

For Dickens, the Government's failure to bestow recognition had a personal meaning, and it was a subject about which he and his fellow authors were hypersensitive. He had recently publicly expressed his annoyance that literary men were never honoured when he gave a speech at the banquet to Literature, Science and Art at the Mansion House on 7 July 1849. In his edition of the *Speeches*, K. J. Fielding gives an account of the misunderstandings which resulted from the occasion (98–100).

O, it was so much better, as it was!

the journey's end]   *Othello* 5.2.270–1: 'Here is my journey's end, here is my butt,/And very sea-mark of my utmost sail'. Esther quotes these words again at the end of chapter 37.

223

Chapter 36

CHESNEY WOLD.

My hair had not been cut off

My hair had not been cut off]   The treatment to relieve the headaches which accompanied fevers was to cut off the hair and apply cold to the head.

Wishing to be fully re-established

a chubby pony . . . I don't know who had given Stubbs his name]   He is named for George Stubbs (1724-1806), the animal-painter best known for his portraits of horses.

Charley and I had reason to call it

a sailor . . . Plymouth]   Plymouth was a historically important city for naval and military preparations. Murray's *Handbook for Travellers in Devon and Cornwall* (3rd edn, 1856) describes the Royal Marine Barracks which could accommodate a thousand men, the Royal Naval Hospital with beds for 1,200, and the dockyard. Construction of the magnificent breakwater of Plymouth Sound, begun in 1806, was not completed until 1840; the lighthouse was completed in 1845.

These are the real feelings that I had.

"Pray daily that the sins of others be not visited upon your head."]   Exodus 20.5: 'for I the Lord thy God am a jealous God, visiting the iniquity of the fathers upon the children unto the third and fourth generation of them that hate me'.

I did not dare to linger

the Ghost's Walk]   Browne's illustration of this scene, 'The Ghost's Walk', is one of the novel's ten so-called 'dark plates', the sinister and sombre effect of which he achieved by machine-ruling the entire plate with fine parallel lines in addition to etching the design. The frontispiece to the first edition and most of the illustrations in the remaining third of the novel are executed in this manner. For discussions of the process and of how the 'dark plates' complement the atmosphere of the text, see Cohen, 1980, 108–12, and Steig, 1978, 148–58.

Chapter 37

JARNDYCE AND JARNDYCE.

The difficulty that I felt

the adage about little pitchers]   The proverb, 'Little pitchers have wide ears'.

"Mister Grubble, miss," returned Charley.

The Dedlock Arms, by W. Grubble]   The usual formula for an inn sign, meaning 'owned and conducted by'.

"Yes, miss. If you please, miss

the cage]   A prison for petty malefactors, a lock-up.

Mr. Grubble was standing in his shirt sleeves

his very clean little tavern . . . his best parlour]   The description of this room derives from one given by Jane Eyre in a similar situation (compare especially Esther's 'a neat carpeted room', 'a coloured print of Queen Caroline', 'either a curious egg or a curious pumpkin . . . hanging from the ceiling'):

> you must fancy you see a room in the George Inn at Millcote, with such large-figured papering on the walls as inn rooms have; such a carpet, such furniture, such ornaments on the mantelpiece, such prints – including a portrait of George the Third and another of the Prince of Wales, and a representation of the death of Wolfe. All this is visible to you by the light of an oil lamp hanging from the ceiling. (11)

a coloured print of Queen Caroline]   See note to chapter 14, p. 134.

"My dear Miss Summerson, here is our friend

Fortune and her train]   By tradition, the followers of Fortune are blind.

"For I am constantly being taken

I am not like the starling; I get out.]   In Sterne's *A Sentimental Journey through France and Italy* (1768), three chapters give the history of a caged starling, encountered in a Paris hotel, which would repeat 'I can't get out – I can't get out' ('The Passport', 'The Captive' and 'The Starling').

225

Bring out Skimpole? <u>Yes</u>

Lady Dedlock. To begin with? – <u>Yes.</u>

Chapter XXXVI.

Chesney Wold.

Esther & Charley at Mr Boythorn's.

Interview with her mother

The Ghosts' Walk

Meeting with Ada.

Chapter XXXVII.

Jarndyce and Jarndyce.

Richard's progress – distrust of Mr Jarndyce naturally
engendered by the suit.

Mr Vholes – supp [supports] Emma, Jane, and

Caroline Vholes – supports aged father in the Vale of Taunton

Driving away to Jarndyce & Jarndyce.
Close with that

Chapter XXXVIII.

A Struggle.

Dancing apprentices. – remind Caddy of "the Sweeps"

Mr Guppy's mother's

"You wouldn't object to admit that, Miss, perhaps?"
Mr Guppy's contention with his legal and illegal angels.

"Friend and legal adviser," said Mr. Skimpole.

if you want common sense, responsibility, and respectability . . . Vholes is the man."]   When he is introduced in his chambers in chapter 39, Vholes is described as 'a very respectable man . . . he is a very respectable man. He is allowed . . . to be a most respectable man' (an allusion to *Julius Caesar* 3.2). His preoccupation with duty, perseverance, financial independence and social ambition (he chiefly desires to leave his daughters ' "some little independence, as well as a good name" ') satirize the preoccupation with respectability which flourished in the mid-nineteenth century and which was widely criticized. For example, Carlyle remarked:

> 'Of all blinds that shut-up men's vision,' says one, 'the worst is Self.' How true! How doubly true, if Self, assuming her cunningest, yet miserablest disguise, come on us, in never-ceasing, all-obscuring reflexes from the innumerable Selves of others; not as Pride, not even as real Hunger, but only as Vanity, and the shadow of an imaginary Hunger for Applause; under the name of what we call 'Respectability'! . . . our England . . . in these days is become the chosen land of Respectability.
>
> (*The Diamond Necklace*, 1837, 1)

The lawyer's name derives from the parasitic water-rat and field-mouse which destroys crops. Used figuratively, 'voling' means to make a clean sweep of the board at cards (Crompton, 1958, 300).

His further consideration of the point

a sallow man with pinched lips . . . a red eruption here and there upon his face, tall and thin]   Sallowness, emaciation and skin eruptions are the symptoms of jaundice, as is Vholes's complaint of impaired digestion (see note to chapter 1, p. 32).

"Indeed?" said Mr. Vholes. "I have the privilege

an aged father in the Vale of Taunton – his native place]   Vholes is concerned to establish his qualifications for respectability: Murray's *Handbook for Travellers in . . . Somersetshire* (1856) describes Taunton as

> an airy, handsome place, seated on the Tone, from which it derives its name, and in a rich and picturesque country, – its famous vale of Taunton Dean being bounded by the wild ranges of the Quantock and Blackdown hills. It is a town of considerable antiquity . . . "The Vale of Taunton," says old Fuller, "is so fruitful, to use their own phrase, with the *zun* and *zoil* alone, that it needs no manuring." (168–70)

We understood from what followed

when the night-travellers were gone.]   At this point in the proofs, Dickens deleted a passage of dialogue in which Richard says: ' "it's very ridiculous, but since it must come out, – there's nothing kept here; there was nothing to be got, but a mourning-coach that happens to be waiting to be taken back; and I am going to drive Mr. Vholes over in that" '. To accord with the deletion, Dickens emended 'ordered the coach' in the next paragraph to 'ordered a gig'.

Richard's high spirits carrying everything

the gaunt pale horse]   The horse of the Apocalypse which emerges when the fourth seal is opened in Revelation 6.8: 'And I looked, and behold a pale horse: and his name that sat on him was Death, and Hell followed with him.'

I look along the road before me

the dead sea of the Chancery suit, and all the ashey fruit it casts ashore] An allusion to the apples of Sodom or Dead Sea fruit. The trees on the shores of the Dead Sea were said to bear lovely fruit, but the apples were filled with ashes (probably the galls produced by insects).

Chapter 38

A STRUGGLE.

"I assure you, my dear," returned Caddy

the Sweeps]   The Chimney Sweepers Regulation Act of 1834 prohibited master-sweeps with no steady clients from sending out their apprentices to solicit business by 'crying the streets'. In 'The Streets – Morning' (*SB*) Dickens described the consequence of the legislation in the account of a little sweep 'who, having knocked and rung till his arm aches, and being interdicted by a merciful legislature from endangering his lungs by calling out, sits patiently down on the door-step, until the housemaid may happen to awake'. By tradition, chimney-sweeps were associated with dancing in springtime. The first of May, the beginning of the slack season of their work, was called the chimney-sweepers' holiday: costumed in tinsel and bright colours, the boys danced in the street and collected coins from the spectators (Phillips, 1963, 28, 40; see also Sydney Smith, 'Climbing Boys', *Edinburgh Review*, 32, 1819, 309–20).

The apprentices were the queerest little people.

cramp-bones] The knee-caps of sheep were believed to be a charm against cramp and were also rolled and tossed in children's games.

"Married woman, I believe?"

within the city of London, but extra-parochial] That is, not included in any parish and exempt from liability to parish obligations.

Chapter 39

Thirteenth monthly number
March 1853

ATTORNEY AND CLIENT.

'The Pilgrim's Progress' is the title which Dickens inserted but then deleted in the corrected proofs of this chapter (*Norton*).

The name of Mr. Vholes

Symond's Inn] One of the Inns of Chancery, in Chancery Lane, it was a series of private tenements let to solicitors and law students. In 1827, when he was 15 and had just left school, Dickens worked for a few weeks for a solicitor who had offices at 6 Symond's Inn, Charles Molloy. The Inn was demolished in 1873.

a little, pale, wall-eyed, woe-begone inn] 'Little, pale' was added in MS. MS additions in eight further places in the paragraphs introducing Mr Vholes intensify his morbid appearance, his dingy surroundings and the immoral quality of his 'respectability'.

a large dust-binn of two compartments and a sifter] Across the top of the bin was a grille or grid for sifting cinders.

Quartered in this dingy hatchment commemorative of Symond, are the legal bearings of Mr. Vholes.] The Inn was probably named after Thomas Simonds, Gent., who was buried in St Dunstan's-in-the-West in June 1621. The wordplay derives from heraldry: a 'quarter' is one of the four divisions of a shield; a 'bearing', a figure on the shield; a 'hatchment', the square panel displaying the coat of arms of a man recently deceased which is hung for a time at the front of his house (and later in church) as a sign of his death. Such a panel adorns the townhouse of Sir Pitt Crawley in chapter 7 of *Vanity Fair* (1847–8).

Mr. Vholes is a very respectable man.

Mr. Vholes is a very respectable man . . . he is a very respectable man. He is allowed . . . to be a most respectable man.]   The allusion is to Mark Antony's reiteration of 'Brutus is an honourable man' in *Julius Caesar* 3.2. For the character of Vholes as a satire on the cult of respectability, see note to chapter 37, p. 228.

making hay of the grass which is flesh]   A conflation of the proverb expressive of opportunism, 'to make hay while the sun shines', and the recurrent biblical association of man with grass, as in the Burial Service (Isaiah 40.6) and 1 Peter 1.24: 'For all flesh is as grass, and all the glory of man as the flower of grass. The grass withereth, and the flower thereof falleth away.'

But, not perceiving this quite plainly

Diligent, persevering, steady, acute in business.]   Compare Romans 12.11: 'Not slothful in business; fervent in spirit; serving the Lord'; and Proverbs 22.29: 'Seest thou a man diligent in his business?' (*Norton*).

blue minutes]   Different colours of paper are used in Parliament for different stages of legislation, as in 'Green Paper', 'White Paper'.

So in familiar conversation

shirt-makers or governesses]   Tailoring, millinery and tutoring were occupations which distressed ladies, forced by circumstances to seek employment, could take up with propriety.

minor cannibal chiefs]   Dickens may have had in mind here the three African chiefs with whom the Niger expedition commissioners made treaties before the expedition itself failed. He mentioned the chiefs and the treaties, some of which concerned 'the abolition of human sacrifices', in his *Examiner* article, 'The Niger Expedition' (see note to chapter 4, p. 55).

The Chancellor is, within these ten minutes

looks the portrait of Young Despair.]   The wealth of Hogarthian emblematic detail in the published version of Browne's illustration of this scene, 'Attorney and Client, Fortitude and Impatience', was not included in the draft illustration (Pierpont Morgan Library). Among the emblems which were added later (most are suggested by the text) are a sheet of law-stationer's 'Foolscap,' a book showing a design for a maze, a time-table, a cat watching a mouse-hole, a bellows, a carving on the mantelpiece of the fable of the fox and the grapes, spiders' webs, fishing-rods and a net, and a pestle and mortar – an allusion to Proverbs 27:22: 'Though thou shouldest bray a fool in a mortar among wheat with a pestle, yet will not his foolishness depart from him.' (I am indebted to K. J. Fielding for this information; see also Cohen, 1980, 108, and Steig, 1978, 143–6.)

Krook's cat.   <u>Yes.</u>

The Smallweeds, in connexion with the house in the Court.

<u>Yes</u>

Sir Leicester Dedlock? – And the cousins?   <u>Yes</u>

Lady Dedlock?   <u>Yes</u>

Finds that Mr. Tulkinghorn has discovered her secret?   <u>Yes.</u>

Their interview at night, at Chesney Wold?   <u>Yes</u>

Wind up with Esther's Narrative?

No – Frenchwoman.   <u>Lay</u>
<u>that ground.</u>

Chapter XXXIX.

Attorney and Client.

Vholes – Symond's Inn

The respectability of the Vholes Legion.   Make man-eating unlawful, and you starve the Vholeses.

Richard's decline – Carry on.

Guppy and Tony – Court – Smallweeds in possession.

Carry on to next.

Chapter XL.

National and Domestic.

Coodle and Doodle. No Govt. without Coodle or Doodle. Only two men in the country.

Volumnia.   Debilitated cousin.   Country house

Electioneering.   Sir Leicester – 658 gentlemen in a bad way.

Carry through Rouncewell and Rosa, to Tulkinghorn's story. So to next.

Chapter XLI.

In Mr Tulkinghorn's Room.

Tulkinghorn's room at night. Lady Dedlock comes to him there.

Begin grim shadow on him

Chapter XLII.

In Mr Tulkinghorn's Chambers.

Lincolns Inn Fields – Tulkinghorn coming back at dusk – London bird.

Begin with Snagsby, and work up to – Frenchwoman.

"A good deal is doing, sir.

We have put our shoulders to the wheel . . . and the wheel is going round."
"Yes, with Ixion on it.]   Vholes alludes to Aesop's fable of the man who lay on his back and cried for help when his cart was stalled. A friend advised him to whip his horses and put his shoulder to the wheel. Richard conflates the fable with the Greek myth of Ixion, who was punished by having his hands and feet chained to a fiery wheel which rolled perpetually in the air (according to the older version), or in the underworld. Carlyle associates Ixion's wheel with Chancery in *Past and Present* 4.3.

"I ought to imitate you, in fact

beating the Devil's Tattoo]   Mr George gives way to this kind of nervous tapping during his interview with Grandfather Smallweed in chapter 26.

Mr. Vholes, after glancing at the official cat

an unclean spirit . . . that will neither come out nor speak out]   A recurrent scriptural expression, for example, Luke 4.36: 'And they were all amazed . . . for with authority and power he commandeth the unclean spirits, and they come out.' It is part of the service for the public baptism of infants in the Book of Common Prayer.

"What are you to do, sir

This desk is your rock, sir!"]   Compare Matthew 7.24–5:

> I will liken him unto a wise man, which built his house upon a rock: And the rain descended, and the floods came, and the winds blew, and beat upon that house; and it fell not: for it was founded upon a rock. (Noted by *Norton*)

"Yes, sir," says Mr. Vholes

ashes were falling on ashes, and dust on dust]   From the Burial Service: 'we therefore commit his body to the ground: earth to earth, ashes to ashes, dust to dust'.

"Mr. C," returns Vholes, "I wish

making arrangements for moving heaven and earth]   An allusion to the boast of Archimedes about the lever: 'Give me a firm spot on which to stand, and I will move the earth.'

Lastly, the client, shaking hands

an earthy cottage situated in a damp garden at Kennington.]   In the eighteenth century Kennington and its common comprised a pleasant country village near Lambeth, but by 1852 the common had become 'but a name for a small grassless square, surrounded with houses, and poisoned by the stench of vitriol works, and by black, open, sluggish ditches' (*Picturesque Sketches in London*, quoted in Thornbury and Walford 6.338). In June 1852 an Act of Parliament converted Kennington Common into a public pleasure-ground, and the dismal waste of twenty acres was prettily laid out with walks and flower-beds. This scheme for civic beautification might have suggested to Dickens the idea of locating Vholes's cottage in Kennington as a reflection of his aspirations to respectability.

Yet the time is so short

his heart is heavy with corroding care]   The cliché derives from Horace, *Odes* 2.2.18: 'Curas edaces dissipat Evivus' ('The god of wine dissolves heart-eating care'); it occurs in Pope's translation of the *Odyssey* 8.163: 'Steal from corroding care one transient day.'

Is Richard a monster in all this

Recording Angel]   The angel who keeps a record of the activities of all persons for production on the Day of Judgement.

"Ah!" says Mr. Guppy

as high as the Monument]   The fluted Doric column 202 feet high was designed by Wren to commemorate the Great Fire of London in 1666.

Never, since it has been a court

the sixpenny history (with highly-coloured folding frontispiece) of Mr. Daniel Dancer and his sister, and also of Mr. Elwes, of Suffolk . . . those authentic narratives]   The miser Daniel Dancer (1716–94) lived in seclusion with his sister, who predeceased him. When he died, he left almost £250,000. John Elwes (1714–89) inherited his miserliness from his mother and paternal grandfather: his mother inherited £100,000 but died of starvation, and his uncle left an estate of £250,000, but never spent more than £110 a year. Elwes inherited his uncle's estate, became an MP in 1772 and was considered a kind man. He left property worth £500,000. Dancer and Elwes became famous through the publication of cheap, crudely printed and sensational accounts of their lives. In *OMF*, for example, the 'life of Mr Elwes' is Mr Boffin's 'favourite subject' (3.6).

"patter" allusions . . . "gags"]   In 'patter', a large number of words are fitted to a few notes and sung rapidly; 'gags' are remarks not occurring in the script but interpolated by the actor.

the revived Caledonian melody of "We're a' nodding," points the senti-

ment that **"the dogs love broo"**]   'We're a' noddin' is one of the two traditional Scots pieces adapted by Robert Burns in his song 'Gudeen to you kimmer'; when the drunken kimmer (gossip) is asked if all her five children are her husband's, she replies:

> Are they a' Johny's?
> Eh! atweel no:
> Twa o' them were gotten
> When Johny was awa.

> *Chorus:* We're a' noddin, nid nid noddin,
>   We're a' noddin at our house at hame,
> We're a' noddin, nid nid noddin,
>   We're a' noddin at our house at hame.

> Cats like milk
>   And dogs like broo;
> Lads like lasses weel,
>   And lasses lads too.
>   We're a' noddin etc.

He addresses this to the astounded Tony

who admits the soft impeachment.]   The admission of Mrs Malaprop in Sheridan's *The Rivals* 5.3: 'Sir Lucius O'Trigger – ungrateful as you are – I own the soft impeachment – pardon my blushes, I am Delia.'

Chapter 40

NATIONAL AND DOMESTIC.

The title alludes to the descriptive headlines given in newspapers to the different categories of news.

England has been

England has been in a dreadful state for some weeks . . . Lord Coodle would go out, Sir Thomas Doodle wouldn't come in . . . there has been no Government.]   For the satiric implications of 'Coodle' and 'Doodle', see note to chapter 12, p. 124. The allusion is to the ministerial crisis of 1851 caused by two changes of government. In February, Lord John Russell and his Whig ministry resigned on account of a no-confidence vote brought about by Russell's losing a dispute with his foreign secretary, Lord Palmerston. A minority Conservative government was formed under the Earl of Derby with Disraeli as Chancellor of the Exchequer. Palmerston was asked to join them but refused. The cabinet that emerged was an unconvincing group which came to be known as the ' "Who? Who" ministry' because in the Lords the elderly and deaf Duke of Wellington would repeat insistently 'Who? Who?' as Lord Derby attempted to tell him the names of the new ministers (Blake, 1966, 313, 322). The cabinet resigned the following December after the defeat of Disraeli's new budget. In January 1853, Lord Aberdeen united the Whigs and Peelites to form a coalition government which the opposition accused of 'factious combination' (Irving, 1869, 237–9). The reconciliation between Coodle and Doodle seems to be an allusion to the Aberdeen ministry.

if both pistols had taken effect]   Duelling was a topical subject in the 1840s. It had been widely discouraged since the turn of the century and had long been a felony: a duellist who killed his adversary would be tried for murder and hanged if found guilty. Duelling was already in decline when the Anti-Duelling Association was formed in 1843 to denounce it and press for its abolition. In 1844 duelling among army officers was prohibited, and during the next few years it became virtually defunct on account of the pressure of public opinion and the ridicule of the press.

having no pilot (as was well observed by Sir Leicester Dedlock) to weather the storm]   In this allusion to 'The Pilot that Weathered the Storm' (1802), the poem by George Canning in praise of William Pitt, Dickens may have had in mind *Latter-Day Pamphlets* numbers 3 and 4 ('Downing Street' and 'The New Downing Street', 1850), in which Carlyle repeatedly borrows Canning's image to describe his ideal reforming statesman. The first stanza of the poem runs:

> If hush'd the loud whirlwind that ruffled the deep,
>   The sky, if no longer dark tempests deform;
> When our perils are past, shall our gratitude sleep?
>   No! – Here's to the pilot that weather'd the storm!

Doodle has found that he must throw himself

the London season]   May, June and July constitute the 'season', the months when the fashionable world assembles in London.

Hence Mrs. Rouncewell, housekeeper

taking Time by the forelock]   The proverb is: 'Take Time by the forelock, for he is bald behind.'

Through some of the fiery windows

casting the shadow of that virgin event before her]   An echo of Thomas Campbell, 'Lochiel's Warning':

237

-Lochiel, Lochiel! beware of the day;
For, dark and despairing, my sight I may seal,
But man cannot cover what God would reveal;
'Tis the sunset of life gives me mystical lore,
And coming events cast their shadows before.

This groom is the pilot-fish

mysterious men with no names]   Election agents.

an auriferous and malty shower]   Periphrasis for the expression denoting bribery which was used by Doodle, 'sovereigns and beer'. For the contemporary scandal about electoral corruption, see note to chapter 6, p. 65.

My lady takes no great pains

basilisk balls]   The basilisk is a fabulous reptile whose hissing drives away all other serpents and whose breath and looks are fatal. 'Basilisk' was substituted in proof for 'state'.

refrigerator]   A cooler; in *LD*, Lord Lancaster Stiltstalking is described as a 'noble Refrigerator' who 'had iced several European courts in his time' (1.26).

The mighty business is nearly over

a bright particular star]   *All's Well That Ends Well* 1.1.79–80: ''Twere all one/That I should love a bright particular star/And think to wed it' (noted by Page).

In fact, as to this question of opposition

Two other little seats]   Even after the Reform Act of 1832 many seats remained uncontested on account of patronage.

Sir Leicester feels it incumbent on him

the ordinary supplication in behalf of the High Court of Parliament]   In the Book of Common Prayer, 'A Prayer for the High Court of Parliament, to be read during their Session' is one of the Prayers and Thanksgivings upon several occasions, to be used during the Litany or Morning and Evening Prayer when Parliament is sitting.

six hundred and fifty-eight gentlemen]   The number of Members of Parliament.

A languid cousin with a moustache

a moustache] For whiskers as a recently introduced fashion, see note to chapter 20, p. 163.

man told him ya'as'dy . . . 'twould be highly jawlly thing] The drawl and slang affected by aristocrats was mocked by G. A. Sala in his *HW* article, 'Slang': 'Young Lord Fitzurse speaks of himself and of his aristocratic companions as "fellows" (very often pronounced "faywows") . . . a vehicle which is not a drag (or dwag) is a "trap" . . . ' (8.76).

Volumnia is charmed to hear

knowing all sorts of things and never telling them! . . . he must be a Freemason.] Jests and satires about the secrecy and ritualism of Freemasonry date from the eighteenth century, the period when the recorded history of Freemasonry in England begins. (Records of lodges in Scotland date from the sixteenth century.) By 1844 there were 723 lodges established in England, and they included prominent noblemen and members of the royal family. In July 1847 a scathing attack on Freemasonry appeared in the *Christian Remembrancer* (14, no. 57, 1–38) in the form of a review by Dr Armstrong (afterwards Bishop of Grahamstown) of five works on Freemasonry published between 1840 and 1846. Armstrong criticized the symbols and secret rites ('the members attend in their symbolical aprons, and, after certain ceremonies, partly childish and partly profane, march off in a tawdry procession'), the vague aim of 'universal benevolence' ('The sympathy of your universal philanthropists is gloriously obscure . . . impracticable, and cheap'), the charity which began and ended at home ('The body helps itself; the members pay and the members receive'), and the anti-Christian doctrines of Freemasonry. All these opinions can be assumed to have been shared by Dickens, who criticized the rituals of Roman Catholicism and the ineffectiveness of Exeter Hall philanthrophy on the same grounds.

"A rat," says my Lady.

"A rat"] Compare Hamlet's remark on slaying Polonius (3.4.23–4): 'How now! a rat?/Dead, for a ducat, dead!' (Leavis, 1970, 222).

Sir Leicester is majestically wroth.

sort of thing that's sure tapn slongs votes – giv'n – Mob.] The cousin's complaint is that the extension of the franchise after 1832 has enabled the supporters of the manufacturing interests to defeat the landowners. One of the arguments against the 1832 Reform Act was that it would make the conduct of government impossible, for Members of Parliament would be so much under the influence of their constituents as to be no longer susceptible to the pressure of their governmental patrons. The extension of the franchise was a topical subject in 1852. In February the prime minister, Lord John Russell, brought before the

House a Bill intended to emend the provisions of the 1832 Reform Act by lowering the thresholds on the amount of annual rent paid by householders and lease-holders, the amount of rent being the qualification for a right to vote. The Bill gained a first reading but was coldly received and was afterwards withdrawn on the defeat of the ministry later that month.

Chapter 41

IN MR. TULKINGHORN'S ROOM.

The title was substituted in proof for 'More to Follow'.

There is a capacious writing-table

the old man's sight for print or writing being defective at night]   Roger Chillingworth, the character in *The Scarlet Letter* on whom Tulkinghorn is partly modelled, also has defective vision. The present chapter shows several aspects of Tulkinghorn's relationship with Lady Dedlock which parallel the relationship between Chillingworth and Hester Prynne. For example, both men admire the women they humiliate, both demand that their victims keep secret their past sins until such time as the men choose, both display a demeanour of formal composure towards the women, and both are repeatedly associated with images of mortality, burial, secrecy and concealment. Moreover, Lady Dedlock's query, ' "I am to remain on this gaudy platform, on which my miserable deception has been so long acted, and it is to fall beneath me when you give the signal?" ' recalls the 'pedestal of infamy' on which Hester and her child are publicly exposed at the beginning of *The Scarlet Letter* (see note to chapter 2, p. 41 and Stokes, 1969, 177, 180–1, 183, 184).

The time was once

The time was once, when men as knowing as Mr. Tulkinghorn would walk on turret-tops in the star-light, and look up into the sky to read their fortunes there.]   A reminiscence of the opening scene of *Hamlet*, in which the soldiers standing watch on the guard-platform of the castle describe the night sky and the appearance of the ghost, likening what they see to the omens which presaged the death of Julius Caesar:

> This bodes some strange eruption to our state . . .
> In the most high and palmy state of Rome,
> A little ere the mightiest Julius fell . . .
> As, stars with trains of fire, and dews of blood,

Disasters in the sun; and the moist star
Upon whose influence Neptune's empire stands
Was sick almost to doomsday with eclipse;
And even the like precurse of fear'd events,
As harbingers preceding still the fates
And prologue to the omen coming on,
Have heaven and earth together demonstrated
Unto our climatures and countrymen. (1.1.69, 113–25)

The same wan day peeps in

Up comes the bright sun, drawing everything up with it . . . the latent vapour in the earth, the drooping leaves and flowers, the birds and beasts and creeping things . . . into the lightsome air.] . A reminiscence of Genesis 1 and 2 which includes a type of chronographia (the rising sun is likened to the awakening of persons and natural objects).

Chapter 42

IN MR. TULKINGHORN'S CHAMBERS.

From the verdant undulations

From the verdant undulations and the spreading oaks . . . Mr. Tulkinghorn transfers himself to the stale heat and dust of London.] This is a reversal of the theme familiar in Roman and English poetry, the joy of leaving the city for the country; here, the allusion is to the classic example, Horace, *Odes* 3.29 (compare especially line 12): 'fumum et opes strepitumque Romae' ('the smoke, the riches, and the din of wealthy Rome'). The idea is extended in the inverted pastoralism of the second paragraph of the chapter.

"Just so sir," returns Mr. Snagsby

Employer . . . a foreign mode of viewing a clerk)] The French for 'clerk', *employé*.

a foreign female . . . formerly connected with a bunch of brooms and a baby, or at the present time with a tamborine and ear-rings.] In the early nineteenth century brooms were hawked in the streets by women chiefly from Flanders and Germany – such as the pedlar described by Louis Hayes, *Reminiscences of Manchester from 1840*: 'a dark-skinned gypsy . . . danced and sang her quaint little songs, whilst her little white wooden broom . . . had always a ready sale' (*Norton*).

Broom-girls were a subject of caricature during the 1820s when Lord Brougham was frequently represented as a Bavarian broom-girl hawking her wares (Patten, 1970, 214–16). The 'tamborine and ear-rings' allude to the Swiss Savoyards and Italians who emigrated to London as itinerant street-musicians throughout the early and middle years of the century.

"So much the poorer you

In this city, there are houses of correction (where the treadmills are, for women)] The City Prison, or Holloway House of Correction for male and female prisoners, was opened in October 1852, shortly before the publication of the present number. A well-ventilated and comfortable prison based on reformatory principles, the whole of its water supply was pumped from a well by the aid of a treadmill. Women were also put to the treadmill at the Female Convict Prison, Brixton, which in 1850 had a reputation for being disorderly, dirty and unhealthy. The treadmill was first employed there in the 1820s, from which time the regime imposed was one of hard labour (Thornbury and Walford 5.376–80, 6.319–20; Timbs 631). For the introduction of treadmills to prisons, see note to chapter 26, p. 192.

Chapter 43   Fourteenth monthly number
                                                                              April 1853

ESTHER'S NARRATIVE.

He lived in a place

a place called the Polygon, in Somers Town]   The Polygon, in Clarendon Square, is a ring of houses with their back gardens and yards facing to the centre of the circle. The houses were built about 1790 for middle-class professional people, but by the mid-1820s The Polygon had become an area of shabby gentility (in 1827, when he was aged 15, Dickens lodged with his parents at number 17). The Polygon also had literary and artistic associations at this time, according to W. H. Wills's 'Forty Years in London', which describes the address in the 1820s:

> When Somer's Town had an aristocracy, its court centre was "The Polygon," in the middle of Clarendon-square . . . In and around it, Art and Literature nestled in cozy coteries . . . I think a royal academician, I know an A.R.A., and a world-famed actor, lived in the Polygon. (*AYR* 13.254)

(I am grateful to Philip Collins for this quotation.)

there were at that time a number of poor Spanish refugees walking about in cloaks, smoking little paper cigars] A group of Spanish exiles who later supported General Torrijos in his abortive attempt to overthrow the Spanish government settled in Somers Town in the 1820s. Dickens would have seen them for himself when he lived at The Polygon, but the reference here seems inspired by Carlyle's description of them in his *Life of John Sterling* (1851):

> Daily . . . you could see a group of fifty or a hundred stately tragic figures, in proud threadbare cloaks . . . Old steel-gray heads, many of them; the shaggy, thick, blue-black hair of others struck you; their brown complexion, dusky look of suppressed fire, in general their tragic condition as of caged Numidian lions. (1.9; noted by House, 1941, 32)

We went up-stairs to the first floor,

furnished with an odd kind of shabby luxury] Carlyle described Leigh Hunt's house in Cheyne Row to his brother following his first visit there in May 1834:

> His House here excels all you have ever read of; a "poetical Tinkerdom" without parallel even in Literature. In his family-room, where are a sickly large Wife and a whole shoal of well-conditioned wild children, you will find half a dozen old rickety chairs gathered from half a dozen different hucksters, and all seemingly engaged, and just pausing, in a violent *hornpipe*; on these, and around them, and over the dusty table and ragged carpet, lie all kinds of litter; books, papers, egg-shells, pil[lows?] and, last night when I was there, the *torn heart* of a half quartern loaf! His own room above stairs, into which alone I strive to enter, he keeps cleaner. (*Collected Letters of Thomas and Jane Welsh Carlyle*, 27 June, 7.225; see also his letter to Jane, 17 May, 7.152–3)

hothouse nectarines . . . grapes . . . sponge-cakes . . . wine] The 'wealthy luxurious individuals who did not hesitate to pamper themselves with hothouse grapes at twenty-five shillings a pound' are mentioned in 'Covent Garden Market', *HW* 7.511.

Mr. Skimpole himself reclined upon the sofa, in a dressing gown] Thornton Hunt wrote of his father: 'Those who knew him best will picture him to themselves clothed in a dressing-gown, and bending his head over a book or over the desk' (*Autobiography*, revised edn, 1860, vi). Carlyle refers to the dressing-gown several times in his letters. The gown was mentioned in a literary attack on Hunt published in the *Morning Post* in 1853 (see Fogle, 1952, 11).

"And not being the richer

trusting in a rotten reed] Isaiah 36.6: 'Lo, thou trustest in the staff of this broken reed, on Egypt; whereon if a man lean, it will go into his hand, and pierce it.'

Mr and Mrs Chadband? <u>No</u>

Allan Woodcourt? <u>Yes</u>. Return

Skimpole? – family? <u>Yes.</u>

Boythorn. – <u>about</u> <u>him,</u> <u>but</u> <u>not</u> <u>himself</u>

Mr Jarndyce. <u>Yes</u> – <u>And</u> <u>his</u> <u>love</u> <u>for</u> <u>Esther</u> <u>to</u> <u>be</u> <u>now</u>
<u>brought</u> <u>out</u>

George – and Bagnets? No. <u>Next</u> <u>No.</u>

Chapter XLIII.

Esther's Narrative.

Skimpole family at home – borders of Somers Town. Polygon

Beauty Daughter, Sentiment daughter, Comedy daughter

Angry baker – such an absurd figure.

Sir Leicester calls <at> on Mr Jarndyce
<Esther tells> "Guardian, Lady Dedlock is my mother

(through Skimpole
Boythorn and Miss
Barbary.

Chapter XLIV.

The Letter and the Answer.

Send Charley "for the letter."

"I have brought the answer guardian"

Chapter XLV.

In trust

Esther to – Plymouth – no – Deal – Ada's letter

Allan Woodcourt comes back

Glad to be thought of, like the dead

Chapter XLVI.

Stop him!

Tom all alone's – Night and morning.

Allan – Jenny – Jo –

Jo tells that he was taken away
by Mr Bucket – Allan takes him

Hearing that his examination

Mrs. Skimpole, who had once been a beauty, but was now a delicate high-nosed invalid, suffering under a complication of disorders.] Carlyle described Marianne Hunt to Jane after his first visit to the Hunt household: 'The Frau Hunt lay drowsing on cushions "sick, sick" with thousand temporary ailments' (*Collected Letters*, 17 May 1834, 7.152). Mrs Hunt had indeed been attractive in youth but became a chronic invalid and an alcoholic, mismanaging the housekeeping and borrowing household items from her neighbours and money from her husband's friends behind his back (Blunden, 1930, 258, 327).

"This," said Mr. Skimpole

my Beauty daughter, Arethusa] The MS reading, 'Juliet – a remembrance of Shakespeare', was revised in proof, doubtless because of the likeness to Julia, the real name of one of Hunt's daughters (*Norton*). In Greek legend, Arethusa was the nymph transformed into a fountain when she fled from Alpheus, the river-god who loved her; but, flowing under the sea, Alpheus became united with the fountain. Dickens may have chosen the name as a compliment to his friend, the society hostess Mrs Thomas Milner Gibson, *née* Susanna Arethusa Cullum, whom he addressed as Mrs Gibson but referred to as Arethusa (see *Letters* 4.106 n., 5.176, 546).

my Sentiment daughter, Laura] The MS refers to her as '– a remembrance of Petrarch'. For the sentimental associations of this name, see note to chapter 13, p. 129 (Mrs Badger is called Laura).

my Comedy daughter, Kitty] The MS reading, 'Susannah – a remembrance of Beaumarchais', was revised in proof; the real name of this particular daughter of Hunt was Jacintha (*Norton*). The revised name alludes to the eighteenth-century comic actress Kitty Clive (1711–85), of whom Dr Johnson remarked to Boswell: 'Clive, Sir, is a good thing to sit by; she always understands what you say. In the sprightliness of humour I have never seen her equalled' (*Life of Johnson*, entry for 1780).

"My dears, it is true," said Mr. Skimpole

like the dogs in the hymn, 'it is our nature to.'] From Isaac Watts's 'Against Quarrelling and Fighting', song 16 in *Divine Songs for Children* (1715):

> Let dogs delight to bark and bite,
> For God hath made them so;
> Let bears and lions growl and fight,
> For 'tis their nature to. (st. 1)

246

"In fact, that is our family department," said Mr. Skimpole

her marrying another child, and having two more, was all wrong in point of political economy]   The problem of an increasing population was one of the concerns of the Political Economy Club, the group of philosophic radicals founded in 1821 on doctrines formulated largely by David Ricardo (1772–1823) and expounded by James Mill, McCulloch and Bentham. Ricardo's disciples became more orthodox than Ricardo himself and in the next generation established political economy as the adversary of the working man. In regard to the implications of population growth, they disagreed among themselves. The Ricardians, or optimists, believed that an increase in numbers is necessarily accompanied not merely by a positive but by a relative increase in productive power. This was disputed by the pessimistic conclusions of Thomas Malthus (1766–1834), himself a close friend of Ricardo. Malthus urged that, however abundant the means of subsistence, population must gradually increase and surpass it, and he condemned the existing Poor Law system for encouraging the growth of poverty through the relief it offered to large families. In the second edition of his *Essay on the Principle of Population* (1803), he suggested that the human race could regulate its own numbers by exercising prudence and moral restraint. Failing this, the natural checks on population growth – war, famine, pestilence, vice and misery – would continue to operate. Liberals and conservatives alike attacked his doctrine as inhumane. Dickens expressed his own criticism through the Malthusian Mr Filer in *The Chimes* (First Quarter): ' "Married! Married!! The ignorance of the first principles of political economy on the part of these people; their improvidence; their wickedness . . . " ' (*DNB*; Finer, 1952, 19–22).

We were all assembled shortly

the ruined old Verulam wall]   Verulam, or Verulamium, was the Roman city founded in AD 50 on the site on which St Albans was built. The Roman theatre was discovered in 1847, and parts of the city walls survive in various places. Skimpole might have sketched the fragments of masonry known as St Germain's block, situated near the Roman causeway, but a more picturesque scene would be the massive walls of flint, mortar and tiles in Verulam Woods, considered one of the prettiest spots in the area (*Gossiping Guide to St Albans*, 1891, 24).

Chapter 45

IN TRUST.

Presently came Charley

Flora] The Roman goddess of flowers and gardens.

It appeared to us that Mr. Vholes

Deal, where Richard was then stationed] Barracks were located nearby at Walmer: built in 1795, they accommodated 1,100 infantry and a troop of horse (Murray's *Handbook for Travellers in Kent and Sussex*, 1863, 221). The work plans show Plymouth to have been Dickens's first choice.

Mr. Vholes, whose black dye

black dye . . . so deep . . . that it had quite steamed before the fire] Mr Vholes wears black crêpe, a fabric exclusively reserved for mourning. The black dye used for crêpe was not fast, and in the rain or when in contact with perspiration the colour ran easily, staining the skin and ruining other fabrics.

It was a night's journey

It was a night's journey in those coach times; but we had the mail to ourselves] The route from London to Deal in those days lay through Canterbury, Littlebourn, Wingham, Ash and Sandwich; the distance was about seventy-five miles. For the mail-coach system, see note to chapter 7, p. 77.

At last we came into the narrow

the narrow streets of Deal] A dense network of streets runs through the late-seventeenth-century town. Numerous lanes connect the High Street with the shore road, and narrow Middle Street threads along between the two.

But when we got into a warm room

numbers of ships . . . were then lying in the Downs.] Between Deal and the treacherous Goodwin Sands lie the Downs, a shallow stretch of breakwater eight miles long by six miles wide. Except in the severest weather, the Downs provided an excellent anchorage and refuge from the notorious storms which periodically ravaged this part of the coast. Deal had long been an important maritime town: Defoe described it in his *Tour Through the Whole Island of Great Britain* (1724–6):

248

This place is famous for the road for shipping, so well known all over the trading world, by the name of the Downs, and where almost all ships which arrive from foreign parts for London, or go from London to foreign parts, and who pass the Channel, generally stop; the homeward-bound to dispatch letters, send their merchants and owners the good news of their arrival, and set their passengers on shore, and the like; and the outward-bound to receive their last orders, letters, and farewells from owners, and friends, take in fresh provision, &c. (Letter 2)

Indiaman]   A ship engaged in the trade with India, but specifically a ship of large tonnage belonging to the East India Company.

"Esther," he returned, "it is indeed.

those who are put in authority over me (as the catechism goes)]   The catechumen replies that his duty is 'To honour and obey the Queen, and all that are put in authority under her: To submit myself to all my governors, teachers, spiritual pastors and masters'.

"You have been in shipwreck

we can hardly call that a misfortune which enabled you to be so useful and so brave]   Both this passage and Esther's account of how she and Charley went to watch the naval officers disembark are reminiscent of the memorable description in Leigh Hunt's *Autobiography* of the heroism and nobleness characteristic of the boatmen at Deal. Hunt describes how, having set sail for Italy with his family in 1821, their ship encountered a storm as they came into the Downs and took on board a Deal pilot to help them into Ramsgate harbour: 'In we turned, to the admiration of the spectators who had come down to the pier, and to the satisfaction of all on board.' Hunt praises the Deal boatmen as 'a well-known race; reverenced for their matchless intrepidity, and the lives they have saved', and he admires 'the fine manly cast of their countenances' and 'their useful and noble lives' (2.17.238–9).

And in his last look as we drove away

I felt for my old self as the dead may feel if they ever revisit these scenes. I was glad to be tenderly remembered, to be gently pitied, not to be quite forgotten.]   A reminiscence of the encounter between Hamlet and the ghost of his father:

Hamlet.   What may this mean
              That thou, dead corse, again in complete steel
              Revisits thus the glimpses of the moon . . .
                            Alas, poor ghost!
Ghost.   Pity me not . . .
              Adieu, adieu, adieu! Remember me.

Hamlet.   . . . Remember thee!
          Ay, thou poor ghost, whiles memory holds a seat
          In this distracted globe. Remember thee!
                         . . . Now to my word:
          It is 'Adieu, adieu! Remember me'.

                              (1.4.51–3, 1.5.4–5, 91, 95–7, 110–11)

Chapter 46

STOP HIM!

Darkness rests upon

Darkness rests upon Tom-all-Alone's . . . blasted by volcanic fires]   The opening paragraph is a reminiscence of Satan's description in *Paradise Lost* of the dry land to which he and his fellows fly from the burning lake:

> Seest thou yon dreary plain, forlorn and wild,
> The seat of desolation, void of light,
> Save what the glimmering of these livid flames
> Casts pale and dreadful? (1.180–3)

This land is later described as burning with solid fire and as seeming torn from Pelorus or Aetna: it is

> a singèd bottom all involved
> With stench and smoke: such resting found the sole
> Of unblest feet. (236–8)

dungeon lights]   Probably the kind of small iron lamp, called by the Scots a 'crusie', which burnt cheap oil or tallow and was commonly used in prisons (*Norton*). As for the kind of light it cast, *OED* quotes the Scottish poet Robert Fergusson (1750–74), 'Farmer's Ingle': 'The cruizy, too, can only blink and bleer.'

The blackest nightmare in the infernal stables]   The wordplay may have been inspired by Charles Lamb, 'Witches, and Other Night-Fears' (1821): 'I confess an occasional night-mare; but I do not, as in early youth, keep a stud of them' (*Norton*).

Much mighty speech-making

Much mighty speech-making there has been, both in and out of Parliament . . . determined spirit.]   The ideas in this paragraph reiterate those in 'A Sleep to Startle Us', a *HW* article by Dickens which was published in the month in which *BH* began serialization. Dickens gives a favourable account of his visit to a privately financed ragged school and dormitory in a London slum, but he is angered that the government provides no assistance for such places:

> My Lords and Gentlemen, can you, at the present time, consider this at last, and agree to do some little easy thing! Dearly beloved brethren elsewhere, do you know that between Gorham controversies, and Pusey controversies, and Newman controversies, and twenty other edifying controversies, a certain large class of minds in the community is gradually being driven out of all religion? Would it be well, do you think, to come out of the controversies for a little while, and be simply Apostolic thus low down! (4.580)

The influence of Carlyle on Dickens's disbelief in the ability of Parliament to ameliorate social abuses was remarked upon by Forster in 1844, apropos of *The Chimes*:

> I had noticed in him the habit of more gravely regarding many things . . . the hopelessness of any true solution of either political or social problems by the ordinary Downing-street methods had been startlingly impressed on him in Carlyle's writings; and in the parliamentary talk of that day he had come to have . . . little faith for the putting down of any serious evil. (2.120–1)

An immense amount of legislation to improve the sanitary conditions in towns and cities, particularly among the poor, began to be enacted from the early 1840s. The guiding force behind the movement for sanitary reform was Edwin Chadwick, whose investigations of fever dens in working-class districts during the previous decade led him to recognize the relationship between epidemic disease and environmental factors (see note to chapter 22, p. 182). The publication of his monumental *Report on the Sanitary Condition of the Labouring Population of Great Britain* (1842) provoked the establishment of royal commissions and private associations and the enactment of major pieces of legislation:

1843–5   Royal Commission on the Sanitary State of Large Towns

1844   Metropolitan Health of Towns Association. (Established to diffuse information about the physical and moral evils resulting from defective sewerage, inadequate supplies of water, air and light, and poorly constructed dwellings. By 1846 branches of the Association had been founded in most major cities.)

1844   Royal Commission on the Sanitary State of Large Towns and Populous Districts

1846   Nuisance Removals Act. (Concerned unwholesome houses, accumulations of filth, foul drains and cesspools.)

1846   Public Baths and Wash-houses Act. (These amenities to be provided by the local authorities.)

1847   Towns Improvement Clauses Act and Towns Police Clauses Act. (Defend the rights of towns to lay water-supplies and main drains and to control nuisances.)

1847	**Water Works Clauses Act**	
	Commissioners Clauses Act } (Helped to expedite private Acts.)	
	Cemeteries Clauses Act	

1848 **Public Health Act.** (Established a General Board of Health and empowered local authorities to establish local boards to manage sewers and drains, wells, water-supplies, gasworks, refuse and sewer systems, and slaughter-houses; to regulate offensive trades, remove nuisances, control cellar dwellings and houses unfit for human habitation; and to provide burial-grounds, parks and public baths.)

1850 **Metropolitan Interments Act.** (Vested the management of burial-grounds in a General Board of Health which was empowered to discontinue interment in certain burial-grounds; to prohibit burials within 200 yards of dwellings; to appoint chaplains and regulate fees associated with burials; and to provide, enlarge, enclose and lay out new grounds.)

Throughout the 1850s, sanitary reform remained a major national issue as smaller, related pieces of legislation were enacted and as interested groups and the periodical press helped to disseminate information among the public (see Winslow, 1944; Frazer, 1950; Finer, 1952; Wohl, 1983).

Whether he shall be put into the main road by constables, or by beadles, or by bell-ringing]   Constables and beadles could instruct vagrants to 'move on' into the jurisdiction of the next parish in order to prevent them from burdening the present parish by receiving poor relief. For the rivalry between policemen and beadles which was generated by the Police Act of 1839, see note to chapter 11, p. 108.

force of figures]   An allusion to the leadership of the Benthamites in the movement for sanitary reform. Chadwick, a disciple of Bentham, was supported in his own use of comparative statistics as a weapon of persuasion by William Farr (1807–83), the statistician at the Office of the Registrar-General, and by the Statistical Society of London, which was strongly reformist in its tendencies (Wohl, 1983, 143–4; see also Cullen, 1975, *passim*).

correct principles of taste]   Among the various and often rival factions which became involved in the sanitary reform movement were the arbiters of taste, who concerned themselves with the debate on interment in metropolitan burial-grounds. For example, in *On the Laying Out, Planting, and Managing of Cemeteries, and on the Improvement of Churchyards* (1843), the landscape gardener and horti-cultural writer J. C. Loudon made controversial proposals for establishing temporary cemeteries in fields rented on a twenty-one year lease; the fields would eventually revert to the landlord for cultivation. Loudon also held opinions on a related issue, allying himself with such other aesthetic reformers as A. W. Pugin and J. H. Markland in supporting proposals to ensure that tombstones be Christian and not pagan in form, and that epitaphs be chaste and decorous. During the 1840s and 1850s, wide coverage in the periodical press ensured that these aesthetic debates retained the attention of the public. (See: *Quarterly Review*, 73, 1844, 438–77; *HW*, 6.105–9; Morley, 1971, 52–62.)

Tom goes to perdition head foremost in his old determined spirit.] An allusion to *Aeneid* 6.126: 'Facilis descensus Averni . . .' ('The way down to hell is easy. The gates of black Dis stand open night and day').

But he has his revenge.

Even the winds are his messengers . . . There is not a drop of Tom's corrupted blood but propagates infection and contagion somewhere . . . through every order of society] This passage is informed by both of the opposing theories of disease which influenced the different groups of sanitary reformers. The miasma (or zymotic, or effluvia) theory held that contagion existed as an evil miasma in the atmosphere, lurking dormant in decaying animal and vegetable matter until it spread by a process analogous to fermentation. From the 1840s onwards, this theory gradually lost ground to the discoveries made by bacteriologists and analytical chemists which proved that disease is spread either through contact or by germs which are airborne or waterborne. These discoveries influenced Edwin Chadwick in his opinion, which became the influential and official view, that disease resulted from predisposing causes such as filth, putrescent deposits and dampness. Carlyle alludes to these theories in an exhortation from *Chartism* (1839) which is one of many examples of his use of the metaphor of the diseased body politic (7), and he pursued the ideas in a passage in *Past and Present* (1843) to which these scenes in Tom-all-Alone's are indebted (as is Woodcourt's refusal, in chapter 47, to put Jo into hospital). In the present chapter, the scene with Woodcourt, Jo and the wife of the poor Irish brickmaker derives from Carlyle's description of the poor Irish widow, based on the true account in *Observations on the Management of the Poor in Scotland*, by William Pulteney Alison, MD (Edinburgh, 1840):

> A poor Irish Widow, her husband having died in one of the Lanes of Edinburgh, went forth with her three children, bare of all resource, to solicit help from the Charitable Establishments of that City. At this Charitable Establishment and then at that she was refused; referred from one to the other, helped by none; – till she had exhausted them all; till her strength and heart failed her: she sank down in typhus-fever; died, and infected her Lane with fever, so that 'seventeen other persons' died of fever there in consequence. The humane Physician asks thereupon, as with a heart too full for speaking, Would it not have been *economy* to help this poor Widow? She took typhus-fever, and killed seventeen of you! – Very curious. The forlorn Irish Widow applies to her fellow-creatures, as if saying, "Behold I am sinking, bare of help: ye must help me! I am your sister . . . !" They answer, "No; impossible; thou art no sister of ours." But she proves her sisterhood; her typhus-fever kills *them*: they actually were her brothers, though denying it! (3.2)

The theme of the spread of contagion across cities and social distinctions is alluded to in *DS* (47) and discussed in three *HW* articles which antedate *BH*: 'The Devil's Acre', 'Health by Act of Parliament' and 'The Pen and the Pickaxe' (1.297–

301; 1.460–3; 3.193–6). Dickens used the image of contagion as spreading, 'when the wind is Easterly', from Gin Lane into Mayfair in his speech at the first-anniversary banquet of the Metropolitan Sanitary Association on 10 May 1851 (*Speeches* 128).

Verily, what with tainting, plundering, and spoiling, Tom has his revenge.] A conflation of Matthew 6.16, 'Verily, I say unto you, They have their reward', and Romans 12.19, 'Vengeance is mine; I will repay, saith the Lord' (Gill, 1967, 153).

It is a moot point whether

it might be better for the national glory even that the sun should sometimes set upon the British dominions]   The originator of the phrase alluded to may have been John Wilson ('Christopher North') in his *Blackwood's* series, *Noctes Ambrosianae* (1822–35), 20, May 1825: 'His Majesty's dominions, on which the sun never sets'.

She has been sitting on her bag

the two come up out of Tom-all-Alone's into the broad rays of the sunlight and the purer air.]   This is a recollection of Dante's description of his ascent from hell at the end of the *Inferno* and the beginning of the *Purgatorio*. Dickens would have known the translation by H. F. Cary (1772–1884), the best-known English edition of the time: 'My guide and I did enter, to return/To the fair world' (*Hell* 34); 'O'er the serene aspect of the pure air,/High up as the first circle, to mine eyes/Unwonted joy renew'd' (*Purgatory* 1).

Chapter 47   Fifteenth monthly number
May 1853

JO'S WILL.

A breakfast-stall at a street corner

A breakfast-stall]   Such stalls were to be found in all the great thoroughfares frequented by working people. Mayhew reported that on the top of a spring barrow, or table, or trestle and board

> are placed two or three, and sometimes four, large tin cans, holding upon an average five gallons each. Beneath each of these cans is a small iron fire-pot, perforated like a rush-light shade, and here charcoal is continually burning, so as to keep the coffee or tea . . . hot throughout the early part of the morning . . .

The coffee-stall keepers usually sell coffee and tea, and some of them cocoa . . . They supply bread and butter, or currant cake, in slices – ham sandwiches, water-cresses, and boiled eggs. (1.184)

A breakfast-stall is the subject of Cruikshank's illustration for 'The Streets – Morning' in *SB*.

What is a dainty repast to Jo is then set before him]   An echo of Milton, Sonnet 20, 9–10: 'What neat repast shall feast us, light and choice,/Of Attic taste, with wine.'

But he is so sick and miserable

But he is so sick and miserable, that even hunger has abandoned him.] This scene seems to derive from a passage in 'The Verdict for Drouet', the final *Examiner* article on the Tooting disaster (see note to chapter 10, pp. 99–100):

> Mary Harris, examined by Mr. Clarkson: – I am a nurse at Holborn Union Workhouse, and went to the Royal Free Hospital, Gray's Inn Road. I recollect Andrews coming with the other boys. He was not well. I gave him some milk and bread.
>
> Mr. Clarkson: Did he eat his bread? – Witness: No; he held up his head, and said, 'O, nurse, what a big bit of bread this is!' Baron Platt: It was too much for him, I suppose?
> 'Oh, nurse!' says the poor little fellow, with an eager sense that what he had longed for had come too late; 'what a big bit of bread this is!' Yes, Mr. Baron Platt, it is clear that it was too much for him. His head was lifted up for an instant, but it sank again. He could not but be full of wonder and pleasure that the big bit of bread had come, though he could not eat it.
> (Brice and Fielding, 1968, 243)

Intending to refer his difficulty

Divan]   An oriental council of state.

"That's he," says Allan.

I am unwilling to place him in a hospital, even if I could procure him immediate admission]   Of the 500 charitable institutions in London, a quarter were general medical hospitals, medical charities and dispensaries supported mostly by donations and annual subscriptions. Such hospitals as the Royal Free in Gray's Inn Road afforded free treatment to the destitute sick. What Woodcourt alludes to is the complex selection procedure of in-patients. A *HW* article of 1851, 'Twenty-four Hours in a London Hospital', describes a crowd of poor people waiting for treatment or admission at St Bartholomew's:

255

Mr Tulkinghorn to be shot. (Pointing Roman)

George to be taken by Bucket. Yes.

Jo? Yes. Kill him.

Allan? – and Richard? Not Richard

Mr Guppy? No.

Smallweeds? No.

Lead up to murder through Chesney Wold? No. Through
                                                                  house in town.

Mrs Bucket? No

Snagsbys? Mr. Slightly

Chadbands? Not yet.

(Bleak House. —— No. XV.)

Chapter XLVII.

Jo's Will.

Esther.

"If it could be written wery large as I didn't go to do it" –

Our father

Dead my Lords and gentlemen

Chapter XLVIII.

Closing in.

Gather up Ironmaster and Rosa

Lady Dedlock and Mr Tulkinghorn

If it said now, Don't go home!   High and mighty street.

Shot.   Pointing Roman

Chapter XLIX.

Dutiful Friendship.

The old girl's birthday.

George

Mr Bucket

Making things pleasant

Hundred Pound reward – Sir Leicester –

George taken.

Handcuffs – and hat over his eyes.

During rapid examination of patients in the reception-room, those who require something more than an off-hand physic ticket, or a trifling operation, are kept back to be prescribed for by the surgeon or apothecary; the worst cases of all receiving letters, and being sent to another apartment, called the admission-room, in which they undergo another and more deliberate examination, after which the worst of all are admitted to the wards . . . The number of vacant beds being reported, the medical officers begin the task of inspection. One after another the names of the patients most in need are written on the petitions. This done, the names of the applicants, to whom beds have been allotted, are read aloud . . .

As the patients thus file off, a balance of rejected candidates are seen being lifted into cabs, or being led by their friends through the hospital gates. (2.461, 462)

The same objection applies to a workhouse; supposing I had the patience to be evaded and shirked . . . in trying to get him into one]   The Workhouse Test for eligibility, which operated under the Poor Law Amendment Act of 1834, aimed to make public relief so unattractive that most paupers would decline to accept it. Paupers could be admitted only by a written order of the Board of Guardians; or by a provisional order signed by an overseer, churchwarden or relieving officer; or by the master of the workhouse without any such order but only in case of urgent necessity. On admission, the pauper would be placed in a probationary ward until an examination by the medical officer (First Annual Report of the Poor Law Commissioners, cited in Anstruther, 1973, 93).

"I take it for granted, sir," he adds

there is no present infection]   Jo is a carrier of smallpox, but his presenting symptoms suggest that he suffers from terminal pneumonia or from the disease endemic to slums, pulmonary tuberculosis (see note to chapter 31, p. 209).

Mr. Squod tacks out

the beasts that perish]   Psalms 49.12, 20: 'Nevertheless, man being in honour abideth not: he is like the beasts that perish . . . Man that is in honour, and understandeth not, is like the beasts that perish.'

"Now I was thinking, sir," says Mr. George

a council of war at a drum-head]   A large drum was used during military operations as a table or desk for the principal officers.

a bath]   Prior to the passage of the Public Baths and Wash-houses Act of 1846, admission to public baths cost sixpence or more, a prohibitive price for the labouring poor. The Act required local authorities to provide two classes of bath and to charge no more than a penny for a cold bath and two pence for a warm one.

Baths and wash-houses were built in Whitechapel (which had a model establishment) and in St Pancras, Marylebone, St Martin-in-the-Fields and other large parishes (Timbs 33; Wohl, 1983, 72–3).

To Cook's Court, therefore, he repairs.

an Indenture of several skins]   A deed or sealed agreement written on parchment.

"There again!" says Mr. Snagsby

this is a private asylum! . . . this is Bedlam]   Private madhouses flourished because of the lack of county asylums. Licensed by the Commissioners in Lunacy, they were operated on a commercial basis by medical doctors or laymen and offered a variety of accommodation, but because they catered for the gentry they attempted to maintain the atmosphere of a country house or gentleman's residence. Since its founding as a public asylum in the Middle Ages, the Hospital of St Mary of Bethlehem had become the archetype of such institutions. The nineteenth-century hospital situated in Liverpool Street, was rebuilt in 1812–15 (Timbs 42–5).

Dead, your Majesty.

Dead, your Majesty. Dead, my lords and gentlemen . . . dying thus around us every day.]   This paragraph derives from 'A Sleep to Startle Us'; see the passage cited in note to chapter 46, pp. 250–51.

Chapter 48

CLOSING IN.

The place in Lincolnshire

fire-eyed carriages]   A lantern was mounted on either side of the front of carriages.

Where the throng is thickest

inconvenient woman – who *will* getoutofbedandbawthstablishment – Shakspeare.]   An allusion to the sleepwalking of Lady Macbeth:

Gentlewoman.	I have seen her rise from her bed, throw her nightgown upon her, unlock her closet, take forth paper, fold it, write upon't, read it, afterwards seal it, and again return to bed . . .
Doctor.	What is it she does now? Look how she rubs her hands.
Gentlewoman.	It is an accustomed action with her, to seem thus washing her hands. (5.1.4.–26)

The spelling 'Shakspeare', which was common in the first part of the nineteenth century, was promoted by the influential Shakespeare scholar, Edmund Malone (1741–1812).

It is a dull street under the best conditions

It is a dull street]   The Georgian domestic architecture which is characteristic of the West End of London was regarded with disdain by the Victorians: in particular, Tennyson, Dickens, Carlyle and Ruskin considered it an abomination. The qualities they disliked are described by Disraeli in *Tancred* (1847):

> It is Parliament to whom we are indebted for your Gloucester Places, and Baker Streets, and Harley Streets, and Wimpole Streets, and all those flat, dull, spiritless streets, resembling each other like a large family of plain children. (2.10)

extinguishers for obsolete flambeaux gasp at the upstart gas.]

> Few and far between are the link-boys in this present 1852. The running footmen with the flambeaux have vanished these many years; and the only mementos surviving of their existence are the blackened extinguishers attached to the area railings of some old-fashioned houses about Grosvenor Square.
>
> ('Things Departed', *HW* 4.401)

a weak little iron hoop . . . sacred to the memory of departed oil. Nay, even oil itself, yet lingering . . . in a little absurd glass pot]   For the introduction of gas street-lighting to London, see note to chapter 1, p. 27. Oil-lamps, consisting of a small pan of oil with a floating wick inside a glass pot, were suspended from a hoop in the ornamental ironwork above the entrance (*Norton* 575).

high and dry]   In the religious debates of the mid-century, 'high and dry' was used to describe the old-fashioned, rigid members of the Anglican church who were opposed to liberalizing tendencies and to enthusiasm of any sort.

Lady Dedlock dines alone in her own room

Sir Leicester is whipped in to the rescue of the Doodle Party]   He has gone to the House of Commons to take part in a crucial vote. The duty of a party whip (originally 'whipper in', a hunting term) is to secure the attendance of the members of his party when there is an important division.

It is a moonlight night

she is sick at heart]   *Hamlet* 1.1.7: 'For this relief much thanks, 'Tis bitter cold,/And I am sick at heart.'

A very quiet night.

A very quiet night . . . pass more tranquilly away.]   The vista described is from the river above London, through the Pool, down to the Essex and Kent marshes. The paragraph derives from Wordsworth's sonnet, 'Composed Upon Westminster Bridge, Sept. 2, 1802' (compare especially 'shipping', 'towers', 'dome', 'smoky housetops', 'fields'):

> silent, bare,
> Ships, towers, domes, theatres, and temples lie
> Open unto the fields, and to the sky;
> All bright and glittering in the smokeless air . . .
> Ne'er saw I, never felt, a calm so deep!
> The river glideth at his own sweet will:
> Dear God! the very houses seem asleep;
> And all that mighty heart is lying still!

In these fields . . . where the shepherds play on Chancery pipes that have no stop, and keep their sheep]   The 'shepherds' are the street-musicians playing Pan-pipes who accompanied Punch and Judy shows, and the allusion is to the noise-nuisance caused by street-musicians in general (see note to chapter 16, pp. 143–4). The pastoral wordplay (suggested by the rural character of Lincoln's Inn Fields, which was used for grazing prior to the nineteenth century) derives from *Hamlet* 3.2.354: 'You would play upon me; you would seem to know my stops . . . 'Sblood, do you think I am easier to be play'd on than a pipe? Call me what instrument you will, though you can fret me, yet you cannot play upon me.' Chancery Lane is described in similar pastoral terms at the opening of chapter 10.

Has Mr. Tulkinghorn been disturbed?

Has Mr. Tulkinghorn been disturbed?]   The scene of Tulkinghorn lying dead in his chambers may have been suggested by the famous chapter 18 in Hawthorne's *The House of the Seven Gables*, which depicts the wicked, dead Judge Pyncheon sitting upright through the day and night whilst the narrator rehearses the important events he is missing (Stokes, 1985, 55–8; Stamon, 1983, 56–8).

Chapter 49

DUTIFUL FRIENDSHIP.

A great annual occasion

Mr. Joseph Bagnet]   Bagnet's first name is Matthew: 'Joseph' is a MS error which remained uncorrected in the proofs (it recurs in chapter 52).

It is not Mr. Bagnet's birthday.

the bank-books of their remembrance]   An echo of Hamlet's 'the table of my memory' (1.5.98).

It is not the birthday

substituting for number three, the question And how do you like that name?]   The actual third question of the Catechism is 'What did your God-fathers and Godmothers then for you?'

On this present birthday

specimens of poultry, which, if there be any truth in adages, were certainly not caught with chaff]   The proverb is 'Old birds are not caught with chaff'.

The old girl has another trial

a confusion of tongues]   At the tower of Babel, the Lord 'did there confound the language of all the earth' (Genesis 11.9).

"I didn't know I looked white," says the trooper

that boy . . . died yesterday afternoon]   The time-sequence between the death of Jo and Tulkinghorn and that of Lady Dedlock spans seven days. Tulking-horn was murdered at 10 p.m. on the day Jo died. George is arrested the next day. Esther's chapters are woven into the scheme in her mention that Jarndyce has gone to visit the dying Jo (chapter 51) and her account of visiting George in prison (chapter 52). Tulkinghorn's funeral takes place on the fourth day (chapter 53), and Bucket exposes Hortense the following day (chapter 54). The events of chapter 55 take place during the night which falls between chapters 53 and 54. Sir Leicester collapses in the afternoon of the day on which Lady Dedlock takes flight, the fifth day (chapter 56). In chapters 57–9, Esther carries on the narrative, describing her journey with Bucket from the night of the fifth day until daybreak on the seventh day, when they discover the body of Lady Dedlock.

"George. Woolwich. Quebec. Malta.

Take a day's march. And you won't find such another.] The proverb, 'You won't find such another in a day's march' (that is, within about fifteen miles).

"Would you believe it, governor," says Mr. Bucket

British Grenadiers] The regimental march of the Grenadier Guards; the words date from the end of the seventeenth century. The chorus runs: 'But of all the world's brave heroes,/There's none that can compare, with a tow, row, row, row, row, to the British Grenadiers.'

Nothing could be more acceptable

receives the harmonious impeachment] A variation on the remark of Sheridan's Mrs Malaprop, cited in note to chapter 39, p. 236.

"Believe me if all those endearing young charms."] The song by Thomas Moore, *Irish Melodies* (1807–35):

> Believe me, if all those endearing young charms,
>   Which I gaze on so fondly to-day,
> Were to change by to-morrow, and fleet in my arms,
>   Like fairy-gifts fading away,
> Thou wouldst still be ador'd, as this moment thou art,
>   Let thy loveliness fade as it will,
> And around the dear ruin each wish of my heart
>   Would entwine itself verdantly still.
> . . . the heart that has truly lov'd never forgets,
>   But as truly loves on to the close,
> As the sun-flower turns on her god, when he sets,
>   The same look which she turn'd when he rose.

It is natural, under these circumstances

a tender eye] *Macbeth* 3.2.47: 'Scarf up the tender eye of pitiful day.'

Chapter 50   Sixteenth monthly number
                                                              June 1853

ESTHER'S NARRATIVE.

"Now, little woman, little woman

Constant dropping will wear away a stone]   The proverb derives from Job
14.19: 'The waters wear the stones.'

"Charming! We must take care

Your necessities are greater than mine."]   The dying words of Sir Philip
Sidney at the battle of Zutphen in 1586: 'Thy necessity is yet greater than mine.'

Chapter 51

ENLIGHTENED.

"I wish, sir," said Mr. Vholes

the labourer is worthy of his hire.]   The proverb derives from Luke 10.7:
'And in the same house remain, eating and drinking such things as they give: for the
labourer is worthy of his hire.'

"Sir," returned Mr. Vholes

it is next door.]   The chapter plan shows Dickens's other ideas for Richard's
address. Carey Street, one of the alternatives, was doubtless considered because it
was tenanted by solicitors and law-stationers. Symond's Inn, the final choice, may
have been chosen not merely for its proximity to Vholes: the *UT* essay, 'Chambers',
discusses the reputation of the legal Inns as places of melancholia, solitude and
suicide. K. J. Fielding has observed that, as well as indicating the care Dickens took
in choosing an exact actual location for the events in his novels, the alternative
addresses here are one of the few instances in the work plans which show a change
of mind, or hesitation. Unlike the work plans for his other novels, which show his
considering alternatives, the plans for *BH* suggest immense assurance and
decision (personal communication).

"A friendly one," he replied

only waiting, as they say ghosts do, to be addressed.]　　It was believed that ghosts could not speak unless addressed first, as Bernardo knows in *Hamlet* 1.1.45: when the ghost of King Hamlet appears, he remarks, 'It would be spoke to'.

"We are doing very well," pursued Richard

We shall rouse up that nest of sleepers]　　The image conflates the proverb, 'to stir up a wasp's nest', with the fable of the Seven Sleepers, as told by Gibbon in his *History of the Decline and Fall of the Roman Empire* (33). Seven noble and Christian youths of Ephesus concealed themselves in a mountain cavern to escape the persecution of the emperor Decius, but they were found out, and the tyrant ordered the entrance to the cave to be blocked up with stone. The youths 'immediately fell into a deep slumber, which was miraculously prolonged, without injuring the powers of life, during a period of one hundred and eighty-seven years'. The stones happening to be removed at the end of that time, the seven sleepers were awakened by the daylight, unaware that almost two centuries had passed, and after they had related their story to the emperor Theodosius, the bishops and the clergy, they peacefully expired. (4.234–6).

Chapter 52

OBSTINACY.

It was a large prison

It was a large prison, with many courts and passages so like one another] This seems a description of Millbank Prison, Westminster, originally named 'The Penitentiary'. Founded on the plans of Bentham's 'Panopticon, or Inspection House', it was begun in 1812 and completed in 1821. The largest prison in London, accommodating 1100 prisoners, Millbank served as the depot for transports waiting to go to other prisons. It was laid out in the form of an octagonal wheel enclosing eighteen acres of ground and various ranges of buildings. The corridors were upwards of three miles long and contained cells which were small, dark and below ground level (Timbs 633; Thornbury and Walford 4.8–9).

I seemed to gain a new comprehension ... of the fondness that solitary prisoners ... have had – as I have read – for a weed, or a stray blade of grass.] Dickens had been profoundly moved by the mental anguish suffered by prisoners in solitary confinement during his visits to American penitentiaries in 1842. He described to Forster his impressions of the Eastern Penitentiary near Philadelphia

Ada and Richard? <u>Yes.</u> Married

Esther and Allan? <u>Yes.</u> Carry on gently.

Lady Dedlock?   d<u>o</u>

Mr George. <u>Yes.</u>

Sir Leicester? Very little. <u>Reserve for next time. Hold him in.</u>

   Boythorn? In connexion with Lady Dedlock?

                              <u>No.</u>

(Bleak House ——— No. XVI.)

Chapter L.

Esther's Narrative.

Caddy Jellyby – Ill

    and a poor little child

      Esther there constantly – Work in Woodcourt

        Observes Ada changing

        "Still the same shadow on my darling"

Chapter LI.

Enlightened.

Allan Woodcourt. Vholes

    Richard living in – Cursitor Street? Carey Street? Dyer's Buildings?
      Symond's Inn

"Not going home, my dear, any more. Richard is my dear husband!

    Esther "Bleak House is thinning fast Little Woman!"

Chapter LII.

Obstinacy.

Mr George in prison

    Object to the breed Sir

      Old girl and Mrs Rouncewell

Chapter LIII.

The Track

          Disconsolate coaches.

Bucket & Sir Leicester – Volumnia & debilitated cousin.

    – Bucket & Mercury.

('a most dreadful, fearful place'), sentiments he elaborated in a chapter of *AN*, 'Philadelphia, and its Solitary Prison':

> I am only the more convinced that there is a depth of terrible endurance in it which none but the sufferers themselves can fathom, and which no man has a right to inflict upon his fellow-creature. I hold this slow and daily tampering with the mysteries of the brain, to be immeasurably worse than any torture of the body.

"I thank you, miss, and gentlemen both

I shall reap pretty much as I have sown.]　　Galatians 6.7: 'Be not deceived; God is not mocked: for whatsoever a man soweth, that shall he also reap.'

The door had been opened

Joseph Bagnet]　　As in chapter 49, 'Joseph' for 'Matthew' as Bagnet's first name is a MS error which remained uncorrected in the proofs.

"Persuade him, sir?" she returned.

an eight-and-forty pounder]　　A size of cannon capable of firing a forty-eight pound shot.

"Why, then, miss," the old girl proceeded

Dover Castle]　　The medieval fortress was erected to protect Dover harbour and a narrow part of the Channel from invasion. Mrs Bagnet would know the castle because a garrison was stationed there.

Chapter 53

THE TRACK.

Mr. Bucket and his

Augurs]　　The religious officials among the Romans whose duty it was to predict events and advise upon the course of public business, in accordance with omens derived from birds.

Time and place cannot bind

Time and place cannot bind Mr. Bucket. Like man in the abstract, he is here

to-day and gone to-morrow] The proverbs are 'Time and tide wait for no man' and 'Man is here today and gone tomorrow'.

A great crowd assembles

A great crowd assembles . . . on the day of the funeral.] The description of Tulkinghorn's funeral procession is partly informed by the recent state funeral of the Duke of Wellington on 19 November 1852. Dickens considered the ceremony indecorous and absurd (see his letters of 3 and 19 November to Miss Coutts) and, in a *HW* article composed on the eve of the funeral itself, he protested against the humbug and commercialism it generated ('Trading in Death', 6.241–5). He had conducted a lifelong personal campaign against the ostentatious funerals which the contemporary concern for 'gentility' necessitated even among the poor, and he used the occasion of Wellington's funeral as the latest example of a social institution in need of reform (see also *HW* 1.241–2).

the amount of inconsolable carriages is immense.] Funeral etiquette allowed that a family could send its carriage to represent it in the funeral procession.

the Heralds' College] The College of Arms in the City: the seat of the official authority in matters of armorial bearings and pedigrees.

Quiet among the undertakers

lattice blinds] The coaches in which mourners travelled usually had the blinds drawn.

He turns the key in the door

(book of fate to many)] Of the three Fates ('Moirae') in Greek mythology, Lachesis is the one who keeps a book in which human destinies are inscribed. In works of art, however, the Fates are usually represented by different attributes, the book being associated with Clotho, the spinning Fate.

Having put the letters

fine old brown East Inder sherry] Casks of wine from Spain and Madeira were sent on voyages to the East Indies and back, often several times, to enhance the flavour and bouquet. A restaurant guide to London mentions 'old Indian Madeira, that has been sent so often to the East, that it has almost become tired of the voyage' (*London at Table*, 1851; 1858 edn, 27–8).

The fair Volumnia, not quite unconscious

cocked-hat notes] Notes folded in on themselves in the form of the cocked-

269

hats made by children. They were sent by ladies in a flirtatious or romantic mood. For instance, Miss Lillerton sends Mr Watkins Tottle 'a little pink note folded like a fancy cocked-hat' (*SB*), and Twemlow receives a highly perfumed cocked-hat and monogram from Mrs Veneering in *OMF* (1.9).

"The ceremony of to-day," continues Sir Leicester

death levels all distinctions]　　The proverb, 'Death is the grand leveller'.

Mr. Bucket sees none now

that charmingly horrible person is a perfect Blue Chamber.]　　'Blue Beard' was one of the fairy-tales collected and published by Charles Perrault (1697) and translated into English by Robert Samber under the title *Tales of Passed Times by Mother Goose* (1729). The merciless tyrant murders six of his seven wives, secreting their bodies in a locked room to which he forbids entrance. The seventh wife is saved by her curiosity and rescued by her brothers – incidents which are alluded to in chapters 56 and 64.

"Are you so much?

Was you ever modelled now?" . . . **a Royal Academy Sculptor, would stand something handsome to make a drawing of your proportions for the marble.]**　　Footmen prided themselves on their fine physiques and particularly on their height and their calves. The sculpture school in the Royal Academy found its models from various sources: it is not recorded if these included footmen, but Guardsmen were popular, as was the first porter of the Academy, John Malin (Hutchison, 1968, 52, 54, 96). In *NN* the footman of Sir Mulberry Hawk has legs which 'although somewhat large for his body, might, as mere abstract legs, have set themselves up for models at the Royal Academy' (27).

"Not to be wondered at!" says Mr. Bucket.

like a fresh lemon on a dinner-table]

> Flowers should invariably be tastefully introduced, as being the most pleasing and agreeable to the eye and senses. Plateaus of fruits complete the ornamental part of the arrangements.
>
> > ('Decoration of the Table', *London at Dinner*, 1851; 1858 edn, 50)

The doors are thrown open

slight mourning]　　A mitigation of the full mourning costume worn for family members and close friends.

This is merely in passing.

murderous groups of statuary]   In Browne's illustration of this scene, 'Shadow', the plaque in front of Lady Dedlock is Bertel Thorwaldsen's popular 'Night', depicting a motherly angel carrying an infant aloft – an emblem which also appears in Browne's illustration for *DS*, 'Florence and Edith on the Staircase' (Steig, 1978, 153). Steig also suggests that the statue at the foot of the stairs represents Abraham and Isaac (102), but the details are so badly drawn and indeterminate (as K. J. Fielding has noticed) that the statue could just as well represent Virginius about to sacrifice his daughter, or Agamemnon about to slay Iphigenia (personal communication).

"You're so well put together

the household troops]   The troops specially employed to guard the monarch: the 1st and 2nd Life Guards, the Royal Horse Guards, and the Grenadier, Coldstream and Scots Guards.

"I was rather in a hurry," returns Mr. Bucket

lives at Chelsea – next door but two to the old original Bun House] 'The old original' (as it was called) Chelsea Bun House stood at the bottom of what is now Pimlico Road until it was taken down in 1839.

Chapter 54   Seventeenth monthly number
                                                    July 1853

SPRINGING A MINE.

Refreshed by sleep,

Mr. Bucket . . . prepares for a field-day.]   The allusion to Inspector Field is a private joke which Dickens made elsewhere, as in his describing as his 'Field-days' his excursions in the company of the metropolitan police (Collins, 1981, 2.326, 329).

"Now, Sir Leicester Dedlock, Baronet," Mr. Bucket

all them ancestors of yours, away to Julius Caesar]   The implied compliment is that Sir Leicester is descended from a line more exalted and more ancient than the Normans. In the first chapter of *CHE* (*HW* 2.409–12), Dickens had recently given a sympathetic account of the contributions to early Britain of the Romans, led by 'their great General', Julius Caesar.

Guppy? <u>Yes.</u>

And Weevle? <u>No.</u>

Smallweeds? Grandfather.

The Chadbands? <u>Yes.</u>

Chapter LIV.

Springing a Mine.

Bucket & Sir Leicester.

So to the Chadbands, Smallweed, Mrs Snagsby

Disclosure of the murder. Madlle Hortense taken.

"My Lodger." All in Bucket's hands

Sir Leicester swoons – compassionate and sorrowful. Not angry.

Chapter LV.

Flight.

Mrs Rouncewell & the old girl.

George and his mother. His brother.

Mrs. Rouncewell & Lady Dedlock. Mr Guppy

"My enemy alive and dead" – Hunted, she flies

Chapter LVI.

Pursuit.

Sir Leicester ill. To him, Mr Bucket. "Save her."

Hurry, in pursuit. Handkerchief. Takes Esther

with him. Hurry, Hurry!

"Sir Leicester Dedlock, the deceased

to reckon up her Ladyship – if you'll excuse my making use of the term we commonly employ]   As explained in one of the *HW* articles on the London detective police:

> So thoroughly well acquainted with these [thieves] are the Detective officers we speak of, that they frequently tell what they have been about by the expression of their eyes and their general manner. This process is aptly termed "reckoning them up."

> ('The Modern Science of Thief-taking', 1.371)

"You don't happen to know

"You don't happen to know why they killed the pig, do you?" . . . "on account of his having so much cheek.]   Presumably this is a pantomime joke, but it has not been found elsewhere.

Mrs. Snagsby is at first prevented

"as well as if a trumpet had spoken it,"]   'The voice of the trumpet' is a scriptural commonplace (Exodus 19.16, Revelation 1.10, 8.13).

"Why, of course, you wanted to get in, " Mr. Bucket

a mag]   A 'magpie', slang for 'halfpenny'.

"The party to be apprehended

nobbiest]   'Nobby' is slang for 'extremely smart' or 'elegant'; Bucket uses the term in the sense of 'most discreet', 'mannerly'.

Mr. Bucket rings, goes to the door

a French woman enters. Mademoiselle Hortense.]   The revelation in the remainder of this chapter of how Hortense has brought shame to Sir Leicester and dishonour to Lady Dedlock seems indebted to Carlyle's account in *The Diamond Necklace* (1837) of the 'Affaire du Collier', one of the events which discredited Louis and Marie-Antoinette. At the centre of the scandal was the queen's confidante, Jeanne de Lamotte, a so-called countess who had begun life as 'a non-descript of Mantuamaker, Soubrette, Court-beggar, Fine-lady, Abigail, and Scion-of-Royalty' (5). Her appearance and demeanour, particularly her feline qualities, resemble those of Hortense:

> our poor High and Puissant Mantuamaker has realised for herself a 'face not beautiful, yet with a certain piquancy' . . . the liveliest glib-snappish tongue, the liveliest kittenish manner (not yet hardened into *cat*-hood) . . . capricious,

coquettish, and with all the finer sensibilities of the heart; now in the rackets, now in the sullens; vivid in contradictory resolves. (5)

The real Jeanne de Lamotte managed to escape punishment, but her last appearance in Carlyle's story resembles the scene between Hortense and Mr Bucket: Carlyle imagines her in prison, defiant in her humiliation:

> 'Sniff not, Dame de Lamotte; tremble thou foul Circe-Megaera; thy day of desolation is at hand! Behold ye the Sanhedrin of Judges . . . as they winnow all her chaff and down-plumage, and she stands there naked and mean? . . . Hark ye! Shrieks of one cast out . . . Weep, Circe de Lamotte; wail there in truckle-bed, and hysterically gnash thy teeth . . . Here at last thou actest not, but art what thou seemest . . . Thou gallows-carrion!'
>
> ('Chapter Last')

"There is no doubt

I found the wadding of the pistol with which the deceased Mr. Tulkinghorn was shot.]   Dickens may have derived this incident from Mrs Gaskell's *Mary Barton* (1848), chapters 21 and 22, in which Mary's aunt discovers a piece of paper used for gun wadding, and this is identified by Mary as evidence that the murderer of Henry Carson is her father and not the suspected man, Jem Wilson (personal communication from Philip Collins).

it begins to look like Queer Street."]   'Queer Street' here means an uncomfortable and awkward situation; the connotation derives from the strict meaning, as given in a *HW* article, 'Slang': 'To say that a man is without money, or in poverty, some persons remark that he is down on his luck, hard up, stumped up, in Queer Street' (8.75).

"Sir Leicester Dedlock, Baronet," proceeds Mr. Bucket

her Ladyship . . . looking . . . like Venus rising from the ocean]   He indecorously alludes to the most famous representation of the classical myth, Botticelli's 'The Birth of Venus', which depicts the naked goddess emerging from the sea on a shell and being received by one of the Hours or Nymphs, holding a purple cloak. Dickens would have seen the painting at the Uffizi during his visit to Florence in the spring of 1845.

they should go, per bus, a little ways into the country, and take tea at a very decent house of entertainment . . . near that house . . . there's a piece of water.]   Dickens may have had in mind one of his favourite rendezvous in the country, the Star and Garter at Richmond. The house is located on a hill just above the Thames. Omnibuses to Richmond and Hampton Court left from St Paul's churchyard.

275

"Angel and devil by turns, eh?"

Let me put your shawl tidy. I've been lady's maid to a good many before now. Anything wanting to the bonnet?]   This scene was suggested by the conflation of two actual events: the recent hanging of the murderess Maria Manning (see note to chapter 12, p. 119) and the execution of Mary Queen of Scots. A month before the publication of the present number, Dickens's own account of Mary's execution was published in *CHE* (*HW* 7.332–6). He seems to have associated the women not merely because both were executed, but also because they shared the same Christian name and because they were both fastidious about their clothes (as Hortense is shown to be). The remarks Mary is reported to have made on the scaffold are given in this way in *CHE*: 'In the morning she dressed herself in her best clothes . . . When her head and neck were uncovered by the executioners, she said that she had not been used to be undressed by such hands, or before so much company' (336).

"That is droll. Listen yet one time.

You are very spiritual.]   Although the French *spirituel* has the same meaning as its English homonym, Hortense employs it in its other sense, 'witty'.

With these last words

enfolding and pervading her like a cloud . . . as if he were a homely Jupiter, and she the object of his affections.]   Zeus, whom the Romans called Jupiter, changed himself into a cloud in order to seduce Io.

Chapter 55

FLIGHT.

Railroads shall soon

Railroads shall soon traverse all this country . . . but, as yet, such things are non-existent in these parts, though not wholly unexpected. Preparations are afoot]   Railway lines were established in the north-east of England considerably later than in the rest of the country. A line to link London with the north-east had been surveyed through Cambridge and Lincoln as early as 1827, and further surveys were carried out during the 1830s, but in the next decade plans to establish the Great Northern Railway were delayed not only by the opposition of landowners but also by the withdrawal from the scheme of Joseph Locke, the chief engineer. The Great Northern finally opened in 1850, providing the first direct link to the north-east. The line ran from King's Cross (from 1852) via Peterborough, then digressed through Boston and Lincoln before rejoining the main line northwards to York at Retford. By 1850, 5,500 miles of railway lines were operating in Britain and Ireland and a further 6,000 were scheduled to be laid (see 'The Railway Wonders of Last Year', *HW* 1.481–2).

Bridges are begun . . . fragments of embankments are thrown up, and left as precipices with torrents of rusty carts and barrows tumbling over them . . . there are rumours of tunnels]   Because it was considered essential that the railway lines should be as level as possible, bridges, viaducts, cuttings, embankments and tunnels were constructed through all but the flattest country-side. To build an embankment, a train of horse-drawn waggons loaded with earth lined up along a wooden track on top of the embankment under construction. One at a time, each horse was made to approach the slope at a trot and then at a gallop, the driver running alongside. Within a few yards of the edge, the driver freed the horse and swung the animal off the track clear of the waggon, which carried on and hit a balk of timber at the end of the track. The shock of the collision lifted the back of the waggon almost vertical, emptying the load of earth down the slope (Rogers, 1961, 99–104).

The frosty night wears away

the Cape of Good Hope, the Island of Ascension, Hong Kong, or any other military station.]   The British took possession of the Cape of Good Hope in 1814 and established the headquarters of the naval squadron in the South Atlantic. Ascension Island, in the middle of the South Atlantic 1,500 miles west of Africa, was originally occupied by the British to prevent its being used to promote the rescue of Napoleon from St Helena, 700 miles to the south-east. Subsequently, Ascension was taken over by the Admiralty and became an important supply station. For both naval and commercial reasons, Hong Kong was of great strategic importance to the British on account of its harbour and its proximity to mainland China.

"Mother, I have been an undutiful trouble

I cared for nobody, no not I, and that nobody cared for me."]   From Isaac Bickerstaff, *Love in a Village* (1762), 1.5, air no. 8:

> There was a jolly miller once,
>   Liv'd on the river Dee;
> He work'd, and sung, from morn till night,
>   No lark more blyth than he.
> And this the burthen of his song,
>   For ever us'd to be,
> I care for nobody, not I,
>   If no one cares for me.

(cited from 11th edn, 1765)

The air became popular after a performance of the opera at Covent Garden in

1762. It is referred to in *OMF* 2.1: 'Like the Miller of questionable jollity in the song, They cared for Nobody, no not they, and Nobody cared for them.'

"No, I don't say that it was so

I, the vagabond boy]   This sounds like a song, but it has not been identified.

'You have made your bed. Now lie upon it.' "]   A variation of the proverb, 'He that makes his bed ill lies there'.

"Why, mother, perhaps not for good and all

his Rip of a brother]   That is, a worthless, dissolute fellow.

"Nor can I," Mr. Guppy returns

darkened these doors again]   The expression had become a cliché by the nineteenth century. According to *OED* it first appeared in print in 1729; it was used by Tennyson in 'Dora' (1842): 'And never more darken my doors again' (30).

"Your Ladyship will remember

Self-praise is no recommendation]   The proverb is: 'He that praises himself spatters himself.'

"Indeed, it has been made so hard," he goes on

I was gravelled]   'Perplexed', 'puzzled'.

Chapter 56

PURSUIT.

Impassive, as behoves

Death and the Lady fused together]   An allusion to the ballad of 'Leonore' by Gottfried Burger (1747–94), translated and imitated by Sir Walter Scott in 'The Chase and William and Helen' (1796). The story tells of a girl who pines for her lover to return from the wars. He arrives at night and asks her to mount his horse behind him, and he will take her to their marriage-bed. But the end of the journey is an open grave, and the lover is suddenly transformed into a ghastly skeleton. Dickens refers to the ballad frequently, and the version he knew was clearly one of the many illustrated ones.

coachmen in flaxen wigs]   It was customary, as late as the 1860s, for a family coachman to wear flaxen curls or a wig.

hammer-cloths]   The traditional name for the pleated valance of the coach-man's seat on a carriage.

Mercuries, bearing sticks of state, and wearing cocked hats broadwise]
When mounted on coaches, footmen carried long staffs and, if dressed in eighteenth-century style livery, they wore a cocked bicorne or tricorne.

a spectacle for the Angels.]   An echo of the Bible and an allusion to lines in *Measure for Measure* which derive from the scriptural passage:

For I think that God hath set forth us the apostles last, as it were appointed to death: for we are made a spectacle unto the world, and to angels and to men.

(1 Corinthians 4.9)

> But man, proud man,
> Dress'd in a little brief authority,
> Most ignorant of what he's most assur'd,
> His glassy essence, like an angry ape,
> Plays such fantastic tricks before high heaven
> As makes the angels weep; who, with our spleens,
> Would all themselves laugh mortal.

(2.2.117–23)

The sprightly Dedlock is reputed

that grass-grown city of the ancients, Bath]   The contemporary resort, much frequented by the elderly, is conflated with the spa of 'ancient' Roman times. For the decline of Bath as a fashionable resort, see note to chapter 28, p. 200.

"So I thought, according to what

as might be showed for models in a caravan.]   Small waxwork exhibitions featuring models of celebrated personages were transported and displayed in horse-drawn caravans which toured provincial towns in the eighteenth and nineteenth centuries. Madame Tussaud, for example, travelled with her exhibition for many years before establishing it permanently in Baker Street in 1833. Mrs Jarley operates a travelling waxworks in *OCS*, and in *MED* (14) a waxworks visits Cloisterham at Christmas-time.

"A spicy boudoir this," says Mr. Bucket

"A spicy boudoir this," says Mr. Bucket, who feels in a manner furbished up in his French]   Dickens ridiculed the use of 'boudoir' and other French terms characteristic of 'silver-fork' novels in his pastiche of the genre in *NN* (28). 'Spicy' is slang for 'smart-looking'.

"One might suppose I was a moving

Almack's]   These elegant assembly rooms on the south side of King Street, St James's, were built by Robert Mylne for a Scotsman named Almack and opened on 12 February 1765. For a subscription of ten guineas, the fashionable could attend a weekly ball and supper during the Season. The ballroom, a hundred feet in length by forty feet wide, was decorated with gilt columns and pilasters, and classical medallions. Mirrors reflected the illumination of 500 candles in cut-glass lustres. In the nineteenth century the rooms were often called Willis's, from the name of their proprietor, and were let for public meetings, dramatic readings, lectures, concerts, balls and dinners. In 1840 the *Quarterly Review* remarked that Almack's had declined of late, 'a clear proof that the palmy days of exclusiveness are gone by in England' (cited in Timbs 3–4).

a swell in the Guards]   The Life Guards, one of two regiments of cavalry which formed, with the Royal Horse Guards, the household cavalry. Because these regiments took precedence over all other corps, commissions in them were sought after by fashionable young men.

There, he mounts a high tower

There, he mounts a high tower in his mind, and looks out far and wide.] Another allusion to the fairy-tale of 'Blue Beard' (see note to chapter 53, p. 270). Having discovered the secret of her husband's previous wives, the seventh bride calls to her sister to look out for her brothers whom she hopes will rescue her:

> 'Sister Anne' (for that was her name) 'go up I beg you, upon the top of the tower, and look if my brothers are not coming; they promised me that they would come to-day' . . . Her sister Anne went up upon the top of the tower, and the poor afflicted wife cried out from time to time, 'Anne, sister Anne, do you see any one coming?' And sister Anne said, 'I see nothing but the sun, which makes a dust, and the grass, which looks green.'

This episode from 'Blue Beard' is alluded to in *MED* (13).

Where is she? Living or dead

If, as he folds the handkerchief . . . it were able, with an enchanted power] A recollection of the magic handkerchief in *Othello* 3.4:

> That handkerchief
> Did an Egyptian to my mother give.
> She was a charmer, and could almost read
> The thoughts of people; she told her, while she kept it.
>
> (55–8)

the gaunt blind horse]   The horse of the Apocalypse, as alluded to in chapter 37.

Chapter 57   Eighteenth monthly number
                                                              August 1853

ESTHER'S NARRATIVE.

We had not driven very far

Two police officers . . . were quietly writing . . . except for some beating and calling out at distant doors underground, to which nobody paid any attention.]   The imperturbability of the British policeman had become a commonplace: see note to chapter 11, p. 109. The description of the police station here suggested the similar scene in *OMF* 1.3.

He gave me his arm

a phaeton or barouche]   A phaeton was a light four-wheeled open carriage. Browne's illustration, 'The Night', depicts a barouche (see note to chapter 5, p. 64).

a dark lantern]   A hand-lantern, the light of which could be obscured by the use of a movable screen.

I was far from sure

a low-lying, water-side, dense neighbourhood . . . there was a bill, on which I could discern the words, "FOUND DROWNED" . . . and an inscription about Drags]   The area described is Limehouse, which lies between the London Docks and the West India docks; Limehouse is the scene of the dredging activities of Gaffer Hexam in *OMF*. Bucket seems to be making inquiries at one of the numerous 'dead-houses' dotted along the shore on either side of the river. Persons found drowned were brought to these unsavoury depositories to await identification or consignment to a nameless grave (Thornbury and Walford 3.303–5).

I had no need to remind myself

A man yet dank and muddy, in long swollen sodden boots and a hat like them, was called out of a boat]   Dredgers, or 'water-finders', retrieved the bodies of persons found drowned in the Thames. A *HW* article published three months before the present number of the novel described a group of dredgers frequenting a waterside public house:

> knots of damp, silent, deep-drinking men, surrounding whom there is a halo of deep and fearful interest . . . These be the searchers of the river, the finders of

All Esther's Narrative? <u>No.</u>

Pursuit interest sustained throughout

Ending with the churchyard gate, and Lady Dedlock
lying dead upon the step.

Mr Bucket and Esther.

Snagsby's and Guster? <u>Yes.</u>

Mr Boythorn? <u>No.</u>

Allan Woodcourt? <u>Yes.</u>

Explain the change of clothes or leave it? Explain it <u>at the last.</u>

Chapter LVII.

Esther's Narrative.

Journey through the snow.   Beginning with the water-side.
Thaw coming on.   Mr Bucket got Jo away, by bribing Mr
                                                   Skimpole. "No idea of money. But he
     Brickmakers   takes it though."

Inn picture.

       Lady Dedlock has changed clothes with Jenny – to
       avoid being traced – has got her to go on, certain miles –
       has herself returned to London.

Mr Bucket<'s excitement> "I have got it by the Lord!"

Chapter LVIII.

     A Wintry day and night.

Carry on suspense

     Impassive House in Town.

    Bring Sir Leicester and George together. Old youthful
feeling of Chesney Wold.   "Who will tell him"
    Night picture – Volumnia and maid – Volumnia's room. George.
                           Solitary house

Chapter LIX.

Esther's Narrative.

Take up from first chapter

> Mr Bucket
> and Mrs Snagsby

     Allan Woodcourt.

Guster causes delay "Bring her round somehow in the Lord's name!"

     "And it was my mother cold and dead."

horrors, the coroner's purveyors, the beadle's informants, the marine store-keeper's customers. When a man is no longer a man, but a body, and drowned, these seek and find him. The neighbouring brokers' stalls and rag-shops have dead men's boots and dead men's coats exposed for sale. These men are quiet, civil sober men enough, and passing honest – only there never was a drowned man found with any money in his pockets. (7.236)

We appeared to retrace the way

the bridge]   Waterloo Bridge, a favourite haunt of suicides, commemorated by Thomas Hood in 'The Bridge of Sighs' (1844), to which the present paragraph seems indebted: compare Esther's remarks on the 'shadowy female figure', 'the homeless woman' and 'a face, rising out of the dreaded water'; 'the profound black pit of water . . . so deathlike and mysterious'; 'the lights upon the bridge'; 'the light of the carriage-lamps reflected back'. Also compare Esther's discovery of her mother's body at the end of chapter 59 (note, p. 288).

He had gone into every

the turnpike-keepers]   Hundreds of turnpike trusts were established from the first decade of the eighteenth century onwards, when Parliament began to grant a Private Act to bodies of trustees appointed to finance the construction and repair of roads.

"Passed through here on foot

"Passed through here on'foot, this evening, about eight or nine.]   Bucket earlier suggested that Lady Dedlock left the house in town between 3 and 5 p.m. (chapter 56). This means that she would have walked the twenty-three miles to St Albans at the clearly impossible rate of 4–6 miles per hour over roads covered in slush and snow. It has been remarked that Dickens sacrificed probability for the sake of excitement, but the belief that Dickens's chronology of the flight is muddled (Fitzgerald, 1916) derives from Fitzgerald's inaccurate and confused reconstruction of the time-scheme. Dickens's chronology, if not always probable, is at least consistent, and the care he took in working out Lady Dedlock's ruse is indicated in the chapter plan.

the archway toll, over at Highgate]   The archway and the archway road were constructed at the top of Highgate hill following the failure of the original idea of driving a tunnel through the hilltop. A toll was levied up until 1876. The road was the main thoroughfare to the north, and the archway marked the place where town and country met.

"Ah!" said Mr. Bucket.

the country house in the Woodpecker-tapping, that was known by the

smoke which so gracefully curled.]   From the song by Thomas Moore, 'Ballad Stanzas':

> I knew by the smoke, that so gracefully curl'd
>   Above the green elms, that a cottage was near,
> And I said, "If there's peace to be found in the world,
>   "A heart that was humble might hope for it here!" (st. 1)

Whenever you find a young man behind the kitchen door, you give that young man in charge on suspicion of being secreted in a dwelling-house with an unlawful purpose."]   Bucket refers to area and lobby sneaks, or 'area-divers', as described by Mayhew:

> Some are ... so venturesome as to enter dwelling-houses through open windows, and conceal themselves in closets, waiting a favourable opportunity to skulk off, unobserved, with plunder ... If the door is open, they enter the kitchen, and steal anything they can find. (3.290–1).

"Bounds, my dear?" returned Mr. Bucket

Fast and loose]   The figurative meaning derives from the name of a cheating game at least as old as the sixteenth century: playing with a stick and a belt or string, the spectator would think he could make the latter fast by placing a stick through its intricate folds, whereas the operator could detach it at once.

Chapter 58

A WINTRY DAY AND NIGHT.

Still impassive

powdered heads . . . looking out at the untaxed powder]   A tax was levied on hair powder by Pitt, who introduced it in order to help finance the war with France. Hundreds of hairdressers went out of business, and many people chose to abandon the fashion of wearing powder rather than to pay the tax (Mayhew 2.300). By the mid-nineteenth century, of course, the fashion was virtually confined to servants in livery.

Rumour, busy overmuch

Not to know that there is something wrong at the Dedlocks' is to augur yourself unknown.]   A punning echo of *Paradise Lost* 4.830–1: 'Not to know me argues yourselves unknown,/The lowest of your throng' (noted by Gill, 1967, 146).

Sir Leicester's application for a bill of divorce.]   Reform of the procedure for divorce was a topical issue. In 1850 a Royal Commission on Divorce was appointed following a series of unsuccessful efforts which began in the 1830s to alter the traditional law under which divorce was granted only on the grounds of adultery, desertion, continued absence or cruelty. The constitution of marriages in England belonged to the jurisdiction of the ecclesiastical courts and the practice became established of granting complete divorces by private Acts of Parliament. Because three suits were required – ecclesiastical, civil and parliamentary – the proceedings were necessarily expensive, so divorce was consequently only for the rich. The Royal Commission issued its report in 1853, recommending the establishment of a civil court empowered to grant divorce and to hear the matrimonial causes then heard by the ecclesiastical courts. The proposals were adopted in 1854 and the Bill submitted led to the Divorce Act of 1857 (Shanley, 1982, 357–8). Dickens had argued for reform of the traditional law in *HT*, where the working man, Stephen Blackpool, is prohibited from taking divorce proceedings against his dissolute wife because of the costs involved.

At Blaze and Sparkle's

If it had been a speculation, sir, it would have brought money.]   A surge in company flotations, share-holding and speculation began in the 1850s and continued for more than a decade. Thousands of small investors, unfamiliar with the commercial world, invested their capital in companies offering high returns and limited risks. The crash of such companies, many of them dishonest, often brought financial ruin to their shareholders.

Thus rumour thrives in the capital

By half-past five, post meridian, Horse Guards' time]   The clock at the Horse Guards held the same popular reputation for correct time in the West End as St Paul's clock held in the City. Much of its reputation may have been conventional, resulting from the punctuality associated with military manoeuvres. The clock was made in 1756 and improved in 1815–16. At night, the dial facing Whitehall was illuminated by a strong light thrown from a lamp with a reflector placed on the projecting roof in front of the clock-tower (Timbs 378–80).

And not the least amazing

the feeble sisters]   The sister arts: the nine Muses, goddesses of song and poetry.

Sir Leicester lying in his bed

some opiate to lull his pain]   This would have been laudanum, (the alcoholic tincture of opium), the sedative most commonly used for all types of illness (see note to chapter 11, p. 107).

The fair Volumnia

her favourite Life Guardsman . . . who was killed at Waterloo.]
Corporal John Shaw; see note to chapter 24, pp. 188–9.

His old housekeeper is the first

it is not growing late.]   A dialogue was deleted in proof at this point, probably for want of space. The scene resulted from the note in the chapter plan to develop Sir Leicester's deep affection for George. The dialogue closes with the lines:

> "Where is your son George? He is not gone? I want him here. I want only you and him; I would rather have no one else to-night."
> "He hoped he might be of some use, and he is not gone, Sir Leicester."
> "I thank him!"
> "Dear Sir Leicester . . .

Chapter 59

ESTHER'S NARRATIVE.

"It looks like Chancery Lane."

"It looks like Chancery Lane."]   The street was not, in fact, ' "christened so" ', as Bucket replies, but was formerly called New Lane and then Chancellor's Lane.

"Don't you be at all put out

'Believe me, if all those endearing, and cetrer']   Bucket sang this song to the Bagnets in chapter 49 (see note, p. 263).

"What does Mr. Bucket mean?"

Go and see Othello acted. That's the tragedy for you."]   Bucket suggests that Mrs Snagsby will be punished, as Othello is, for her suspicions and jealousy. His analogy seems based upon the same one made by the narrator in *Tom Jones*, in the scene showing Mrs Partridge's unfounded suspicions of her husband's relationship with Jenny Jones.

"And Toughey – him as you call Jo

whole bileing]   The 'whole lot', referring to washing all the clothes together by boiling them in the copper over the fire.

"And yet she was so well spoken," said the girl

I had been a poor child myself, and it was according to parishes. But she said she meant a poor burying-ground not very far from here]   Although the precise location of the burying ground is not specified in the novel, Dickens stated in 1868 that the place he had in mind imaginatively was the one in Drury Lane (see his letter to Miss Palfrey, cited in note to chapter 11, p. 113). However, it has been pointed out that Dickens was legally in error to bury Nemo here, for Hawdon died in the parish of Chichester Rents, in the Rolls parish, which had its burying-ground in Breams Buildings, whereas the Drury Lane burying-ground is half a mile away from Chichester Rents and outside the Rolls parish. Because the cost of burying a pauper was incurred by the rates of the parish in which the pauper died, one parish would consequently refuse to be responsible for paying the burial expenses of a person who had died in another parish (Miller, 1930, 84).

I passed on to the gate

I lifted the heavy head, put the long dank hair aside . . . it was my mother, cold and dead.]   This scene is reminiscent of Thomas Hood's 'The Bridge of Sighs' (see note to chapter 57, p. 284); compare especially:

> Take her up tenderly,
> Lift her with care . . .
>
> Loop up her tresses
> Escaped from the comb,
> Her fair auburn tresses;
> Whilst wonderment guesses
> Where was her home? (5–6, 31–5)

Chapter 60   Nineteenth and twentieth monthly numbers
(Final double number)
September 1853

PERSPECTIVE.

"Ah, Dame Trot, Dame Trot!"

He no more gathers grapes from thorns, or figs from thistles]   Matthew 7.16: 'Ye shall know them by their fruits. Do men gather grapes of thorns, or figs of thistles?'

"Why – yes – perhaps,"returned my guardian

there is a medical attendant for the poor to be appointed at a certain place in Yorkshire.] Yorkshire had a high rate of poverty, but Dickens's choice of locale may also have been influenced by a story by Harriet Martineau which was serialized in *HW* in 1850, *The Sickness and Health of the People of Bleaburn*, a fictionalized account of the work of the American sanitary reformer Mary Pickard Ware to improve the health and housing conditions among the poor in a Yorkshire village (1.193–9, 230–8, 256–61, 283–8).

"Nor to hear, miss,"returned Mr. Vholes.

"A little music does occasionally stray in; but we . . . soon eject it.] For the nuisance caused by street-musicians, see note to chapter 16, pp. 143–4.

"I have not the pleasure

good report and evil report] Philippians 4.8: 'whatsoever things are of good report; if there be any virtue, and if there be any praise, think on these things'.

Chapter 61

A DISCOVERY.

"On the contrary,"said Mr. Skimpole

I am not warped by prejudices, as an Italian baby is by bandages.] In *Rome and Venice . . . in 1866–7* (1869), G. A. Sala describes having seen babies 'swaddled after the fashion of the Roman fasces in their ligatures' ('Rome and the Romans', 351). Dickens would have seen such babies during his visit to Italy in 1844.

as far above suspicion as Caesar's wife."] 'Caesar's wife must be above suspicion' is a traditional saying, based on Plutarch's *Life of Julius Caesar* 10.6.

"Observe the case,

like the house that Jack built.] The familiar cumulative nursery rhyme:

> This is the house that Jack built.
> This is the malt that lay in the house that Jack built.
> This is the rat that ate the malt that lay in the house
>   that Jack built . . .

<u>Richard's death.</u>

Vholes and Conversation Kenge <u>at the end of</u>
<u>the suit.</u>

Grandfather Smallweed and the will?

George and his brother. Betrothal day

Esther and Allan Woodcourt

of instructions
Her father. The letter ∧ George gave Mr Tulkinghorn

Sir Leicester, in connexion with

Boythorn

Mrs Rouncewell

The old girl and   Volumnia

the Bagnet family

Debilitated Cousin

George?

Mr Snagsby. <u>No</u>

Mr Guppy's handsome proposal – His mother. Tony Jobling

Jellybys and Turveydrops – Deportment

Chesney Wold Picture. Sir Leicester and George. <u>Boythorn</u>
obliged to pretend to be still in opposition – Lady Dedlock
in the Mausoleum – without being found very
Charley.   much to disturb the deceased Dedlocks.

Miss Flite and her birds –   Mr Skimpole

(Bleak House. ——— Nos. XIX and XX.)

Chapter LX.

Perspective.

Mrs Woodcourt and Allan. Prepare the way.
Ada and Richard – Prepare the way. Vholes, the evil genius

Ada's secret – "<The> And something else upholds me Esther."
        – "That he may not live to see the child
            who is to do so much

Chapter LXI.

A Discovery

Mr Skimpole. Life afterwards written. "Jarndyce Incarnation of
                selfishness."

Allan Woodcourt's declaration

Chapter LXII.

Another Discovery

Mr Bucket and the will
      Smallweed
Esther and Mr Jarndyce

Chapter LXIII.

Steel and Iron.

George and his brother's family
      His letter to Esther about the paper

Chapter LXIV.

Esther's Narrative

Mistress of Bleak House
  Mr Guppy's magnanimity

Chapter LXV.

Beginning the world.

Richard's death.

Chapter LXVI.

Mr Boythorn –   Down in Lincolnshire

<Chesney Wold> Mausoleum Peace.

Chapter XLVII. [sic]

Wind up. End   The Close of Esther's Narrative.

As it so happened that I

a diary ... with letters and other materials towards his Life; which was published] 'The diary-writing I took from Haydon, not from you,' Dickens told Leigh Hunt, when he tried to deny that Hunt was the model for Skimpole (Forster 3.8). Dickens's contemporary readers would have recognized allusions to Hunt's *Autobiography* (1850) and also (in Skimpole's unkind comment on Jarndyce) to *Lord Byron and Some of His Contemporaries* (1828). During 1821 to 1823, Hunt and his large family were the guests and dependants of Byron in Italy, but the two men were thoroughly uncongenial, their relations broke down, and Hunt vented his anger by publishing a mean and ungrateful attack on his host and benefactor. Subsequently, while insisting everything he had said was true, he regretted his imprudence (see his *Autobiography* 3.1–6).

Chapter 62

ANOTHER DISCOVERY.

I had not the courage

my tears might a little reproach me.] Psalms 69.10: 'When I wept, and chastened my soul with fasting, that was to my reproach.'

A servant came to the door

chair that there Member] This practice is illustrated in Hogarth's painting in the *Election* series, 'Chairing the Member', which shows the triumphal candidate in a parliamentary election about to be toppled from his chair which is being borne through the streets.

"And as you say, Mr. Vholes

when the Cause is in the paper next Term] The 'paper' is the list of causes or cases intended for argument, called 'the paper of causes'.

Chapter 63

STEEL AND IRON.

As he comes into

the iron country farther north . . . a heavy never-lightening cloud of smoke]
Yorkshire, Lancashire and Durham are the industrial counties north of Lincolnshire, but the description here condenses the panorama of a Midlands industrial
scene given in *OCS* (45), a scene based on a tour of the Midlands which Dickens
made in 1838 (see his letter to his wife on 1 November 1838 in *Letters* 1.447).

The trooper thanks his informant

Rouncewell's hands] The use of 'hands' for 'workmen' dates from the seventeenth century, but examples cited in *OED* suggest that the usage became widespread during the Industrial Revolution.

He comes to a gateway

**a great perplexity of iron lying about, in every stage, and in a vast variety of
shapes . . . and a Babel of iron sounds.]**

> The iron wealth of England is a proverb in the most remote corners of the
> world. It produces the enormous amount of three millions of tons annually. We
> export to all parts of the world iron and steel to the yearly value of ten millions
> sterling, and machinery and tools to the extent of two millions; sums that equal
> the revenue of more than one kingdom.
> In travelling through the iron districts of England, it is impossible to avoid
> being struck with the vastness of the works carried on in those places.
>
> ('Important Rubbish', *HW* 11.376)

(Also compare Carlyle's astonished impressions of a Birmingham ironworks in his
letter of 10 August 1824 in *Collected Letters of Thomas and Jane Welsh Carlyle* 3.121.)
Descriptions of industrial towns and manufactories are frequent in the novels of
the period; for example, In Disraeli's *Sybil* (1845) and in Mrs Gaskell's *Mary
Barton* (1848) and *North and South* (1854–5). The description of a mighty iron
foundry in William Sewell's *Hawkstone* (1845) (2.5) is an interesting anticipation
of the present passage.

steam hammer] Invented and patented by James Nasmyth in 1840, the
steam-hammer had wide applications and was an immediate success. In his

293

Industrial Biography (1863), Samuel Smiles devotes nine pages to the steam-hammer, describing it as a 'recognised power in modern mechanics' (288). The machine consisted of an anvil, a block of iron constituting the hammer and an inverted steam-cylinder with a piston-rod to which the hammer was attached. The steam-activated piston raised the hammer, and when steam was allowed to escape the hammer fell upon the work placed on the anvil.

Mr. George is so entirely overcome

waltzing, after the German manner]   That is, with the partners holding each other in a close hold. The waltz was considered indelicate when it was introduced to England from Germany around 1812, but it gradually gained acceptance. Byron satirized it in 'The Waltz: An Apostrophic Hymn' (1813; 1824):

> Oh, Germany! how much to thee we owe . . .
> Who sent us – so be pardon'd all her faults –
> A dozen dukes, some kings, a queen – and Waltz.

Chapter 64

ESTHER'S NARRATIVE.

"Well, guardian," said I

"without thinking myself a Fatima, or you a Blue Beard]   In the fairy-tale 'Blue Beard', the curiosity of Fatima, the seventh wife, leads her to discover the fate of her predecessors. She herself is rescued when her two brothers arrive and kill Blue Beard (see notes to chapters 53 and 56, pp. 270, 280).

"I have some connexion," pursued Mr. Guppy

Walcot Square, Lambeth]   Like Penton Place, Pentonville, Guppy's former address, Lambeth, on the south bank of the Thames between Vauxhall and Southwark, had long been celebrated for its places of public amusement, such as Vauxhall Gardens and Astley's. In the mid-nineteenth century it was a district of indifferent character bisected by the South-Western Railway and densely populated by small tradesmen, boat-yards, timber-wharves, glassworks, potteries, breweries, and chemical, soap and candle works.

"It's a six-roomer

with a sentimental air, "from boyhood's hour?"]   The wordplay alludes to a much parodied passage of Thomas Moore, *Lalla Rookh* (1817):

Oh, ever thus, from childhood's hour,
   I've seen my fondest hopes decay;
I never loved a tree or flower,
   But 'twas the first to fade away.
I never nursed a dear gazelle,
   To glad me with its soft black eye,
But when it came to know me well,
   And love me, it was sure to die!

('The Fire-Worshippers')

Chapter 65

BEGINNING THE WORLD.

"And Patience has sat upon

"And Patience has sat upon it a long time,"]   *Twelfth Night* 2.4.113–14: 'She sat like Patience on a monument,/Smiling at grief.'

"Very well indeed, sir," returned Mr. Kenge

the Woolsack]   A large square cushion of wool without back or arms, like an ottoman, which is the seat of the Lord Chancellor in the House of Lords. On the cover of the monthly parts, the top centre panel shows lawyers tripping over the woolsack as they play Blind Man's Buff (Plate 1).

Chapter 66

DOWN IN LINCOLNSHIRE.

The only great occasions

Then is she kind and cruel]   *Hamlet* 3.4.178: 'I must be cruel only to be kind.'

295

Chapter 67

THE CLOSE OF ESTHER'S NARRATIVE.

The help that my dear counted on

its power was mighty to do it.]   Daniel 8.24: 'And his power shall be mighty, but not by his own power.'

Caddy Jellyby passed her very last

full two miles further westward than Newman Street.]   She now lives in the fashionable West End.

Caddy ... learns ... innumerable deaf and dumb arts, to soften the affliction of her child.]   During his visit to America in 1842, Dickens was deeply affected by the case of Laura Bridgman, a blind, deaf and dumb girl whom he met at the Boston asylum for the blind, and he published a lengthy and touching account of her history in *AN* (3). In 1843 he made a speech in London at a dinner given by the Charitable Society for the Deaf and Dumb (*Speeches* 41–2), and during his stay in Switzerland in 1846 he took an interest in deaf and dumb children at an institution for the blind (*Letters* 4.584–6). His decision to make Caddy's child deaf and dumb may have been influenced by recent and forthcoming contributions to *HW* of Harriet Martineau, who had become deaf in childhood. 'The Deaf Playmate's Story' was one of the tales in 'A Round of Stories by the Christmas Fire' (6, Extra Christmas number, 27–30). She pursued the subject of the proper treatment and training of deaf, dumb, blind and mentally defective children in a series of articles published in the spring of 1854 which Dickens may well have had in hand during the composition of the last number of *BH*: 'Deaf Mutes', 'Idiots Again', 'Three Graces of Christian Science' and 'Blindness' (9.134–8; 197–200; 317–20; 421–5).

A night or two

A night or two ago . . . I was sitting out in the porch . . . "The moon is shining so brightly, Allan, and the night is so delicious, that I have been sitting here] A reminiscence of the scene in the garden at Belmont in the *Merchant of Venice* 5.1:

> *Lorenzo.*   The moon shines bright. In such a night as this,
> When the sweet wind did gently kiss the trees,
> And they did make no noise – in such a night,
> Troilus methinks mounted the Troyan walls,

And sigh'd his soul toward the Grecian tents,
Where Cressid lay that night.

Jessica.   In such a night
Did Thisby fearfully o'ertrip the dew . . .

Lorenzo.   In such a night
Stood Dido with a willow in her hand . . .

Jessica.   In such a night
Medea gathered the enchanted herbs . . .

Lorenzo. How sweet the moonlight sleeps upon this bank!
Here will we sit and let the sounds of music
Creep in our ears; soft stillness and the night
Become the touches of sweet harmony.
Sit, Jessica. (1–14, 54–8)

APPENDIX
ALTERNATIVE TITLES

A transcript of the ten half-sheets containing Dickens's alternative titles for the novel (see p. 13). The titles are transcribed in the order in which they appear in the manuscript. Dickens customarily used short double underlines to indicate a word to be printed in capitals.

Tom-All-Alone's

The Ruined House

Tom-All-Alone's

The Solitary House

<That never knew happiness>

That was always shut up

Bleak House Academy

The East Wind

Tom-All-Alone's

Building
Factory
Mill
The Ruined House

That got into Chancery

and never got out

Tom-All-Alone's

The Solitary House

where the grass grew

Tom-All-Alone's

The Solitary House

That was always shut up
never lighted

Tom-All-Alone's

The Ruined Mill

That got into Chancery

and never got out

Tom-All-Alone's

The Solitary House

Where the Wind howled

Tom-All-Alone's

        House
The Ruined <Mill>

That got into Chancery

And never got out

Tom-All-Alone's

The Ruined House

<In Chancery>

That got into Chancery

And never got out

Bleak House

and the East Wind

How they both got into Chancery

And never got out

Bleak House

299

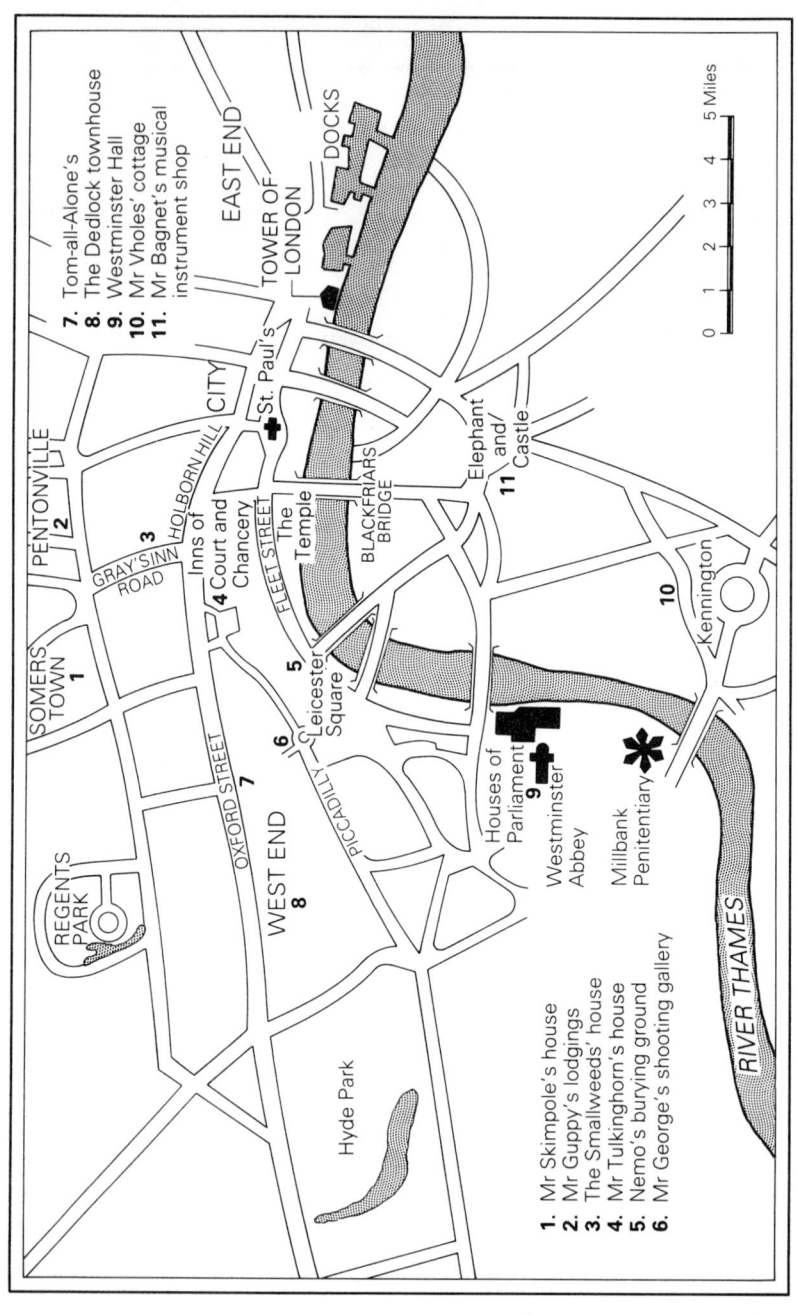

1. Mr Skimpole's house
2. Mr Guppy's lodgings
3. The Smallweeds' house
4. Mr Tulkinghorn's house
5. Nemo's burying ground
6. Mr George's shooting gallery

7. Tom-all-Alone's
8. The Dedlock townhouse
9. Westminster Hall
10. Mr Vholes' cottage
11. Mr Bagnet's musical
    instrument shop

16   A map of the London of *Bleak House*

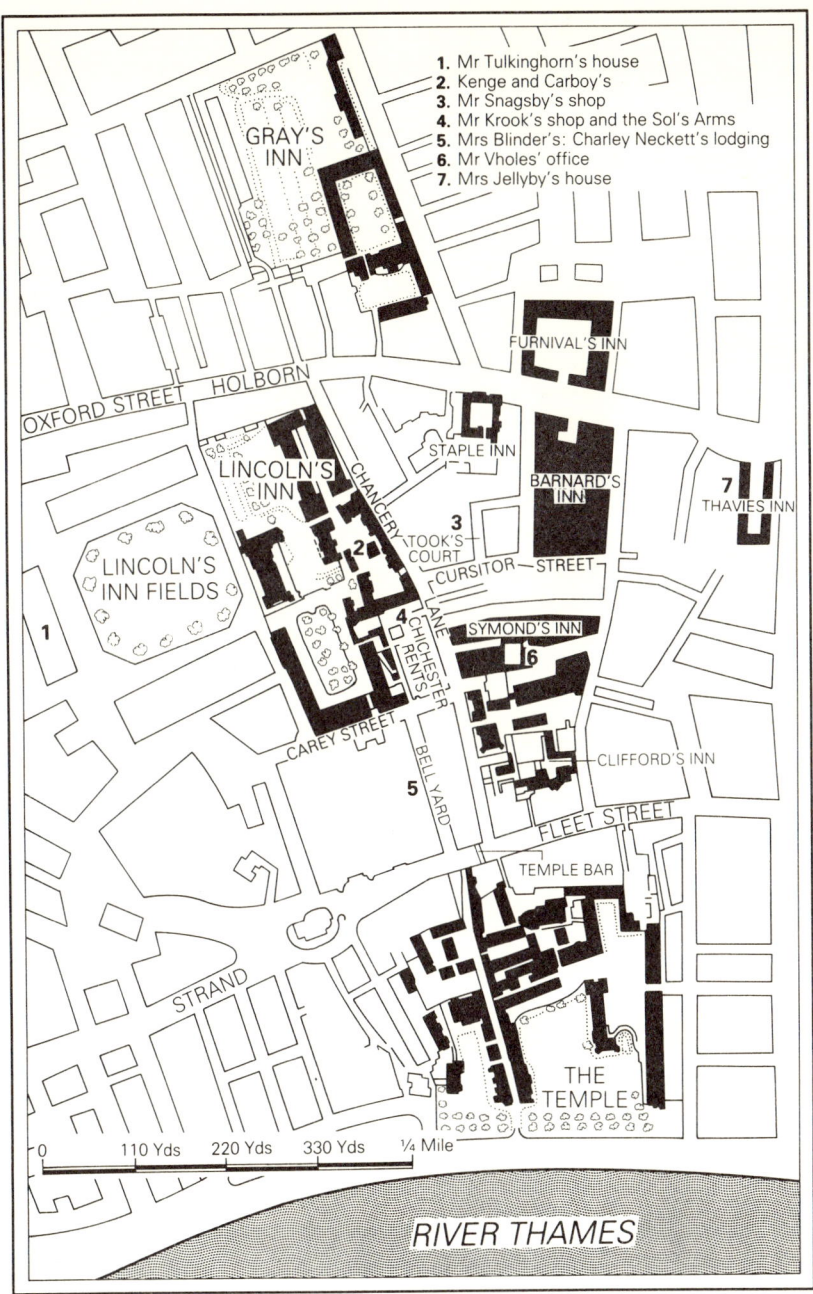

Map labels:

1. Mr Tulkinghorn's house
2. Kenge and Carboy's
3. Mr Snagsby's shop
4. Mr Krook's shop and the Sol's Arms
5. Mrs Blinder's: Charley Neckett's lodging
6. Mr Vholes' office
7. Mrs Jellyby's house

GRAY'S INN

FURNIVAL'S INN

OXFORD STREET   HOLBORN

LINCOLN'S INN

STAPLE INN

BARNARD'S INN

THAVIES INN

LINCOLN'S INN FIELDS

CHANCERY LANE

TOOK'S COURT

CURSITOR STREET

SYMOND'S INN

CHICHESTER RENTS

CAREY STREET

BELL YARD

CLIFFORD'S INN

FLEET STREET

TEMPLE BAR

STRAND

THE TEMPLE

0   110 Yds   220 Yds   330 Yds   ¼ Mile

RIVER THAMES

17   A map of the Inns of Court and Inns of Chancery

SELECT BIBLIOGRAPHY

With the exception of *Household Words* and *All the Year Round*, articles in contemporary periodicals (*Blackwood's, Punch, Quarterly Review*, etc.) are not listed, for complete bibliographical information is given in the text.

(i)   *Works by Dickens*

The Clarendon Dickens (Oxford: Clarendon Press, 1966–) is the edition cited in quotations from:

David Copperfield, ed. Nina Burgess (1981)
Dombey and Son, ed. Alan Horsman (1974)
Little Dorrit, ed. Harvey Peter Sucksmith (1979)
Martin Chuzzlewit, ed. Margaret Cardwell (1982)
The Mystery of Edwin Drood, ed. Margaret Cardwell (1972)
Oliver Twist, ed. Kathleen Tillotson (1966)

The Norton Critical Edition (New York/London: W. W. Norton) is cited in quotations from:

Bleak House, ed. George Ford and Sylvère Monod (1977)
Hard Times, ed. George H. Ford and Sylvère Monod (1966)

The Penguin English Library (Harmondsworth: Penguin Books) is the source of quotations for:

Barnaby Rudge, ed. Gordon Spence (1973)
The Christmas Books, ed. Michael Slater, 2 vols (1971)
Great Expectations, ed. Angus Calder (1965)
Nicholas Nickleby, ed. Michael Slater (1978)
The Old Curiosity Shop, Angus Easson (1972)
The Pickwick Papers, ed. Robert L. Patten (1972)
A Tale of Two Cities, ed. Robert L. Patten (1972)

The Oxford Illustrated Dickens, 21 vols (London: Oxford University Press, 1947–58) is the source of quotations for:

American Notes and *Pictures from Italy*
A Child's History of England (this volume includes *Master Humphrey's Clock*)
The Christmas Stories (this volume includes *A Lazy Tour of Two Idle Apprentices*)
Sketches by Boz (this volume includes *Sketches of Young Gentlemen* and *Sketches of Young Couples*)
The Uncommercial Traveller and Reprinted Pieces (this volume includes *To Be Read at Dusk, Hunted Down, Holiday Romance* and *George Silverman's Explanation*)
Memoirs of Joseph Grimaldi, edited by Dickens, ed. Richard Findlater (London: MacGibbon & Kee, 1968).
Miscellaneous Papers, ed. B. W. Matz, 2 vols (Vols 35 and 36 in the Gadshill Edition) (London: Chapman & Hall, 1897–1908).
Collected Papers, Nonesuch Edition, 2 vols (London: Nonesuch Press, 1938).
The Letters of Charles Dickens, Pilgrim Edition, 5 vols to date (Oxford: Clarendon Press, 1965–). Vols 1 and 2, ed. Madeline House and Graham Storey; Vol. 3, ed. Madeline House, Graham Storey and Kathleen Tillotson; Vol. 4, ed. Kathleen Tillotson; Vol. 5, ed. Graham Storey and K. J. Fielding.

302

The Letters of Charles Dickens, ed. Walter Dexter, Nonesuch Edition, 3 vols (London: Nonesuch Press, 1938).

Letters from Charles Dickens to Angela Burdett-Coutts, 1841–1865, ed. Edgar Johnson (London: Jonathan Cape, 1953).

The Speeches of Charles Dickens, ed. K. J. Fielding (Oxford: Clarendon Press, 1960).

Charles Dickens' Book of Memoranda, ed. Fred Kaplan (New York: New York Public Library, 1981).

(ii)   *Articles in* Household Words

Bell, Robert, 'The Overland Mail Bag', 4 (29 November 1851), 229–34.

Blanchard, Sidney Laman, 'Student Life in Paris', 3 (14 June 1851), 286–8.

Blanchard, Sidney Laman, 'The True Bohemians of Paris', 4 (15 November 1851), 190–2.

Capper, John, 'Important Rubbish', 11 (19 May 1855), 376–9.

Cole, Alfred W., 'The Martyrs of Chancery', 2 (7 December 1850), 250–2; (with W. H. Wills), 2 (15 February 1851), 493–6.

Costello, Dudley, 'The Modern "Officer's" Progress', 1 (22 June 1850), 304–7; 1 (29 June 1850), 317–20; 1 (6 July 1850), 353–6.

Costello, Dudley, 'The Modern Soldier's Progress', 2 (18 January 1851), 391–5; 2 (25 January 1851), 427–31; 2 (1 February 1851), 451–5.

Dickens, Charles, 'A Child's History of England', 2 (25 January 1851), 409–12, and 38 following numbers (not consecutive) concluding with 8 (10 December 1853), 360.

Dickens, Charles, 'A Crisis in the Affairs of Mr. John Bull. As Related by Mrs. Bull to the Children', 2 (23 November 1850), 193–6.

Dickens, Charles, 'A Detective Police Party', 1 (27 July 1850), 409–14; 1 (10 August 1850), 457–60.

Dickens, Charles, 'A Flight', 3 (30 August 1851), 529–33.

Dickens, Charles, 'A Monument of French Folly', 2 (8 March 1851), 553–8.

Dickens, Charles, 'A Preliminary Word', 1 (30 March 1850), 1–2.

Dickens, Charles, 'A Sleep to Startle Us', 4 (13 March 1852), 577–80.

Dickens, Charles, 'A Walk in a Workhouse', 1 (25 May 1850), 204–7.

Dickens, Charles, 'The Amusements of the People', 1 (30 March 1850), 13–15.

Dickens, Charles, 'The Begging-Letter Writer', 1 (18 May 1850), 169–72.

Dickens, Charles, 'Frauds on the Fairies', 8 (1 October 1853), 97–100.

Dickens, Charles, 'From the Raven in the Happy Family', 1 (11 May 1850), 156–8; 1 (8 June 1850), 241–2.

Dickens, Charles, 'The Guild of Literature and Art', 3 (10 May 1851), 145–7.

Dickens, Charles, 'Home for Homeless Women', 7 (23 April 1853), 169–75.

Dickens, Charles, 'The Last Words of the Old Year', 2 (4 January 1851), 337–9.

Dickens, Charles, 'Lying Awake', 6 (30 October 1852), 145–8.

Dickens, Charles, 'The Noble Savage', 7 (11 June 1853), 337–9.

Dickens, Charles, 'On Duty with Inspector Field', 3 (14 June 1851), 265–70.

Dickens, Charles, 'Our Watering Place', 3 (2 August 1851), 433–6.

Dickens, Charles, 'Pet Prisoners', 1 (27 April 1850), 97–103.

Dickens, Charles, 'Red Tape', 2 (15 February 1851), 481–4.

Dickens, Charles, 'Sucking Pigs', 4 (8 November 1851), 145–7.

Dickens, Charles, 'Three "Detective" Anecdotes', 1 (14 September 1850), 577–80.

Dickens, Charles, 'Trading in Death', 6 (27 November 1852), 241–5.

Dickens, Charles, 'Whole Hogs', 3 (23 August 1851), 505–7.

Dickens, Charles, and Chisholm, Caroline, 'A Bundle of Emigrants' Letters', 1 (30 March 1850), 19–24.

Dickens, Charles, and Horne, R. H., 'The Great Exhibition and the Little One', 3 (5 July 1851), 356–60.

Dickens, Charles, and Wills, W. H., 'Spitalfields', 3 (5 April 1851), 25–30.

Dodd, George, 'A Brilliant Display of Fireworks', 8 (10 September 1853), 45–8.

Dodd, George, 'Bouquets', 8 (5 November 1853), 230–3.

Gaskell, Elizabeth, 'Visiting at Cranford', 5 (3 April 1852), 55–64.

Haly, William Taylor, and Wills, W. H., 'The Royal Rotten Row Commission', 1 (15 June 1850), 274–6.

Hannay, James, 'Graves and Epitaphs', 6 (16 October 1852), 105–9.

Hannay, James, 'Lambs to be Fed', 3 (30 August 1850), 544–9.

Hoare, Mrs [W.], 'An Irish Peculiarity', 1 (14 September 1850), 594–6.

Hogarth, George, and Wills, W. H., 'Heathen and Christian Burial', 1 (6 April 1850), 43–8.

Horne, Richard H., 'Ballooning', 4 (25 October 1851), 97–105.

Horne, Richard H., 'The Cattle-Road to Ruin', 1 (29 June 1850), 325–30.

Horne, Richard H., 'The Cow with the Iron Tail', 2 (9 November 1850), 145–51.

Horne, Richard H., 'Father Thames', 2 (1 February 1851), 445–50.

Horne, Richard H., 'The Pen and the Pickaxe', 3 (24 May 1851), 193–6.

Horne, Richard H., 'The True Story of a Coal Fire', chapter 3, 1 (20 April 1850), 90–6.

Hunt, Frederick Knight, 'How to Spend a Summer Holiday', 1 (6 July 1850), 356–8.

Hunt, Frederick Knight, 'The Hunterian Museum', 2 (14 December 1850), 277–82.

Hunt, Frederick Knight, 'Twenty-four Hours in a London Hospital', 2 (8 February 1851), 457–65.

Hunt, Frederick Knight, 'Wings of Wire', 2 (7 December 1850), 241–5.

Hunt, James Henry Leigh, 'Gore House', 7 (20 August 1853), 589–93.

Jerrold, William Blanchard, 'Deadly Lively', 9 (25 March 1854), 138–40.

Jerrold, William Blanchard, 'The Iron Seamstress', 8 (11 February 1853), 575–6.

Jerrold, William Blanchard, and Wills, W. H., 'The Subscription List', 2 (28 September 1850), 10–12.

Knight, Charles, 'The Law', 2 (18 January 1851), 407–8.

Leigh, Percival, 'Address from an Undertaker to the Trade', 1 (22 June 1850), 301–4.

Lewis, John Delaware, 'Chip: A Voice from a "Quiet" Street', 2 (2 November 1850), 143–4.

Lewis, John Delaware, 'City Graves', 2 (14 December 1850), 277.

Mackay, Alexander, 'The Devil's Acre', 1 (22 June 1850), 297–301.

Macpherson, Ossian, 'Chip: The Smithfield Model of the Model Smithfield', 2 (8 March 1851), 572–3.

Martineau, Harriet, 'Blindness', 9 (17 June 1854), 421–5.

Martineau, Harriet, 'Deaf Mutes', 9 (25 March 1854), 134–8.

Martineau, Harriet, 'The Deaf Playmate's Story', 6 (Extra Christmas number, 1852), 27–30.

Martineau, Harriet, 'Idiots Again', 9 (15 April 1854), 197–200.

Martineau, Harriet, 'Malvern Water', 4 (11 October 1851), 67–71.

Martineau, Harriet, 'The Sickness and Health of the People of Bleaburn', 1 (25 May 1850), 193–9; and three following numbers concluding with 1 (15 June 1850), 283–8.

Martineau, Harriet, 'Three Graces of Christian Science', 9 (20 May 1854), 317–20.

Morley, Henry, 'The Horse Guards Rampant', 8 (31 December 1853), 428–31.

Morley, Henry, 'Our Phantom Ship on an Antediluvian Cruise', 3 (16 August 1851), 492–6.

Morley, Henry, 'The Water-Drops. A Fairy Tale', 1 (17 August 1850), 482–9.

Morley, Henry, and Wills, W. H., 'Why Shave?', 7 (13 August 1853), 560–3.

Murray, Grenville, 'The Roving Englishman: His Hints to Travellers', 6 (13 November 1852), 211–14.

Sala, George Augustus, 'The Key of the Street', 3 (6 September 1851), 565–72.

Sala, George Augustus, 'Legal Houses of Call', 7 (14 May 1853), 253–7.

Sala, George Augustus, 'Old Clothes!', 5 (17 April 1852), 93–8.

Sala, George Augustus, 'Powder Dick and His Train', 7 (7 May 1853), 235–40.

Sala, George Augustus, 'Slang', 8 (24 September 1853), 73–8.

Sala, George Augustus, 'Things Departed', 4 (17 January 1852), 397–401.

Sidney, Samuel, 'Chips: Family Colonisation Loan Society', 1 (24 August 1850), 514–15.

Sidney, Samuel, 'A Fashionable Forger', 4 (15 November 1851), 178–82.

Thomas, William Moy, 'Covent Garden Market', 7 (30 July 1853), 505–11.

Thomas, William Moy, 'A Guild Clerk's Tale', 2 (1 February 1851), 437–44.

Thomas, William Moy, 'Market Gardens', 7 (2 July 1853), 409–14.

Thomas, T. M., 'A Suburban Connemara', 2 (8 March 1851), 562–5.

Wills, W. H., 'Chip: From Mr Thomas Bovington', 1 (13 July 1850), 377.

Wills, W. H., 'Chip: Torture in the Way of Business', 1 (14 September 1850), 587–8.

Wills, W. H., 'A Coroner's Inquest', 1 (27 April 1850), 109–13.

Wills, W. H., 'For India Direct', 5 (1 May 1852), 141–5.

Wills, W. H., 'Health by Act of Parliament', 1 (10 August 1850), 460–3.

Wills, W. H., 'The Modern Science of Thief-taking', 1 (13 July 1850), 368–72.

Wills, W. H., 'The Monster Promenade Concerts', 2 (19 October 1850), 95–6.

Wills, W. H., 'The Railway Wonders of Last Year', 1 (17 August 1850), 481–2.

Wills, W. H., 'The Troubled Water Question', 1 (13 April 1850), 49–54.

Wills, W. H., and Morley, Henry, 'Chips: Soldiers' Wives', 3 (6 September 1851), 561–2.

Wills, W. H., and Parry, John Docwra, 'Nice White Veal', 1 (10 August 1850), 467–8.

(iii) *Articles in* All the Year Round

Dickens, Charles, 'Leigh Hunt. A Remonstrance', 2 (24 December 1859), 206–8.

Meason, Malcolm Ronald Laing, 'Accommodation', 13 (8 April 1865), 260–4.

Meason, Malcolm Ronald Laing, 'How I Discounted My Bill', 13 (8 July 1865), 557–61.

Meason, Malcolm Ronald Laing, 'Wanted to Borrow, One Hundred Pounds', 13 (11 March 1865), 164–8.

Wills, W. H., 'Forty Years in London', 13 (8 April 1865), 253–6.

(iv) *Other Material*

Alexander, Doris, 'The poet in Grandfather Smallweed', *Dickensian*, 80 (1984), 66–73.

Alison, Archibald, 'Hints to the aristocracy: a retrospect of forty years, from the 1st January, 1834', *Blackwood's Edinburgh Magazine*, 35 (1834), 68–80.

Allingham, William, *William Allingham, a Diary*, ed. H. Allingham and D. Radford (London: Macmillan, 1907).

Altick, Richard D., *Paintings from Books: Art and Literature in Britain, 1760–1900* (Columbus, Ohio: Ohio State University Press, 1985).

Altick, Richard D., *The Shows of London* (Cambridge, Mass./London: Harvard University Press, 1978).

'Ancient and Modern Freemasonry', *Christian Remembrancer*, 57 (1847), 1–38.

Anson, Peter F., *The Call of the Cloister; Religious Communities and Kindred Bodies in the Anglican Communion* (London: SPCK, 1955).

Anstruther, Ian, *The Scandal of the Andover Workhouse* (London: Geoffrey Bles, 1973).

Ashton, John, *Modern Street Ballads* (1888; reissued New York/London: Benjamin Blom, 1968).

Axton, William, 'Esther's nicknames: a study in relevance', *Dickensian*, 62 (1966), 158–63.

Beckwith, Marc, 'Catabasis in *Bleak House*: Bucket as Sibyl', *Dickens Quarterly*, 1 (1984), 2–6.

Beeton, Isabella, *The Book of Household Management* (London: S. O. Beeton, 1861).

Bernard, Catherine A., 'Dickens and Victorian dream theory', in James Paradis and Thomas Postlewait (eds), *Victorian Science and Victorian Values: Literary Perspectives* (New York: New York Academy of Sciences, 1981).

Berridge, Virginia, 'Victorian opium eating: responses to opiate use in nineteenth-century society', *Society for the Social History of Medicine Bulletin*, 22 (1978), 11–16.

Blunden, Edmund, *Leigh Hunt: A Biography* (London: Cobden-Sanderson, 1930).

Brewer, Luther A., *Leigh Hunt and Charles Dickens: The Skimpole Caricature* (Cedar Rapids, Iowa: privately printed, 1930).

Brice, A. W. C. and Fielding, K. J., 'Dickens and the Tooting disaster', *Victorian Studies*, 12 (1968), 235–9.

Briggs, Katharine M., *A Dictionary of British Folk-Tales in the English Language: Folk Narratives*, 2 vols (London: Routledge & Kegan Paul, 1970).

Brumleigh, T. Kent, 'Notes on *Dombey and Son*', *Dickensian*, 38 (1941–2), 211–17.

Butt, John, '*Bleak House* in the context of 1851', *Nineteenth-Century Fiction*, 10 (1955), 1–21.

Butt, John, '*Bleak House* once more', *Critical Quarterly*, 1 (1959), 302–7.

Butt, John and Tillotson, Kathleen, *Dickens at Work* (1957; reprinted London: Methuen, 1968).

Clubbe, John (ed.), *Selected Poems of Thomas Hood* (Cambridge, Mass.: Harvard University Press, 1970).

Cohen, Jane R., *Charles Dickens and His Original Illustrators* (Columbus, Ohio: Ohio State University Press, 1980).

Collins, Philip, '*Bleak House* and Dickens's *Household Narrative*', *Nineteenth-Century Fiction*, 14 (1960), 345–9.

Collins, Philip, *Dickens and Crime* (London: Macmillan, 1962).

Collins, Philip, *Dickens and Education* (1963; revised edn London: Macmillan, 1964).

Collins, Philip, 'Dickens on the education of girls', *Dickensian*, 57 (1961), 86–96.

Collins, Philip, *Dickens: Interviews and Recollections*, 2 vols (London: Macmillan, 1981).

Collins, Philip, 'Inspector Bucket visits the Princess Puffer', *Dickensian*, 60 (1964), 88–90.

Collins, Philip, review, *Dickensian*, 70 (1974), 135–6.

Collins, Philip, *Tennyson, Poet of Lincolnshire*, an address to the Tennyson Society, 21 May 1983 (Lincoln: Tennyson Society, 1984).

Cook, E. T. and Wedderburn, Alexander (eds), *The Complete Works of John Ruskin*, 37 vols (London: George Allen/New York: Longmans Green, 1903–12).

Cope, Zachary, *The Royal College of Surgeons of England: A History* (London: Anthony Blond, 1959).

Cotsell, Michael, *The Companion to 'Our Mutual Friend'* (London: Allen & Unwin, 1986).

Crompton, Louis, 'Satire and Symbolism in *Bleak House*', *Nineteenth-Century Fiction*, 12 (1958), 284–303.

Crosse, V. Mary, *A Surgeon in the Early Nineteenth Century: The Life and Times of John Green Crosse, 1790–1850* (Edinburgh/London: E. & S. Livingstone, 1968).

Cullen, M. J., *The Statistical Movement in Early Victorian Britain: The Foundations of Empirical Social Research* (Sussex: Harvester Press/New York: Barnes & Noble, 1975).

Cunningham, Peter, *A Handbook for London, Past and Present*, 2 vols (London: John Murray, 1849).

Davies, John D., *Phrenology, Fad and Science: A 19th-Century American Crusade* (New Haven, Conn.: Yale University Press, 1955).

De Vries, Duane (ed.), *Charles Dickens: 'Bleak House'* (New York: Thomas Y. Crowell, 1971).

Denman, Peter, 'Krook's death and Dickens's authorities', *Dickensian*, 82 (1986), 131–41.

Dickens, Charles, the younger, 'Notes on Some Dickens Places and People', *Pall Mall Gazette*, 9 (1896), 342–55.

Dodd, George, *Curiosities of Industry and the Applied Sciences . . . Supplement to the National Cyclopaedia. Part VI. Corn and Bread . . . and A Ship, in the Nineteenth Century* (London: Charles Knight, 1852).

Dodd, George, *Dictionary of Manufactures, Mining, Machinery, and the Industrial Arts* (London: Virtue & Co., n.d. [1869]).

[Dodd, George, (ed.)], *The Land We Live In. A Pictorial and Literary Sketch-Book of the British Empire*, 3 vols (London: Charles Knight, n.d. [1847]).

Duman, Daniel, *The Judicial Bench in England 1727–1875: The Reshaping of a Professional Elite* (London: Royal Historical Society, 1982).

Dunn, Richard J., 'Dickens and Mayhew once more', *Nineteenth-Century Fiction*, 25 (1970), 348–53.

Engel, Monroe, 'The politics of Dickens' novels,' *PMLA*, 71 (1956), 945–74.

Ericksen, Donald H., 'Harold Skimpole: Dickens and the early "art for art's sake" movement', *Journal of English and Germanic Philology*, 72 (1973), 48–59.

Fielding, K. J., 'Leigh Hunt and Skimpole: another remonstrance', *Dickensian*, 64 (1968), 5–9.

Fielding, K. J. and Brice, Alec W., '*Bleak House* and the graveyard', in Robert B. Partlow, Jr (ed.), *Dickens the Craftsman: Strategies of Presentation* (Carbondale/Edwardsville, Ill.: Southern Illinois University Press, 1970).

Fielding, K. J. and Brice, Alec W., 'Charles Dickens on "the exclusion of evidence" ', *Dickensian*, 64 (1968), 131–40 (part 1); 65 (1969), 35–41 (part 2).

Finer, S. E., *The Life and Times of Sir Edwin Chadwick* (London: Methuen, 1952).

Fitzgerald, Percy, *Bozland: Dickens's Places and People* (London: Downey, 1895).

Fitzgerald, Percy, 'A Dickens perplexity', *Dickensian*, 12 (1916), 42–6.

Fogle, Stephen F., 'Skimpole once more', *Nineteenth-Century Fiction*, 7 (1952), 1–18.

Ford, George H., 'The brass bassoon in *Bleak House*', *Dickensian*, 68 (1972), 104.

Ford, George H., 'The titles for *Bleak House*', *Dickensian*, 65 (1969), 84–9.

Ford, John, *Prizefighting: The Age of Regency Boximania* (Newton Abbot: David & Charles, 1971).

Forster, John, *Walter Savage Landor: A Biography*, 2 vols (London: Chapman & Hall, 1869).

Franks, Alan, 'As funny as a crippling case of gout', *The Times*, 24 January 1984, p. 10.

Frazer, W. M., *A History of English Public Health, 1834–1939* (London: Baillière Tindall & Cox, 1950).

Friedman, Stanley, 'The *Bleak House* "East Wind" and Pope's *Rape of the Lock*', *Dickens Quarterly*, 3 (1986), 90–2.

Galignani, A., *Galignani's New Paris Guide* (Paris: A. and W. Galignani, 1842).

Gallagher, Catherine, *The Industrial Reformation of English Fiction, 1832–1867* (Chicago, Ill: University of Chicago Press, 1985).

Gaskell, E., 'More about spontaneous combustion', *Dickensian*, 69 (1973), 25–35.

Georgas, Marilyn, 'Dickens, Defoe, the Devil and the Dedlocks: the "Faust motif" in *Bleak House*', *Dickens Studies Annual*, 10 (1982), 23–44.

Gerson, Stanley, *Sound and Symbol in the Dialogue of the Works of Charles Dickens* (Stockholm: Almquist & Wiksell, 1967).

Gill, Stephen C., 'Allusion in *Bleak House*: a narrative device', *Nineteenth-Century Fiction*, 22 (1967), 145–54.

Gossiping Guide to St Albans (St Albans: Gibbs & Bamforth, 1891).

Gould, Robert Freke, *The History of Freemasonry*, 3 vols (Edinburgh: T. C. & E. C. Jack, n.d. [*c*. 1890]).

Haig, Stirling, 'Frenglish in *A Tale of Two Cities*', *Dickens Studies Newsletter*, 14 (1983), 93–7.

Haight, Gordon S., 'Dickens and Lewes on spontaneous combustion', *Nineteenth-Century Fiction*, 10 (1955), 53–63.

Hall, Samuel Carter, *Retrospect of a Long Life* (London: Bentley, 1883).

Hamer, Douglas, 'Dickens: the old Court of Chancery', *Notes & Queries*, NS, 17 (1970), 341–7.

Harries-Jenkins, Gwyn, *The Army in Victorian Society* (London: Routledge & Kegan Paul/ Toronto and Buffalo: University of Toronto Press, 1977).

Harris, Wendell V., 'Jo at the inquest and the reports of parliamentary commissions', *Dickensian*, 64 (1968), 48–9.

Harrison, Brian, *Drink and the Victorians: The Temperance Question in England, 1815–1872* (London: Faber & Faber, 1971).

Hayes, Henry, letter to the editor, *Dickensian*, 32 (1936), 151.

Heads of the People; or, Portraits of the English, drawn by Kenny Meadows (London: Robert Tyas, 1840); supplemented by a second volume of essays under the same title (London: Robert Tyas, 1841).

Henderson, E. M. A., letter to the editor, *Dickensian*, 20 (1924), 158.

Hern, Anthony, *The Seaside Holiday: The History of the English Seaside Resort* (London: Cresset Press, 1967).

Holdsworth, William S., *Charles Dickens as a Legal Historian* (New Haven, Conn.: Yale University Press, 1928).

[Hotten, John Camden] ('Theodore Taylor'), *Charles Dickens: The Story of His Life*, 2nd edn (London: John Camden Hotten, 1874).

[Hotten, John Camden] ('Theodore Taylor'), *A Dictionary of Modern Slang, Cant, and Vulgar Words . . . by a London Antiquary*, 2nd edn (London: John Camden Hotten, 1860).

[Hotten, John Camden] ('Theodore Taylor'), *A Hand-book to the Topography and Family History of England and Wales* (London: John Camden Hotten, 1863).

[Hotten, John Camden] ('Theodore Taylor'), *Thackeray, the Humourist and the Man of Letters* (London: John Camden Hotten, 1864).

House, Humphry, *The Dickens World* (Oxford: Oxford University Press, 1941).

Howarth, S. F. D., letter to the editor, *Dickensian*, 34 (1937–8), 69–70.

[Hunt, James Henry Leigh], *The Autobiography of Leigh Hunt; with Reminiscences of Friends and Contemporaries*, 3 vols (London: Smith, Elder, 1850).

[Hunt, James Henry Leigh], *The Autobiography of Leigh Hunt. A new edition, revised by the author; with further revisions, and an introduction, by his eldest son* (London: Smith, Elder, 1860).

Hutchison, Sidney C., *The History of the Royal Academy, 1768–1968* (London: Chapman & Hall, 1968).

Irving, Joseph, *Annals of Our Time* (London: Macmillan, 1869).

Jacobson, Wendy S., *The Companion to 'The Mystery of Edwin Drood'* (London: Allen & Unwin, 1986).

Langton, Robert, *The Childhood and Youth of Charles Dickens* (London: Hutchinson, 1891).

Larson, Janet, 'Biblical reading in the later Dickens: the Book of Job according to *Bleak House*', *Dickens Studies Annual*, 13 (1984), 35–83.

Leavis, F. R. and Leavis, Q. D., *Dickens the Novelist* (1970; reprinted Harmondsworth: Penguin, 1980).

308

Lewis, J. R., *The Victorian Bar* (London: Robert Hale, 1982).

Lohrli, Anne (ed.), *Household Words: A Weekly Journal, 1850–1859, Conducted by Charles Dickens. A Table of Contents, List of Contributors and Their Contributions Based on the 'Household Words' Office Book* . . . (Toronto: University of Toronto Press, 1973).

London at Table; or, How, When and Where to Dine and Order a Dinner, and Where to Avoid Dining . . . (1851; reprinted 1858; reprinted as *London at Dinner: Where. to Dine in 1858*, Newton Abbot: David & Charles, 1969).

Low, Sampson, *The Charities of London. Comprehending the Benevolent, Educational, and Religious Institutions. Their Origin and Design, Progress, and Present Position* (London: Sampson Low, 1850).

McLean, Robert Simpson, 'Tory noodles in Sydney Smith and Charles Dickens: an unnoticed parallel', *Victorian Newsletter*, 38 (1970), 24–5.

McMaster, R. D., 'Dickens and the horrific', *Dalhousie Review*, 38 (1958), 18–28.

Matthews, Leslie G., *History of Pharmacy in Britain* (Edinburgh/London: E. & S. Livingstone, 1962).

Maxwell, Constantia, *The English Traveller in France, 1698–1815* (London: George Routledge, 1932).

Maxwell, Richard C., Jr, 'G. M. Reynolds, Dickens and the mysteries of London', *Nineteenth-Century Fiction*, 32 (1977), 188–213.

Mayhew, Henry, *London Labour and the London Poor*, 3 vols and an 'Extra Volume' (London: Griffin, Bohn, 1861–2).

Mayhew, Henry, *The Upper Rhine* (London: George Routledge, 1858).

Melada, Ivan, *The Captain of Industry in English Fiction, 1821–1871* (Albuquerque, N. Mex.: University of New Mexico Press, 1970).

Miller, W., 'Poor Jo's graveyard: where Dickens erred', *Dickensian*, 26 (1930), 84.

Miller, Michael G., 'The *Bleak House* number cover: which way is the wind blowing?', *Dickens Quarterly*, 3 (1986), 93–4.

Mingay, Gordon E. (ed.), *The Victorian Countryside*, 2 vols (London/Boston, Mass.: Routledge & Kegan Paul, 1981).

Moers, Ellen, '*Bleak House*: the agitating women', *Dickensian*, 69 (1973), 13–24.

Moers, Ellen, *The Dandy: Brummell to Beerbohm* (London: Secker & Warburg, 1960).

Monod, Sylvère, 'Some stylistic devices in *A Tale of Two Cities*', in Robert B. Partlow, Jr (ed.), *Dickens the Craftsman* (Carbondale, Ill.: Southern Illinois University Press, 1970).

Morley, John, *Death, Heaven and the Victorians* (London: Studio Vista, 1971).

Murray, John, *A Handbook for Travellers in Constantinople*, new edn, revised (London: John Murray, 1871).

Murray, John, *A Handbook for Travellers in Devon and Cornwall*, 3rd edn, revised (London: John Murray, 1856).

Murray, John, *A Handbook for Travellers in Egypt* [by Sir Gardner Wilkinson] (London: John Murray, 1847).

Murray, John, *A Handbook for Travellers in Kent and Sussex* (London: John Murray, 1863).

Murray, John, *A Handbook for Travellers in Turkey*, 3rd edn, revised and augmented (London: John Murray, 1854).

Murray, John, *A Handbook for Travellers in Wiltshire, Dorsetshire, and Somersetshire* (London: John Murray, 1856).

Murray, John, *Murray's Handbook for Modern London; or, London As It Is* (London: John Murray, 1851).

Newman, Charles, *The Evolution of Medical Education in the Nineteenth Century* (London: Oxford University Press, 1957).

Newsom, Robert, *Dickens on the Romantic Side of Familiar Things: 'Bleak House' and the Novel Tradition* (New York: Cornell University Press, 1977).

Owen, David, *English Philanthropy, 1660–1960* (Cambridge, Mass./London: Harvard University Press, 1975).

Owen, Richard, *Geology and Inhabitants of the Ancient World* (London: Crystal Palace Library/Bradbury & Evans, 1854).

Page, Norman (ed.), *Bleak House* (Harmondsworth: Penguin, 1971).

Page, Norman, *Speech in the English Novel* (London: Longmans, 1973).

Paterson, Daniel, *Paterson's Roads* . . . 18th edn, revised by Edward Mogg (London: J. G. & F. Rivington, Longman *et al.*, 1826; 1829).

Patten, Robert L., 'Portraits of Pott: Lord Brougham and *The Pickwick Papers*', *Dickensian*, 66 (1970), 205–24.

Paul, Howard, *Dinners with Celebrities, Anecdotal, Descriptive, Characteristic* (London: Newton & Eskell, n.d. [dedication dated 1896]).

Perkins, George, 'Death by spontaneous combustion in Marryat, Melville, Dickens, Zola and others', *Dickensian*, 60 (1964), 57–63.

Pope, Norris, *Dickens and Charity* (London: Macmillan, 1978).

Prochaska, F. K., *Women and Philanthropy in Nineteenth-Century England* (Oxford: Clarendon Press, 1980).

Rogers, H. C. B., *Turnpike to Iron Road* (London: Seeley, Service, 1961).

Rogers, Pat, 'The rise and fall of gout', *The Times Literary Supplement*, 20 March 1981, pp. 315–16.

Rolfe, Franklin P., 'More letters to the Watsons', *Dickensian*, 38 (1942), 161–6.

Rumbelow, Donald, *I Spy Blue: The Police and Crime in the City of London from Elizabeth I to Victoria* (London: Macmillan, 1971).

Sala, George Augustus, *Gaslight and Daylight, with Some London Scenes That They Shine Upon* (London: Chapman & Hall, 1859).

Sala, George Augustus, *Rome and Venice, with Other Wanderings in Italy, in 1866–7* (London: Tinsley Bros, 1869).

Sanders, Charles Richard and Fielding, Kenneth J. (eds), *The Collected Letters of Thomas and Jane Welsh Carlyle* (Durham, NC: Duke University Press, 1970). Eleven volumes published to date.

Searle, Mark (ed.), *Turnpikes and Toll-Bars*, 2 vols (London: Hutchinson, 1930).

Ser, Cary D., letter to the editor, *Dickensian*, 65 (1969), 111.

Shanley, Mary Lyndon, ' "One must ride behind": married women's rights and the Divorce Act of 1857', *Victorian Studies*, 25 (1982), 355–76.

Shatto, Susan, 'Byron, Dickens, Tennyson and the monstrous efts', *Yearbook of English Studies*, 6 (1976), 144–55.

Shatto, Susan, 'A commentary on Dickens's *Bleak House*', unpublished dissertation, the Shakespeare Institute, University of Birmingham, 1974.

Shatto, Susan, ' "A complete course, according to question and answer" ', *Dickensian*, 70 (1974) 113–20.

Shatto, Susan, 'New notes on *Bleak House*', *Dickens Studies Newsletter*, 6 (1975), 78–82 (part 1); 108–15 (part 2).

Sheppard, Francis, *London, 1808–1870: The Infernal Wen* (London: Secker & Warburg, 1971).

Shiman, Lilian Lewis, 'The Band of Hope movement: respectable recreation for working-class children', *Victorian Studies*, 17 (1973), 49–74.

Smiles, Samuel, *Industrial Biography: Iron Workers and Tool Makers* (London: John Murray, 1863).

Smith, Grahame, *Charles Dickens: 'Bleak House'* (London: Edward Arnold, 1974).

Stamon, Peggy, 'Dickens' and Hawthorne's "castles in the air": *Bleak House* and *The House of the Seven Gables*', unpublished dissertation, University of California at San Diego, 1983.

Steig, Michael, 'The critic and the illustrated novel: Mr Turveydrop from Gillray to *Bleak House*', *Huntington Library Quarterly*, 36 (1972), 55–67.

Steig, Michael, *Dickens and Phiz* (Bloomington, Ind./London: Indiana University Press, 1978).

Steig, Michael, 'Dickens, Hablot Browne and the tradition of English caricature', *Criticism*, 11 (1969), 230–1.

Stevenson, Lionel, 'Who was Mr Turveydrop?' *Dickensian*, 44 (1948), 39–41.

Stock, David, 'London street-musicians: their social history and influence', typescript, 1982.

Stokes, Edward, ' "Bleak House" and "The Scarlet Letter" ', *Journal of the Australasian Universities Language and Literature Association*, 32 (1969), 177–89.

Stokes, Edward, *Hawthorne's Influence on Dickens and George Eliot* (Queensland: University of Queensland Press, 1985).

Stone, Harry, 'Dark corners of the mind: Dickens' childhood reading', *Hornbook Magazine*, 39 (1963), 306–21.

Stone, Harry (ed.), *The Uncollected Writings of Charles Dickens: 'Household Words,' 1850–1859* (London: Allen Lane, 1968).

Stone, Marjorie, 'Dickens, Bentham, and the fictions of the law: a Victorian controversy and its consequences,' *Victorian Studies*, 29 (1985), 125–54.

Sucksmith, Harvey Peter, 'Dickens at work on *Bleak House*: a critical examination of his memoranda and number plans', *Renaissance and Modern Studies*, 9 (1965), 47–85.

Sucksmith, Harvey Peter, 'Sir Leicester Dedlock, Wat Tyler and the Chartists: the role of the Ironmaster in *Bleak House*', *Dickens Studies Annual*, 4 (1975), 113–31.

Suddaby, John, 'The crossing sweeper in *Bleak House*: Dickens and the original Jo', *Dickensian*, 8 (1912), 246–50.

Sullivan, A. E., 'Soldiers of the queen – and of Charles Dickens', *Dickensian*, 46 (1950), 138–43.

Super, R. H., *Walter Savage Landor: A Biography* (1954; reissued London: John Calder, 1957).

Suzannet, A., 'Sloman's; another Dickens original', *Dickensian*, 36 (1939–40), 180.

Tarr, Rodger, L., 'The "Foreign Philanthropy Question" in *Bleak House*: a Carlylean influence', *Studies in the Novel*, 3 (1971), 275–83.

Taylor, Tom, *Leicester Square; Its Associations and Its Worthies* (London: Bickers & Son, 1874).

Thornbury, George Walter and Walford, Edward, *Old and New London*, 6 vols (London: Cassell, Petter & Galpin, 1873–8).

Thorne, James, *Handbook to the Environs of London*, 2 vols (London: John Murray, 1876).

Tillotson, Kathleen, *Novels of the Eighteen-Forties* (1954; reprinted Oxford: Clarendon Press, 1971).

Timbs, John, *Curiosities of London* (London: David Bogue, 1855).

Trustram, Myna, *Women of the Regiment: Marriage and the Victorian Army* (Cambridge: Cambridge University Press, 1984).

Turner, Ernest Sackville, *Taking the Cure* (London: Michael Joseph, 1967).

Tye, J. R., 'Legal caricature: Cruikshank analogues to the *Bleak House* cover,' *Dickensian*, 69 (1973), 39–41.

Walder, Dennis, *Dickens and Religion* (London: Allen & Unwin, 1981).

Walder, Dennis, 'Dickens and the Reverend David Macrae', *Dickensian*, 81 (1985), 45–51.

Wallins, Roger P., 'Dickens and decomposition', *Dickens Studies Newsletter*, 5 (1974), 68–70.

Warren, Samuel, 'The Baronet's Bride', chapter 15 of *Passages from the Diary of a Late Physician, Blackwood's Edinburgh Magazine*, 35 (1834), 81–121.

Warrington, William, *The History of Wales* (London: J. Johnson, 1786).

Wellcome Institute for the History of Medicine, *Morbid Cravings: The Emergence of Addiction*, exhibition catalogue (London: Wellcome Institute, 1984).

Wiley, Elizabeth, 'Four strange cases', *Dickensian*, 58 (1962), 120–5.

Wilkins, Michael, 'Dickens's portrayal of the Dedlocks', *Dickensian*, 72 (1976), 67–74.

Winslow, C. E. A., *The Conquest of Epidemic Disease* (Princeton, NJ : Princeton University Press, 1944).

Wohl, Anthony S., *Endangered Lives; Public Health in Victorian Britain* (London: Dent, 1983).

Wright, Lawrence, *Clean and Decent: The Fascinating History of the Bathroom and Water Closet* (London: Routledge & Kegan Paul, 1960).

Wright, Lawrence, *Home Fires Burning: The History of Domestic Heating and Cooking* (London: Routledge & Kegan Paul, 1964).

Yamamoto, Tadao, *Growth and System of the Language of Dickens* (Osaka: Kansai University Press, 1952).

A NOTE ON THE INDEX

This is an A to Z index of *The Companion to 'Bleak House'*: it is not an index of Dickens's novel. Variant readings in the manuscript are not indexed, nor are the work plans. References to Dickens's other writings and quotations from them are indexed only when they are considered to be of major significance in the annotation.

Literary allusions and references are indexed only when a note gives a probable allusion by Dickens: references which are merely illustrative, or which are examples of typical phrases, are not indexed. Allusions and references are given title entries in the following cases only: (i) anonymous works other than books of the Bible, nursery rhymes, nursery tales, and songs; (ii) works by Dickens.

Because of the density of information contained in the text, it has not been possible to index all *mentions* of names, places and so on. Notes on the names of characters are entered under the character's surname.

Filing order is word by word rather than letter by letter: thus 'De Quincey' comes before 'Defoe'.

The abbreviation *BH* is used for *Bleak House*.

INDEX

Abercrombie, Dr John, *Inquiries Concerning the Intellectual Powers* 221
Aberdeen, fourth Earl of *see* Hamilton-Gordon, George, fourth Earl of Aberdeen
academies: dancing 131
accidents: firework factories 3, 196; gasworks 3, 193, 196
Accountant-General 94
acrobatics 176
Acts of Parliament. *See under title of Act*
Addison, Joseph 129; 'The Spacious Firmament on High' 199, 200; *Spectator* 67, 122
Adelphi Theatre 96
Administrative Reform Association 34
advertising phraseology: 'desirable property' 142; 'something to his advantage' 175
advocates *see* barristers
Aesop's Fables 76, 129, 234
Africa 154, 277; expeditions to 152; fever 55, 129; and missionaries and philanthropists 54–5; Niger expedition 2, 55, 129, 231; 'Noble Savage' 208; slavery 54, 131, 152; tribes 115
Agar Town 91
Ajax 150
Albaro 30, 151
alcoholic drinks *see* drinks; drunkenness
Aldgate 130
Alexander the Great 41
Alfred, King 87
Alison, Archibald 6, 35; 'Hints to the Aristocracy' 6, 35–6
Alison, Dr William Putney, *Observations on the Management of the Poor in Scotland* 253
Allingham, William, *A Diary* 71–2
Almack's 280
Alpheus 246
allusions, literary. *See under author of work referred to; for books of the Bible, see under* Bible; *for anonymous works, see title. See also* classical allusions; emblematic figures; gods and goddesses
amateur theatricals 13, 72
America: Dickens's visits 87, 152, 296; Indians 87; penitentiaries 265, 268; slavery 152; *see also* British North America; South America
American Indians 87

Amorites 171
analytical chemists 253
angels 119, 279; cherubim 173; Recording Angel 235; Seraphim 47
Anglicans *see* Church of England
animals: badgers 91; bears 96; cats 63; cattle 23, 130–1, 143, 191; cocks 98, 191; cows 99; monkeys: caricature of the French 119, organ grinders' 172–3; pigs 169, 274; sheep 101, 130; voles 228; whales 159; wolves 64; *see also* birds; dogs; horses
Anne, Queen 57
Annual Register 216, 222
antiquarianism (in fine arts) 123–4, 203
Anti-Duelling Association 237
Anti-Slavery Society 131; *see also* Africa; slavery
Apjohn, Dr James, *Cyclopaedia of Practical Medicine* 217
Apollo 129
apothecaries 106, 182–3; *see also* chemists; doctors; medicine
Apothecaries Act (1815) 182–3
apples 189; pies 83
apprentices and servants-of-all-work 2, 3, 62, 99–100
Apprentices and Servants Act (1851) 2, 3, 100
apprenticeship: articles of 204
aprons: ticket-porters 155; tradesmen 72
Arabian Nights 140, 173, 175; *see also* Perrault, Charles; nursery rhymes and tales
Archimedes 234
architectural design. *For specific buildings, see under the name of the building. See also* churches
architecture: Georgian domestic 260
Arctic: Franklin expedition 3, 151–2
area sneaks 285; *see also* crime; thieves
Argus 210
aristocracy: carriages 116, 188; conduct 35, 36, 116; drawl 239; in fashionable novels 35, 36, 37, 124; in government 35–6, 124, 125, 201, 236–7; marriage with industrialists' families 202; in newspapers 38; Norman descent 202, 271; opposition to industrialists 76, 201, 239; portraits 124, 168, 203; *see also* fashionable society; footmen; holidays and resorts; liveried servants
Arkwright, Richard 136

Army: bands 198; chaplains 199; compared to Prussians 187; foreign service: 198, British North America 174, Caffre War 115, India 149; garrisons 198, 268; Horse Guards 187, 286; professionalization 5, 28, 174, 176, 187; reasons for enlistment 75, 163; surgeons 127; troop transports 197; *see also* Household troops; military; officers; regiments, soldiers

arrest warrants 189

arrows: and bows 189; *see also* duelling; firearms

Arthur, King 173

articled clerks 156, 162, 204; *see also* lawyers' clerks

articles of apprenticeship 204

artificial flower making 173–4

artillerymen 5, 174, 198

artists: models: footmen 270, Guardsmen 189, 270, lay-figures 190; self-portraits 71–2

arts: pictorial: artists' self-portraits 71–2, frescoes 30, illustrations for books 122, 168, 278, for newspapers 218, painted ceilings 101–2, 144; styles and movements: antiquarianism 123–4, 203, bohemianism 71, Gothic revival 85, pre-Raphaelitism 71, religious 183; *see also* artists; caricatures; crafts; emblematic figures; entertainments; fashionable portraits; music; ornaments; sculpture

Ascension Island 277

Astley's 151, 175–6, 294

astronomy 23; nebular hypothesis 25

asylums: Bedlam 163, 259; for orphans 85; private and public 259; wrongful imprisonment 1, 14

attorneys 20, 42, 162, 204; *see also* barristers; solicitors; law

Augurs 268

autobiographical elements in *BH*. *See* Dickens, Charles

Austin, Henry 26, 114

Australia: emigration 52, 126, 149; and Mrs Chisholm 52; transportation of criminals 52, 127, 160

Austria: quicksilver mines 127; William Tell 188–9

Azores: Saint Michael's oranges 74

baby farms: Tooting 2, 99–100, 255

Badger, Mr Bayham 128

Badger, Mrs Bayham (Laura) 129

badger-drawing 91

badgers 91

baggage-waggons 197

Bagnet, Mr Matthew: characterization revision 218

bailiffs *see* sherriff's officers

Baker Street 279

ballads *see* songs

ballooning 26–7

bamboo convertible furniture 67

Band of Hope (temperance) Plate 8; 2, 87–8

Bandi, Cornelia, Countess 216

bands: regimental 198; street- 143; *see also* music; street-music

Bank of England 94

bankruptcy: Dickens's father's insolvency 4, 205; list of bankrupts 186, 205; 'gone through the Gazette' 205; 'whitewashing' 218; *see also* finance

banshees 103

baptism 111, 234

baptism service *see Book of Common Prayer*

bards: Welsh 149

Barnaby Rudge 131, 140, 154–5, 163

Barnet 64, 65

Barnum, P. T. 43

barouches 64, 281

barrel organs 144, 173

Barrière de l'Etoile 117, 118

barristers 20, 30, 34, 102, 155; *see also* attorneys; solicitors; law

Barrow, Charles 4, 205

basilisks 238

bassoons 198

Bass's Bill 144; *see also* street-music

Bath 200, 279

baths and showers: Dickens's 4, 219; hip 68; public 258–9; *see also* boilers; plumbing

Battle Bridge 169

Battle of Barnet 65

Battle of Waterloo 174, 189, 205

battledore and shuttlecock 30

Bayham Street 100, 128

bayonets 198

beadles 108, 171; 'moving on' 252; redundancy of 2, 108

bear's grease (hairdressing) 96

Beaumarchais, Pierre 246

Beauty (emblem) 246

Bedlam 163, 259; *see also* asylums

beds 67, 193

beer 58, 211; 'swipes' 176

bees 79, 210

Beeton, Isabella, *Household Management* 71, 74

begging-letters 71, 125

beheadings 28, 276; *see also* executions

Belfast 187

Belgrave Square 38

Bell Yard 140

bells (street-music) 144; *see also* Bow Bells

benchers 33

Bentham, Jeremy 29, 247, 252; *Book of Fallacies* 124; 'Panopticon' 265
Bermondsey 163
Bethnal Green 130
Bianchini, J. 216
Bible 88, 124, 171; Lord's Prayer said backwards 190; New Testament 191–2; books: Genesis 23, 46, 58, 67, 79, 107, 119, 120, 190, 192, 199–200, 241, 262; Exodus 46, 67, 83, 148, 190, 224, 274; 1 Samuel 186; 1 Kings 191; Esther 46; Job 33, 34, 210, 264; Psalms 49, 67, 116, 151, 210, 258, 292; Proverbs 188, 231; Ecclesiastes 117–18; Isaiah 191, 203, 231, 243; Ezekiel 67, 173; Daniel 296; Zechariah 191; Matthew 31, 49, 93, 115, 140, 209, 234, 254, 288; Mark 47, 90, 93, 139; Luke 31, 58, 76, 209, 234, 264; John 46, 47; Acts 115, 157; Romans 231, 254; 1 Corinthians 115, 151, 279; Galatians 268; Philippians 289; 1 Peter 79, 231; Revelation 51–2, 101, 229, 274, 280; *see also* biblical; proverbs
biblical: criticism 23, 123; names: Esther 46, Rachael 46, Sarah 191; phraseology: 31, 49, 58, 101, 117–18; *see also* Bible; proverbs
Bickerstaffe, Isaac, *Love in a Village* 277
bill-discounting 169, 172
billiards 118
bills of mortality 32
biology 23
Bird, Mr and Mrs 3, 100
birds: Dickens's canary 4, 94; game 213; gold-finches 63; larks 63; linnets 63; trained 75–6; *see also* animals
bishops: Church of England 72; Roman Catholic 2, 6, 85
black draught (medicine) 173
Blackfriars Bridge 6, 101, 161, 197
blacking bottles 62
Blackstone, Sir William, *Commentaries on the Laws of England* 30, 141, 148
Bleak House. See composition of *BH*; Dickens, Charles: autobiographical elements in *BH*; French speech in *BH*; illustrations to *BH*; 'originals' depicted in illustrations to *BH*; setting of *BH*; titles of *BH*; see also Summerson, Esther
Blessington, Marguerite, Countess of 35, 67
Bloomsbury 150
Blower, Joseph 33
blue bags: barristers' 34
blue minutes 231
boat-yards 294
boats: cargo 101; collier brigs 26; manure barges 23; rowing 126–7; to the Continent 116; *see also* Navy; nautical phraseology; seamen; ships
bodices: stays 75; tight-lacing 99
bohemians 71
boilers (hot water systems) 57; *see also* baths and showers; plumbing
Bollingers (hats) 65
Bonchurch 219
bone-houses 211
bones: cramp 230; *see also* waste
bonnets 119
book illustrations: dandies 122; 'Death and the Lady' 278; 'Hampton Court Beauties' 168
Book of Common Prayer 78; Baptism 111, 234; Burial Service 103, 113, 177, 231, 234; Catechism 48, 111, 151, 202, 249, 262; Evening Prayer 238; Litany 196, 238; Morning Prayer 151, 238; Solemnization of Matrimony 71, 97, 99, 191, 192; prayers: for Charles I 78, from the Litany 196, for Parliament 238; *see also* prayers
Book of Fate 269
boots: postilions' 116
botany 129
Botticelli, Sandro, 'Birth of Venus' 275
bottles: blacking 62; rag and bottle shops 59, 62; *see also* waste: glass
Bow Bells 65
bowlers (hats) 65
bows and arrows 189; *see also* duelling; firearms
boxing: John Shaw 186; phraseology 'in chancery' 28, 'to come up to the scratch' 158, 'tough subject' 182, use by noncon-formists 158; popularity 176; promotion bills 196; *see also* sports
Boyle, Mary 57, 82
Boythorn, Mr Lawrence: characterization revisions 94
branding-irons 192
brandy balls 110
brass buttons 40
bread 62, 72, 166; and butter 174, 255; sand-wiches 255
breakfast-stalls 254–5
breaking on the wheel 221–2
Brentford 25
breweries 294
bribery *see* electoral corruption
brickmakers 2, 91, 253
brick-making 91
Bridgman, Laura 290
Bright, John 79, 84
Brighton 116, 136
Bristol board 72
Britannia 155
British Constitution 81, 274

British holidays *see* holidays and resorts
British North America 174; *see also* America; South America
Brixton Prison 192, 242
Broadstairs 13, 143
Bronte, Charlotte, *Jane Eyre* 7, 45–6, 47, 225
broom-girls 241–2
brooms: crossing-sweepers' 112–13
Brougham, Henry Peter, Baron Brougham and Vaux 126, 242
Brown, Charles Brockden, *Wieland* 216
Browne, Hablot Knight 70, 102, 177; *see also* illustrations to *BH*; 'originals' depicted in illustrations to *BH*
Brummell, George ('Beau') 40, 120, 122
Buckland, William 23
buckskins 122
bull's-eyes (lanterns) 181
bulls 191; *see also* cattle
Bulwer, Sir Edward Lytton 13, 35, 72
Bunyan, John, *The Pilgrim's Progress* 118, 230
Burdett, Angela *see* Coutts, Angela Burdett
burial clubs 113
burial grounds 113–15; burial by parish 288; Christian rites disregarded 113, 115–16; financial irregularities 113; nonconformist 113; regulated by Parliament 2, 114, 252; sanitary abuses 113–14, 211; speculation in 113; *see also* death; funerals; pollution; sanitary reform and sanitation
burial service *see Book of Common Prayer*
Burns, Robert, 'Gudeen to you kimmer' 236
butter 160, 174, 255
butter paddles 160
buttermen 160
buttons: brass 40
Buxton, Sir Thomas Fowell 55, 129; *see also* Niger expedition
Byron, George Gordon, sixth Baron 6, 44, 48, 51, 292, 294; *Beppo* 129; *Childe Harold's Pilgrimage* 177; 'I would I were a careless child' 136

cab drivers 65
cabbage 197
cabooses 26
cadavers (for dissection) 113, 193; Samuel Rogers 169
Cade, Jack 35
Caesar, Julius 240, 271
Caffre War 115
'cage', the, 225; *see also* prisons
cake: currant 255; sponge 72
Calcraft, William 110–11
'Caledonian melody' 235–6; *see also* songs
calves: padded (of dandies) 122

Cambridge 20, 103, 276
Camden Town 128
Campbell, Thomas, 'Lochiel's Warning' 237–8
Canada *see* British North America
Canadian giant 43
canals: London 23
canaries: Dickens's 4, 94
candle works 294
candles 27, 102, 103
canes: gold-headed 188; *see also* walking sticks
cannibals 231
Canning, George, 'The Pilot that Weathered the Storm' 237
cannon 268
Canova, Antonio 'The Graces' 73
Cape of Good Hope 277
caps: cat-skin 62–3
captains of industry 3, 36, 201–2; heroism 201; *see also* industrialism
caravans: wax-works 279
Carey Street 140, 264
cargo boats 101
caricatures: of dandies 122; the French 119; George IV 131, 186; lawyers 30
Carlyle, Thomas 6, 25, 57, 72, 141, 251, 260; 'heroes' 3, 201; *Collected Letters* (quoted) 70, 243, 293; works: *Chartism* 253; *The Diamond Necklace* 16, 228, 274–5; *Excursion (Futile Enough) to Paris . . .* 117; *The French Revolution* 6, 117, 119–20, 183; 'The Nigger Question' 55, 87, 152; *Latter-Day Pamphlets* 6, 30, 86, 112, 237; *Life of John Sterling* 1, 4, 243; *Past and Present* 6, 91, 107, 120, 201, 234, 253; *Sartor Resartus* 6, 35, 120, 123
Caroline of Brunswick-Wolfenbuttel (wife of George IV) 134, 225
Carpenter, W. B., *Principles of General and Comparative Physiology* 217
carriages *see* coaches and carriages
Carstone, Richard: characterization revisions 126, 229, 264
Cartwright, Edmund 76
casinos 156
Cassandra 150
Catechism *see Book of Common Prayer*
catechism: teetotal 88; *see also* temperance movement
cat-gut manufacturers 211; *see also* waste
Catlin, George 205, 208
cat-skin caps 62–3
cats 63; in songs 236
cavalry: officers and whiskers 163; regiments 174, 280
cellars: cider 96; cow 99
Cemeteries Clauses Act (1847) 252
cemeteries: in Paris 118; *see also* burial grounds

Cerjat, W. F. de 16
Cervantes, Miguel de, *Don Quixote* 152–3; paintings 203
Chadband, Rev. 157; characterization revisions 157, 158–9, 160
Chadband, Mrs (formerly Mrs Rachael) 46; characterization revisions 159
Chadwick, Edwin 176, 252; reforms affecting: Army 176; police 5, 176, 179; 'omni-competence' 5, 108; sanitation 114, 182, 251, 253; *Report on the Sanitary Condition of the Labouring Population* 182, 251
chairs: convertible bamboo 67; porter's 167, 172
Challinor, W. 15
Champs Elysées 117
Chancery Commission 28, 33; *see also* Chancery, Court of
Chancery, Court of Plates 2, 4
  abuses 14, 15, 29, 32, 33
  associated Acts of Parliament: Chancery Procedure Act (1852) 2, 29, 31, 33, 102; Common Law Procedure Act (1854) 29; Court of Chancery Act (1850) 29; Court of Chancery Act (Ireland) (1850) 29; Judicature Act (1873) 29, 82; Suitors in Chancery Relief Act (1852) 29, 33, 102
  associated buildings: King's Bench Office 102; Lincoln's Inn 20, 49, 56; Rolls House 101; Westminster Hall 20, 153, 154
  Dickens's experiences of 20, 29
  'in chancery' 28
  jurisdiction 28, 31, 82; Commissioners in Lunacy 14
  officials 28, 31, 94; Six Clerks' Office 2, 28, 33
  reform movement 2, 15, 28–9, 33, 154
  suits, nonfictional 1–2, 15–16, 29, 56
  terms 20, 154
  wards of court 48–9, 51; *see also* attorneys; barristers; Chancery Commission; Inns of Chancery; Inns of Court; judges; law; law-writers; lawyer's clerks; legal phraseology
Chancery Lane 20, 49, 59, 73, 97, 101, 110, 153, 154; origin of name 287
Chancery Reform Association 15
chaplains: Army 199
characterization in *BH. See* composition of *BH*; *see also* Summerson, Esther
charades 145
charities *see* philanthropy
charity schools 171
Charles I 78, 97
Charles II 155, 168, 186
Charon 211, 212
Chartism 2, 44, 76
Chatham 13, 101, 205

Cheapside 48
Chelsea 73, 128–9, 138, 271
Chelsea Bun House 4, 115, 271
Chelsea figures (ornaments) 73
Cheltenham 156
chemical works 294
chemists: 182–3; dispense opium 107; analytical 253; *see also* apothecaries; doctors; medicine
cherubim 213
Chesney Wold 39, 40, 125, 150
Chesterfield, fourth Earl of *see* Stanhope, Philip Dormer, fourth Earl of Chesterfield
Cheyne Row 70, 73, 243
Chichester Rents 38, 59, 288
children: Band of Hope (temperance) 87–8; crimes against 100, 113; deaf and dumb 7, 85, 296; deaths of 92, 99–100, 111, 113; in employment: apprentices and servants 2, 3, 99–100, chimney sweepers 229, crossing-sweepers 112–13; and New Testament 191–2; orphans 52, 82, 85, 100; philanthropic involvement 88; of soldiers 197–8; swaddling clothes 289; testimonies in court 111–12; vaccination 209; *see also* baby farms; education; nursery rhymes and tales; schools
Child's History of England, A 44, 131, 276
Chimes, The 40, 155, 160, 247, 251
chimney sweepers 229
Chimney Sweepers Regulation Act (1834) 229
China 109, 277; missionary and philanthropic involvement in 54; and Overland Mail 222; subject of popular knowledge 130; *see also* Chinese
China oranges 74
Chinese: art 68, 94, 96, 130; Exhibition 2, 130; Junk 2, 130; manufacturing 68; Opium War 130; sailors 107; *see also* China
Chisholm, Archibald 56
Chisholm, Caroline Plate 5; 2, 4, 52, 54, 56, 86
chocolate 63, 255
cholera 100, 114, 182
Christianity: missionaries: domestic and foreign 2, 54–5, 56, 85, 143; Muscular 68; sectarianism 191–2, 208; *see also* Church of England; Freemasonry; nonconformists; philanthropy; religious beliefs; Roman Catholics
Christmas Carol, A 29, 162
Christopherson, Henry 143
Church of England
  Anglicans: philanthropic activities 88, 92; phraseology 260
  burial service 113

military chaplains 199
Oxford Movement 2, 5, 86; Dickens's attitude towards 85, 86; sisterhoods 85; Young England 3, 123; *see also Book of Common Prayer*; Christianity; non-conformists; philanthropy, religious beliefs; Roman Catholics
church organs 139
churches: Notre Dame cathedral 118; Shoreditch Church 96; St Albans Abbey 79; St Andrew's, Holborn 98; St Dunstan's, Fleet Street 219; St Luke's, Old Street Road 96; St Martin-in-the-Fields 113; St Paul's cathedral 22, 28, 161, 286
churchyards *see* burial grounds
cider 96
cider cellars 96
cigar-ends 58; *see also* waste
circuses 176; *see also* Astley's
City, the 28, 92, 97, 111, 155, 230, 286
Civil List 200
civil servants: East India Company 149
Clare, Ada 51
Clarendon Square 242
claret 72
Clarke, Tom 13
classical allusions: Archimedes 234; Augurs 268; basilisks 238; 'fidus Achates' 167; Olympus 204; Palladium 156; 'Poeta nascitur . . .' 128; Sibyls 219; *see also* gods and goddesses
Clerkenwell 97, 193
clerks *see* lawyers' clerks
clichés *see* phraseology
Clive, Kitty 246
cloaks 243
clocks: eight-day 150; Horse Guards' 286; 'Parliamentaries' 58; St Paul's 286
clockwork bottle-jacks (spits) 172
coaches and carriages 25, private 67, 116, 188, spikes 128; barouches 64, 281; cabs 3, 49, 65, 112, 188; caravans 279; flys 49; gigs 77; hackney-coaches 3, 188; hansoms 49; mourning 229, 269; omnibuses 112, 275; post-chaises 93; stage-coaches 48, 65, 197; *see also* baggage-waggons; mail-coaches
coal: and air pollution 25; coke 103, 130; collier brigs 26; fuel 27, 75; producing gas 27
coats: blue 40, 72; dandies' 122; gold lace 43; policemen's 109; red 72; spencers 188; *see also* costume and appearance
Cobbett, William 54, 126
Cobden, Richard 79
cock and bull story 191
'cocked-hats' (folded notes) 269–70
cocked hats: footmen's 279
cockneys 97

cocks 98, 191
cod's head and shoulders 74
coffee 63, 254–5
coffee-houses 138, 188; *see also* dining places
coke 103, 130
Coldstream Guards 271
Cole, Alfred, 'The Martyrs of Chancery' 29, 32
College of Arms 269
collier brigs 26
Combe, George 139
Comedy (emblem) 246
comic singers 157, 216; *see also* music; songs
Commissioner of Woods and Forests 3, 124
Commissioners Clauses Act (1847) 252
Commissioners in Lunacy 14
commonplaces *see* phraseology
composition of *BH* 34–5, 45, 64, 77, 264, period of 29, 44, 124, setting in time 1; characterization revisions: Bagnet 218, 268, Boythorn 94, Richard Carstone 126, 229, 264, Chadband 157, 158–9, 160, Mrs Chadband 159, Jarndyce 93, Jo 141, Sir Leicester 44, 202, 287, Mrs Pardiggle 87, Skimpole 64, 70, 72, 208, 246, Smallweed family 171, Vholes 229, 230, 264; plot 6, 34–5, 65, 72, 82, 262; stylistic revisions: 16, 67, 151, 152, 248, 264; *see also* Dickens, Charles: autobiographical elements in *BH*; Forster, John; French speech in *BH*; illustrations to *BH*; 'originals' depicted in illustrations to *BH*; setting of *BH*; Summerson, Esther; titles of *BH*
confectionery 110
conjuring 4, 42; *see also* magic
Conservatives *see* Torys
Constitution, British 36, 142
construction of *BH see* composition of *BH*
consumption *see* tuberculosis
contagion: theories of 253–4; *see also* disease
continental holidays *see* holidays and resorts
contributions to charity 88, 90; *see also* philanthropy
convertible bamboo furniture 67
Cook, Captain James 68
cookery: English *vs* French 138; *see also* food; drinks
Copley, John Singleton, the younger, first Baron Lyndhurst 2, 20
copying-clerks *see* law-writers
cordials 213
Cornwall 196
coroner's juries *see* inquests
Corrupt Practices at Elections Act (1852) 65
corsets 122
costume and appearance
clothing: aprons: ticket-porters 155, trades-

men 72; belts: policemen's 109; bodices: stays 75, tight-lacing 99; bonnets 119; boots: postilions' 116; buttons: brass 40; caps: catskin 62–3; cloaks 143; corsets 122; counsellors' bands 62; cravats 122; dresses 119; dressing gowns: Leigh Hunt's 243; gaiters 43; garters: footmen 43, Order of the Garter 136, 189; gloves 96; gowns: barristers' 30; knee-breeches 43, buckskins 122; old clothes 62; sandals: pattens 56, winged 42; shirt-frills 40; shirts 71; sleeves 72; stockings 43, 122; swaddling 289; trousers 43, nankeen 200; waistcoats 40, 43
fashions: canes 188; French 116; walking sticks 197
jewellery: earrings 242; hair 63; mourning 179, 181; pearl 200
wearers and purposes: broom-girls 242; cab drivers 65; charity school uniforms 171; children 289; chimney sweepers 229; clerical 72; coachmen in livery 278; cockney swells 97; disguises: of Inspector Field 188; footmen 42–3, 279, 285; gentlemen 40, 43, 122; legal 30, 51, 62; lower class 62–3; military 72; Naval 72; mourning 179, 181, 248, 270; organ-grinders' monkeys 172–3; physicians 188; policemen 109; postilions 116; Quakers 84; servants-of-all-work 56; tradesmen 72; see also coats; dandies; hats; hairdressing; Maria Manning; Mary, Queen of Scots; neck-wear
cotton-spinning 79, 56
counsellors' bands 62
country dancing 213
Court of St James's 43, 123–4; presentations 120; see also Royal Household
Coutts, Angela Burdett 52, 84, 85, 114, 192, 201, 269
Covent Garden (opera house and theatre) 43, 128, 277
cover design of BH. See illustrations to BH
cows 99
crafts: artificial flower making 173–4; tambour work 222; see also arts
cramp-bones 230
cravats 122
crime: against children 100, 113; area sneaks 285; investigation: detective policemen 5, 177, 179; Newgate Calendar 193; prostitutes 84, 85, 112, 123; sherriff's officers 140; sponging houses 2, 73; see also death; executions; police; prisons; punishment; thieves
Crimean War 163, 174, 187
criminals see crime; executions; police; prisons; punishment; thieves
criticism: biblical 23, 123

crossing-sweepers 102, 112–13; police protection of 112, 159; and 'street-orderlies' 113
Cruickshank, George 30, 136, 186
crusies (lamps) 250
Crystal Palace: Sydenham 23; see also Great Exhibition
Cubitt, William 192
culture: French 116–17
currant cake 255
Cursitor Street 73, 97, 101

'Dance of Death' 82
Dancer, Daniel 235
dancing: academies 131; chimney sweepers 229; country- 213; waltzes 294; see also music
dancing academies 131
dandies 120, 122; and George IV 120, 131; and Beau Brummell 122; and fine arts 124; and Oxford Movement and Young England 123; see also fashionable society
Dante, Divine Comedy: Inferno 203, Purgatorio 254
'darbies' (handcuffs) 179
David Copperfield 64, 100, 162, 171, 190
De Quincey, Thomas, Confessions of an English Opium-Eater 7, 220–1
dead cats 63; see also waste
dead-houses (Thames-side morgues) 281
Dead Sea fruit 229
deaf and dumb children 7, 85, 296
Deal 248–9
death: bills of mortality 32; burial-clubs 113; cadavers 113, 193; children and infants 92, 99–100, 111, 113; 'The Dance of Death' 82; dead-houses 281; dredgers (waterfinders) 281, 284; dying words: Pitt 136, Sir Philip Sidney 264; exhumation 204; 'Found drowned' bills 281; inquests 100, 110; spontaneous combustion 3, 16, 34, 211, 216–18; see also burial grounds; crime; executions; funerals; mourning; suicide
Death and the Lady (ballad) 278
debtors see finance
Dedlock, Sir Leicester 39, 40; characterization revisions 202, 287
Dedlock, Miss Volumnia 200
Defoe, Daniel, Political History of the Devil 42; Robinson Crusoe 92–3
Denman, Thomas, first Lord Denman 54
dens: fever 182, 251; opium 179; thieves' 181, 182
Deptford 163
Derby, fourteenth Earl of see Stanley, Edward George Geoffrey Smith, fourteenth Earl of Derby
Devil: 'Devil's Tattoo' 234; proverb 175; 'sold himself to the devil' 64; and Tulkinghorn 42

Devon 145
Dickens, Catherine 62, 77
Dickens, Charles
  attitudes towards: administrative reform 34;
    baby farms 100; begging-letter writers 125;
    Charles I 78; China 96, 130; classical educa-
    tion 126; deaf and dumb children 7, 296;
    divorce 286; entertainment 172; fairy tales
    172; funerals 269; Georgian architecture
    260; honours system 7, 223; inadmissible
    evidence of children 111; iron masters 201;
    the law 29; missionaries 55, 92; New
    Testament 191–2; nonconformist
    preachers 158; Oxford Movement 85, 86;
    Parliamentary ineffectiveness 34, 125,
    251; philanthropy 52, 54, 55, 83–4, 86;
    phrenology 139; pre-Raphaelitism 71;
    punishment of attempted suicides 160;
    religious beliefs 85, 191–2; Roman
    Catholicism 85, 118; sabbatarianism 172;
    sanitary reform 26, 114, 251; sectarianism
    191–2, 208; slavery 152; solitary confine-
    ment 7, 265, 268; spontaneous combustion
    216–18; street-music 143–4; temperance
    movement 88; Wat Tyler 44; water pollution
    26; women's rights 86–7, 208
  autobiographical elements in *BH*: canary 4, 94;
    conjuring 42; family relations 4, 205; hotel in
    Paris 117; Somers Town lodging 242
  homes, *see* Albaro; Bayham Street; Broad-
    stairs; Chatham; Gad's Hill; Gower Street;
    Somers Town
  knowledge and experience: amateur
    theatricals 13, 72; America, 1842 tour 87,
    152, 296; conjuring 4, 42; country dancing
    213; Court of Chancery 29; dream theories
    221; France 117; Italy 71, 118, 275;
    journalism 110; Midlands, 1838 tour 293;
    office boy in law firm 20; The Polygon 242;
    prisons 265, 268; shorthand writer 20, 140;
    shower-baths 4, 219; 'sitting for his portrait'
    177, 179; sponging houses 73; St Giles's
    rookery 179; St Albans 65; thieves' dens 181;
    trials and executions 119
  library: statue of 'The Graces' 73; books on
    dreams 221, drunkenness 216; De
    Quincey's *Confessions* 220
  relationships: Austin, Henry 26, 114; Boyle,
    Mary 57, 82; Bulwer-Lytton, Edward 13, 35;
    Chisholm, Caroline 52; Coutts, Angela
    Burdett 52, 84, 85, 114, 192; Dickens,
    Catherine 62; Dickens, John 4, 73, 205;
    Dickens, Frederick 65; Forster, John 26, 29,
    39, 62, 65, 93, 119, 143–4; Hunt, Leigh 68,
    70, 71, 292; Landor, Walter Savage 57,
    93–4; Rogers, Samuel 169, 171; Talfourd,

Serjeant Thomas Noon 29; Watson, Hon.
    Mr and Mrs Richard 16, 39, 68, 93; Wills,
    W. H. 15, 49, 68
  writings *see under* individual titles
Dickens, Charles, the younger: quoted 39, 59,
    102, 110
Dickens, Elizabeth Ball 75
Dickens, Frederick 65
Dickens, John 4, 73, 205
diets: of dandies 122; of Leigh Hunt 72; for tight-
    waisting 99
dining habits: Jacobite toasts 173; table decora-
    tions 270
dining places: providing newspapers 166;
    Almack's 280; breakfast-stalls 254–5;
    Chelsea Bun House 4, 115, 271; cider
    cellars 96; coffee houses 138, 188;
    restaurants 138; 'slap-bangs' 163, 166;
    Vauxhall Gardens 157, 294; *see also* public
    houses
dinosaurs Plate 3, 2, 23
disease: African fever 55, 129; cholera 100, 114,
    182; 'fever' (typhus) 3, 182, 251; high
    temperature complicating smallpox 224;
    gout 2, 40; jaundice 32, 228; nausea on visit-
    ing thieves' dens 181; pneumonia 258;
    smallpox 3, 209, 258; theories of contagion
    253–4; tuberculosis (consumption) 182,
    209, 258; *see also* doctors; medicine; opium;
    sanitary reform and sanitation
disguises: of Inspector Field 188
Disraeli, Benjamin 237; *Coningsby* 201–2;
    Henrietta Temple 73; *Sybil* 201, 293; *Tancred,
    or The New Crusade* 38, 260; Young England
    123
dissenters *see* nonconformists
district visitors 2, 88, 91–2; *see also* philanthropy
divorce 4, 286; *see also* marriage
Divorce Act (1857) 286
docks: London 26, 107, 130, 198, 281; Plymouth
    224; Portsmouth 205
doctors: French quacks 118; heroism 5, 107;
    hospital admission procedure 258; medical
    reform movement 5, 106; prescribe opium
    107; professionalization 5, 28, 106; Scottish
    103, 106, 217; *see also* chemists; hospitals;
    medicine; physicians; surgeons
Doctors' Commons 20, 140
dogs: drawing badgers 91; drover's 144; hunting
    213; performing 118; in songs 236, 246; *see
    also* animals
dolly shops (pawnbrokers) 62
Dombey and Son 106, 126, 158, 171, 253, 271
dominoes 118
Dover 116
Dover Castle 268

Downs 211, 248–9
drawl: aristocratic 239
dream theories 221
dredgers (water-finders) 281, 284
dress *see* costume and appearance
dresses 119
dressing gowns: Leigh Hunt's 243
drinking *see* drinks; drunkenness
drinks: beer 58, 211; 'swipes' 176; cordials 213; negus 209; port 40; rum 167; shrub 213; chocolate 63, 255; coffee 63, 254–5; effervescent 162; ginger beer 155; milk 58, 99; tea 63, 68, 254–5; vinegar and lemon juice 99; *see also* drunkenness; wine
dripping (grease) 59, 60; *see also* waste
Drouet, Peter 2, 99–100, 255
drovers' dogs 144
drugs *see* medicine
Druids 174
drunkenness 88; associated with the Irish 91, Mrs Leigh Hunt 246, Puritans 57, spontaneous combustion 216–17; song 'Bibo and Charon' 211–12; *see also* temperance movement; drinks
Drury Lane 113, 288
Drury Lane Theatre 128
Dryden, John, 210; *Aeneid* (trans.) 99, 153, 181–2, 203, 253
Dublin 187
Dudley, first Earl of *see* Ward, John William, first Earl of Dudley 124
duelling: abolished 3, 237; in Leicester Square 176; *see also* firearms; weapons
Dulwich College 183
dust-bins 230
dust contractors 58
dust heaps 63, 130, 169; *see also* waste
dustmen 130
dwarfs 43
dying words: Pitt 136; Sir Philip Sidney 264

earings (ropes) 145
earrings: of broom-girls 242
East End: Limehouse 281; opium dens 107, 179
East India Company 52, 148, 149
East India docks 130
East Indiamen 222, 249
East Indies 269
east wind 7, 67
eating *see* food; drink
Ecclesiastical Titles Assumption Act (1851) 2, 85
Edinburgh 103, 253
education: classical 126; medical 103, 106, 128; military 176, 187; questions and answers 171; teachers and teaching 48; *see also* schools

effervescent drinks 162
Egan, Pierce, *Life in London* 40
eggs 166, 255
Egypt 156
eight-day clocks 150
elections 2, 65, 292; election agents 238; extension of franchise 3, 125, 239–40; *see also* electoral corruption; government; Parliament; Reform Act (1832)
electoral corruption 2, 65, 238; Corrupt Practices at Elections Act (1852) 2, 65
Elephant and Castle 197
Eliot, George, *Adam Bede* 90
Elliotson, Dr John, *Human Physiology* 221
Ellis, Mrs Sarah, *The Daughters of England, The Mothers of England, The Wives of England* 86
Ellis and Blackmore 20
Elwes, John 235
embezzlement 205; *see also* bankruptcy; finance
emblematic figures: Beauty 246; Comedy 246; Fates 269; Muses 286; passions as horses 189; Recording Angel 235; Sentiment 246; Truth 148; *see also* gods and goddesses
embroidery: tambour work 222
emigration 52, 54, 149
Engels, Friedrich, *The Condition of the Working Class in England* 142
engines: fire 213; steam- 75, 76
engineers 26, 276; deserving honours 223
England. *For individual areas see under the area, e.g.* London.
entertainments: acrobatics 176; Almack's 280; amateur theatricals 13, 72; Astley's 175–6, 294; ballooning 26–7; circuses 176; knee-puppets 173; lectures 280; Leicester Square 176; panoramas 176; pantomime 175, 274; Parisian 118; Punch and Judy shows 109, 261; shooting galleries 176; Vauxhall Gardens 157, 294; *see also* exhibitions; games; holidays and resorts; music; sports; theatres
epidemics 251; smallpox 3, 209; typhus fever 182; *see also* disease
epitaphs 252
Essex marshes 261
'Ethiopian' street-musicians 143
evangelicals (Methodists) 2; philanthropic activities 84, 86, 88, 92; phraseology 157–8, 177, 190–1; sympathy with Africans 54–5; 'inner light' 190; preaching from waggons 90; *see also* Christianity; Church of England; nonconformists
Evening Prayer *see Book of Common Prayer*
Exeter Hall 55; Band of Hope meeting 2, 87; in *BH* cover design 54, 84; and sectarianism, philanthropy, politics 208

executions 28, 122, 221, Mary Furly's commuted 160; beheadings 28, 276; hangings 110–11, 119, 237, of the Mannings 2, 111, 119; *see also* prisons

exhibitions: African trophies 152; American Indians 3, 205, 208; Chinese 2, 130; Crystal Palace (Sydenham) 23; dinosaurs 23; dwarfs and giants 43; fireworks 157, 176; Great Exhibition 2, 23; Leicester Square 176; wax-works 179; *see also* entertainments

exhumation 204

expeditions: Arctic 151–2; African 152; Niger 2, 55, 129, 231; Himalayan 94

extension of franchise 3, 125, 239–40; *see also* elections; government; Parliament; Reform Act (1832)

fables: cock and bull story 191; the Seven Sleepers 265

factories *see* industrialism

fairy tales *see* nursery rhymes

Family Colonisation Loan Society 54

Farr, William 252

fashionable ('silver fork') novels: burlesqued 44, 124; characteristics 35, 44, 124; novelists 35; *Passages from the Diary of a Late Physician* 36–7

fashionable portraits: antiquarianism 124, 203; 'beauties' 168; smirks 168

fashionable society: dandies 120, 122, 123–4; entertainments 138, 157; in novels 35, 36–7, 124; phraseology 35, 39, 40, 41, 166, 168, 279; portraits 124, 168, 203; presentation at Court 120; regiments 187, 280; 'the season' 37, 237; *see also* aristocracy; footmen; holidays and resorts; liveried servants

fashions: canes 188; French 116; walking sticks 197; *see also* costume and appearance; dandies

fast and loose (game) 285

Fates 269

Fawkes, Guy 94, 196

feminism *see* women's rights

fever: African 55, 129; dens 182, 251; high temperature associated with smallpox 224; typhus ('fever') 3, 182, 251

fiddles 144

Field, Inspector Charles Plate 14; 3, 4, 177, 182; similarity to Mr Bucket 179, 183, 188

Fielding, Henry, *Tom Jones* 287; *Tom Thumb* 124

finance: Bank of England 94; bill-discounting 169, 172; contributions to charity 88, 89; dolly shops (pawnbrokers) 62; embezzlement 205; fortune-making in India 148; free-trade 79; insurance: fire 212, marine

158; Jewish money-lenders 172, 219–20; Leigh Hunt's insolvency 72; misers 235; 'Queer Street' 275; Royal Mint 219; speculation: burial-grounds 113; shares 286; sponging houses 2, 73; *see also* bankruptcy

firearms: cannon 268; pistols 96, 176, 237, 275; rifles 176; spring-guns 151; *see also* duelling; weapons

fire engines 213

fire-grates 75

fire insurance 213

fires: Great Fire of London 161; Houses of Parliament: burnt down (1834) 34, Guy Fawkes 94, 196; *see also* spontaneous combustion

firemen 213

fireworks: displays 157, 176; factories 3, 196

fish 138; cod's head and shoulders 74, pies 110, shellfish 155

Fitz- (name prefix) 138

Flanders 241

Fleet Prison 3, 14, 29, 189

Fleet River 25, 101

Fleet Street 27, 140, 197, 219

Flemish broom-sellers 241

'flimsy' (tissue-paper) 212

Flite, Miss 31

flogging 112

Flora 248

flowers: artificial 173–4; nosegays 59

Flying Dutchman 154

fogs 22, 25; 'London particulars' 49; and bull's-eyes 181

folios 102

food

   cookery: English *vs* French 138; diets: of dandies 122; of Leigh Hunt 72; for tight-waisting 99

   bread and cakes: bread 62, 72, 166, 174, 255; sandwiches 255; currant cake 255, sponge cake 72

   butter and dripping: butter 160, 174, 255; dripping 59, 60; 'kitchen-stuff' 59, 62

   confectionery: brandy balls 110

   eggs 166, 255

   fish 138; cod's head and shoulders 74; -pies 110; shellfish 155

   fruit: apples 189; hothouse 72; lemons 270; -pies 110; rhubarb 163; Saint Michael's oranges 74

   honey 79

   meat 138; 'junk' 145; on spits 172; -pies 110

   pies: fish 110; fruit 110; meat 110

   poultry 138

   puddings: marrow 166

   vegetables: cabbage 197; marrows 166;

potatoes 2, 91, 203 *see also* dining habits; dining places; drinks; drunkenness

footmen 42–3; mounted on coaches 279; physiques 270; powdered wigs 42, 43, 285

forfeits 190

Forster, John: quoted or mentioned 6, 72, 94, 101, 181, 191, 251
   comments on *BH* 15, 65, 72, 126
   friendship with Dickens 26, 29, 39, 62, 65, 93, 119, 143–4

Fortunatus 150

'Found drowned' bills 281

France: artificial flower making 173–4; British fear of invasion by 173; British visitors to 2, 94, 116–17, 155; exile of Charles Edward Stuart 173; loses Quebec 198; *see also* French; Paris

franchise: extension of 3, 125, 239–40; *see also* elections; government; Parliament; Reform Act (1832)

Franklin, Sir John 3, 151–2; *see also* Niger expedition

Freemasonry 239

free-trade 79

French: cookery 138; culture 116–17; doctors (spontaneous combustion) 217; fashions 116–17; the French caricatured as monkeys 119; French speech in *BH* 120; giants 43; navy 198; novels 123; quack doctors 118; Revolution 35, 117, 119–20, 183; *see also* France; Paris

fruit: apples 189; hothouse 72; lemons 270; -pies 110; rhubarb 163; Saint Michael's oranges 74; *see also* Dead Sea fruit

Fuller's earth 199

funerals: and burial-clubs 113; Dickens's attitude towards 269; of the Duke of Wellington 4, 269; of pagans 115; of the poor 113–14, 288; of the rich 269; of soldiers 175; *see also* burial grounds; death; mourning

Furley, Mary 160

furnishings: furniture: beds 67, 193; chairs 67, porter's 169, 172; clocks: eight-day 150, 'Parliamentaries' 58; fire-grates 75; sofas 67; tables: gilt 44; ornaments: artificial flowers 173–4; Chelsea figures 73; Chinese ivory 94, 96; styles: convertible bamboo 67; eighteenth-century 68; gilt 44

Gad's Hill: Dickens's cast of 'The Graces' 73

gaiters 43

Gall, Franz Joseph 139

game birds 213

games: battledore and shuttlecock 30; billiards 118; Blind Man's Buff 30; charades 145; chess 30; children's 30, 230; dominoes 118;

fast and loose 285; forfeits 190; Turvey 134; *see also* sports; toys

gardens: cemetery landscaping 252; market 163; Parisian 117, 118

garrisons 198, 268; *see also* Army

garters: footmen's 43; *see also* Order of the Garter; Star and Garter

gas lighting 27, 144, 260; *see also* lighting

Gaskell, Elizabeth, *Cranford* 138; *Mary Barton* 275, 293; *North and South* 201–2, 293

gasworks 103; accidents 3, 193, 196

Gay, John, *The Beggar's Opera* 211

genealogy: Welsh 148–9

General Board of Health 26, 114, 252

Gentlemen's Magazine 216

geology 23, 129, 145

George III 122, 157

George IV Plates 11, 12; 3, 4, 131, 134; at Brighton 68, 136; portraits of 131, 136, 186, 225

Georgian architecture 260

German: broom-sellers 241, 242; street-musicians 143; waltzes 294; *see also* holidays and resorts

ghosts: Flying Dutchman 154; in *Hamlet* 99, 265; 'popular ghost' 158

Ghost's Walk 7, 77, 224

giants 43

Gibbon, Edward, *History of the Decline and Fall of the Roman Empire* 265

Gibson, Mrs Thomas Milner 246

Gillray, James 136, 186

gilt tables 44

ginger beer 155

girls' schools 48

Glasgow 103

glass 59, 60; *see also* waste

glass-works 294

glee singers 144; *see also* music; songs

Gloucestershire 65

gloves 96

gods and goddesses: Alpheus 246; Apollo 129; Fates 269; Flora 248; Graces 73; Jupiter 204, 276; Mercury 42, 204, 210, 279; Minerva 150; Pallas Athene 156; Venus 275; *see also* classical allusions; emblematic figures

gold-headed canes 188; *see also* walking sticks

goldfinches 63

Goldsmith, Oliver 83

Goodwin Sands 248

Gordon-Cumming, George 3, 152

Gore, Mrs Catherine 35

Gothic revival 85; *see also* arts

gout 2, 40

governesses 48

government: British constitution 36, 142; coalition of 1853 237; Civil List 200; Commissioner of Woods and Forests 124; Dickens's attitude towards 34, 125, 251; extension of franchise 3, 125, 239–40; honours system 3, 7, 222–3; *London Gazette* 186; ministerial crisis (1851) 124, 125, 236–7; pocket boroughs 238; political phraseology 110, 124, 260, 292; Young England 3, 123, 124; *see also* elections; electoral corruption; House of Commons; House of Lords; Parliament; political parties; Reform Act (1832)

Gower Street 100

gowns: dressing- 243; barrister's silk 30

Graces, Three 73

Gravesend 157

graveyards *see* burial grounds

Gray's Inn 20

Gray's Inn Road 169

grease 59, 62; *see also* waste

Great Exhibition 2, 23; *see also* Crystal Palace

Great Expectations 62, 68, 193

Great Fire of London 161

Great North Road 65

Great Northern Railway 276

Great Seal of England 51–2

Great Turnstile 101

Greenwich 163

Greenwich Hospital 26; pensioners 26

Grenadier Guards 263, 271

Grey, Lady Jane 63

Guest, Lady Charlotte, *Mabinogion* 149

Guild of Literature and Art 13

Guildhall 111

Gunpowder Plot 94, 196

Guppy, Mr 33

Guy Fawkes 94, 196

hairdressing: bear's-grease 96; moustaches 163, 239; powder 42–3, 285; whiskers 3, 163, 'Newgate frill' 163, 'Newgate knockers' 179; *see* costume and appearance; wigs

Hamilton-Gordon, George, fourth Earl of Aberdeen 237

Hampstead 101

Hampton Court 275

'Hampton Court Beauties' 168

handcuffs: 'darbies' 179

Handel, George Fredrick, 'Harmonious Blacksmith' 140; *Saul* 175

handkerchiefs: magic 280

handwriting: law-hand 44

hangings 110–11, 119, 237; of the Mannings 2, 111, 119

Hanging-Sword Alley 197

hard labour 242

Hard Times 172, 286

Harlequin 175

harmonic meetings 110, 216; *see also* music; songs

hatchments 230

hats: Bollingers 65; bowlers 65; cocked 43, 279; gentlemen's 84, 162; glazed 109, 116; Quakers' 84

Hatton Garden 193, 205

Hawthorne, Nathaniel 6–7; *English Notebooks* 100–1

   The House of the Seven Gables 6; influences depictions of: Bleak House 7, 67, Chesney Wold 7, 39, 77, Esther 7, 45, Skimpole 7, 68, 70–1, Tulkinghorn 7, 41–2, 261, Volumnia 7, 200

   The Scarlet Letter 6, 46; influences depictions of: Lady Dedlock 6–7, 46, 240, Tulkinghorn 6–7, 41–2, 240

Haydon, Benjamin Robert 292

Haymarket 176

health *see* chemists; disease; doctors; hospitals; medicine; sanitary reform and sanitation

heathens: religious beliefs 115

Her Majesty's Theatre 138

heraldry 116, 230, 269

Hermes *see* Mercury

heroism: captains of industry 201; Carlyle's concept 3, 201; doctors 5, 107; policemen 5; soldiers 5, 174

Hertfordshire 28

High Church *see* Oxford Movement

High Court terms 20

Highgate 64, 284

Hilary term 20

Hill, Sir Rowland 223

Himalaya Mountains 188

Hittites 171

Hogarth, William 231, 292

Holbein 82

Holborn 130; Circus 56, 193, 205; High Street 49, 101, 193; Hill 25, 98; Viaduct 25

holidays and resorts

   aristocratic and fashionable: Bath 156, 200, 279; Brighton 136; France 116–17; German spas 155, 156

   British: Bath 156, 200, 279; Brighton 136; Cheltenham 156; Gravesend 157; Leamington 156; Malvern 156; Margate 157; Ramsgate 157; Tunbridge Wells 57

   continental: France 116–18, 155; Germany 155, 156

   Middle East: Egypt and Turkey 155, 156; *see also* entertainments

Holland 43

Holland, Henry 136

Holland House 47–8

Holloway 64, 65

Holloway House of Correction 3, 192, 242

Holyhead 187

honey 79

Hong Kong 277

honours system 3, 7, 222–3

Hood, Thomas 219; 'The Bridge of Sighs' 6, 160, 284, 288; 'Moral Reflections on the Cross of St Paul's' 6, 161

Horace, *Odes* 235, 241

Horne, Richard Hengist 27, 72, 174, 181, 188, 198

Horse Guards 187; clock 286; *see also* Royal Horse Guards

horse of the Apocalypse 229, 280

Horsemonger Lane Gaol 111, 119

horses: cavalry 174; emblematic of the passions 189; painted by Stubbs 224; performing 175–6; and manure 23; and postilions 116; and vehicles: caravans 279, carriages and coaches 77, 93, 116, 188, carts 76, 130, 277; *see also* horse of the Apocalypse

hospitals 127, 128; admission procedures 253, 255, 258; cadavers 193; general 84, 129, 255; medical education 106, 128; specialist 85; *see also* chemists; doctors

hotels: French 117, 119

houris 175

House of Commons 25, 127; burnt down in 1834 34; and Guy Fawkes 94, 196; 'whipping in' 260; *see also* extension of franchise; government; House of Lords; Parliament; political parties

House of Lords: burnt down in 1834 34; and Guy Fawkes 94, 196; Speaker 20; woolsack 20, 30, 295; *see also* government; House of Commons; Parliament; political parties

Household Narrative of Current Events 100, 111, 114

Household troops 174, 270; Coldstream Guards 271; Grenadier Guards 263, 271; Life Guards 189, 271, 280, 287; Royal Horse Guards 271, 280; Scots Guards 271; *see also* Army; officers; regiments; soldiers

housekeepers 74–5, 77, 78

houses *see* lodging-houses; public houses

Hugo, Victor, *The Hunchback of Notre-Dame* 204; *Notre-Dame de Paris* 37

Hunt, Leigh Plates 6, 7; *A Jar of Honey from Mount Hybla* 79; *Autobiography* 6, 70, 71, 72, 292; original of Skimpole 2, 4, 64, 68, 70–3, 243, 246, 292; reviews *George Selwyn* 122

Hunt, Marianne 71, 246

Hunterian Museum 128

Hyde Park Corner 115, 136, 138, 152

illegitimacy: Esther's nicknames 83; Fitz- (name prefix) 138

illustrations to *BH*: 'Attorney and Client' 231; 'Coavinses' 73; cover design Plate 1, 68, 137, 169, 551; dark plates 224; 'The Ghost's Walk' 224; 'The Lord Chancellor Copies from Memory' 62; 'Mr. Chadband "Improving" a Tough Subject' 190; 'Mr. Guppy's Entertainment' 163; 'The Night' 281; 'Shadow' 271; *see also* 'originals' depicted in illustrations

illustrations for books *see* book illustrations; for newspapers 218

immigrants: Flemish broom-sellers 241; German broom-sellers 241, 242, street-musicians 143; Italian street-musicians 242; Swiss Savoyard broom-sellers 242; Tyrolean street-musicians 173; *see also* Irish

inadmissible evidence 111; *see also* law

indentures 259

India 67, 198, 269; East Indiamen 222, 249; English marriage market 149; Englishmen make fortunes 148; Overland Route 155, Mail 222; missionary and philanthropic involvement 52, 54

Indians: American 87, craze for 3, 205, 208; West: missionary and philanthropic involvement 54–5, 56, 87, 152

industrial novels 201–2, 293

industrial regions: counties north of Lincolnshire 54, 76, 136, 293; Manchester 79; Midlands 293

Industrial Revolution 76, 79, 136, 201; *see also* industrial regions; industrialism; inventions; inventors

industrialism 201–2; aristocratic marriages 202; 'captains of industry' 3, 36, 201–2; iron masters 201–2; iron works 293; workers 76, 201, 293; *see also* industrial regions; Industrial Revolution; inventions; inventors

'inner light' (doctrine) 190; *see also* nonconformists

Inner Temple *see* Inns of Court

inns *see* public houses

Inns of Chancery 20, melancholy associations 264; Clifford's Inn 20, 219; Serjeants' Inn 20, 155; Staple Inn 20, 100–1; Symond's Inn 20, 230; Thavies Inn 20, 56, 64; *see also* Chancery, Court of; Inns of Court

Inns of Court 20, melancholy associations 264; Gray's Inn 20; Lincoln's Inn 20, 49, 56, Fields 20, 100, 101, Old and New Halls 20, Old and New Squares 49, 59, 110; Temple, The (Inner and Middle) 20, 28, 100, 102, 197; *see also* Chancery, Court of; Inns of Chancery

inquests 100, 110
insurance: fire 212; marine 158
interment *see* burial grounds
inventions: power looms 76; spinning machines 136; steam-engines 75, 76; steam hammers 4, 293–4; *see also* Industrial Revolution; industrialism; inventors
inventors: Arkwright, Richard 136; Cartwright, Edmund 76; Hill, Roland 223; Nasmyth, James 293; Watt, James 44, 75; *see also* industrialism; Industrial Revolution; inventions
investigation: criminal *see* crime
Io 210, 276
Ireland: civil unrest 3, 187; potato famine 2, 55, 91, 103; railway construction 277; *see also* Irish immigrants
Irish immigrants: brickmakers 2, 91, 253; 'Irish' fever (typhus) 182; in low lodging-houses 91, rookeries 142; name: Anastasia 111; *see also* Ireland
iron masters 201–2
iron works 293
Irving, Washington, *The Sketch Book* 37
Isle of Wight 219
Isleworth 25
Islington 64
Italians: immigrant street-musicians 173, 242; swaddled children 289
Italy 289; visited by Dickens 71, 275; Leigh Hunt 292; Landor 94
Ixion 234

Jacobite toasts and songs 173
Jarndyce, John 32, 65; characterization revisions 93
jaundice 32, 228
Jellyby, Caddy 57
Jerrold, Douglas 219
jewellery: earrings 242; hair 63; mourning 179, 181; pearl 200
Jews: money-lenders 172, 219–20; wearing whiskers 163
Jo 2, 111–12; characterization revisions 141
'John Doe and Richard Roe' 166
Johnson, Dr Samuel 134, 172, 246
journalism *see* newspapers
judges 30, 31, 59; *see also* Chancery, Court of; law; Lord Chancellor; Masters
Judicature Act (1873) 83
Julius Caesar 240, 271
'junk' (salt-meat) 145
Jupiter 204, 276
justices of the peace 189
Juvenal, *Satires* 41

Keeper of the Privy Purse 31

Kenge, 'Conversation' 2, 4, 47–8
Kennington 197
Kensington 136, 138
Kent 65; marshes 193, 261
King Arthur 173
King's Bench Office 102
King's Cross 169, 276
King's Dragoon Guards 174
Kingsley, Charles 68
kitchen maids 62
kitchen-stuff 59, 62
knee-breeches 43; buckskins 122
knee-puppets 173
Knights of the Bath 189

ladies' maids 71
Lamb, Charles, 'Witches, and Other Night-Fears' 250
Lambeth 97, 197, 235, 294
lamps *see* lighting
Lancashire 196, 202
Landor, Walter Savage Plate 9; 2, 4, 57, 93–4, 96 depicted by Browne as John Jarndyce Plate 6; 65, 94
landscaping *see* gardening
Landseer, Sir Edwin Henry 168
Lansdowne, Henry Petty-Fitzmaurice, 3rd Marquess of 2, 40
lanterns: bull's-eyes 181; carriage 259; hand- 281; *see also* lighting
Laplace, Pierre 25
larks 63
Latin phrases: 'classic shades' 128; 'trusty' 167
laudanum *see* opium
Laurie, Sir Peter 160
law: arrest warrants 189; common 82; Dickens's knowledge and experience of 20, 29, 140; Doctors' Commons 140; and Equity 82; -hand 44; High Court terms 20, 154, 162; inadmissible evidence of children 111; inquests 100, 110; justices of the peace 189; magistrates 196; paper of causes 186, 292; nosegays 59; sponging houses 6, 73; -stationers 97, 98, 264; Westminster Hall 20, 153, 154; *see also* barristers; Chancery, Court of; crime; Inns of Court; Inns of Chancery; judges; law-writers; lawyers' clerks; legal; Lord Chancellor; Masters; police; solicitors
Law Courts 154
law-hand (handwriting) 44
Law List 163
law-writers 97; copying by hand discontinued 2, 33; law-hand 44; payment per folio 102; *see also* lawyers' clerks
lawyers' clerks: articled 156, 162, 204; articles of

apprenticeship 204; salaried 96, 156, 204; *see also* law-writers

Lawrence, Sir Thomas, 'George IV' (painting) Plate 11; 136, 186, 189

lawyers *see* attorneys; barristers; solicitors; Queen's Counsel

Leamington 156

legal: district of London 28, 97–8; fictions: 'John Doe and Richard Roe' 3, 166; phraseology 28, 32, 188, 230

Leicester Square 176, 192

Lely, Sir Peter, 'Hampton Court Beauties' 168

lemons 99, 213, 270

letters: of administration 213; begging- 71, 125; penny postage 223

Lewes, G. H. 217

Life Guards 271, 280, 287

lighting: bull's-eyes 181; candles 27, 102, 103; carriage lanterns 259; crusies 250; gas 27, 144, 260; hand-lanterns 281; Horse Guards' clock 286; lucifer matches 211; street lighting 27, 144, 260; *see also* oil

lignum vitae 218

Limehouse 281

Lincoln's Inn *see* Inns of Court

Lincoln's Inn Fields 20, 100, 101

Lincolnshire 39, 150, 276

linnets 63

Litany *see Book of Common Prayer*

Little Dorrit 107, 123, 238

liveried servants: coachmen 278; *see also* footmen

Liverpool 187

Livingstone, David 3, 132

Locke, Joseph 276

lodging houses 91, 179, 182

London (map) 300; areas:

    central

        Baker Street 279; Bell Yard 140; Bloomsbury 150; Carey Street 140, 264; Chancery Lane 20, 49, 59, 73, 97, 101, 110, 153, 154, 287; Chichester Rents 38, 59, 288; City 28, 92, 97, 111, 155, 230, 286; Clerkenwell 97, 193; Cursitor Street 73, 97, 101; Drury Lane 113, 288; Fleet Street 27, 140, 197, 219; Gower Street 100; Great Turnstile 101; Hanging-Sword Alley 197; Hatton Garden 193, 205; Holborn 130; Circus 56, 193, 205; High Street 49, 101, 193; Hill 25, 98; Viaduct 25; Leadenhall Market 28; Leadenhall Street 28; Lincoln's Inn Fields 20, 100, 101; Ludgate Hill 22; New Oxford Street 141; Newman Street 131, 138; Queen Square 150; Russell Street 113; Saffron Hill 193; Soho 176, 186, 192; St Giles's 3, 4, 141–2, 179, 182; St Martin's Lane 197; Strand 27; Temple 126, 154–5;

        Temple Bar 27–8; Took's Court 97; Tower 26, 130, 219; Whitefriars 197

    West End 260, 286, 296

        Belgrave Square 38; Haymarket 176; Hyde Park Corner 115, 136, 138, 152; Leicester Square 176, 192; Mayfair 38, 67, 254; Oxford Street 131, 141; Pall Mall 143, 156; Piccadilly 49; Soho 176, 186, 192; Vauxhall 294; Westminster 126–7, 265; White Horse Cellar 49; Whitehall 109, 187, 286

    East End 179

        Aldgate 130; Limehouse 281; Mile End Road 130; Newgate Market 64; Old Street Road 96; Whitechapel 130, 182; Smithfield 130, 193; Smithfield Market 3, 4, 22, 130–1, 143, 193

    north

        Agar Town 91; Battle Bridge 169; Bayham Street 100, 128; Camden Town 128; Clarendon Square 242; Gray's Inn Road 169; Hampstead 101; Highgate 64, 284; Holloway 64, 65; Islington 64; King's Cross 169, 276; Pentonville 96–7, 294; Polygon 242; Somers Town 242, 243

    south-east

        Bermondsey 163; Cheapside 48; Elephant and Castle 197; Greenwich 163; Kennington 197; Lambeth 97, 197, 235, 294; New Kent Road 197; Rotherhithe 163; Southwark 294; Tooting 99–100; Walworth 197; Waterloo 197; Woolwich 198

    south-west

        Chelsea 73, 128–9, 138, 271; Cheyne Row 70, 73, 243; Kensington 136, 138; Vauxhall 294

    bridges: Blackfriars 6, 101, 161, 197; Vauxhall 196; Waterloo 197, 284; Westminster 155, 197, 261

    City Corporation: ticket-porters 155

    docks: 26, 107, 130, 198, 281

    slums: Agar Town 91; St Giles's rookery 3, 4, 141–2, 179, 182; *see also* churches; Inns of Court; Inns of Chancery; prisons; sewerage; Thames River; theatres

London and Southwestern Railway 197, 294

London Gas Company 196

London Gazette 186, 205

'London particular' 49

Long Vacation 20, 154, 162

Longfellow, Henry Wadsworth 181

Lord Chamberlain of the Household 123

Lord Chancellors 33, 51, 52, 101; Lord Lyndhurst 2, 20; woolsack 20, 30, 295; *see also* Chancery, Court of; judges; Masters; law

Lord Great Chamberlain 123, 212

Lord Mayors 65, 223
Lords of the Admiralty 109; *see also* Navy
Lord's Prayer: said backwards 190; *see also* Bible; prayers
Loudon, J. C., *On . . . Cemeteries, and . . . Churchyards* 252
Louis XVI 117, 274
Lovell, Francis 204
lucifer matches 211
Ludgate Hill 22
lunacy *see* asylums
Lunardi, Vincenzo 27
Lyceum Theatre 128
Lyndhurst, first Baron *see* Copley, John Singleton, the younger, first Baron Lyndhurst
Lytton, Sir Edward *see* Bulwer, Sir Edward Lytton

machines *see* inventions
Maclise, Daniel 169, 181
MacNish, Robert, *The Anatomy of Drunkenness* 216; *Philosophy of Sleep* 216, 221
Madeira (wine) 269
madhouses *see* asylums
magic: conjuring 4, 42; handkerchiefs 280; necromancers 125; witches 190
magistrates 196
maids: kitchen 62; ladies' 71
mail-coaches 49, 93; cease operating 1, 2, 77, 248; *see also* coaches and carriages
Malta 156, 198
Malthus, Thomas 247, *Essay on the Principle of Population* 247
Malvern 156
Manchester 56, 79
Manchester School 79
Mangnall, Richmal, *Historical and Miscellaneous Questions* 171
Manners, Lord John 3, 124
Manning, Maria Plate 10; 2, 119–20, 276
Manning, Frederick George 2, 119
Mansion House 1, 14, 223
man-traps 151
manufacturing *see* industrial regions; industrialism; Industrial Revolution; textile manufacture
manure: 22–3; *see also* mud
Margate 116, 157
Marie-Antoinette 117, 274
marine insurance 158
marine-stores 59, 62; *see also* waste
market-gardens 163
marriage: Army policy towards 197–8; between aristocrats and industrialist families 202; divorce 4, 286; spinsters visiting Bath 200, India 149

marrow pudding 166
Marryat, Captain Frederick, *Jacob Faithful* 216
Marshalsea Prison 189
marshes of Essex 261; Kent 193, 261
Martin Chuzzlewit 75–6, 163, 202
Martineau, Harriet, articles on deaf and dumb children 296; *The Sickness and Health of the People of Bleaburn* 289
Mary, Queen of Scots 276
Master of the Rolls 31
Masters (judges) 28, 31, 102; *see also* Chancery, Court, of; judges; law
matches: lucifers 211
Mayfair 38, 67, 254
Mayhew, Augustus 112
Mayhew, Henry, *The Upper Rhine* 166
meat 138; 'junk' 145; on spits 172; -pies 110
medical education 103, 106
Medical Reform Act (1858) 103, 106
medical reform movement 5, 106
medicine: black draught 173; dispensing 182–3; and lignum vitae 218; quack medicines: French 118, for gout 40; vaccinations 209; *see also* chemists; disease; doctors; opium
Medway 193
Megalosaurus Plate 3; 2, 23
Melville, Herman, *Redburn* 216
'mendicity tickets' 84; *see also* philanthropy
Mercury (Hermes) 42, 204, 210, 279
metal *see* waste
Methodists *see* evangelicals
Metropolitan Health of Towns Association 251
metropolitan interment *see* burial grounds
Metropolitan Interments Act (1850) 2, 114, 252
Metropolitan Police Acts (1829, 1839) 108, 159
Metropolitan Sanitary Association 67, 92, 254
Michaelmas term 20
Middle Temple *see* Inns of Court
Midlands 293
Mile End Road 130
military: education 176, 187; funerals 175; music 197, 198, 263; phraseology 258, 263; *see also* Army; Household troops; officers; regiments; soldiers
milk 58, 99
Mill, James 247
Millbank Prison 192, 265
Milton, John, *Comus* 151; *Paradise Lost* 74, 203, 250, 285; *Sonnets* 255
Minerva 150; *see also* Pallas Athene
mines: quicksilver 127
ministerial crisis (1851) 124, 125, 236–7
misers 235
missionaries: domestic and foreign: 2, 56, 143; societies 54–5, 85, 143; *see also* philanthropy
Mohammedans 175

Molière, *L'Avare* 166
monarchs and rulers: Alfred 87; Anne 57; Arthur 173; Charles I 78, 97; Charles II 155, 168, 186; George III 122, 157; Julius Caesar 240, 271; Louis XVI 117, 274; Marie-Antoinette 117, 274; Mary, Queen of Scots 276; Napoleon 174, 277; Richard III 204; *see also* George IV
money *see* finance
money-lenders; Jewish 172, 219–20
monkeys: caricature of the French 119; organ-grinders' 172–3
Montgolfier brothers 27
Monument, The 235
Moore, Thomas 6, 48, 177; 'Ballad Stanzas' 285; *Irish Melodies* 73–4, 263; *Lallah Rookh* 175, 294–5; 'M.P.; or, The Blue-Stocking' 140; 'Sound the Loud Timbrel' 190
morgues: dead-houses 281
Morning Prayer *see Book of Common Prayer*
Mornington, first Earl of *see* Wellesley, Garrett, first Earl of Mornington
Mother Goose 83, 270
Mother Shipton 83
mourning: coaches and carriages 229, 269; costume 248, 270; hatchments 230; jewellery 179, 181; *see also* death; funerals
moustaches 163, 239; *see also* hairdressing
mud 22–3, 112
Mudfog and Other Sketches, The 56, 172–3
Muscular Christianity 68
music: Leigh Hunt 72–3; military sheet music 197; phraseology 210, 213, 235; singers: comic 157, 216, glee 144; venues: harmonic meetings 110, 216, music halls 110, public houses 110, 212, 'song and supper rooms' 110, Vauxhall Gardens 157, 294; *see also* bands; dancing; entertainments; musical instruments; opera; songs; street-music
music halls 110
musical instruments: barrel organs 144, 173; bassoons 198; bells 144; church organs 139; fiddles 144; Pan-pipes 261; tabors 173; tamborines 242; timbrels 190; violins 144; whistles 173; *see also* music
Mystery of Edwin Drood, The 84, 101, 107, 112, 139, 158, 202, 204

names: biblical: Esther 46, Rachael 46, Sarah 191; nicknames: of Esther 83; of Caddy 138. *For other characters' names, see under the surname, e.g.* Chadband, Rev.
nankeen trousers 200
Napoleon 174, 277
Nash, John 136, 138
Nasmyth, James 293

National Philanthropic Association 113
nausea in thieves' dens 181
nautical phraseology 129, 145
Navy: French 198; Greenwich Hospital 26; Lords of the Admiralty 109; Pay Office 205; Plymouth 224; Russian 198; squadrons 54, 277; stations 198; surgeons: pay disparity with Army 3, 5, 106, 127; *see also* boats; nautical phraseology; seamen; ships
nebular hypothesis 25
necromancers 125; *see also* magic
negus 209
Nero 192
New Kent Road 197
New Oxford Street 141
New Testament: Dickens contrasts with sectarianism 191–2; *see also* Bible
Newgate Calendar 193
'Newgate frill' (whiskers) 163
'Newgate knockers' (whiskers) 179
Newgate Market 64
Newgate Prison 192–3
Newman Street 131, 138
newspapers: in dining places 166; 'flimsy' 212; illustrations 218; and Overland Mail 222; phraseology 38, 110, 175
Nicholas Nickleby 35, 48, 114, 168, 222, 270, 279
nicknames: of Esther 83; of Caddy 138; *see also* names
Niger expedition 2, 55, 129, 231
'Noble Savage' 208
nonconformists
    evangelicals (Methodists): burial grounds 113; 'inner light' 190; philanthropic activities 2, 84, 86, 88, 92; phraseology 157–8, 161, 177, 190–1; preachers 90, 158; sympathy with Africans 54–5
    Quakers 84, 88
    Wesleyans 88; *see also* Christianity; Church of England; Exeter Hall; religious beliefs; Roman Catholics
'noodle' 124
Normans 271; compared to Saxons 202; 'Fitz-' 138
Northamptonshire 39, 134, 150
nosegays 59
Notre Dame cathedral 118
Nova Scotia 174
novels: fashionable 35, 36–7, 44, 124; French 123; industrial 201–2, 293; 'romance' 6, 8, 16; 'urban Gothic' 37
Nuisance Removals Act (1846) 251
nursery rhymes and tales: 'A Frog He Would a-Wooing Go' 139; 'A was an apple-pie' 83; Dickens's attitude towards 172; 'Goosey, goosey gander' 74; 'Jack the Giant Killer'

173; 'Little old woman, and whither so high?' 83; *Mother Goose* 83, 270; 'Old Mother Hubbard' 83; 'The Three Bears' 168; *see also Arabian Nights*; Perrault, Charles; songs

officers, Army 258; duelling prohibited 237; education 187; in India 149; purchase system abolished 187; retire to Bath 200; whiskers acceptable on cavalry officers 163; *see also* Army; Household troops; regiments; soldiers

oil: lamps 27, 250; lanterns 181; street-lighting 260; 'train' 159; *see also* lighting

Ojibbeways 205, 208

old clothes 62; *see also* waste

Old Curiosity Shop 48, 158, 279

Old Ship tavern 110

Old Street Road 96

Oliver Twist 63, 100, 108, 110, 193

Olympic Theatre 128

omnibuses 112, 275

'omnicompetence' 5, 108; *see also* police

opera: Covent Garden 277; Opera Colonnade 138; Royal Italian 43, 277; swooning 122; *see also* entertainments; music; theatres

opium 103, 107; causing death 2, 107; De Quincey's *Confessions* 220–1; dens 107, 179; laudanum 107, 286; *see also* medicine

oranges: Saint Michael's 74

Order of the Garter 136, 189; *see also* Star and Garter (public house); garters

organ-grinders 172, 173; *see also* street-music

organs: barrel 144, 173; church 139

'originals' depicted in illustrations to *BH*: George IV as Mr Turveydrop Plates 11 and 12, 131, 136, 186; Inspector Field as Mr Bucket Plates 14 and 15, 177; Samuel Rogers as Grandfather Smallweed Plate 13, 169; Skimpole as Leigh Hunt Plates 6 and 7, 70; W. S. Landor as John Jarndyce Plates 6 and 9, 65, 94; *see also* illustrations to *BH*

ornaments: artificial flowers 173–4; Chelsea figures 73; Chinese ivory 94, 96; *see also* furnishings

orphans 52, 82, 100; asylums 85; *see also* children

Our Mutual Friend 63, 110, 123, 142, 163, 235, 278

Overland Mail 222

Overland Route 155

Ovid, *Metamorphoses* 129, 150

Owen, Sir Richard 23

Oxford 20, 85, 96

Oxford Movement 2, 85, 86; relationship to Roman Catholics 85; sisterhoods 85; and Young England 3, 123; *see also* Church of England

Oxford Street 131, 141

padded calves 122

paddles: butter 160

painted ceilings 101–2, 144

paintings and engravings. *For specific works, see under the name of the artist; see also* arts; portraits

Pall Mall 143, 156

Pallas Athene 156; *see also* Minerva

Palmerston, third Viscount *see* Temple, John Henry, third Viscount Palmerston

'Panopticon' 265

panoramas 176

Pan-pipes 261

pantomime 175, 274

papal aggression 2, 6, 85; *see also* Church of England; Roman Catholics

papal bull *see* papal aggression

paper 62; *see also* waste

paper of causes 186, 292

Pardiggle, Mrs: characterization revisions 87

Paris: attractions 117–18; bohemians 71; Catlin's American Indians 208; cemeteries 118; Dickens's fondness for 117; fashionable resort for the British 116–17; travel to 2, 116; *see also* France; French

Parliament: blue minutes 231; criticized for aristocratic exclusiveness 35–6, 125, 201; Dickens's attitude towards 34, 251; divorce jurisdiction 286; extension of franchise 3, 125, 239–40; members of 238; turnpike trusts 284; Westminster Hall 154; 'whips' 260; *see also* elections; government; House of Commons; House of Lords; Torys; Whigs

'Parliamentaries' (clocks) 58

pattens 56

Paul, Howard 157

'Paul Pry', *Oddities of London Life* 31

pawnbrokers: dolly shops 62

Paymaster-General 94

pearl jewellery 200

peas 122

Peasants' Revolt 44; *see also* Wat Tyler

penitentiaries in America 265, 268; *see also* prisons

'penny-a-line' 110; *see also* newspapers

penny postage 223

pens 56

Pentonville 96–7, 294

Pentonville Prison 192

performing: dogs 118; horses 175–6; *see also* trained birds

Perrault, Charles, *Contes du Temps Passé* 38, 46, 57, 270, 280, 294; *see also Arabian Nights*; nursery rhymes and tales

'petit bag' 31
Petrarch 129, 246
Phaethon 129
phaetons 281
Pharmacy Act (1852) 183
Pharmacy Act (1868) 107
philanthrophy: Band of Hope Plate 8; 2, 87–8; charities 83–5, 86–7, 88, 90, 91–2; charity schools 171; childrens' involvement 87–8; contributions 88, 90; district visitors 2, 88, 91–2; management committees 84, 86; missionaries 2, 54–5, 56, 85, 143; subscription cards 84, 86; tracts 88, 92; *see also* Christianity; Church of England; Exeter Hall; nonconformists
Philosophical Transactions 216
Phoenix Fire Insurance 213
phraseology: advertising 142, 175; biblical 31, 49, 58, 101, 117–18; boxing 28, 158, 182; clichés 35, 76, 88, 163, 167, 278; colloquialisms 74, 75, 159, 163, 166, 167; commonplaces 67, 102; fashionable 35, 39, 40, 41, 166, 168, 279; financial 218, 275; humorous 49, 58, 74; Latin 128, 167; legal 28, 30, 32, 102, 158, 166, 188; marine insurance 158; military 258, 263; musical 210, 213, 235; nautical 129, 145; newspaper 38, 110, 175; policemen's 109, 159, 182, 252, 274; political 110, 124, 260, 292; puns 159, 250, 271; religious 88, 157–8, 161, 177, 260; slang 91, 159–60, 162, 166, 167, 179, 182; *see also* proverbs
phrenology 139, 171
physicians 103, 106, 188; *see also* chemists; doctors; hospitals; medicine; surgeons
Piccadilly 49
Pickwick Papers, The 29, 49, 73, 88, 102, 157–8, 167, 177
Pictures from Italy 118
piemen 110
pies: fish 110; fruit 110; meat 110
pigs 169, 274
pins 58; *see also* waste
pipe-clay 145
Piper, Anastasia 111
Piranesi 220–1
pistols 96, 176, 237, 275
Pitt, William, the younger 136, 237, 285
Plato, *Republic* 189
plot of *BH*. *See* composition of *BH*
plumbing 57, 199, 242; *see also* baths and showers; boilers
Plymouth 224, 248
pneumonia 258
poachers 151
pocket boroughs 238

polar expeditions 3, 151–2
police: constables 108, 109; costume 109; crossing-sweepers protected 112, 159; detectives 5, 177, 179; heroism 5; imperturbability 109, 281; 'omnicompetence' 5, 108; phraseology: 'darbies' 182, 'moving on' 109, 159, 252, 'reckoning up' 274; professionalization 5, 28, 108, 179; redundancy of beadles 2, 108; Towns Police Clauses Act (1847) 251; *see also* crime; law
Police Acts (1829, 1839) 5, 252
political economy 4, 247
political parties: radicals 201; Torys 35–6, 124, 201, 236–7; Whigs 36, 124, 236, 237; *see also* government; House of Commons; House of Lords; Parliament; Young England
political phraseology: 'chairing the Member' 292; 'noodle' 124; 'rally round' 110; 'whip' 260
politics *see* government
pollution: burial grounds 113–14, 211, 251, 252; fog and coal smoke 22, 25, 49; mud and manure 22–3, 251; water 26, 251, 252; *see also* sanitary reform and sanitation; Smithfield Market
Polygon, The 242
Poole, John, *Paul Pry* 91
Poor Law Amendment Act (1834) 258
Poor Law Commission 176
poor relief 252
Pope, Alexander 172; *An Essay on Criticism* 32, 210; *Epistles and Satires of Horace, Imitated* 145; *Moral Essays* 102
porter's chairs 169, 172
portraits: fashionable 124, 168, 203; artists' self-71–2; 'sitting for your portrait' 177; *see also* arts
Portsmouth 205
postage, penny 223
post-chaises 93
postilions 93, 116
potatoes 2, 91, 103
potboys 58, 211
potteries 294
poultry 138
power-looms 76
prayers: for Charles I 78; Litany 196; Lord's Prayer backwards 190; for Parliament 238; *see also* Book of Common Prayer
pre-Raphaelitism 71
presentation at Court 120; *see also* fashionable society
Prince Regent *see* George IV
Princess's Theatre 128
Prior, Matthew 212

prisons: attempted suicides sentenced 3, 160; Brixton 192, 242; 'the cage' 225; 'crusies' (lighting) 250; Fleet 3, 14, 29, 189; Holloway House of Correction 3, 192, 242; Horsemonger Lane Gaol 111, 119; Marshalsea 189; Millbank 192, 265; Newgate 192–3; 'Panopticon' 265; penitentiaries in America 265, 268; Pentonville 192; Queen's 189; Queen's Bench 189; 'sitting for your portrait' 177; solitary confinement 7, 265, 268; transportation 52, 127, 160; treadmills 3, 192, 242; turnkeys 177; *see also* executions; punishment

prize fighting *see* boxing

Procter, B. W. 216

professionalization: Army 5, 28, 174, 176, 187; church 28; doctors 5, 28, 106; government 5, 28; law 5, 28; police 5, 28, 108, 179

promotion bills (boxing) 196

prostitutes 112, 123; philanthropic schemes 84, 85; St Giles's 142

proverbs: biblical 264; secular 30, 64, 138, 183, 200, 269, 270, 278; *see also* Bible; phraseology

Prussian army 187

public baths and wash-houses 4, 258–9

Public Baths and Wash-houses Act (1846) 4, 251, 258

public health *see* sanitary reform and sanitation

Public Health Act (1848) 252

public houses: dancing and music 212; Elephant and Castle 197; inquests 110; Old Ship 110; potboys 58, 211; provision of newspapers 166; signs 225; 'song and supper rooms' 110; Star and Garter 275; St Giles's 182; waterside 281; White Conduit House 97; 'wine vaults' 213; *see also* dining places

public schools 126

puddings: marrow 166

pugilism *see* boxing

Pugin, A. W. 252

Punch and Judy shows 109, 261

punishment: of attempted suicides 3, 160; branding-irons 192; breaking on the wheel 221–2; flogging 110–11; hard labour 160; quicksilver mines 127; transportation 52, 127, 160; treadmills 3, 192, 242; *see also* executions; prisons

puns *see* phraseology

puppets: knee- 173

purchase system 187; *see also* Army; officers

Puritans 57

Pusey, Dr Edward 85, 86

quack doctors and medicines: French 118, for gout 40

Quakers 84, 88

Quebec 174, 198

Queen Square 150

Queen's Bench 189

Queen's Counsel 30, 34; *see also* barristers

Queen's Prison 189

'Queer Street' 275

quicksilver mines 127

radicals 201; *see also* government; Parliament; political parties

rag-and-bottle shops 59, 62

Ragged School Union 112

ragged schools 112, 192, 251

rags *see* refuse

railways: construction 1, 2, 197, 276–7; to France 2, 116; Great Northern 276–7; London and South Western 197, 294; replace coaches 2, 77, 197; troop transports 197

Ramsgate 116, 157

Reading 48

Recording Angel 235

recreation *see* entertainments; games; holidays and resorts; music; sports

red tape 98

redundancy of beadles 2, 108; *see also* police

Reform Act (1832) 76, 201, 238, 239; *see also* elections; electoral corruption; government; Parliament

refrigerators 238

Regency 122, 176, 200; *see also* George IV

regiments: bands 198; cavalry 174, 280; 'Rough riders' 174, 187; fashionable 187, 280; King's Dragoon Guards 174; Scottish: Coldstream Guards 271, Royal Highlanders 205, Scots Guards 271; *see also* Army; Household troops; military; officers; soldiers

Registrar General 252

Reid, W., *Temperance Encyclopaedia* 217

religious beliefs: Army chaplains 199; Druids 174; Freemasonry 239; heathens 115; Mohammedans 175; Romans 268; *see also* Christianity; Church of England; nonconformists; Roman Catholics

religious phraseology: 'very prettily done' 88; 'vessel' 157–8; 'improving' 161; 'exertions' 177; 'high and dry' 260

Repton, Humphry 138

resorts *see* holidays and resorts

respectability: cult of 228, 231

restaurants: Opera Colonnade 138; *see also* dining places; public houses

revision of characterization in *BH see* composition of *BH*

Reynolds, G. M., *The Mysteries of London* 37; *The Seamstress* 37

Reynolds, Sir Joshua 168
Ricardo, David 247
Richard III 204
rifles 176, 189
River Thames *see* Thames River
Rochester 48, 193
Rochester Cathedral 148
Rockingham Castle 39, 40, 125, 150, 213
Rogers, Samuel Plate 13; 3, 4, 169, 171, 213
Rogers, Sarah 3, 169
Roman Catholics: Army chaplains 199; bishops in England 2, 6, 85; Dickens's attitude towards 85, 118, 239; names 87; papal aggression 2, 6, 85; relationship to Oxford Movement 85; *see also* Christianity; Church of England
romance (novels) 6, 8, 16; *see also* novels
Romans: Augurs 268; in Britain 271, 279; classical poetry 241; ruins 247; swaddling children 289
Rome 289
Romney, George 168
rookeries 141–2; *see also* slums
Rotherhithe 163
'Rough riders' 174, 187; *see also* cavalry
rowing boats 126–7
Royal Academy 203, 242, 270
Royal Arsenal 198
Royal College of Physicians 103
Royal College of Surgeons 103, 106, 127
Royal Commission on Divorce 286
Royal Commission on the Sanitary State of Large Towns 251
Royal Exchange 145
Royal Family *see* Court of St James's; Royal Household
Royal Highlanders 205
Royal Horse Guards 271, 280; *see also* Horse Guards
Royal Household 31, 271; *see also* Court of St James's
Royal Italian Opera 43, 277
Royal Mint 219
Royal Navy *see* Navy
Royal Pavilion 68, 136
Royal Society 90
Ruby, George 2, 111
rum 167
Ruskin, John 260
Russell, Lord John, first Earl Russell 3, 236, 239
Russell Street 113
Russia 174, 198

sabbatarianism 172
Saddler's Wells Theatre 128
Saffron Hill 193

sailors *see* seamen
Saint Michael's oranges 74
Sala, G. A. 41, 97, 142, 144, 179
salaried clerks 96, 156, 204; *see also* lawyers' clerks
sandals: pattens 56; winged 42
Sandwich Islands 68
sandwiches 255
sanitary reform and sanitation: Acts of Parliament associated with 251–2; cow sheds 99; Dickens's attitude towards 26, 114, 251; district visitors 2, 88, 91–2; doctors' interest in 106; rookeries and slums 91, 141–2, 182, 251–2; tracts 92; water pollution 26, 251–2; *see also* burial grounds; disease; Metropolitan Sanitary Association; pollution; sewerage; Smithfield Market
Savoyard street-musicians 173, 242
Saxons characteristics 202
scavengers *see* street-finders and scavengers
schools: charity 171; dancing 131; girls' 48; medical 103, 106; public 126; ragged 112, 192, 251; *see also* education sciences: anatomy 23; astronomy 23, 25; biology 23; botany 129; geology 23, 129, 145; *see also* phrenology; scientists
scientists and spontaneous combustion 217
Scotland 32, 43, 253; 'Caledonian melody' 235–6; Mary, Queen of Scots 276; medical schools 103, 106; *see also* doctors; regiments
Scott, Sir Walter, 'The Chase and William and Helen' 278
sculpture: life models 189, 270; Thorwaldsen 271; 'Three Graces' 73; Tuileries 118; *see also* arts
seamen: Captain Cook 68; Chinese sailors 107; Deal boatmen 249; Greenwich pensioners 26; phraseology of 129, 145; Plymouth 224; 'ship fever' 182; *see also* boats; Navy; ships
seamstresses 149, 197, 231
'season, the' 37, 237
sectarianism 191–2, 208; *see also* Christianity
Selwyn, George Augustus 122
Sentiment (emblem) 246
seraphim 47
serjeants-at-law 155
Serjeants' Inn 20, 155
servants-of-all-work *see* apprentices
setting of *BH* 39, 40, 65, 125; *see also* composition of *BH*
'Seven Sleepers' (fable) 265
Sewell, William, *Hawkstone* 293
sewerage 26, 141–2, 182, 251, 252, 253; *see also* sanitary reform and sanitation
Shakespeare, William 8, 183, 'Hem! Shakes-

peare!' 167; *All's Well That Ends Well* 238; *A Midsummer Night's Dream* 118; *Antony and Cleopatra* 72; *Coriolanus* 200, 212; *Hamlet* 8, 41, 98, 99, 172, 210, 240–1, 249–50, 261, 262, 265, 295; *Henry IV* 99; *Julius Caesar* 171, 228, 231; *Macbeth* 58, 82, 113, 115, 186, 204, 213, 259–60; *Measure for Measure* 279; *The Merchant of Venice* 8, 175, 296–7; *A Midsummer Night's Dream* 83; *Othello* 8, 41, 47, 159, 222, 223, 280, 287, paintings 203; *Romeo and Juliet* 115, 129; *Sonnets* 14–15, 73; *The Tempest* 118; *Twelfth Night* 295

shares *see* speculation

Sharp, Richard 2, 4, 47–8

Shaw, Corporal John 189

sheep 101, 130

sheet music: military 197

Shelley, Percy Bysshe 72

shellfish 155

Sheridan, Richard Brinsley, *The Rivals* 41, 236

sherriff's officers (bailiffs) 73, 140

sherry 138, 269

ship fever (typhus) 182; *see also* disease

ships: sailing: 26, 109, 145, 248–9, Chinese Junk 130, clippers 154; East Indiamen 222, 249, 269, Flying Dutchman 154; steamers 126–7, 157, 187; *see also* boats; nautical phraseology; Navy; seamen

Shipton, Mother 83

shirt-frills 40

shirts 71

shoemakers 159

shooting 176; *see also* sports

Shoreditch church 96

showers *see* baths and showers; *see also* plumbing

shrub 213

Sibthorp, Colonel 39

Sibyls 219

Sidney, Sir Philip: dying words 264

'silver fork' novels *see* fashionable novels

singers: comic, 157, 216; glee 144; *see also* music; songs

sisterhoods 85

Six Clerks' Office 33

Skelton, John Henry 3, 131, 134

Sketches by Boz 73, 108, 110, 137, 188, 211, 255

Skimpole, Arethusa 246

Skimpole, Harold: characterization revisions 64, 70, 72, 208, 246

Skimpole, Kitty 246

Skimpole, Laura 246

slang *see* phraseology

slap-bangs 163, 166; *see also* dining places

slaughterhouses 211; *see also* Smithfield Market

slavery 54, 131, 152

sleeves: lawn 72

Sloane, Mr and Mrs George 3, 100

Sloman's sponging house 2, 73

slums: Agar Town 91; St Giles's rookery 3, 4, 141–2, 179, 182

smallpox 3, 209, 258

Smallweed family: characterization revisions 171

Smiles, Samuel, *Industrial Biography* 201, 294

smirks: fashionable portraits 168

Smith, Sidney, 'Noodle's Oration' 124

Smithfield Market 3, 4, 22, 130–1, 143; slaughterhouses 211; *see also* sanitary reform and sanitation; waste

soap-boilers 62

soap-works 294

society *see* aristocracy; fashionable society

Society for the Propagation of the Gospel 3, 143

Soho 176, 186, 192

soldiers: artillerymen 5, 174, 198; costume 72; children of 197–8; education 176; habits 193; heroism 5, 174; reputation for irresponsibility 75, 163, 198; serious demeanour 174, 198; 'to go for a soldier' 75; wives of 197–8; *see also* Army; Household, troops; officers; regiments

Solemnization of Matrimony *see* Book of Common Prayer

solicitors 20, 30, 33, 42; *see also* attorneys; barristers; law

solicitors' clerks *see* lawyers' clerks

solitary confinement 7, 265, 268

Somers Town 242, 243

'song and supper rooms' 110; *see also* dining places; public houses

songs: 'Against Idleness and Mischief' 79; 'Against Quarrelling and Fighting 246; 'Ballad Stanzas' 285; 'Believe me, if all those endearing young charms' 263, 287; 'British Grenadiers' 263; 'Bibo and Charon' 211–12; 'The Children in the Wood' 51; 'Dame Durden' 83; *Divine Songs for Children* 79, 246; 'The Fire-Worshippers' 294–5; 'The Girl I Left Behind Me' 218; 'Gudeen to you kimmer' 236; 'Harmonious Black-smith' 140; 'Here, in cool grot' 210; 'How Stands the Glass Around?' 219; *Irish Melodies* 73, 263; 'King Death' 216; 'Miller of Dee' 277–8; 'Over the Water to Charlie' 173; 'The Peasant Boy' 209; 'Pray, Fair One, Be Kind' 211; 'Sound the Loud Timbrel' 190; 'The Spacious Firmament on High' 199, 200; 'Young Love' 140; 'The Young May Moon' 73–4; 'The Workhouse Boy' 109; *see also* music; nursery rhymes and tales

South America 218; *see also* America; British North America
south bank *see* Thames River
South Seas 54
Southampton 116
Southern Africa 115
Southey, Robert, *The Doctor* 168
Southwark 294
Spain 43, 269
Spanish exiles 1, 4, 243
Speaker of the House of Lords 20
Spectator 67, 82
speculation: burial grounds 113; shares 286
speech: aristocratic drawl 239; French in *BH* 120
spencers 188
spikes (on coaches and carriages) 126
spinsters: visit Bath 200; visit India 149; *see also* marriage
Spitalfields 49
spits: clockwork bottle-jacks 172
sponge cake 72
sponging houses 2, 73
spontaneous combustion 3, 16, 34, 211, 216–18
sports: badger-drawing 91; shooting 176; *see also* boxing; games
spring-guns 151
Spurzheim, J. G. 139
squadrons: naval 54, 277
St Albans 64, 79; electoral corruption 2, 65; Verulam 247
St Andrew's, Holborn 98
St Dunstan's, Fleet Street 219
St Giles's rookery 3, 4, 141–2, 179; lodging-houses 182
St Helena (island) 277
St Luke's, Old Street Road 96
St Martin-in-the-Fields 113
St Martin's Lane 197
St Paul's cathedral 22, 28, 161, 286
Staffordshire 15
stamp duty 204
Stanhope, Philip Dormer, fourth Earl of Chesterfield 3, 4, 131
Stanley, Edward George Geoffrey Smith, fourteenth Earl of Derby 237
Staple Inn 20, 100–1
Star and Garter (public house) 275; *see also* garters; Order of the Garter
starch 122
starlings 225
stationers: law 97, 98
stationery 56, 72, 98, 162; cocked-hats 269–70; red tape 98
stations: naval 198
Statistical Society of London 252

statisticians 252
stays (bodices) 75
steam-engines 75, 76
steam hammers 4, 293–4
steamers 126–7, 157, 187; *see also* boats; ships
Stephenson, George 223
stepmothers (fairy tale) 46
Sterne, Laurence, *The Life and Opinions of Tristram Shandy* 191, 225
Stevenage 13
Stewart, Dugald, *Elements of the Philosophy of the Human Mind* 221
stockings 43, 122
Stonehenge 174
Stowe, Harriet Beecher, *Uncle Tom's Cabin* 54
Strand 27
street-buyers *see* street-traders
street cries: chimney-sweepers 229; dustmen 130
street-dirt *see* manure; mud
street-finders and scavengers 23, 58, 63; *see also* waste
street-lighting 27, 144, 160; *see also* lighting
street-music: 3, 143–4, 242, 261, 289, organ-grinders 172–3; *see also* music; musical instruments
Street Music (Metropolis) Act (1864) 144
street-orderlies 113
street-traders: birds 63; breakfast-stalls 254–5; brooms 241–2; coke 103; confectionery 110; effervescent drinks 162; gingerbeer 155; glass 62; lucifers 211; 'open air' 155, 162; pies 110; rag-and-bottle 62; shellfish 155
Stroudwater Valley 65
Stuart, Charles Edward 173
Stubbs, George 224
stylistic revisions of *BH*. *See* composition of *BH*
subscription cards 84, 86; *see also* philanthropy
Sue, Eugéne, *The Mysteries of Paris* 37
Suffolk 16
suicide: punishment for attempts 3, 160; using opium 2, 107; Waterloo Bridge 284; *see also* death
Suitors in Chancery Relief Act (1852) 2, 33, 102
Summerson, Esther: characterization 6, 7, 45, 82; illegitimacy 83, 138; name 46
Sunday Under Three Heads 158
supernatural *see* ghosts
superstitions 103, 190, 212
surgeons 103, 106; Army and Navy pay disparity 3, 5, 106, 127; education 103, 106; instructing students 128; *see also* chemists; doctors; hospitals; medicine; physicians
Surgeons' Hall 127–8
'swells' 97, 156, 163
Swift, Jonathan, *A Tale of a Tub* 38; *Gulliver's Travels* 44

'swipes' 176; *see also* beer
Swiss Savoyards: immigrant street-musicians 173, 242
Switzerland 37
swooning at opera and theatre 122
swords 176, 189
Symond's Inn 264

tables 44
tabors 173
Tale of Two Cities, A 120
Talfourd, Serjeant Thomas Noon 29, 72
tallow-makers 62
tamborines 242
tambour work 222
Taunton, Vale of 228
taverns *see* public houses
tea 63, 68, 254–5
teachers and teaching *see* education; schools
teetotal catechism 88; *see also* temperance movement
tee-totum 143
telegraphy 108–9
Tell, William 188–9
temperance movement: Band of Hope Plate 8; 2, 87–8; teetotal catechism 88; writers 217; *see also* drinks; drunkenness
Temple *see* Inns of Court
Temple Bar 27–8
Temple, John Henry, third Viscount Palmerston 236, 237
Tennyson, Alfred, first Baron 6, 150, 260; *In Memoriam* 25; *The Princess* 96
Terrific Register, The 216
Thackeray, William Makepeace 149; *The Book of Snobs* 35, 148; *Pendennis* 129, 175, 216; *Punch's Prize Novelists* 35, 44; *Vanity Fair* 35, 73, 149
Thames River: dead-houses 281; docks 26, 107, 130, 198, 281; manure barges 23; pollution 26; rowing-boats 126–7; sewerage 26; shipping 26; south bank 157, 163, 175, 196, 294; suicides from Waterloo Bridge 284; water-finders 281, 284
Thavies Inn 20, 56, 64
theatres: Adelphi 96; Covent Garden 43, 128; Drury Lane 128; Her Majesty's 138; Leicester Square 176; Lyceum 128; Olympic 128; Princess's 128; Royal Italian Opera 43; Sadler's Wells 128; swooning 122; tickets 96, 113, 128; *see also* entertainments; opera; music
Theatres Act (1737) 212
theatricals, amateur 13, 72
thieves: area sneaks 285; dens 181, 182; 'gonophs' 159–60; St Giles's 142; *see also* crime

Thomas, William Moy, 'A Guild Clerk's Tale' 6, 82
Thorwaldsen, Bertel 271
'Threatening Letter to Thomas Hood . . .' 160
'Three Graces' 73
'Thumb, General Tom' 43
tickets: mendicity 84; theatre 96, 113, 128; ticket-porters 155, 188
tight-lacing 99
timbrels 190
tissue-paper: 'flimsy' 212
titles of *BH* 13, 65, Appendix
toasts: Jacobite 173
Took's Court 97
Tooting baby-farm 2, 99–100, 124, 255
Torrijos, General 4, 243
Torys: aristocracy in government 35–6, 124; government of 1851 124, 236–7; *vs* radicals 201; *see also* aristocracy; government; Parliament; political parties
Tower of London 26, 130, 219
Towns Improvement Clauses Act (1847) 26
Towns Police Clauses Act (1847) 251
toys: cramp-bones 230; tee-totums 143; *see also* games; sports
tracts 88, 92; *see also* philanthropy
tradesmen: Hatton Garden 193; Lambeth 294
'train oil' 159
trained birds 75–6; *see also* performing dogs, horses
transport *see* boats; carriages and coaches; railways; ships
transportation of criminals 52, 127, 160; *see also* crime; prisons; punishment
treadmills 3, 192, 242; *see also* prisons, punishment
tribes: African 115
Trinity term 20
trousers: nankeen 200
Truth (emblem) 148
tuberculosis (consumption) 182, 209, 258
Tuileries 117, 118
Tulkinghorn, Mr 41–2, 43
Tunbridge Wells 57
Turkey 156, 159, 174
turnkeys: 'sitting for your portrait' 177
turnpike trusts 284
Turvey (game, town) 134
Tussaud's wax-works 279
Twickenham 25
Tyler, Wat 35, 44, 76
typhus ('fever') 3, 182, 251
Tyrolean immigrant street-musicians 173

Uncommercial Traveller, The 48, 88, 92–3, 97, 114, 153, 179, 264

Index

Uffizi palace 71, 275
Urania Cottage 84
'urban Gothic' (novels) 37

vaccination: smallpox 209
Vaccination Extension Act (1840) 209
Vale of Taunton 228
Vauxhall 294
Vauxhall Bridge 196
Vauxhall Gardens 157, 294
vegetables: cabbage 197; marrows 166; potatoes
2, 91, 203
venues: musical *see* music
Venus 275
Verulam 247
Vholes, Mr 228; characterization revisions 229,
230

vinegar 99
violins 144
Virgil, *Aeneid*, 99, 153, 181–2, 203, 253
visiting societies 91–2; *see also* philanthropy
voles 228

waistcoats 40, 43
walking sticks 197; *see also* canes
Walpole, Horace 122
Walpole, Sir Robert 124
Walworth 197
Ward, John William, first Earl of Dudley 124
Ware, Mary Pickard 289
Warren, Samuel, *Passages from the Diary of a Late
Physician* 35, 36–7
Warren's blacking warehouse 62
Wars of the Roses 65
Warwickshire 157
wash-houses: public 4, 251, 258–9
washing: Army wives 197; 'whole bileing' 287
waste: bones 58, 59, 62; cigar-ends 58; dead cats
63; dripping 59, 62; dust heaps 63, 130, 169;
glass 59, 62; grease 59, 62; kitchen-stuff 59,
62; manure 22–3; marine stores 59, 62; old
clothes 62; paper 62; pins 58; rag and bottle
shops 59, 62; slaughterhouses 211; *see also*
street-finders and scavengers
water-cures 68, 156
water-finders (dredgers) 281, 284
water-systems: boilers 57; *see also* baths and
showers; plumbing
Water Works Clauses Act (1847) 252
Waterloo, Battle of 174, 189, 205
Waterloo Bridge 284
Watson Hon. Mr and Mrs Richard 16, 39, 68, 93,
213
Watt, James 44, 75
Watts, Isaac, *Divine Songs for Children* 79, 246

wax-works 279
weapons: bows and arrows 189; *see also* duelling;
firearms
Wellesley, Arthur, first Duke of Wellington 124,
174, 205, 237; funeral 4, 269
Wellesley, Garrett, first Earl of Mornington,
'Here, in cool grot' 210
Wellington, first Duke of *see* Wellesley, Arthur,
first Duke of Wellington
Welsh: bards 149; genealogy 148–9
West Country 49
West End 286, 296
West Indies 218; philanthropic involvement 54,
55, 56, 87, 152
Westminster 126–7, 265
Westminster Bridge 175, 197
Westminster Hall 153, 154
Whigs 36, 124, 236, 237; *see also* government;
Parliament; political parties
'whips' 260
whiskers 3, 163; 'Newgate frill' 163; 'Newgate
knockers' 179; *see also* hairdressing
whistles 173
White Conduit House 97
White Horse Cellar 49
white lime 199
Whitechapel 130, 219
Whitefriars 197
Whitehall 187, 286
Whittington, Richard 64–5
wigs 30, 51, 63, 278; *see also* hairdressing
Willis's *see* Almack's
Wills, W. H. 15, 49, 68, 110, 179, 242
Winchester School 126
Windsor 48
wine 138; claret 72; Madeira 269; sherry 138,
269; *see also* drinks
witches 83, 190; *see also* magic
wives: of soldiers 197–8; *see also* marriage
wolves 64
women's rights 2, 3, 86–7, 153, 208
Woods and Forests Commission 3, 124
woolsack 20, 30, 295
Wordsworth, William 6; 'Composed Upon Westminster Bridge' 155, 261; *The Excursion* 7, 221
workers: industrial 76, 293
Workhouse Trust 258
workhouses 100, 193, 208, 258
Wren, Christopher 27, 28, 98, 161

Yorkshire 54, 83, 289
Young England 3, 40, 123, 124

Zeus *see* Jupiter
zymotic theory 253; *see also* disease; sanitary
reform and sanitation